PENGUIN BOOKS

GRASSES

Charles Edward Hubbard was born at Appleton, Norfolk, in 1900. After intensive training in horticulture in the Royal Gardens, Sandringham, and Oslo, Norway, and service in the Royal Air Force, he entered the Royal Botanic Gardens, Kew, in 1920. He became keenly interested in the large collection of living plants for which Kew is world-renowned. This interest led to his transference to the Herbarium in 1922 where he assisted the distinguished botanists of that famous institution, gaining experience in the classification and identification of flowering plants. After 1926 he specialized in the study of grasses, and for many years was in charge of the section devoted to these plants, publishing many studies of them. He was appointed Keeper of the Herbarium and Library in 1957, and Deputy Director of the Royal Botanic Gardens, Kew, in 1959. In 1930 he was sent to Australia to revise grass-collections in the Brisbane Herbarium, and during extensive travels in Australia he gathered numerous specimens for Kew. The University of Reading conferred on him the Honorary Degree of Doctor of Science in 1960. In 1954 he was awarded the OBE and in 1965 the CBE; and in 1967 h̶ received the Linnean Gold Medal and in 1970 the V̶ ̶ ̶orial Medal of the Royal Horticultural Soc̶ ̶ ̶ ̶ ̶1965 but continued to add to his lis̶ ̶ ̶ ̶ ̶ to give freely of his specialist ̶ ̶ ̶ ̶ ̶980.

GRASSES

A GUIDE TO THEIR STRUCTURE, IDENTIFICATION,
USES, AND DISTRIBUTION IN THE
BRITISH ISLES

BY

C. E. HUBBARD

THIRD EDITION
REVISED BY J. C. E. HUBBARD

WITH ILLUSTRATIONS MAINLY BY

JOAN SAMPSON

PENGUIN BOOKS

PENGUIN BOOKS

Published by the Penguin Group
Penguin Books Ltd, 27 Wrights Lane, London W8 5TZ, England
Penguin Putnam Inc., 375 Hudson Street, New York, New York 10014, USA
Penguin Books Australia Ltd, Ringwood, Victoria, Australia
Penguin Books Canada Ltd, 10 Alcorn Avenue, Toronto, Ontario, Canada M4V 3B2
Penguin Books India (P) Ltd, 11, Community Centre, Panchsheel Park, New Delhi – 110 017, India
Penguin Books (NZ) Ltd, Private Bag 102902, NSMC, Auckland, New Zealand
Penguin Books (South Africa) (Pty) Ltd, 5 Watkins Street, Denver Ext 4, Johannesburg 2094, South Africa

Penguin Books Ltd, Registered Offices: Harmondsworth, Middlesex, England

First published in Pelican Books 1954
Second Edition 1968
Third Edition 1984
Reprinted in Penguin Books 1992
5

Copyright © C. E. Hubbard, 1954, 1968
Copyright © J. C. E. Hubbard, 1984

Printed in England by Clays Ltd, St Ives plc
Set in Linotron Times

CONTENTS

In October 1979 my father wrote: 'I had hoped to complete the revision of the text for the third edition, but at that time I became ill and was unable to finish it. I had planned to include twelve additional drawings of such grasses as *Gaudinia fragilis* (now well established in parts of South England and Ireland); various subspecies of *Festuca rubra* (such as those used in horticulture, etc., as subsp. *litoralis*, and subsp. *megastachys*); various *Agrostis* and several aliens of common occurrence, including *Panicum miliacium, Setaria italica, Echinochloa utilis*.'

Sadly, he was unable to finish the work, so the third edition is a compilation made from an amended copy of the book found amongst his papers, plus extracts from the voluminous notes which he had continued to accumulate up to the time of his death. No changes have been made to nomenclature in spite of the subsequent publication of Part 5 of the *Flora Europaea* which deals specifically with the classification of the *Gramineae*. This book has been regarded as a standard work and, as such, it should stand without alteration, particularly as many of the name changes are merely the use of synonyms already listed here. In other instances, and particularly in the subspecies of *Festuca rubra*, there is a divergence of opinion over whether species' or subspecies' names should be utilized. In the case of *Festuca rubra*, my father had compiled a classification of subspecies which was included in the *Flora of Moray, Nairn and East Inverness*, published in 1978. The classification is now added to this work, together with brief descriptions of these grasses gleaned from unpublished notes. The information is intended to be of use to devotees of amenity grassland where the subspecies of *Festuca rubra* are of economic importance. The same applies to the description of *Agrostis castellana* and to the amended key to the identification of grasses in lawns. Generally, the name used in the *Flora Europaea* has been placed at the bottom of each page of description so as to assist the reader who wishes to maintain continuity in dealing with ecological and farming literature, etc.

There have been recent and major changes in the use of grasses so I am greatly indebted to Mr J. O. Green and Mr J. P. Sheldrick for revising the sections of this book dealing with the economic uses of grasses, for their advice over improving the key and for recent additions to the bibliography.

J. C. E. Hubbard
December 1982

LIST OF ABBREVIATIONS USED IN THE ILLUSTRATIONS AND TEXT

In order to facilitate comparison of the drawings of different grasses, the following system of lettering has been used to indicate similar parts of the plants illustrated.

AU	auricle, at apex of sheath or base of blade
AW	awn
BL	blade of leaf
BR	bristle ·
C	caryopsis or grain
CE	caryopsis, back view, showing embryo
CH	caryopsis, front view, showing hilum
CS	caryopsis, side view
F	floret
FS	florets
FL	flower, with or without lodicules, enlarged
G_1	lower or first glume
G_2	upper or second glume
GS	glumes
L	lemma
LL	lower lemma
L_2	upper lemma
LI	ligule
LO	lodicules, much enlarged
P	palea
P_1	lower palea
P_2	upper palea
PE	pedicel
PL	pistil (ovary, style, and stigmas), enlarged
R	rhachilla
S	spikelet
SB	spikelet, back view
SF	spikelet, front view
ST	stamens
TF	fertile lemma
TS	transverse section, of leafy shoot, or of stem, etc.

Ch. no. Chromosome number (at end of each description)

MEASUREMENTS

The measurements given in the keys and descriptions are in the metric system. Approximate equivalents in inches and feet are given below.

       1 mm. = $\frac{1}{25}$ inch
       2·5 cm. (25 mm.) = 1 inch
       30 cm. = 1 foot
       1 m. (100 cm.) = 39 inches

A centimetre scale is provided down the edge of this page for use in the field.

INTRODUCTION

Most visitors to the British Isles are deeply impressed by the luxuriance of our meadows and pastures, as well as by the fine crops of the cereal grasses – wheat, barley, oats, and rye of arable land. The rich growth of the herbage grasses gives one the impression that here is a land ideally suited for such plants. This inference is correct, for our climate is most favourable for the production of this luscious green growth during a large part of the year. It is not realized, however, that these associations of grasses are almost entirely artificial in origin and due to the continuous labours of many generations of our ancestors, together with the cumulative action of the grazing and treading of their domestic animals. Under our climatic conditions and on most soils, these artificial grasslands, when removed from the control of man and beast and left to the effects of competition and natural selection, gradually revert to scrub, and in most cases from scrub to forest. As proof that such a change is inevitable, one has only to recall the years immediately preceding World War II for an example of what happens when man's controlling hand is removed. At that time, owing to the precarious state of British agriculture, much outlying land on farms, together with the so-called marginal lands, was so neglected that in almost every county one could find grassland with a gradually increasing infiltration of hawthorns, sloes, brambles, and roses, besides numerous other invaders. For botanists these were areas of much interest, not only because they provided excellent examples of the effects of competition and selection, and of the development of a different local flora, but also because they gave some of the less common and agriculturally unimportant grasses a chance to increase and spread, or at least to hold their own. Such a situation in an overcrowded country was, of course, only a passing phase, and the food shortages of the last war soon provided the necessary incentive for agricultural improvement in every direction. The derelict lands were cleared of trees and bushes, rush-infested fields were drained, and the grasslands with a very high percentage of weeds were ploughed up, and some were sown with pedigree strains of grasses and clovers. In this way the area of improved grassland and of arable land was increased to a record high level. Fortunately most of our grasses are tolerant of adverse conditions, and whilst some have lost favourable habitats to agricultural crops, and others have been reduced in numbers, the majority have persisted in the natural and semi-natural communities still available on sand-dunes, shingle-banks, salt-marshes, cliffs, river-, lake- and pond-margins, freshwater swamps, heaths and moorlands, hill and mountain grassland, and in hedgerows and woodland. Through the centuries special associations of grasses have developed in these habitats, many of which have provided a safe refuge for ancient species which but for such situations would have long since disappeared.

It is estimated that in the whole world there are about 620 genera and 10,000 species of grasses. Of these, only 54 genera and between 150 and 160 species are indigenous to or naturalized in the British Isles, 158 of which are illustrated in this book. Contrasting our grass flora with those of other areas similar in size, one is impressed by its poverty both in number of species and in its representation of the main groups of grasses. There is such a wide range of suitable habitats, soil types, and even minor climatic zones that one might well expect to find a richer flora. The absence of certain continental genera and species is due no doubt to the several glaciations to which these islands have been subjected and to their isolation from the big land masses.

Several of our species include a wide range of variants, in particular *Agropyron repens, Agrostis stolonifera, Festuca rubra, Koeleria cristata, Molinia caerulea, Poa nemoralis, P. pratensis*, and *Puccinellia maritima*. This variability is due to several causes, in some instances to past interspecific and intervarietal hybridization, particularly in self-sterile grasses, to polyploidy and apomixis, and to adaptation to a limited range of habitat. Thus in *Agrostis stolonifera* there are distinct variants, in chalk grassland, arable land, salt-marshes, sand dunes, and margins of ponds and streams, which maintain their growth-forms under cultivation.

As our grasses become more and more the subject of intensive study, numerous hybrids, intergeneric and interspecific, are being discovered, indicating a close relationship between the genera and species concerned. Thus eleven male-sterile or partially fertile intergeneric hybrids have now been recorded. They comprise: 1. × *Agrohordeum langei* (*Agropyron repens × Hordeum secalinum*), 2. × *Agropogon littoralis* (*Agrostis stolonifera × Polypogon monspeliensis*), 3. × *Ammocalamagrostis baltica* (*Ammophila arenaria × Calamagrostis epigejos*), 4. × *Festulolium loliaceum* (*Festuca pratensis × Lolium perenne*), 5. × *Festulolium braunii* (*Festuca pratensis × Lolium multiflorum*), 6. × *Festulolium holmbergii* (*Festuca arundinacea × Lolium perenne*), 7. × *Festulolium* (*Festuca arundinacea × Lolium multiflorum*), 8. × *Festulolium brinkmannii* (*Festuca gigantea × Lolium perenne*), 9. *Festuca rubra* subsp. *rubra × Vulpia membranacea*, 10. *Festuca rubra* subsp. *rubra × Vulpia myuros*, and 11. *Festuca rubra* subsp. *rubra × Vulpia bromoides*. Others will no doubt be found, including the hybrid between *Elymus arenarius* and *Agropyron junceiforme*, which has been recorded from coastal dunes on the Continent.

In addition to these intergeneric hybrids, there are about thirty-two interspecific hybrids in the genera listed below, the number in each genus being given in parentheses; the majority are referred to after the individual descriptions, as far as possible, of the species concerned. With the exception of *Lolium × hybridum* (*L. perenne × L. multiflorum*) and

14

Bromus hybrids, most of the hybrids appear to be male-sterile, their anthers remaining closed and containing imperfectly developed pollen. This characteristic, as well as a structure more or less intermediate between the putative parents, is helpful in recognizing such hybrids, although confirmation by genetical and cytological studies is essential. Interspecific hybrids occur in the following genera: *Agropyron* (3), *Agrostis* (6), *Alopecurus* (2), *Avena* (1), *Bromus* (4), *Calamagrostis* (1), *Catapodium* (1), *Festuca* (4), *Glyceria* (2), *Holcus* (1), *Lolium* (1), *Poa* (2), *Puccinellia* (3), and *Spartina* (1).

In addition to our established grasses, species of other genera are occasionally found on rubbish-tips in the vicinity of large towns, in similar places on waste ground at ports, on roadsides, and on arable fields manured with 'shoddy' (wool-cleanings); their seeds having been introduced with wool, grain, packing materials, ballast, etc. They include species of *Cenchrus, Chloris, Dactyloctenium, Danthonia, Diplachne, Eleusine, Eragrostis, Panicum, Sorghum, Sporobolus, Stipa, Tragus*, and *Zea*, besides species of genera already represented here by native species. Numerous grasses have been recorded as a result of studies of our rich alien flora, about 200 having been recorded as being introduced with imported wool. Other genera, such as *Triticum* (wheat), *Hordeum* (barley), *Avena* (oats), and *Secale* (rye), are cultivated as crop plants, whilst other grasses, including *Phalaris tuberosa* and overseas strains of herbage plants, are occasionally sown for grazing or hay. Species of *Arundo, Cortaderia* (Pampas-grass), *Miscanthus*, as well as of many other herbaceous grasses, and of the bamboo genera *Arundinaria, Phyllostachys, Sasa*, and *Shibataea*, are grown on account of their ornamental value in our parks and gardens.

THE STRUCTURE OF GRASSES

Many people capable of identifying common wild plants bearing coloured flowers experience considerable difficulties when they attempt to name grasses. These difficulties are due to the small size of the floral organs, to the use of special terms for the scales enclosing the flower, but mainly on account of an imperfect knowledge of the apparently complicated structure of the flower-head. It is true their real flowers are small, but except where sexual differences are used to separate genera, it is not necessary to study them in detail when naming many of our grasses. Furthermore, the flower-heads of British grasses, though appearing complex at first, will soon become comparatively simple to those who examine them thoroughly.

The genera of grasses are distinguished from one another mainly in the arrangement, form, and modification of the miniature leaf-like scales enveloping the flowers, whilst the species are usually separated by differences in duration, form of growth, and in the size and shape of the stems, leaves, and of the flower-head and its parts.

For the examination of the grass flowers and the scales that cover them, the following articles are all that are required at first: a hand-lens (× 5 or × 10), a sharp penknife, and one or two dissecting needles (stiff needles mounted in wooden handles). A dissecting microscope with lens (× 10 and × 20) is an asset to the more ambitious student, particularly if the smaller seeds of grasses and the minute parts of the flower are to be examined.

I. Structure of the Common Oat (*Avena sativa*)

As an introduction to the study of grasses, the cultivated cereal, *Avena sativa*, illustrated on pages 18 and 20, has been selected for examination because it is generally available and the parts of the flower-head are comparatively large and easy to recognize even without a lens. The plants should be complete, that is with roots, stem, leaves, and flower-head.

The stem or haulm of grasses, bearing leaves and the flower-head, is known botanically as the *culm*. At its base are roots which anchor the plant in the soil and conduct water and food materials in solution from the soil to the culm. In the oat, as in most grasses, the culm is formed of several cylindrical tubes of unequal length, closed at the joints by solid tissue. The position of the join is marked externally by a narrow dark-coloured zone encircling the culm immediately above the solid part. The joints are termed *nodes* and the hollow portions between them are *internodes*.

17

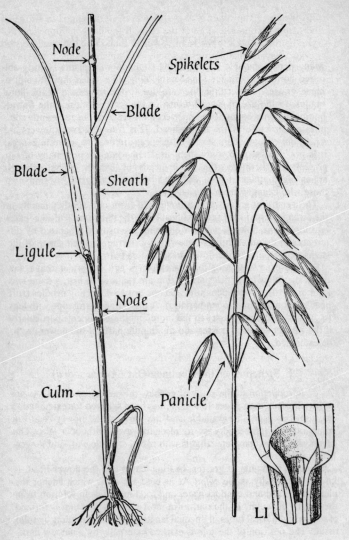

Common Oat, *Avena sativa*, × ½.

In the oat, as in other grasses, the leaves are arranged in two rows alternating on opposite sides of the culm. If the flattened upper part of a leaf be traced back to the culm, it will be found that the basal portion is cylindrical and that it arises at a node. The upper expanded part is the *blade* and the basal part is the *sheath*. The latter closely embraces the culm, but is open along one side, with one margin overlapping the other. On the inside of the leaf, at the junction of the sheath and blade and at the point where the latter diverges from the culm, there is a thin whitish membranous outgrowth, the *ligule* (LI, × 3).

The flower-head of the oat terminates the culm. It consists of a main-axis from which arise, at intervals, clusters of slender spreading branches. These branches bear at their tips rather long slender green structures known as *spikelets* (S, × 2). The stalks on which these are borne are *pedicels*. This branched type of flower-head is a *panicle*.

If the spikelets (S) are examined closely, it will be seen that they are formed of scales borne alternately in two rows on opposite sides of an extremely short thread-like axis (or *rhachilla*). In the fresh state these scales are green and somewhat fleshy, but on ripening they become yellowish and leathery. The two outer scales (G_1, G_2) are similar, narrow, and finely pointed; for some time they envelop the rest of the spikelet, but diverge at flowering time and at maturity. They are the *glumes*; the outer or first is the *lower glume* (G_1) and the next is the *upper glume* (G_2).

The glumes should be pushed on one side or cut away at the base to disclose the rest of the spikelet (FS, × 2). This consists of 2 or 3 slender tapering structures, each composed of two scales (L, P), smaller than, yet somewhat similar to, the glumes. The outer scale of each pair is the *lemma* (L), also known as the flowering glume, lower or outer pale; it frequently bears a bristle on its rounded back. Its margins tightly embrace the narrower and shorter inner scale known as the *palea* (P), also termed upper or inner pale. The palea is flattened on the back and is next to the spikelet-axis. With the use of a needle or knife-point, the lemma and palea may be prised apart and, if care is taken, the delicate flower of the oat will be seen at the base between them. The lemma should be removed, leaving the flower between the two inflexed margins of the palea, from which it can be extracted by using the fine point of a knife. The lower two pairs of lemmas and paleas each enclose a flower, but the third pair may be empty.

The flower (FL, × 6) should be examined with a hand-lens. It consists of three parts: 1, two small narrow scales at the base termed *lodicules* (LO); 2, three stamens (male part of flower), with each stamen formed of a stalk (or *filament*) and a terminal 2-celled part (*anther*) containing pollen; 3, a rounded hairy body, the *ovary* (female part of flower), bearing at its apex two whitish feathery organs (*stigmas*) on very short stalks (*styles*), the whole termed the *pistil*. The ovary contains a single *ovule*,

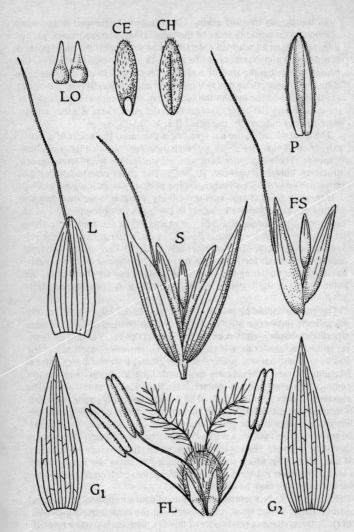

Common Oat, *Avena sativa*, FL, LO, × 6; rest, × 2.

spikelets are seated on the main-axis itself, the flower-head or ear is known as a spike *e.g.Agropyron, Lolium*).

Panicles may be loose, contracted, or narrow and dense when they are said to be spike-like (e.g. *Phleum*). Some grasses have panicles with branches spreading in all directions round the main-axis, whilst in others they are directed to one side (*e.g. Dactylis, Cynosurus*). The spikes or racemes may be asymmetrical, the spikelets being borne on one side of the axis only (e.g. *Digitaria, Spartina, Mibora*); or symmetrical, with the spikelets in two rows on opposite sides of the axis (e.g. *Lolium, Brachypodium*).

4. SPIKELETS

The *spikelets* (S) of species belonging to the same genus, although usually different in shape and size, possess certain characteristics in common which give them such a distinctive appearance that one is able, after some experience, to recognize the genus without detailed study. In British grasses, many genera have the same basic spikelet-structure as the common oat, although in some instances possessing only one flower (e.g. *Agrostis*), in others with up to 20 or more (e.g. *Brachypodium*). The number of flowers in each spikelet is sometimes characteristic of a genus; for example there is only one in *Phleum*, and two in *Aira* and *Corynephorus*. The spikelets of all such grasses possess two glumes at the base, with one or more florets (F, FS) above, each with a lemma and palea usually enclosing a bisexual flower (stamens and pistil). The axis of the spikelet is minute in spikelets with one floret, but elongated when there are many. There are exceptions to the normal type of spikelet referred to above, in which, instead of all the florets being bisexual, some of them may have male organs only, as in *Holcus, Hierochloë*, and *Arrhenatherum*, or be completely barren as in the lower two florets of the spikelets of *Anthoxanthum*. An extreme example may be seen in the genus *Phalaris*, in which the lower two florets are reduced to small or minute scales at the base of the fertile floret. There are many other modifications of the sexual nature of the spikelets. For example in *Zea mays* (Maize, Sweet Corn), the sexes are in distinct flower-heads, the male spikelets being borne in a terminal panicle, and the female in thick spikes in the axils of the sheaths. The male and female spikelets are borne in separate panicles, on different plants, in the Pampas Grass (*Cortaderia selloana*), cultivated in gardens. In the genus *Cynosurus* also, there are two kinds of spikelets, but these are in the same spike-like panicle, some spikelets being bisexual and partially covered by others which are entirely sterile.

In some genera, the spikelets are typically large (e.g. *Avena*), in others rather small (e.g. *Agrostis*), whilst a few genera show a considerable range in spikelet-size (e.g. *Festuca*). Spikelets may be strongly flattened, either from the side or from the back, or they may be quite plump or even circular in section. In outline they also exhibit a large series of variations. Their sides are parallel in those narrowly to broadly oblong, or they may be widest at the base and taper above in shapes described as lanceolate or ovate, or widest at the middle in those termed elliptic.

One of the most important characteristics of the spikelet is the way in which fractures develop in various parts of its axis at maturity, thus freeing the seed from the parent plant. This is of considerable importance in the distinction of genera and species. For an account of this method of seed-dispersal the reader is referred to the chapter on the 'seeds' of grasses on page 402.

The *glumes* (GS, G_1, G_2 and *lemmas* (L) provide numerous distinctive features in their relative sizes, shape, texture, nervation, and in the presence or absence of various types of outgrowth such as hairs and bristles. For example, the glumes may be shorter (e.g. *Festuca*), as long as (e.g. *Apera*) or longer than the lemmas (e.g. *Avena*), in the last providing increased protection for the flowers. The glumes may be similar or dissimilar when the lower is usually narrower and shorter. In a few genera the lower glume is minute (e.g. *Digitaria*), or absent (e.g. *Lolium*), whilst both glumes are almost suppressed in *Leersia*.

The *lemmas* (L) are more diverse in structure than the glumes, as the drawings in this book show. They are consequently of great importance for both specific and generic separation. In addition to differences in shape and size, their tips may be pointed, blunt, or variously toothed. They may be rounded on the back or compressed and keeled there; such differences are seen in the lemmas of *Festuca* and *Poa* respectively. Lemmas may be similar to the glumes in texture. Usually, however, they show a greater range in thickness, from the delicate ones of *Agrostis* to the green somewhat fleshy lemmas of *Bromus* which become hardened and rigid as the seeds mature. The number of ribs or nerves in the lemma is constant or nearly so in the species of many genera, for example, there are three in *Catabrosa* and *Cynodon*, five in *Poa* and *Puccinellia*, and seven in *Glyceria*. Such lemmas are referred to in the descriptions as being 3-, 5-, or 7-nerved.

Modifications which ensure a wider distribution of the seed are prominent in the lemma. Thus its base may be hardened, pointed or blunt, forming a thickening (*callus*) which is barbed with minute or short hairs (e.g. *Avena*), or provided with a ring of long hairs (e.g. *Calamagrostis*). In many grasses the middle nerve or midrib of the lemma is produced into a bristle or *awn*. This may arise from near the base of the lemma, at any point on the back, or from the tip. Awns may be straight, flexuous, or after drying they may become bent at or about the middle, with the part below the bend twisted.

The *palea* (P) provides fewer distinguishing features than the lemma. It is mostly narrow, with parallel sides, and about the same length as the lemma or shorter. Usually it has two ribs or nerves, rarely 1 or 3, which in some grasses project as prominent keels. The keels may bear hairs or minute rough points, or be quite smooth.

The *flower* (FL) being small is generally disregarded, although it does provide valuable clues to generic relationships. The parts of the perianth are usually represented by 2 (rarely 3) minute scales – the *lodicules* (LO) – at one side of the ovary. These vary somewhat in shape, being lanceolate, elliptic, or oblong, entire or 2-toothed; they are free from each other, rarely united by their margins as in *Glyceria* and *Melica*. These differences in the lodicules often provide useful characters for the identification of grass fruits (mature florets). There are none in *Alopecurus, Anthoxanthum, Spartina,* and *Nardus*. Usually there are 3 stamens but 2 only are present in the flowers of *Anthoxanthum* and often 1 in those of species of *Vulpia*. The ovary is generally hairless, rarely hairy all over as in *Avena* and a few other genera, or hairy only at the tip as in *Bromus, Brachypodium, Hordeum,* etc. It bears at or near the tip, 2 (rarely 3 or 1) styles which are tipped by the long- or short-haired stigmas.

The grains of grasses are described in the section dealing with the seeds on page 402.

III. Flowering in Grasses

Most of our grasses flower during May, June, and July, the greatest number being in bloom towards the end of June and early in July. At that period their graceful flower-heads are an attractive feature of grasslands, although the abundant pollen liberated from their anthers on hot dry days is most objectionable to those who suffer from hay-fever. Flowering is not confined to the spring and summer months, since even in December and January during mild winters up to 20 species with fully developed flower-heads have been seen at Kew. *Poa annua* also is generally in bloom throughout the year, except during very cold winters. With these exceptions, the first grass to flower is *Hierochloë odorata*, a few panicles of which may be out by the end of March. *Alopecurus pratensis* and *Anthoxanthum odoratum* follow in April, *Poa* and *Bromus* spp. towards the end of April and in May, and in June various species of *Festuca* and numerous other genera are flowering. Most of the species of *Agrostis* and *Agropyron* are in bloom by the end of June and throughout July. These and other grasses may continue into August when the species of *Molinia, Phragmites, Spartina, Leersia,* and *Digitaria* extend the grass-flowering season into November. Woodland and mountain species generally flower later than species of the same genera from open situations in the lowlands or from the south.

Individual grasses have fairly regular daily flowering periods, although naturally this is affected by the weather, as the florets remain closed on dull or wet days. In the majority, flowering takes place in the early

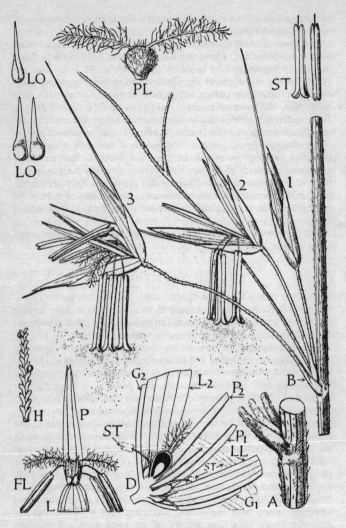

Arrhenatherum elatius (L.) Beauv. ex J. & C. Presl

A, part of panicle with swollen bases of branches; B, part of panicle, with 3 spikelets (1, 2, 3); D, diagrammatic representation of section through flowering spikelet.

morning (mainly 4–9 a.m.), in a few about midday, and in others during the afternoon and evening (3–7 p.m.). Most species flower only once a day but *Anthoxanthum odoratum* and *Holcus lanatus* flower twice daily (5–10 a.m., 5–7 p.m.). Flowering lasts for about 4–12 (mostly 7–8) days, depending on the type and size of flower-head.

The majority of our grasses are chasmogamous, their florets opening for the exsertion of the anthers and stigmas. There are, however, a few species such as *Leersia oryzoides*, *Sieglingia decumbens*, *Bromus*, and *Vulpia* spp. which are partially or completely cleistogamous, pollination taking place within the closed florets. Many of our perennials and a few of our annuals are self-sterile, developing seed only after cross-pollination, whereas the annuals are mainly self-fertile. The cross-pollinated species usually have large anthers which become fully exserted from the floret, their pollen being carried to the stigmas of other plants by the wind. The self-fertile annuals on the other hand often have very small anthers, the pollen of which falls on to the stigmas of the same plant. In *Alopecurus*, *Anthoxanthum*, *Spartina*, and other grasses lacking lodicules, the stigmas are exserted from the florets before the anthers, the interval being 2 to 5 days in species of *Alopecurus*.

For an interesting account of flowering and seed-setting in grasses, the reader should consult A. R. Beddow's long paper on self-and cross-fertility and flowering habits of many grasses, published in Bulletin H12 (1931) of the Welsh Plant Breeding Station.

Flowering is best observed in grasses with large spikelets, such as the widespread *Arrhenatherum elatius,* illustrated in this condition on page 26. In this grass, just before flowering commences, the previously erect branches and branchlets of the panicle are forced apart and away from the main-axis and each other by the small cushions of spongy tissue in their axils (A) becoming swollen with sap, and the spikelets (B, 1, 2, 3) become evenly distributed round the panicle. When the florets are completely developed and climatic conditions are favourable, the lower portion of each lodicule (LO) becomes swollen with sap and exerts great pressure at the base of the lemma (L) and palea (P), forcing them apart (B 2, 3; FL) to an angle of 33°–45° (see D). The filaments of the stamens next elongate rapidly causing the three anthers to be pushed over the sides and hang from the floret (B 2, 3). At the same time the white brush-like stigmas (PL) spread and project laterally one on each side of the open floret (FL). The tip of each anther-lobe (ST) gradually diverges and splits along a line on the outside, becoming open and boat-like, disclosing the minute yellow grains of pollen. At each movement of the panicle, the pollen is shaken out and scattered by the wind, some adhering to the hairs of the stigmas (H). After pollination is completed, the lodicules shrivel and the floret gradually closes.

In a few British grasses, the spikelet-axis continues to grow from the tip, bearing a succession of small leaves, and forming a miniature plant which may terminate in a small inflorescence. The culms bearing such plantlets bend under the extra weight and touch the ground, or the plantlets become detached and fall, and root in the soil. This form of proliferation has been erroneously known as 'vivipary', and such species or variants in which it occurs have often been given the name *'vivipara'*. Examples among the British grasses are *Deschampsia alpina*, *D. caespitosa* var. *vivipara*, *Festuca vivipara*, *Poa alpina* var. *vivipara*, P. × *jemtlandica*, and *P. bulbosa* var. *vivipara*. Proliferation also occasionally occurs in late summer or autumn, with shorter day-lengths, and especially during long periods of dull weather, in various grasses, such as species of *Cynosurus*, *Dactylis*, *Lolium*, *Molinia*.

GRASSES LISTED UNDER HABITATS

The following lists are intended to serve two purposes. First, as the word habitat implies, to give the places in which our grasses are to be found, and second, to enable those studying grasses in a particular type of habitat to name their plants more easily by limiting the number of species to be considered. All except a few very rare or introduced grasses have been listed, and where rare grasses have been included, they are indicated by the letter R. The figures in brackets refer to the pages on which the grasses are described.

1. Coastal Sand-dunes and Shingle-banks

Agropyron obtusiusculum (101)
Agropyron junceiforme (103)
Agropyron pungens (99)
Agrostis stolonifera (303)
Agrostis tenuis (299)
× *Ammocalamagrostis baltica* (R) (285)
Ammophila arenaria (287)
Arrhenatherum elatius (on shingle) (233)
Bromus thominii (77)
Catapodium marinum (207)

Corynephorus canescens (R) (255)
Cynodon dactylon (R) (361)
Elymus arenarius (105)
Festuca juncifolia (R) (139)
Festuca rubra subsp. *arenaria* (377)
Mibora minima (R) (337)
Phleum arenarium (315)
Poa bulbosa (R) (169)
Poa subcaerulea (191)
Vulpia ambigua (R) (159)
Vulpia membranacea (R) (161)

2. Salt-marshes, Coastal Mud-flats, Sea-banks or in Silts near Sea

× *Agropogon littoralis* (R) (307)
Agropyron pungens (99)
Agropyron repens (97)
Agrostis stolonifera (303)
Alopecurus bulbosus (329)
Festuca rubra (137, 375, 376)
Hordeum marinum (111)
Parapholis incurva (341)
Parapholis strigosa (339)

Polypogon monspeliensis (309)
Puccinellia capillaris (197)
Puccinellia distans (199)
Puccinellia fasciculata (195)
Puccinellia maritima (201)
Puccinellia rupestris (203)
Spartina anglica (357)
Spartina maritima (353)
Spartina × *townsendii* (355)

3. Freshwater Habitats: Ditches, Streams, Ponds, Lake-margins, River-banks, Marshes, and Fens

Alopecurus aequalis (327)
Alopecurus geniculatus (331)
Agrostis stolonifera var. *palustris* (303)
Calamagrostis canescens (281)

Calamagrostis epigejos (283)
Calamagrostis scotica (R) (277)
Calamagrostis stricta (R) (279)
Catabrosa aquatica (221)
Deschampsia caespitosa (251)

Deschampsia setacea (R) (247)
Glyceria declinata (115)
Glyceria fluitans (117)
Glyceria maxima (123)
Glyceria × *pedicellata* (119)
Glyceria plicata (121)

Hierochloë odorata (R) (265)
Leersia oryzoides (R) (345)
Molinia caerulea (349)
Phalaris arundinacea (273)
Phragmites communis (347)

4. Low-lying Meadows and Pastures, Water Meadows; on Moist Loamy or Heavy Soils, Sometimes Cut for Hay

Agrostis stolonifera (303)
Alopecurus pratensis (333)
Anthoxanthum odoratum (269)
Briza media (213)
Bromus commutatus (85)
Bromus mollis (77)
Bromus racemosus (83)
Cynosurus cristatus (219)
Dactylis glomerata (215)
Deschampsia caespitosa (251)
Festuca arundinacea (143)

Festuca pratensis (141)
Festuca rubra (137)
× *Festulolium loliaceum* (147)
Helictotrichon pubescens (229)
Holcus lanatus (261)
Hordeum secalinum (113)
Lolium perenne (149)
Phleum pratense (321)
Poa pratensis (189)
Poa subcaerulea (191)
Poa trivialis (185)

5. Pastures, Good to Poor Grades; on Well-drained Soils

Agrostis stolonifera (303)
Agrostis tenuis (299)
Alopecurus pratensis (333)
Cynosurus cristatus (219)
Dactylis glomerata (215)
Festuca pratensis (141)
Festuca rubra (137)

Hordeum secalinum (113)
Lolium perenne (149)
Phleum bertolonii (319)
Phleum pratense (321)
Poa pratensis (189)
Poa trivialis (185)
Trisetum flavescens (245)

6. Hayfields (Sown)

Bromus commutatus (85)
Bromus lepidus (79)
Bromus mollis (77)
Bromus racemosus (83)
Bromus thominii (77)
Dactylis glomerata (215)
Holcus lanatus (261)

Lolium × *hybridum* (151)
Lolium multiflorum (151)
Lolium perenne (149)
Phleum pratense (321)
Vulpia bromoides (155)
Vulpia myuros (157)

7. Lawns, Greens, and Sports-grounds

Agrostis canina (295–7)
Agrostis tenuis (299)
Agrostis stolonifera (303)
Cynosurus cristatus (219)
Dactylis glomerata (215)

Deschampsia flexuosa (249)
Festuca longifolia (131)
Festuca ovina (129)
Festuca rubra (133, 375, 376)
Festuca tenuifolia (127)

Holcus lanatus (261)
Holcus mollis (263)
Koeleria cristata (241)
Lolium perenne (149)
Nardus stricta (343)
Phleum bertolonii (319)
Poa annua (167)

Poa nemoralis (175)
Poa pratensis (189)
Poa trivialis (185)
Puccinellia maritima (sea-washed turf) (201)
Sieglingia decumbens (351)

8. Arable and Waste Land

Agropyron repens (97)
Agrostis gigantea (301)
Agrostis stolonifera (303)
Agrostis tenuis (299)
Aira caryophyllea (257)
Alopecurus myosuroides (325)
Apera spica-venti (289)
Arrhenatherum elatius (233)
Avena fatua (237)
Avena ludoviciana (239)
Briza minor (R) (209)
Bromus commutatus (85)
Bromus lepidus (79)
Bromus mollis (77)
Bromus secalinus (87)
Bromus sterilis (61)

Bromus thominii (77)
Cynosurus echinatus (217)
Dactylis glomerata (215)
Festuca rubra (135, 137, 378)
Gastridium ventricosum (311)
Holcus lanatus (261)
Holcus mollis (263)
Hordeum murinum (109)
Lolium multiflorum (151)
Lolium perenne (149)
Phalaris canariensis (271)
Poa annua (167)
Poa pratensis (189)
Poa trivialis (185)
Vulpia bromoides (155)
Vulpia myuros (157)

9. Rough Grassland (Especially Waste Land near Towns), Roadsides, Field-margins

Agropyron repens (97)
Agrostis gigantea (301)
Agrostis stolonifera (303)
Agrostis tenuis (299)
Arrhenatherum elatius (233)
Bromus diandrus (R) (67)
Bromus mollis (77)
Bromus sterilis (61)
Dactylis glomerata (215)
Deschampsia caespitosa (251)

Festuca arundinacea (143)
Festuca rubra (135, 137, 378)
Holcus lanatus (261)
Holcus mollis (263)
Hordeum murinum (109)
Hordeum secalinum (113)
Lolium perenne (149)
Poa pratensis (189)
Poa trivialis (185)
Trisetum flavescens (245)

In addition to the above, grasses from adjacent grassland may be found on roadsides and field-margins.

10. Shaded Habitats: Woodlands and Hedgerows

Agropyron caninum (95)
Agrostis canina subsp. *canina* (295)
Anthoxanthum odoratum (269)

Brachypodium sylvaticum (89)
Bromus benekenii (R) (69)
Bromus ramosus (71)

Calamagrostis epigejos (wet places) (283)
Deschampsia caespitosa var. *parviflora* (251)
Festuca altissima (R) (125)
Festuca gigantea (145)
Festuca heterophylla (R) (133)
Holcus mollis (263)
Hordelymus europaeus (107)
Melica nutans (223)
Melica uniflora (225)
Milium effusum (275)
Poa chaixii (R) (183)
Poa nemoralis (175)

11. Commons, Heaths, Moors; on Sandy, Stony, or Peaty Soils

Agrostis canina (295–297)
Agrostis setacea (293)
Agrostis tenuis (299)
Aira caryophyllea (257)
Aira praecox (259)
Anthoxanthum adoratum (269)
Apera interrupta (R) (291)
Catapodium rigidum (205)
Deschampsia flexuosa (249)
Festuca ovina (129)
Festuca rubra (137)
Festuca tenuifolia (127)
Holcus lanatus (261)
Koeleria cristata (241)
Molinia caerulea (wet places) (349)
Nardus stricta (343)
Phleum bertolonii (319)
Phleum phleoides (R) (317)
Poa annua (167)
Poa pratensis (189)
Sieglingia decumbens (351)
Vulpia ambigua (R) (159)
Vulpia bromoides (155)

12. Hill and Downs Grassland; Calcareous Soils, on Chalk or Limestone

Agrostis stolonifera (303)
Agrostis tenuis (299)
Anthoxanthum odoratum (269)
Arrhenatherum elatius (233)
Brachypodium pinnatum (91)
Briza media (213)
Bromus erectus (73)
Catapodium rigidum (205)
Cynosurus cristatus (219)
Dactylis glomerata (215)
Festuca arundinacea (143)
Festuca ovina (129)
Festuca rubra (135, 137)
Helictotrichon pratense (231)
Helictotrichon pubescens (229)
Holcus lanatus (261)
Koeleria cristata (241)
Koeleria vallesiana (R) (243)
Lolium perenne (149)
Nardurus maritimus (R) (163)
Phleum bertolonii (319)
Poa angustifolia (187)
Poa compressa (193)
Sesleria caerulea (limestone) (227)
Trisetum flavescens (245)

13. Hill Grassland; on Sandy, Stony, or Shaly Soils

Agrostis canina subsp. *montana* (297)
Agrostis tenuis (299)
Aira caryophyllea (257)
Aira praecox (259)
Anthoxanthum odoratum (269)
Catapodium rigidum (205)
Deschampsia flexuosa (249)
Festuca ovina (129)
Festuca rubra (137)
Festuca tenuifolia (127)
Holcus lanatus (261)

Nardus stricta (343)
Poa pratensis (189)

Sieglingia decumbens (351)
Vulpia bromoides (155)

14. Mountains; in Grassland, on Rocks, Cliffs, etc.

Agropyron donianum (R) (93)
Agrostis canina (295–7)
Agrostis stolonifera (303)
Agrostis tenuis (299)
Aira caryophyllea (257)
Aira praecox (259)
Alopecurus alpinus (R) (335)
Anthoxanthum odoratum (269)
Briza media (213)
Deschampsia alpina (R) (253)
Deschampsia caespitosa (251)
Deschampsia flexuosa (249)
Festuca ovina (129)
Festuca rubra (137, 379)

Festuca vivipara (129)
Helictotrichon pratense (231)
Molinia caerulea (349)
Nardus stricta (343)
Phleum alpinum (R) (323)
Poa alpina (R) (171)
Poa annua (167)
Poa balfouri (R) (177)
Poa flexuosa (R) (173)
Poa glauca (R) (179)
Poa nemoralis (175)
Poa subcaerulea (191)
Sesleria caerulea (227)
Sieglingia decumbens (351)

HOW TO USE THE KEYS

The main key on page 35 (as well as the keys for special purposes on p. 387 and p. 407) is provided for more speedy identification of grasses than would be possible by examining each illustration and description. It is composed of pairs of sets of contrasting characters. The first set of characters of each pair is prefaced by a number, e.g., 1, 2, 3, 4, and so on; the second or contrasting set has the same number as the first, but with the addition of the letter a, e.g. 1a, 2a. After the specimen for naming has been thoroughly examined, it should be compared with the sets of characters given in 1 and 1a to decide with which it agrees best. If it has the structure described in 1, the reader proceeds to 2 and then considers whether the plant fits the characteristics given in 2 or its alternative 2a; if with 2, he proceeds to 3 and 3a; and so on. If, however, the plant has the structure described in 1a, then the next sets of contrasting characters are those of 36 and 36a. The search is continued in this way until, by a process of elimination, the name of the grass is eventually reached. Each pair of sets of contrasting characters may be adjacent as are 4 and 4a, or separated by several paragraphs like 3 and 3a, or by one or more pages as 1 and 1a, but in the last mentioned the page of the contrasting set (1a) is given with the first set. No key is perfect, and as the grasses are so variable in many of their characteristics, particularly in size, colour, and degree of hairiness or smoothness, the supplementary characters included in the key should always be read, and the identification finally confirmed by checking with the illustration and description.

KEY FOR NAMING WILD AND
AGRICULTURAL GRASSES

*The figures in parentheses refer to the pages on which the grasses are
described or mentioned*

1 Spikelets stalkless or with very short stalks (pedicels), arising on one
  side or on opposite sides of the axes of spikes or racemes (to
  p. 39).
2 Spikelets in one or more rows along one side of the axis only (to
  p. 36).
  3 Culm terminated by a single spike or raceme:
    4 Densely tufted wiry perennial, with coarse roots; lemma short-
      awned from the tip; leaf-blades bristle-like, hard, stiff;
      spikelets 1-flowered, narrow; moors, heaths

                                                  Nardus stricta (343)
    4a Annuals; lemmas blunt, awnless, or pointed and awned in
      Nardurus:
      5 Spikelets 1-flowered, 1·8–3 mm. long; leaf-blades delicate, about
        0·5 mm. wide; racemes thin, 0·5–2 cm. long, up to 1 mm.
        wide; culms hair-like; coastal sands..... **Mibora minima** (337)
      5a Spikelets 2–12-flowered, 4–9 mm. long:
        5* Lemmas lanceolate, pointed, tipped with a fine straight awn
          1–6 mm. long, usually minutely hairy; thin grassland or dis-
          turbed soil .... **Nardurus maritimus** (163)
        5a* Lemmas broader, blunt, awnless, mainly smooth:
          6 Lemmas 2–2·5 mm. long; glumes up to 2 mm. long; spikelets
            narrowly oblong, 1–1·5 mm. wide; pedicels up to 1·5 mm.
            long; dry places .... **Catapodium rigidum** (205)
          6a Lemmas 2·5–3·8 mm. long; glumes 2–3·5 mm. long; spikelets
            wider; pedicels shorter; coastal sands

                                              Catapodium marinum (207)
  3a Culm bearing two or more spikes or racemes at or towards the
    apex, rarely 1 in *Spartina maritima:*
    7 Spikes or racemes scattered along the main-axis of the inflor-
      escence (to p. 36):
      8 Ligule a dense fringe of hairs; spikelets flattened, overlapping,
        awnless; maritime perennials, with rhizomes:
        9 Anthers 8–13 mm. long; ligular-hairs mostly 2–3 mm. long;
          spikelets mostly 2·5–3 mm. wide, 14–21 mm. long, hairy;
          leaf-blades 6–15 mm. wide; culms up to 130 cm. high;
          coastal mud-flats and salt-marshes **Spartina anglica** (357)

9a Anthers 4–8 mm. long; ligular-hairs 0·2–2 mm. long; spikelets slightly narrower, 11–18 mm. long:

9* Anthers remaining closed, containing imperfect pollen; spikelets obscurely hairy; upper glume 1–3-nerved; leaf-blades 4–12 mm. wide; culms 30–130 cm. high; coastal mud-flats and salt-marshes **Spartina × townsendii** (355)

9a* Anthers opening when mature, with good pollen:

10 Spikelets softly hairy; upper glume 3-nerved, leaf-blades finally deciduous; culms 15–50 cm. high; salt-marshes
Spartina maritima (353)

10a Spikelets almost hairless; upper glume 5–9-nerved; leaf-blades persisting on the sheaths; culms 40–100 cm. high; coastal mud-flats, very rare **Spartina alterniflora** (359)

8a Ligule absent; spikelets plump, pointed or awned, 3–4 mm. long, bearing short spiny hairs; annual; leaf-blades 8–20 mm. wide; arable and waste land ...... **Echinochloa crus-galli** (363)

7a Spikes or racemes clustered at or near the apex of the culm:

11 Ligule a dense fringe of hairs; perennial, with tough rhizomes and creeping stolons; spikelets strongly compressed, breaking up at maturity, the glumes persisting; coastal sands, S.W. England .... **Cynodon dactylon** (361)

11a Ligule membranous; annuals; spikelets falling entire at maturity; arable and waste land:

12 Leaf-sheaths usually hairless; upper glume about as long as the spikelet; spikelets 2–2·5 mm. long
Digitaria ischaemum (369)

12a Leaf-sheaths usually hairy; upper glume up to half the length of the spikelet; spikelets 2·5–3·3 mm. long
Digitaria sanguinalis (371)

2a Spikelets borne in two rows on opposite sides of the axes of solitary spikes or racemes:

13 Spikelets normally solitary at each node of the axis of the spike or raceme (to p. 38):

14 Spikelets sunken in hollows in the jointed fragile axes of slender cylindrical spikes, 1-flowered, awnless; lemmas membranous, 3-nerved, enclosed by the glumes; salt marshes:

15 Anthers 0·5–1 mm. long; spikes rigid, 1–8 cm. long, often incurved .... **Parapholis incurva** (341)

15a Anthers mostly 2–4 mm. long; spikes stiff, up to 20 cm. long, usually straight .... **Parapholis strigosa** (339)

14a Spikelets appressed to the axis or spreading from it, 2- or more-flowered; spikes not cylindrical; lemmas 5–9-nerved, firm to tough, exceeding the glumes:

16 Spikelets borne on short stalks in spike-like racemes (to p. 37):

17 Leaf-blades with small spreading auricles at the base (junction

with sheath), glossy beneath; lemmas awnless; sterile hybrid between *Lolium perenne* and *Festuca pratensis*

× **Festulolium loliaceum** (147)

17a Leaf-blades without auricles, dull green beneath; lemmas awned:

18 Rhizomes well developed; leaf-sheaths and culms mostly hairless; lemmas tipped with awns 1–5 mm. long; grassland

Brachypodium pinnatum (91)

18a Rhizomes absent; leaf-sheaths loosely hairy; culms hairy at the nodes; lemmas tipped with awns up to 12 mm. long; woods

Brachypodium sylvaticum (89)

16a Spikelets without stalks, borne directly on the spike-axis:

19 Spikelets with their narrower edges fitting into depressions in the spike-axis, the upper glume external:

20 Lower glume developed; sterile hybrid between *Lolium perenne* and *Festuca pratensis* .... × **Festulolium loliaceum** (147)

20a Lower glume absent in all except the terminal spikelets:

21 Upper glume normally much shorter than the rest of the spikelet; florets oblong or lanceolate-oblong, not turgid:

22 Perennial; leaf-blades folded about the midrib when young; lemmas awnless, blunt or slightly pointed; grassland

Lolium perenne (149)

22a Annual or biennial; leaf-blades rolled when young; lemmas awned from near the tip; hay-fields and waste land

Lolium multiflorum (151)

21a Upper glume reaching to or exceeding the uppermost lemma; florets elliptic to ovate, turgid, awnless or awned; annual; waste land .... **Lolium temulentum** (153)

19a Spikelets with their broader sides adjacent to the spike-axis, their glumes both developed and placed laterally:

23 Perennials, tufted, or with spreading rhizomes; grain tightly enclosed between the lemma and palea and adhering to the latter (to p. 38):

24 Spikelets falling entire at maturity or the whole spikelet breaking up; anthers 3·5–8 mm. long; plants with creeping rhizomes:

25 Leaf-blades densely and minutely hairy on the upper surface along the prominent ribs; spike-axis fragile, readily breaking just above each spikelet; lemmas awnless; plants bluish-grey; sand-dunes ..**Agropyron junceiforme** (103)

25a Leaves sparingly hairy or hairless above; spikes not fragile, their axes tough; lemmas awnless or awned:

26 Leaf-blades prominently and closely ribbed on the upper surface, the ribs usually rough, the blades often tightly inrolled (to p. 38):

27 Spikelets closely overlapping, one-fifth to half their length apart, 10–20 mm. long; spikes dense; anthers with good pollen; salt-marshes and dunes

Agropyron pungens (99)

27a Spikelets half their length or more apart, 15–28 mm. long; spikes loose; anthers sterile; pollen shrivelled, translucent; sterile hybrids between *A. junceiforme* and *A. pungens* or *A. repens*

27* Leaf-blades minutely rough on the closely and prominently ribbed upper surface

Agropyron × obtusiusculum (101)

27a* Leaf-blades with short-haired less-ribbed upper surface.

Agropyron × laxum (101)

26a Leaf-blades usually flat, without prominent ribs, the upper surface with short scattered hairs or hairless; lemmas awnless or awned; arable and waste land

Agropyron repens (97)

24a Spikelets breaking up at maturity, the glumes persisting on the spike-axis; anthers 2–3·5 mm. long; plants tufted, without rhizomes:

28 Lemmas narrowed into a straight or wavy awn 7–20 mm. long; spikes usually curved or nodding; woodlands

Agropyron caninum (95)

28a Lemmas tipped with a straight awn up to 3 mm. long; spikes mostly straight; Scottish mountains

Agropyron donianum (93)

23a Annuals; grain free between the lemma and palea; cultivated cereals:

29 Glumes broad, bulging on the back, 5–7-nerved; spikelets 2–5-flowered; lemmas broad, rough on the keels, awnless or awned; Wheat ....**Triticum aestivum** (425)

29a Glumes very narrow, 1-nerved; spikelets usually 2-flowered; lemmas narrow, stiffly hairy on the keels, awned; Rye

Secale cereale (425)

13a Spikelets in twos or threes at each node of the spike-axis:

30 Spikelets usually in pairs, 3–6-flowered; spikes stout, 15–35 cm. long; leaf-blades 8–20 mm. wide; a robust bluish-grey perennial; sand-dunes ....**Elymus arenarius** (105)

30a Spikelets usually in threes, 1- rarely 2-flowered:

31 Spike-axis tough, continuous, persistent (to p. 39):

32 Spikelets breaking up at maturity, the glumes persisting on the spike-axis; lemmas with straight awns 1·5–2·5 cm. long; tufted perennial; woods ....**Hordelymus europaeus** (107)

32a Spikelets breaking up only when threshed; lemmas with stiff awns mostly 10–20 cm. long; annuals; cultivated cereals:

33 Spikes with six rows of fertile spikelets, all spikelets producing
   seed; Barley ....**Hordeum vulgare** (425)
33a Spikes with two rows of fertile spikelets, the lateral spikelets
   sterile; Barley ....**Hordeum distichon** (426)
31a Spike-axis fragile, readily fracturing at maturity beneath each
   cluster of spikelets; only the central spikelet of each three fertile; wild grasses:
34 Glumes of the central spikelet of each three fringed with hairs in
   the lower part; fertile lemma 7–12 mm. long, tipped with an
   awn 18–50 mm. long; arable and waste land
                                             Hordeum murinum (109)
34a Glumes all hairless, rough; fertile lemma 6–9 mm. long:
   35 Spikes 1·5–3 cm. wide, with the awns finally widely spreading;
      glumes of the lateral spikelets dissimilar, one bristle-like, the
      other much wider; annual; salt-marshes
                                             Hordeum marinum (111)
   35a Spikes 0·7–1·5 cm. wide, with the awns erect or slightly spread-
      ing; glumes similar, bristle-like; perennial; grassland
                                             Hordeum secalinum (113)
1a Spikelets on long or short stalks, on the branches of loose or dense
   panicles, rarely in loose racemes, or if in cylindrical spike-like
   panicles, then the spikelets crowded all round the axis:
36 Spikelet-stalks (pedicels) bearing one to several stiff bristles (modified branchlets) which project beyond the spikelets; panicles
   spike-like; annuals; waste and arable land:
37 Bristles bearing barbs pointing backwards, these acting like hooks;
   upper glume as long as the spikelet; panicle greenish or purplish
                                             Setaria verticillata (365)
37a Bristles with barbs pointing forwards (i.e. not hooked):
   38 Upper glume covering the nearly smooth upper lemma; bristles
      green or purplish; spikelets elliptic-oblong
                                             Setaria viridis (365)
   38a Upper glume much shorter than the prominently wrinkled upper
      lemma; bristles yellowish or reddish-yellow; spikelets broadly
      elliptic .... **Setaria glauca** (367)
36a Spikelet-stalks without bristles, but sometimes bearing fine hairs:
39 Spikelets 1-flowered, each formed of 2 to 4 scales (but see *Phalaris*)
   in addition to the flower (to p. 45):
40 Glumes feathery-hairy, 8–10 mm. long, each tapering into a fine
   bristle; lemma with an awn 8–18 mm. long from the back; panicles very dense, globose to oblong-cylindrical, very softly
   hairy; annual; cultivated land; Channel Isles
                                             Lagurus ovatus (313)
40a Glumes hairless or shortly hairy, the panicles not as above:
   41 Lemmas surrounded by fine white hairs from the base, the hairs

39

one-third the length of to much longer than the lemmas; perennials, with rhizomes:
42 Spikelets 3–7 mm. long:
43 Lemma smooth, half to two-thirds the length of the glumes, shortly or much exceeded by a ring of hairs from the base; damp woods and fens:
44 Leaf-blades hairless; panicles dense; hairs much exceeding the lemma; ligules 4–12 mm. long

Calamagrostis epigejos (283)
44a Leaf-blades hairy on the upper surface; panicles moderately loose; hairs slightly exceeding the lemma; ligules 2–5 mm. long ....**Calamagrostis canescens** (281)
43a Lemma minutely rough, with a ring of hairs from the base up to three-fourths its length; lemma three-fourths to four-fifths the length of the glumes:
45 Spikelets 4·5–6 mm. long; glumes finely pointed; N. Scotland only; wet places, very rare ...**Calamagrostis scotica** (277)
45a Spikelets 3–4 mm. long; glumes pointed or somewhat blunt; wet places, rare ....**Calamagrostis stricta** (279)
42a Spikelets 9–16 mm. long; panicles very dense, spike-like:
46 Panicles tapering upwards, linear-lanceolate to lanceolate, purplish; leaf-blades flat or becoming inrolled; glumes lanceolate; anthers about 4 mm. long; sterile hybrid between *Calamagrostis epigejos* and *Ammophila arenaria*; sand-dunes .... × **Ammocalamagrostis baltica** (285)
46a Panicles cylindrical, pale; leaf-blades tightly inrolled, rigid, sharp-pointed; glumes oblong; anthers 4–7 mm. long, fertile; sand-dunes ....**Ammophila arenaria** (287)
41a Lemmas hairless at the base or with only a tuft of very short hairs there:
47 Glumes conspicuously awned from the tip:
48 Awns 4–7 mm. long; panicles very dense and and bristly, covered with the fine awns; spikelets falling from the stalks at maturity; annual; salt-marshes

Polypogon monspeliensis (309)
48a Awns up to 2 mm. long; panicles less dense, slightly bristly; spikelets persisting; perennial; sterile hybrid between *Polypogon monspeliensis* and *Agrostis stolonifera*; salt-marshes; rare .... × **Agropogon littoralis** (307)
47a Glumes without awns, or if with very short awns, then the panicles narrowly cylindrical and the glumes persisting on their stalks at maturity:
49 Panicles loose, or contracted, but not very dense, cylindrical and spike-like (to p. 42):
50 Glumes absent, the spikelet being composed only of the

40

lemma, palea, and flower; lemma and palea fringed with short stiff hairs; spikelets oblong, flattened, 4–5 mm. long; palea 3-nerved; leaf-sheaths rough with reflexed spiny hairs between the ribs; perennial; wet places; rare

Leersia oryzoides (345)

50a Glumes present, well developed, half as long as to longer than the lemma:

51 Glumes about half the length of the lemma; leaf-sheaths strongly compressed and keeled; panicles loose; lemma 3-nerved; stoloniferous perennial; wet places

Catabrosa aquatica (221)

51a Glumes nearly as long as to longer than the lemma; leaf-sheaths rounded on the back:

52 Lemmas with fine straight awns 4–10 mm. long; lemma equalling or slightly exceeding the glumes; annuals:

53 Panicles usually open and very loose, 3–15 cm. wide; anthers 1–2 mm. long; arable and waste land

Apera spica-venti (289)

53a Panicles narrow, contracted, dense and continuous, or interrupted, 0·4–1·5 cm. wide; anthers 0·3–0·4 mm. long; sandy places .... **Apera interrupta** (291)

52a Lemmas awnless or short-awned, the awn if up to 5 mm. long then bent when dry; glumes longer than the lemmas:

54 Glumes swollen, hardened and shining near the base; panicles narrow, contracted and dense before and after flowering, 2–10 cm. long, 5–12 mm. wide; annual; grassland and arable land

Gastridium ventricosum (311)

54a Glumes not swollen at the base:

55 Lemmas thinly membranous, more delicate than the glumes; spikelets compressed from the side, with the glumes keeled; perennials (to p. 42):

56 Glumes persisting on the pedicels after the seeds have fallen; palea shorter than the lemma; anthers 1–2 mm. long (to p. 42):

57 Ligules (upper) of the vegetative shoots as long as or longer than wide (to p. 42):

58 Ligules of upper culm-leaves narrow, usually pointed; palea very small, less than one-fourth the length of the lemma; lemmas usually awned (to p. 42):

59 Basal leaf-blades very fine, bristle-like, 0·2–0·3 mm. wide, with a single groove; densely tufted perennial, without rhizomes or stolons; panicle dense and spike-like before and after flowering,

0·5–1·5 cm. wide; heaths and moors
Agrostis setacea (293)
59a Basal leaf-blades flat or inrolled, 1–3 mm. wide;
perennials with rhizomes or stolons; panicles up
to 7 cm. wide:
60 Mat-forming; spreading by leafy creeping stolons;
leaves soft; panicles usually rather loose; damp
grassland
Agrostis canina subsp. **canina** (295)
60a Tuft-forming; spreading by slender scaly underground rhizomes; leaves firm to somewhat stiff;
panicles usually somewhat dense; dry grassland
Agrostis canina subsp. **montana** (297)
58a Upper ligules very blunt; palea half to two-thirds the
length of the lemma; lemmas usually without
awns:
61 Panicles usually open and very loose; perennial with
tough creeping rhizomes; arable and waste land
Agrostis gigantea (301)
61a Panicles contracted and usually dense after flowering; perennial with trailing leafy stolons forming
a loose to close turf; grassland
Agrostis stolonifera (303)
57a Ligules of vegetative shoots shorter than wide;
panicles usually open and very loose; perennials,
with rhizomes; grassland .... **Agrostis tenuis** (299)
56a Glumes falling with the rest of the spikelet at maturity;
panicle dense; palea about as long as the lemma;
anthers about 0·5 mm. long; perennial, with trailing
leafy stolons; rare introduced grass; Channel Isles
Agrostis semiverticillata (305)
55a Lemmas hardened, thickened and shining, much firmer
than the membranous glumes, awnless; spikelets compressed from the back; panicles loose or contracted:
62 Panicles very loose, 10–40 cm. long by up to 20 cm.
wide; leaf-blades 10–30 cm. long, 5–15 mm. wide;
perennial; woods .... **Milium effusum** (275)
62a Panicles contracted, 1·5–5 cm. long, narrow; leaf-
blades up to 5 cm. long and 1·5–3 mm. wide; annual;
Channel Isles .... **Milium scabrum** (275)
49a Spikelets in very dense narrowly cylindrical or oblong spike-
like panicles (3–12 mm. wide):
63 Lemmas awnless; glumes pointed or with short awns at the
tips, persisting on their stalks after the rest of the spikelet
has fallen; panicles very stiff and rough (to p. 43):

64 Annual; glumes gradually narrowed to sharply pointed tips; anthers 0·3–1 mm. long; panicles usually narrowed at the base; sand-dunes .... **Phleum arenarium** (315)

64a Perennials; glumes abruptly pointed or very blunt; anthers 1–2 mm. long:

65 Panicles oblong, broadly cylindrical, 1–5 cm. long, 6–12 mm. wide; awns of glume 2–3 mm. long; mountains (610–1220 m.) .... **Phleum alpinum** (323)

65a Panicles narrowly cylindrical; awns of glumes up to 2 mm. long:

66 Glumes very blunt (truncate); leaf-blades 2–9 mm. wide; culms often swollen and bulbous at the base; ligules up to 6 mm. long:·

67 Panicles mostly 1–6 cm. long by 3–5 mm. wide; leaf-blades 3–12 cm. long; spikelets 2–3 mm. long; glumes with awns 0·4–1 mm. long; grassland
Phleum bertolonii (319)

67a Panicles mostly 6–15 cm. long by 6–10 mm. wide; leaf-blades up to 45 cm. long; spikelets 3–4 mm. long; glumes with awns 1–2 mm. long; grassland
Phleum pratense (321)

66a Glumes abruptly narrowed into a rough point up to 0·5 mm. long; leaf-blades 1–2·5 mm. wide; culms never swollen at the base, densely tufted; ligules up to 2 mm. long; dry grassland .... **Phleum phleoides** (317)

63a Lemmas usually awned; glumes awnless; spikelets jointed below the glumes and falling as a whole at maturity; panicles soft:

68 Panicles broadly cylindrical or ovoid, 1–3 cm. long by 7–12 mm. wide, silkily hairy; loosely tufted perennial; mountains .... **Alopecurus alpinus** (335)

68a Panicles narrowly cylindrical or cylindrical, 3–10 mm. wide:

69 Culms bulbous at the base; glumes sharply pointed; leaf-blades 1–3·5 mm. wide; panicles 3–5 mm. wide; spikelets 3–4 mm. long; salt-marshes
Alopecurus bulbosus (329)

69a Culms not bulbous at the base:

70 Margins of glumes united only near the base; keels of glumes fringed with fine hairs; perennials or annuals (to p. 44):

71 Awn conspicuous, projecting from the glumes; anthers yellow or purple; spikelets 2·5–6 mm. long (to p. 44):

72 Culms erect or spreading, 30–120 cm. high; panicles 5–10 mm. wide; spikelets 3·5–6 mm. long; anthers 2–3·5 mm. long; meadows and damp places (to p. 44):

72* Uppermost ligule 1–2·5 mm. long; spikelets 4–6 mm.

43

long; culms mostly erect; anthers 2–3·5 mm. long,
opening, with good pollen; meadows

Alopecurus pratensis (333)

72a* Uppermost ligule up to 5 mm. long; spikelets
3·5–4·5 mm. long; culms spreading and geniculate;
anthers 2 mm. long, remaining closed, with imperfect pollen; wet places

Alopecurus × hybridus (331)

72a Culms spreading, usually ascending from a bent or
prostrate base and rooting at the nodes; panicles
3–7 mm. wide; spikelets 2·5–3·5 mm. long; anthers
1·5–2 mm. long; wet places

Alopecurus geniculatus (331)

71a Awn enclosed by the glumes or very slightly protruding
from them; anthers bright orange or golden-yellow;
spikelets 2–2·5 mm. long; panicles 1–5 cm. long,
3–6 mm. wide; wet places **Alopecurus aequalis** (327)

70a Margins of glumes united up to half their length; keels of
glumes minutely hairy; spikelets 4·5–7 mm. long;
annual; arable and waste land

Alopecurus myosuroides (325)

39a Spikelets 2- to many-flowered, rarely with only one flower, and
then formed of at least six scales (*Phalaris*):

39* Spikelets borne in two opposite rows on the axis of a spike,
annual, or rarely perennial (?) .... **Gaudinia fragilis** (245)

39a* Spikelets stalked and borne in panicles:

73 Both glumes, or upper only, as long as or longer than the lowest
lemma and usually as long as the whole spikelet and enclosing
all the lemmas; lemmas awnless (*Koeleria, Phalaris*), or frequently awned from the back, the awn usually bent at or near
the middle when dry (to p. 48):

74 Lemmas without awns, or very rarely with a very short awn from
the tip (to p. 45):

75 Ligule a dense fringe of short hairs; lemmas 3-toothed at the tip;
spikelets 4–6-flowered, plump, 6–12 mm. long; panicles
compact or loose; moors, heaths

Sieglingia decumbens (351)

75a Ligules membranous; lemmas not 3-toothed; spikelets 1–3-
flowered:

76 Ligules up to 1 mm. long; spikelets 2–3-flowered; panicles
spike-like, glistening; densely tufted perennials; leaf-blades
1–3 mm. wide (to p. 45):

77 Base of plant thickly coated with a dense network of fibrous
remains of the old leaf-sheaths; Somerset hills

Koeleria vallesiana (243)

77a Base of plant not so clothed; dry grassland
Koeleria cristata (241)
76a Ligules 3–10 mm. long; spikelets 1-flowered; fertile lemma 1,
with 2 much smaller sterile lemmas at its base, the lemmas
enclosed by the glumes; leaf-blades 4–18 mm. wide:
78 Reed-like perennials, with stout erect culms 60–200 cm. high;
panicles lanceolate to oblong, up to 25 cm. long and 4 cm.
wide; wèt places .... **Phalaris arundinacea** (273)
78a Annuals; panicles dense, ovate to ovate-oblong, 1–6 cm.
long, 8–22 mm. wide; waste and arable land:
79 Spikelets all fertile and alike in structure, their glumes persisting on the pedicels after the seeds have fallen:
80 Spikelets 6–10 mm. long up to 6 mm. wide
Phalaris canariensis (271)
80a Spikelets 4·5–5·5 mm. long, 2·5–3 mm. wide
Phalaris minor (271)
79a Spikelets in clusters of 6 or 7, the central one of each cluster
fertile, the others sterile, smaller and different in structure, each cluster falling as a whole at maturity
Phalaris paradoxa (271)
74a Lemmas usually with an awn arising from the back:
81 Spikelets 11–32 mm. long; awns 12–55 mm. long; ovary and
grain hairy (to p. 46):
82 Tufted perennials 30–100 cm. high; spikelets erect or spreading; glumes 1–3-nerved; awns 12–22 mm. long:
83 Leaf-sheaths without hairs; panicles erect, contracted; spikelets 3–6-flowered; spikelet-axis with hairs 1–2 mm. long;
dry grassland .... **Helictotrichon pratense** (231)
83a Leaf-sheaths softly hairy; panicles erect or finally nodding,
loose; spikelets 2–3-flowered, the spikelet-axis conspicuously hairy with white hairs up to 7 mm. long; grassland
Helictotrichon pubescens (229)
82a Annuals, up to 180 cm. high; spikelets pendulous; glumes
closely 7–11-nerved; awns 20–55 mm. long:
84 Lemma with two fine bristles 3–7 mm. long from the apex, in
addition to the awn (20–35 mm.) on the back; without an
articulation between the lemmas or a scar at the base of
the second lemma; arable land; sometimes cultivated
Avena strigosa (235)
84a Lemma without bristles at the apex, toothed only there:
85 Lemmas densely bearded at the base; axis of spikelet readily
disarticulating between the upper glume and lowest
lemma; lowest lemma with a thickened horse-shoe-
shaped scar at the base:

86 Axis of spikelet readily disarticulating between the lemmas, the second lemma with a scar at the base; third lemma when present awned; arable and waste land
Avena fatua (237)

86a Axis of spikelet tough and continuous between the lemmas, the second lemma without a scar at the base; third lemma when present awnless; arable and waste land ....**Avena ludoviciana** (239)

85a Lemmas without hairs; axis of spikelet not articulated either above the glumes or between the lemmas, but fracturing irregularly when threshed; cultivated cereal; Common Oat .... **Avena sativa** (17–21, 427)

81a Spikelets 2–11 mm. long; awns up to 17 mm. long:

87 Longer awns 10–17 mm. long; spikelets 7–11 mm. long; lowest floret usually male; ovary and grain hairy; perennial; rough grassland .... **Arrhenatherum elatius** (233)

87a Awns up to 10 mm. long; spikelets up to 10 mm. long; ovary and grain hairless:

88 Lowest flower in each spikelet bisexual (with stamens and ovary); leaves not scented when bruised (e.g. with coumarin) (to p. 47):

89 Glumes falling with the rest of the spikelet at maturity, dull; spikelets strongly flattened; lower lemma awnless; perennials:

90 Tufted perennial, softly hairy all over, with short hairs at the nodes of the culms; awn of the upper lemma becoming hook-like, hidden by the glumes; grassland
Holcus lanatus (261)

90a Perennial, with tough creeping rhizomes; nodes bearded with spreading or reflexed hairs; awn of upper lemma becoming slightly bent, protruding from the glumes: shady places, arable land .... **Holcus mollis** (263)

89a Glumes persisting on the pedicels after the rest of the spikelet has fallen, shining, especially at the margins; lower lemma awned:

91 Awns very slender, the upper part of each finer than the lower (to p. 47)

92 Lemmas with the awn arising about the middle of the back; spikelets 2–4-flowered, usually yellowish, 5–7 mm. long; perennial; grassland
Trisetum flavescens (245)

92a Lemmas with the awn arising near the base, very rarely above; spikelets usually 2-flowered:

93 Perennials, densely tufted; spikelets mostly 4–7 mm.

long (rarely only 2·5); lemmas with broad, toothed
tips:
94 Leaves bristle-like, 0·2–0·8 mm. wide; awns 4–7 mm.
long:
95 Ligules blunt, 0·5–3 mm. long; leaf-sheaths often
slightly rough; lemmas 3·5–5·5 mm. long; moors,
heaths .... **Deschampsia flexuosa** (249)
95a Ligules finely pointed, 2–8 mm. long; leaf-sheaths
smooth; lemmas 2·5–3 mm. long; wet places
Deschampsia setacea (247)
94a Leaves flat or inrolled, 2–5 mm. wide, prominently
ribbed on the upper surface; awns up to 4 mm. long:
96 Awn arising near the base of the lemma; spikelets usually sexual, very rarely proliferous; wet grassland,
woods .... **Deschampsia caespitosa** (251)
96a Awn arising from the middle of the lemma or above
the middle; spikelets mostly proliferous (bearing
miniature plants); mountains

Deschampsia alpina (253)
93a Annuals; leaf-blades thread-like, 0·3–0·5 mm. wide;
culms very slender; spikelets 2·5–3·5 mm. long;
lemmas finely 2-toothed at the tip; sandy places:
97 Panicles very loose and spreading, 1–12 cm. long and
wide; leaf-sheaths minutely rough in the upper part
Aira caryophyllea (257)
97a Panicles spike-like 0·2–0·8 cm. wide; leaf-sheaths
smooth .... **Aira praecox** (259)
91a Awns with the terminal portion thickened and club-
shaped, and the lower portion orange or brown, the
junction of the two parts marked by a ring of minute
hairs; densely tufted perennial, with bristle-like leaf-
blades 0·3–0·5 mm. wide; panicles rather dense,
0·5–1·5 cm. wide; sand-dunes

Corynephorus canescens (255)
88a Lower two flowers of each spikelet male or barren, the third
bisexual; leaf-blades aromatic (strongly scented with
coumarin when bruised):
98 Spikelets golden-brown in the upper part, 3·5–5 mm. long,
borne in loose panicles up to 8 cm. wide; glumes equally
long; lower two flowers male, their lemmas awnless; wet
places; rare; N. Ireland and Scotland

Hierochloë odorata (265)
98a Spikelets green or purplish, 5–10 mm. long, in spike-like
panicles 0·6–1·5 cm. wide; lower glume about half the

length of the upper; lower two florets barren (without stamens or ovary), their lemmas awned:

99 Perennial; culms unbranched; glumes thinly hairy; grassland
Anthoxanthum odoratum (269)

99a Annual; culms branched, especially in the lower part; glumes hairless; arable and waste land
Anthoxanthum puelii (267)

73a Glumes usually shorter than the lowest lemma; the other lemmas distinctly exceeding the glumes (except *Melica*): lemmas awnless or with a straight or flexuous awn from or near the tip or from between two apical teeth:

100 Ligule a fringe of hairs:

100* Spikelets unisexual, the sexes on different plants; forming dense tussocks, up to 300 cm. high; leaf-blades 90–270 cm. long; panicles 30–120 cm. long; escape from cultivation
Cortaderia selloana (347)

100a* Spikelets bisexual; leaf-blades and panicles smaller:

101 Culms 140–300 cm. high; leaf-blades 10–30 mm. wide; panicles deep purple, finally silky; spikelets 10–16 mm. long; fetile lemmas 9–13 mm. long, surrounded by fine white hairs from the base up to 9 mm. long; wet places
Phragmites communis (347)

101a Culms 15–120 cm. high; leaf-blades 3–10 mm. wide; spikelets 4–9 mm. long; lemmas 4–6 mm. long, hairless; wet peaty places .... **Molinia caerulea** (349)

100a Ligule membranous, sometimes very short:

102 Spikelets of two kinds, fertile and sterile mixed in dense clusters and borne on one side of the main axis of spike-like panicles, the sterile spikelets composed of numerous persistent stiff scales which more or less conceal the fertile spikelets:

103 Perennial; culms unbranched; leaf-blades 1–4 mm. wide; panicles narrowly oblong, 4–10 mm. wide; fertile spikelets 3–6 mm. long; lemmas usually tipped with an awn to 1 mm. long; grassland .... **Cynosurus cristatus** (219)

103a Annual; culms often branched; leaf-blades 3–10 mm. wide; panicles ovate to oblong, bristly, 10–20 mm. wide; fertile spikelets 8–14 mm. long; lemmas tipped with awns 6–16 mm. long; arable and waste land
Cynosurus echinatus (217)

102a Spikelets all alike in the same panicle:

104 Lemmas with a broad 3–5-toothed tip; panicles spike-like, 1–3 cm. long, 5–10 mm. wide, usually bluish- or purplish-grey; tufted perennial; calcareous grassland
Sesleria caerulea subsp. **calcarea** (227)

104a Lemmas entire or only 2-toothed, very rarely 3-toothed and then with loose panicles:

105 Lemmas keeled, laterally compressed, not rounded on the back; spikelets less than 10 mm. long, flattened (to p. 51):

106 Spikelets borne in dense one-sided clusters on the branches of a panicle; lemmas tipped with a rigid awn up to 1·5 mm. long; tufted perennials:

107 Lemmas usually hairy on the keels, tipped with rough awns up to 1·5 mm. long; grassland **Dactylis glomerata** (215)

107a Lemmas minutely rough on the keels, tipped with smooth shorter awns; woods; very rare

Dactylis polygama (215)

106a Spikelets borne in loose or contracted panicles; lemmas not awned:

108 Leaf-blades 5–10 mm. wide, up to 45 cm. long; lemmas minutely rough, hairless; tufted perennial, 60–120 cm. high, with strongly flattened shoots, without rhizomes; ligules up to 1·5 mm. long; woods ... **Poa chaixii** (183)

108a Leaf-blades mostly less than 5 mm. wide; lemmas hairy, rarely hairless and then quite smooth:

109 Plants without rhizomes; loosely to densely tufted perennials or annuals (to p. 50):

110 Basal leaf-sheaths enlarged and fleshy, forming a bulbous thickening at the base of the shoots; perennial, 5–40 cm. high; ligules up to 4 mm. long; leaf-blades 1–2 mm. wide; coastal sands

Poa bulbosa (169)

110a Basal leaf-sheaths thin; shoots not bulbous at the base:

111 Ligules of culm-leaves mostly 2–10 mm. long; annuals, or perennials (to p. 50):

112 Branches of panicles usually in pairs or solitary; plants 1–40 cm. high (to p. 50):

113 Densely tufted perennials, with unbranched mostly erect culms, coated at the base with old leaf-sheaths; mountain grasses (to p. 50):

114 Leaf-blades blunt or abruptly pointed at the tip, 2–4 mm. wide; spikelets sexual, 4–7 mm. long, or proliferous .... **Poa alpina** (171)

114a Leaf-blades gradually tapering to a pointed tip, 1–2 mm. wide:

115 Spikelets sexual, 4–5·5 mm. long; rare

Poa flexuosa (173)

115a Spikelets proliferous; rare

Poa × jemtlandica (173)

113a Annuals, or rarely short-lived perennials: culms erect, spreading or prostrate, very slender, weak, often branched towards the base; spikelets always sexual:

116 Anthers 0·2–0·5 mm. long; lemmas 2–2·5 mm. long, separate; Cornwall and Channel Isles
Poa infirma (165)

116a Anthers 0·7–1·3 mm. long; lemmas 2·5–4 mm. long, overlapping; widespread and common grass on arable and waste land .... **Poa annua** (167)

112a Branches of panicles in clusters of 3 to 7; plants 20–150 cm. high:

117 Ligules pointed, 4–10 mm. long; leaf-sheaths usually rough; lemmas with rather prominent nerves; plants with creeping leafy stolons; grassland, etc.
Poa trivialis (185)

117a Ligules blunt, 2–5 mm. long; leaf-sheaths smooth; lemmas obscurely nerved; loosely tufted plants without stolons; wet places ... **Poa palustris** (181)

111a Ligules of culm-leaves 0·3–3 mm. long, blunt; loosely tufted perennials:

118 Ligules up to about 0·5 mm. long; leaves usually green; panicles usually nodding; lower glume lanceolate; woods and other shady places
Poa nemoralis (175)

118a Ligules 1–3 mm. long; leaves bluish-grey or bluish-green; mountain grasses:

119 Panicles mostly nodding; lower glume lanceolate; lemmas 3·5–5 mm. long. .... **Poa balfouri** (177)

119a Panicles stiffly erect and usually open; lower glume ovate; lemmas 3–4 mm. long .. **Poa glauca** (179)

109a Plants with rhizomes; ligules 0·5–3 mm. long:

120 Culms flattened, wiry, 4–6 noded, in loose tufts, or scattered; spikelets 3–8 mm. long, 3–10-flowered; lemmas 2·5–3 mm. long; dry places
Poa compressa (193)

120a Culms circular in section, 1–4 noded:

121 Basal leaf-blades bristle-like, 1–2 mm. wide; lemmas 2–3 mm. long; culms and shoots in small compact erect tufts; dry grassland ..... **Poa angustifolia** (187)

121a Basal leaf-blades 2–4 mm. (rarely more) wide, folded or flat; lemmas 3–5 mm. long:

122 Panicle-branches mostly in clusters of 3 to 5 at a node; culms in tufts; glumes abruptly pointed; grassland, etc. .... **Poa pratensis** (189)

122a Panicle-branches usually in pairs or threes; culms mostly scattered and solitary; glumes tapering to a finely pointed tip: damp places

Poa subcaerulea (191)

105a Lemmas rounded on the back especially in the lower part, or if keeled then only in the upper part, or the spikelets more than 12 mm. long (*Bromus* spp.):

123 Lemmas awnless, with blunt tips, these often thin and whitish (to p. 53):

124 Spikelets 1- to 3-flowered:

125 Leaf-sheaths tubular, their margins united, cylindrical or 4-angled; glumes almost enclosing the 7–9-nerved lemmas; spikelet-axis terminated by a club-shaped mass of sterile lemmas; spikelets nodding; woodland grasses, with slender rhizomes:

126 Leaf-sheaths with a bristle-like outgrowth at the apex; spikelets in a spreading panicle, each spikelet with one bisexual flower .... **Melica uniflora** (225)

126a Leaf-sheaths without a bristle at the apex; spikelets usually in a nodding one-sided narrow raceme, each spikelet with two or three bisexual flowers

Melica nutans (223)

125a Leaf-sheaths compressed and keeled, with free margins; glumes shorter than the 3-nerved lemmas; spikelets with one to three bisexual flowers; aquatic grass, with creeping leafy stolons

Catabrosa aquatica (221)

124a Spikelets 3- to 20-flowered:

127 Spikelets nodding, 3–15 mm. wide, plump, on curved hair-like pedicels; glumes and lemmas hooded at the apex; lemmas very broad, cordate at the base (to p. 52):

128 Spikelets 14–25 mm. long, 8–15 mm. wide, 7–20-flowered; panicles sparingly divided, bearing few spikelets; annual; cultivated grass; Channel Isles

Briza maxima (211)

128a Spikelets 3–7 mm. long and wide, 4–12-flowered; panicles loosely divided, usually with many spikelets:

129 Annual; ligules 3–6 mm. long; leaf-blades 3–9 mm. wide; lemmas up to 3·5 mm. long, their tips inflexed at maturity; anthers 0·6 mm. long; arable and waste land .... **Briza minor** (209)

129a Perennial; ligules 0·5–1·5 mm. long; leaf-blades 2–4 mm. wide; lemmas 4 mm. long, their tips not inflexed; anthers 2–2·5 mm. long; grassland

Briza media (213)

127a Spikelets erect or spreading, generally narrow, on stiff pedicels: lemmas not cordate at the base:

130 Leaf-sheaths with their margins united; lemmas prominently 7-nerved, minutely rough; freshwater aquatic grasses:

131 Plants reed-like, 90–250 cm. high, with stout to robust culms; leaf-blades 30–60 cm. long by 7–20 mm. wide; spikelets 5–12 mm. long; lemmas very blunt, 3–4 mm. long .... **Glyceria maxima** (123)

131a Plants 10–100 cm. high, slender to somewhat stout but not reed-like; leaf-blades 3–30 cm. long by 1·5–14 mm. wide; spikelets 10–35 mm. long:

132 Lemmas 6–7·5 mm. long, blunt or slightly pointed; anthers 2–3 mm. long; panicles narrow after flowering .... **Glyceria fluitans** (117)

132a Lemmas 3·5–5·5 mm. long; anthers less than 2 mm. long:

133 Lemmas usually 3-toothed or 3-lobed at the tip, 4–5 mm. long; paleas with their two sharply pointed apical teeth projecting from the tip of the lemma; anthers 0·8–1 mm. long; leaves greyish-green .... **Glyceria declinata** (115)

133a Lemmas blunt, not conspicuously lobed; tips of paleas not projecting beyond the lemmas; anthers 1–1·8 mm. long; leaves mostly green:

134 Spikelets fragile, readily breaking up beneath each lemma at maturity; lemmas 3·5–5 mm. long; anthers opening, with good pollen
Glyceria plicata (121)

134a Spikelets persisting; lemmas mostly 5–5·5 mm. long; anthers remaining closed, without good pollen; sterile hybrid between *G. fluitans* and *G. plicata* .... **Glyceria × pedicellata** (119)

130a Leaf-sheaths with the margins free and with one folding over the other; lemmas 5-nerved, smooth; salt-marsh or dry land grasses:

135 Panicles very loose and open, up to 14 cm. wide; branches clustered, bare for up to half their length, becoming deflexed; lemmas 2–2·5 mm. long; salt-marshes ....**Puccinellia distans** (199)

135a Panicles mostly contracted and dense, or if loose then with some at least of the branches bearing spikelets to the base; branches not becoming deflexed:

136 Plants with creeping stolons, these rooting at the nodes

and forming a dense turf; lemmas 3–5 mm. long;
anthers 2–3 mm. long; salt-marshes

Puccinellia maritima (201)

136a Plants tufted, perennial or annual; anthers 0·3–
1·2 mm. long:
137 Lemmas minutely hairy at the base; salt-marshes:
138 Tufted perennials; lemmas 1·8–3 mm. long:
138* Leaf-blades 1–2 mm. wide; lemmas 2–3 mm.
long, the middle nerve not reaching the tip; N.
Scottish coasts ....**Puccinellia capillaris** (197)
138a* Leaf-blades 1·5–5 mm. wide; lemmas 1·8–
2·3 mm. long, the middle nerve minutely projecting from the tip .... **Puccinellia fasciculata** (195)
138a Annual or biennial; lemmas 3–4 mm. long

Puccinellia rupestris (203)

137a Lemmas hairless; annuals:
139 Panicle spike-like, narrow, rigid, branched in the
lower part; main-axis rigid, flattened on the back;
spikelets borne in two rows on one side of the
main-axis and its branches, almost stalkless; lemmas 2·5–3·8 mm. long; coastal sands

Catapodium marinum (207)

139a Panicle loose or dense, stiff, with slender main-axis
and branches; spikelets on short stalks; lemmas
2–2·5 mm. long; dry places

Catapodium rigidum (205)

123a Lemmas awned or with pointed tips:
140 Basal leaf-blades bristle-like, numerous, mostly hairless,
0·2–1·5 mm. wide, tightly inrolled or infolded, stiff to
rigid; ligules extremely short; perennial grasses; spikelets 3–18 mm. long; lemmas awnless or tipped with an
awn up to 6 mm. long (to p. 54):
141 Plants densely tufted, without rhizomes (to p. 54):
142 Lemmas finely pointed, usually awnless, 2·5–3·5 mm.
long; leaf-blades hair-like, 0·2–0·4 mm. in diameter:
spikelets 3–7 mm. long; acid grassland

Festuca tenuifolia (127)

142a Lemmas 3:5–8 mm. long, tipped with a fine awn up to
6 mm. long; or spikelets proliferous:
143 Leaf-blades alike, those at the base being similar to
those higher on the culm (to p. 54):
144 Leaves green or greyish-green (to p. 54):
145 Leaf-blades 0·3–0·6 mm. wide; lemmas tipped with
an awn 0·5–1·5 mm. long; leaf-sheaths with free
margins:

53

146 Spikelets sexual; heaths, hill and mountain grassland .... **Festuca ovina** (129)
146a Spikelets proliferous; hills and mountains
                              Festuca vivipara (129)
145a Leaf-blades 0·5–1 mm. wide; lemmas with awns up
    to 4 mm. long:
 147 Leaf-sheaths with free margins; dry grassland
                              Festuca longifolia (131)
147a Leaf-sheaths tubular, with the margins united, but
    soon splitting; lawns, greens, etc
                     Festuca rubra subsp. **commutata** (135)
144a Leaves bluish-white (covered with a whitish wax);
    East Anglian heaths; cultivated in gardens
                              Festuca glauca (131)
143a Leaf-blades of two kinds, green, the basal very fine,
    0·3–0·5 mm. wide, infolded, those of the culm flat,
    2–4 mm. wide; spikelets 7–14 mm. long; lemma
    tipped with an awn up to 6 mm. long
                              Festuca heterophylla (133)
141a Plants forming loose to dense mats, or with scattered
    shoots and culms; rhizomes present, very slender,
    extensively creeping; leaf-blades 0·5–1·5 mm. wide:
 148 Lemmas 5–6 (rarely 7) mm. long, hairless or hairy;
    anthers 2–3 mm. long; spikelets 5–14 mm. long; leaf-
    blades blunt or abruptly pointed; grasslands; salt-
    marshes ......,.............. **Festuca rubra** subsp. (137)
148a Lemmas 7–10 mm. long, usually softly hairy; anthers
    4–5 mm. long; spikelets 10–18 mm. long; leaf-blades
    with a hard sharply pointed tip; sand-dunes
                              Festuca juncifolia (139)
140a Basal leaf-blades flat or folded, generally much wider
    than the above, or if slender then the lemmas with
    longer awns and the plants all annuals:
 149 Leaf-sheaths with narrow spreading auricles at the apex;
    lemmas 6–9 mm. long; tufted perennials (to p. 55):
 150 Lemmas awnless or with awns up to 4 mm. long:
 151 Panicle-branches in pairs, the shorter one of each pair
    bearing one or two spikelets; auricles at sheath-apex
    quite hairless; lowland grassland
                              Festuca pratensis (141)
151a Shorter panicle-branch of each pair bearing three or
    more spikelets; auricles fringed with minute hairs;
    grasslands .... **Festuca arundinacea** (143)
150a Lemmas awned, the awns 4–18 mm. long; auricles

hairless; leaf-blades bright green, 4–18 mm. wide; woods and shady places;

150* Leaf-blades glossy beneath; sheaths hairless; lemma-awns 10–18 mm. long ....**Festuca gigantea** (145)

150a* Leaf-blades dull green beneath; lower sheaths softly to stiffly hairy with reflexed hairs; lemma-awns 4–8 mm. long:

151* Upper leaf-sheaths hairless or minutely hairy; ligules 1–3 mm. long; panicles contracted, their branches bearing 1–3 spikelets, the lowest with a hairless scale at the base ....**Bromus benekenii** (69)

151a* Upper leaf-sheaths stiffly hairy; ligules up to 6 mm. long; panicles loose and open, with spreading and drooping branches bearing up to 9 spikelets, the lowest branch with a ciliate scale at the base
Bromus ramosus (71)

149a Leaf-sheaths without auricles:

149* Spikelets strongly compressed and flattened, 20–45 mm. long; lemmas keeled:

150† Lemmas awnless or with an awn from the tip 1–3 mm. long; waste and cultivated ground
Bromus unioloides (71)

150a† Lemmas tipped with an awn 5–10 mm. long; waste ground; often near rivers (Kew, Oxford)
Bromus carinatus (71)

149a* Spikelets and lemmas not as above; the latter usually rounded on the back:

152 Lower glume very narrow, narrowly lanceolate, usually 1- rarely 3-nerved; upper glume usually 1–3 nerved (to p. 57)

153 Lemmas finely pointed, awnless, 4–6 mm. long; spike-lets 5–8 mm. long; tufted perennial; leaf-blades 4–14 mm. wide; woods and other shady places
Festuca altissima (125)

153a Lemmas usually awned, or if awnless then more than 6 mm. long:

154 Annuals; spikelets gaping, finally wider at the apex than the base; lemmas narrowly lanceolate (to p. 57):

155 Lower leaf-sheaths hairless; leaf-blades 0·5–3 mm. wide; glumes very unequal (to p. 56):

156 Lemmas 8–16 mm. long, each tipped with a fine awn up to 25 mm. long; glumes extremely unequal the lower 0·2–1·6 mm., the upper

10–14 mm. long; panicles erect, dense; coastal
sand-dunes .... **Vulpia membranacea** (161)

156a Lemmas 4–9 mm. long, each tipped with a fine
awn up to 15 mm. long; glumes less unequal:

156* Lemmas with fine hairs on the margins of the
upper part; cultivated and waste ground
Vulpia megalura (157)

156a* Lemmas hairless, only minutely rough:

157 Lower glume half to three-fourths the length of
the upper; upper glume 3-nerved; panicles
loose to compact, lanceolate to narrowly
oblong; arable and waste land
Vulpia bromoides (155)

157a Lower glume one-sixth to nearly half the length
of the upper; upper glume mostly 1-nerved;
panicles usually linear:

158 Panicles mostly curved or nodding; spikelets
7–10 mm. long; lemmas 5–7 mm. long; arable
and waste land .... **Vulpia myuros** (157)

158a Panicles stiffly erect; spikelets 5–7 mm. long;
lemmas 4–5 mm. long; sandy places; locally
common .... **Vulpia ambigua** (159)

155a Lower leaf-sheaths loosely hairy; leaf-blades
2–8 mm. wide; glumes slightly unequal; lemmas
9–36 mm. long, bearing awns 10–60 mm. long:

159 Spikelets 2·5–6 cm. long (including awns); awns
10–30 mm. long (to p. 57):

160 Panicles contracted and rather dense, or somewhat loose; branches short, awns 10–18 mm.
long:

161 Longer panicle-branches bearing up to 8 spikelets; panicles drooping to one side, glistening;
spikelets 2·5–3·5 cm. long (with the awns);
waste and arable land; rare
Bromus tectorum (63)

161a Longer panicle-branches bearing one or two
spikelets; panicles erect or slightly inclined;
spikelets 3·5–6 cm. long (with the awns); dry
banks, waste land; rare
Bromus madritensis (65)

160a Panicles open and very loose, nodding, up to
25 cm. long and wide, with the branches widely
spreading and bearing usually a single spikelet;
arable and waste land; common
Bromus sterilis (61)

159a Spikelets 7–9 cm. long (with awns); awns
35–60 mm. long; panicles very loose, nodding,
the branches bearing one or two spikelets; arable
and waste land; roadsides; locally common
Bromus diandrus (67)

154a Perennials; spikelets not gaping, equally wide or
nearly so throughout or narrowed upwards, narrowly lanceolate or narrowly oblong:

162 Lemmas usually blunt and awnless; leaves hairless;
plants with extensively creeping rhizomes
Bromus inermis (73)

162a Lemmas pointed and with an awn 2–8 mm. long
from the tip; leaves usually hairy; plants densely
tufted, without rhizomes .... **Bromus erectus** (73)

152a Lower glume wider, lanceolate to ovate, oblong or
elliptic, 3–7-nerved; upper glume 5–9-nerved;
annuals; awns up to 10 mm. long:

163 Lower leaf-sheaths softly hairy; lemmas overlapping;
spikelets fragile, readily breaking up at maturity (to
p. 58):

164 Anthers 3–4·5mm. long; panicles open and very
loose, up to 20 cm. broad, with widely spreading
branches; arable and waste land
Bromus arvensis (75)

164a Anthers 0·2–3 mm. long; panicles loose or dense:

165 5·5–6·5 mm. long; hairy top of grain visible at the tip
of the lemma; spikelets mostly hairless; hayfields,
waste land .... **Bromus lepidus** (79)

165a Lemmas 6·5–11 mm. long; hairy top of grain
enclosed by the lemma and palea:

166 Spikelets stalkless or nearly so, in small dense clusters, in a narrow erect oblong interrupted panicle
2–9 cm. long and up to 2 cm. wide, softly hairy;
palea divided to the base between the keels; hayfields and arable land; very rare
Bromus interruptus (81)

166a Spikelets short- or rather long-stalked; palea not
divided:

167 Lemmas somewhat thin, with rather prominent
nerves; panicles contracted and dense,
especially after flowering or always; pedicels
shorter than the spikelets; anthers rarely more
than 1 mm. long (to p. 58):

168 Lemmas 8–11 mm. long, mostly hairy; grassland,
waste places .... **Bromus mollis** (77)

168a Lemmas 6·5–8 mm. long:
   169 Spikelets usually hairless; awns mainly straight; hayfields and waste land
Bromus thominii (77)
  169a Spikelets very densely hairy; awns curving outwards; coastal grassy and rocky places
Bromus ferronii (77)
167a Lemmas thicker, tough, the nerves not prominent; pedicels rather long; anthers mostly 1·5–2·5 mm. long; spikelets usually hairless:
  170 Spikelets 12–16 mm. long; lemmas 6·5–8 mm. long; panicles erect, rather stiff and open, finally somewhat contracted and nodding; meadows, arable land **Bromus racemosus** (83)
  170a Spikelets 18–28 mm. long; lemmas 8–11 mm. long; panicles loose, soon drooping to one side; meadows, arable land
Bromus commutatus (85)
163a Lower leaf-sheaths hairless or very obscurely hairy; margins of lemmas becoming incurved; spikelets slowly breaking up at maturity, hairless or hairy; lemmas 7–9 mm. long; arable and waste land
Bromus secalinus (87)

DESCRIPTIONS
AND ILLUSTRATIONS
OF INDIVIDUAL
GRASSES

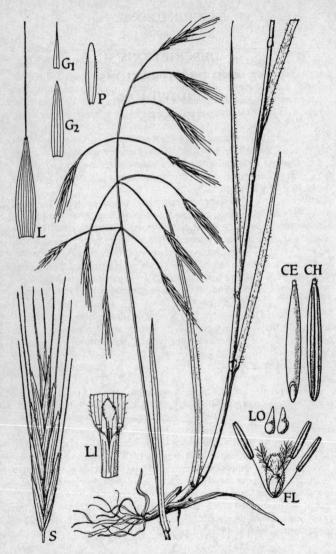

Bromus sterilis. Common; arable and waste land.

BARREN BROME
Bromus sterilis L.

Annual or biennial, 15–100 cm. high. Culms loosely tufted or solitary, erect or spreading, slender to somewhat stout, unbranched, 3–5 noded, smooth. Leaves green or purplish; sheaths tubular, soon splitting, rounded on the back, shortly and softly hairy, the upper often hairless; ligules (LI, × 2) membranous, 2–4 mm. long, toothed; blades finely pointed, 5–25 cm. long, flat, 2–7 mm. wide, flaccid to firm, softly and shortly hairy, rough. Panicles very loose and open, nodding, variable in size, up to 25 cm. long and wide, but sometimes reduced to a single spikelet, green or purplish; branches widely spreading, up to 10 cm. long, flexuous, unequal, slender, rough, each bearing usually 1 spikelet or the longest with up to 5.

Spikelets (S, × 1½) loosely scattered and drooping, oblong, becoming wedge-shaped and gaping, compressed, 4–6 cm. long (including awns), 4–10-flowered, breaking up at maturity beneath each lemma. Glumes (G$_1$, G$_2$ × 1½) persistent, unequal, narrow, finely pointed; lower subulate, 6–14 mm. long, 1-nerved; upper narrowly oblong-lanceolate, 10–20 mm. long, 3-nerved. Lemmas (L, × 1½) at first overlapping, later separate, each with a blunt hard base, linear-lanceolate in side view, finely pointed, slightly keeled or becoming rounded on the back, finely 2-toothed at the tip (teeth 1–3 mm. long), 13–23 mm. long, minutely rough, 7-nerved, firm except for the narrow shining membranous margins, with a fine rough straight awn 15–30 mm. long from just below the tip. Paleas (P, × 1½) shorter than the lemmas, the two keels fringed with very short stiff hairs. Anthers (FL, × 7) 1–1·8 mm. long. Grain (CE, CH, × 3) hairy at 'the tip, tightly enclosed by the hardened lemma and palea. *Ch. no.* 2n = 14.

A common weed of open situations, on waste and cultivated land, of waysides, hedgerows, and field margins, usually on well-drained soils. Widely distributed in the British Isles but most abundant in the lowlands; uncommon to rare in mountainous regions, especially in Wales, N. England and Scotland. Throughout the greater part of Europe and in S.W. Asia; introduced into N. America, etc. Flowering: May to July.

The species of *Bromus* may be recognized by their very distinctive ovary; this, when examined with a lens (× 10), will be found to bear a lobed hairy apical appendage (FL), with the two stigmas borne on one side at the base of the latter. This hairy portion persists at the tip of the grain. Their grains consist mainly of simple starch granules, resembling those of the Couch and related grasses.

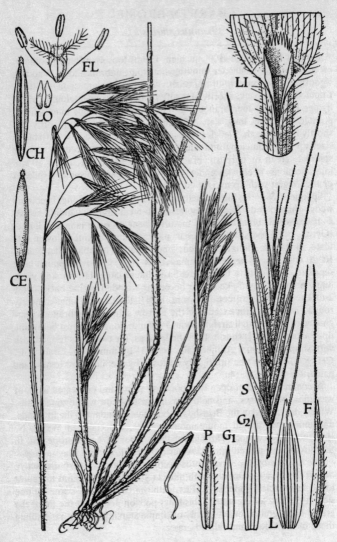

Bromus tectorum. Rare; mostly waste and arable land.

DROOPING BROME

Bromus tectorum L.

Annual, 10–60 cm. high. Culms loosely tufted or solitary, slender, unbranched, 2–5 noded, minutely hairy or smooth. Leaves green; sheaths tubular, soon splitting, rounded on the back, softly hairy, or the upper hairless; ligules (LI, × 3) membranous, up to 5 mm. long, jagged; blades finely pointed, 3–16 cm. long, flat, 2–4 mm. wide, softly hairy. Panicles loose, or contracted and rather dense, drooping to one side, 4–18 cm. long, green or purplish, glistening; branches clustered, fine, flexuous, spreading, shortly hairy or rough, the longer bearing up to 8 spikelets.

Spikelets (S, × 3) nodding, narrowly oblong, becoming wedge-shaped, gaping, 2·5–3·5 cm. long (including awns), compressed, 4–8-flowered, breaking up at maturity beneath each lemma. Glumes (G_1, G_2, × 3) persistent, finely pointed, thinly membranous; lower subulate, 5–8 mm. long, 1-nerved; upper narrowly oblong-lanceolate, 7–11 mm. long, 3-nerved. Lemmas (F, L, × 3) overlapping, linear-lanceolate in side view, finely pointed, 9–13 mm. long, finely 2-toothed at the tip (teeth 1–2 mm. long), becoming rounded on the back, with thinly membranous margins, rough, 7-nerved, with a fine straight rough awn 10–18 mm. long from just below the tip. Paleas (P, × 3) shorter than the lemmas, with the two keels loosely fringed with short stiff hairs. Anthers (FL, × 6) 3, 0·5–1 mm. long. Grain (CE, CH, × 4) hairy at the tip, tightly enclosed by the lemma and palea. *Ch. no* 2n = 14.

A native of the Mediterranean Region; widely distributed in Europe. Introduced into the British Isles; naturalized and rare in W. Norfolk and W. Suffolk (1978); of rare occurrence on waste and cultivated land in S. England, and on rubbish-tips in various parts of Britain. Introduced into America, Australia, New Zealand, etc. A variety with hairy spikelets, var. *hirsutus* Regel (var. *longipilus* Borb.), is occasionally found on waste ground. Known in the United States as Downy Chess. Flowering: May to July.

Bromus tectorum L., as well well as B. *diandrus*, B. *madritensis*, B. *rigidus*, B. *rubens*, and B. *sterilis*, are sometimes classified as a separate genus *Anisantha*; the species of this group are all annuals or biennials, with long-awned wedge-shaped spikelets, broader at their tips, subulate or narrowly lanceolate 1–3 nerved glumes, and hairy-keeled paleas. They have no value for fodder in the British Isles and are generally regarded as weeds. A few species are occasionally cultivated for their ornamental inflorescences.

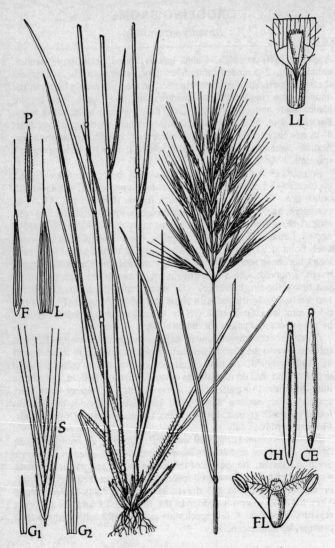

Bromus madritensis. Rare; dry banks, rocks, waste land.

COMPACT BROME
Bromus madritensis L.

Annual, 10–60 cm. high. Culms loosely tufted or solitary, erect or spreading, slender, unbranched, 2–4-noded, smooth, or rarely minutely hairy beneath the panicle. Leaves green; sheaths tubular, soon splitting, the lower softly hairy, the upper hairless; ligules (LI. × 3) membranous, jagged, 1·5–4 mm. long; blades finely pointed, 3–20 cm. long, flat, 2–5 mm. wide, short-haired or hairless. Panicles erect or slightly inclined, contracted and rather dense, or somewhat loose, 4–15 cm. long, 1·5–6 cm. wide, purple or green; branches clustered, fine, unequal, erect or slightly spreading, minutely rough, 0·5–3·5 cm. long, bearing 1–2 spikelets.

Spikelets (S. × 1½) oblong, becoming wedge-shaped and gaping, compressed, 3·5–6 cm. long (including awns), loosely 6–13-flowered, breaking up at maturity beneath each lemma. Glumes (G_1, G_2 × 1½) persistent, narrow, unequal, finely pointed; lower subulate, 6–11 mm. long, 1-nerved; upper linear-lanceolate, 10–16 mm. long 3-nerved. Lemmas (F, L, × 1½) at first overlapping, later with tightly incurved margins, linear-lanceolate in side view, finely pointed, 12–19 mm. long, finely 2-toothed at the tip (teeth 1–2 mm. long), finally rounded on the back, rough, with narrow shining membranous margins, 7-nerved, awned from just below the tip, with the fine rough awn slightly diverging and 12–18 mm. long. Paleas (P, × 1½) shorter than the lemmas, with the two keels loosely fringed with short stiff hairs. Anthers (FL, × 6) 2, 0·5–1 mm. long. Grain (CE, CH, × 3) hairy at the tip, tightly enclosed by the hardened lemma and palea. *Ch. no.* 2n = 28.

A rare grass of a few scattered localities in S. England, S. Wales, S. Eire, and Channel Isles, perhaps native on dry open banks and rocky slopes such as on the carboniferous limestone near Bristol, well established elsewhere on old walls and ruins, also occurring occasionally on waste and cultivated ground and on port dumps. Native of the Mediterranean Region, now widespread in Europe; introduced into N. and S. America, South Africa, and Australia. Known also as Stiff, Wall, Madrid or Upright Annual Brome. Flowering: May to July.

A variety (var, *ciliatus* Guss.), with hairy spikelets, is sometimes introduced. Another Mediterranean Region annual species of *Bromus*, *B. rubens* L., is found rarely on port tips and waste ground. It is closely related to *B. madritensis*, differing mainly in its very dense stiffly erect panicles, and in the culms being densely pubescent beneath the panicles.

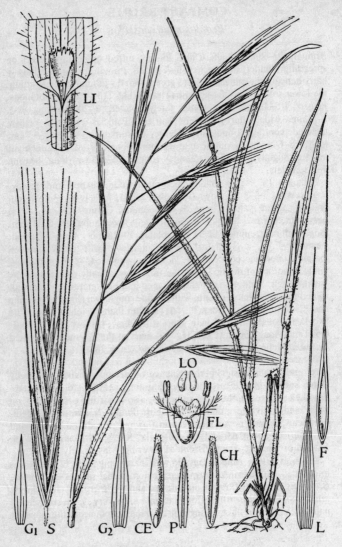

Bromus diandrus. Rare; waste and arable land.

GREAT BROME
Bromus diandrus Roth

Annual, 35–80 cm. high. Culms loosely tufted or solitary, erect or usually spreading, slender to relatively stout, unbranched, 3–6 noded, usually hairy near the panicles. Leaves green; sheaths tubular, soon splitting, rounded on the back, loosely hairy with spreading hairs; ligules (LI, × 3) membranous, jagged, 3–6 mm. long; blades finely pointed, 10–25 cm. long, flat, 4–8 mm. wide, thinly to loosely hairy, rough. Panicles very loose, nodding, very variable in size, up to 25 cm. long and wide, bearing few to many spikelets, green or purplish; branches in clusters of 2–4, up to 10 cm. long, spreading, unequal, very rough, bearing 1 spikelet, or the longest with 2.

Spikelets (S, × 1½) finally drooping, loosely scattered, oblong, becoming wedge-shaped and gaping, compressed, 7–9 cm. long (including awns), loosely 5–8-flowered, breaking up at maturity beneath each lemma. Glumes (G_1, G_2, × 1½) persistent, unequal, narrow, finely pointed; lower subulate, 15–23 mm. long, 1–3-nerved; upper narrowly lanceolate, 20–32 mm. long, 3–5-nerved. Lemmas (F, L, × 1½) overlapping, narrowly lanceolate in side view, finely pointed, 22–36 mm. long, finely 2-toothed at the tip (teeth 4–7 mm. long), broadly rounded on the back, with the middle nerve projecting, very rough, 7-nerved, firm except for the narrow membranous margins, with a straight stout rough awn 3·5–6 cm. long from just below the tip. Paleas (P, × 1½) shorter than the lemmas, with the two keels fringed with short stiff hairs. Anthers (FL, × 4) 2–3, 0·8–1·5 mm. long. Grain (CE, CH, × 2) hairy at the tip, tightly enclosed by the hardened lemma and palea. *Ch. no.* 2n = 56.

A native of the Mediterranean Region, introduced into the British Isles, occasionally occurring on waste land, roadsides and rubbish tips, and as a weed of cultivated land; naturalized in several places in S. and E. England, and in sandy places in the Channel Isles. Introduced into N. and S. America, Australia, New Zealand, etc. The name *Bromus maximus* Desf. has been misapplied to this species. Flowering: May to July.

Bromus rigidus Roth, a Mediterranean Region grass, is sometimes found on waste ground and roadsides. It is similar to B. *diandrus*, but differs in having stiff contracted erect panicles, with shorter branches (0·5–2·5 cm. long). In the United States, where it is a bad weed, it is known as Ripgut Grass, on account of the basally pointed fruits, which enter the mouths and noses of grazing animals and work their way into the flesh. *Ch. no.* 2n = 42.

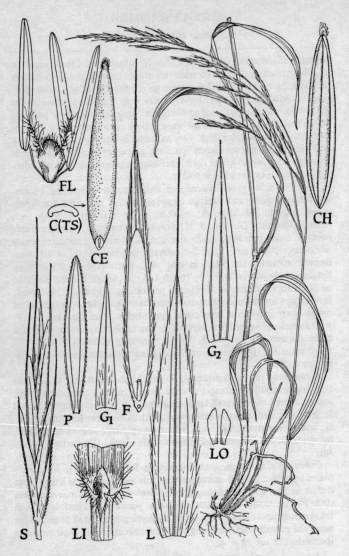

FL

C(TS)

CE

CH

P

G_1

F

G_2

LO

S

LI

L

Bromus benekenii. Rare; woodlands on chalk and limestone.

LESSER HAIRY BROME
Bromus benekenii (Lange) Trimen

A perennial, forming small tufts, 45–120 cm. high. Culms erect or ascending, slender to somewhat stout, few-noded, minutely and obscurely hairy. Leaves dull green; sheaths tubular, splitting,.with short pointed auricles at the tip (LI, × 3), the lower densely to loosely hairy with short, reflexed soft hairs, the upper minutely hairy or hairless; ligules (LI, × 3) blunt, membranous, 1–3 mm. long; blades finely pointed, 10–25 cm. long. flat, 4–12 mm. wide, drooping, shortly hairy or almost hairless, somewhat rough. Panicles rather narrow, contracted, nodding in the upper part, 12–20 cm. long, moderately loose to rather dense, green; branches 1–3 together, more or less appressed, not spreading, very slender, rough, bearing 1–3 spikelets, the lower up to 7·5 cm. long, the lowest with a hairless scale at the base; pedicels 3–6 mm. long, very slender, rough.

Spikelets (S, × 3) lanceolate to oblong, compressed, 1·5–2·5 cm. long, 3–5-flowered, breaking up beneath each lemma. Glumes (G$_1$, G$_2$, × 5) persistent, keeled, unequal, membranous; lower linear-lanceolate, or narrowly lanceolate, finely pointed, 7–9 mm. long, 1-nerved; upper oblong-lanceolate, pointed, 9–11 mm. long, 3-nerved. Lemmas (F, L, × 5) narrowly lanceolate-oblong or oblong, pointed or blunt, 11–14 mm. long, slightly keeled or rounded on the back, becoming firm, 5-nerved, appressed hairy near the margins, rough on the back, tipped with a fine rough awn, 5–8 mm. long, Paleas (P, ×5) shorter than the lemmas, with minutely hairy or rough keels. Anthers (FL, × 10) 2·8–3 mm. long. Grain (CE, CH, × 5) hairy at the tip, enclosed by the lemma and palea. *Ch. no.* 2n = 28.

A rare grass of shaded places; in woodland (especially beech) and hedgerows, mostly on shallow calcareous soils; recorded from relatively few widely scattered localities in England, Wales, and Scotland, from Monmouth and Radnor, eastwards in Kent, Surrey, Berkshire, Oxfordshire, Gloucestershire and Hertfordshire, and northwards to Perthshire; usually with or near *Bromus ramosus*, and perhaps sometimes overlooked because of its close similarity to that species. Also in various parts of Europe and temperate Asia. Flowering: June to August.

Distinguished from *B. ramosus* by its hairless or minutely hairy upper leaf-sheaths, shorter ligules, mostly shorter and narrower leaf-blades, contracted panicles, with branches shorter, not stiff and widely spreading, bearing fewer spikelets, and with a hairless scale at the base of the lowest cluster, and by its smaller fewer-flowered spikelets and smaller anthers.

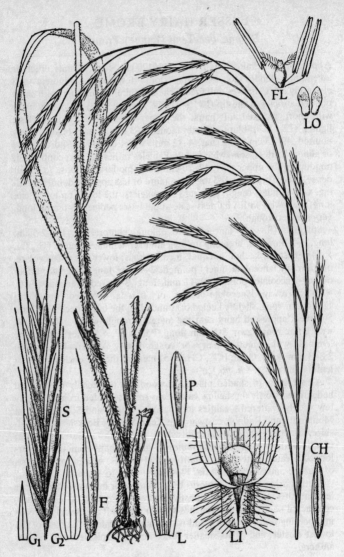

Bromus ramosus. Common; woodland, hedgerows.

HAIRY or WOOD BROME
Bromus ramosus Huds.

A loosely tufted perennial, 45–190 cm. high. Culms erect, slender to stout, unbranched, 3–5 noded, hairy. Leaves dark green; sheaths tubular, splitting, rounded on the back, hairy with stiff reflexed hairs, with narrow auricles at the tip (LI); ligules (LI, × 3) firm, jagged, up to 6 mm. long; blades finely pointed, up to 60 cm. long, flat, 6–16 mm. wide, drooping, rough. Panicles loose, open, nodding, 15–45 cm. long, green or purplish; branches usually in pairs, spreading and drooping, divided, rough, bearing up to 9 spikelets, the lowest branch with a minute ciliate scale at the base; pedicels 6–30 mm. long.

Spikelets (S, × 2½) pendulous, narrowly lanceolate to narrowly oblong, compressed, 2–4 cm. long, 4–6 mm. wide, loosely 4–11-flowered, breaking up beneath each lemma. Glumes (G_1, G_2, × 2½) persistent, keeled; lower subulate, 6–8 mm. long, 1-nerved; upper oblong-lanceolate, abruptly pointed, 9–11 mm. long, 3–5-nerved. Lemmas (F, L, × 2½) at first overlapping, later with incurved margins, narrowly oblong-lanceolate, pointed, 10–14 mm. long, keeled or becoming rounded on the back, firm except for the narrow membranous margins, 7-nerved, with short hairs near the margins and on the back, and a fine, straight awn 4–8 mm. long from near the tip. Paleas (P, × 2½) shorter than the lemmas, with rough keels. Anthers (FL, × 4) 3–4 mm. long. Grain (CH, × 2) hairy at the tip, enclosed by the lemma and palea. *Ch. no.* 2n = 42.

Widespread in the British Isles, except N. and Central Scotland; in partial shade on moist soils; in open woodland, wood-margins, and hedgerows; sometimes persisting on roadsides and ditch-banks in areas originally wooded. Throughout Europe and temperate Asia; N.W. Africa. Flowering: July and August.

Bromus erectus, B. benekenii and *B. ramosus* have been placed in the genus *Zerna*, perennial species, with lanceolate or oblong spikelets and mostly 1–3-nerved glumes. *B. unioloides* H.B.K., Rescue Grass, of S. and N. America, is occasionally introduced. *Ch. no.* 2n = 28, 42. It has strongly compressed 6–12-flowered spikelets 16–40 mm. long, and pointed or short-awned 9–13-nerved lemmas (awn 1–3 mm). *B. carinatus* Hook. & Arn., California Brome, of N. America, is naturalized in various places. *Ch. no.* 2n = 56. It differs from *B. unioloides* by its longer-awned 7–8-nerved lemmas (awn 5–10 mm. long). Its florets are first chasmogamous with large exserted anthers, later cleistogamous with small enclosed anthers. These two short-lived perennials are sometimes placed in *Ceratochloa*.

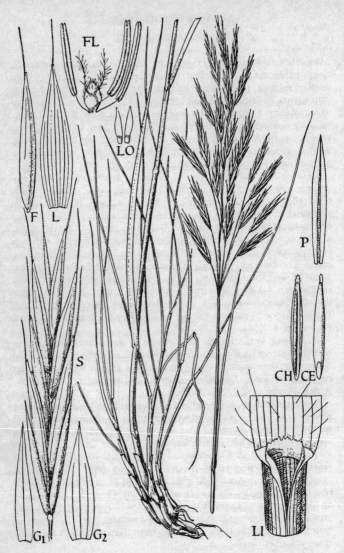

Bromus erectus. Common; calcareous grassland.

UPRIGHT BROME
Bromus erectus Huds.

A densely tufted perennial, 40–120 cm. high. Culms erect or slightly spreading, slender to stout, stiff, 3–4-noded, smooth, rarely hairy. Leaf-sheaths tubular, rounded on the back, the lower sparsely hairy with spreading hairs, or hairless, the upper usually smooth; ligules (LI, × 4) membranous, up to 3 mm. long; blades finely pointed, loosely hairy or hairless, tough, green, rough, the basal inrolled or flat, up to 30 cm. (or more) long, and 2–3 mm. wide, the upper broader, flat, up to 6 mm. wide. Panicles erect or rarely nodding, loose or rather dense, 10–25 cm. long, purplish, reddish or green; branches clustered, erect or spreading, mostly short, rough, bearing 1–4 spikelets.

Spikelets (S, × 3) narrowly lanceolate to narrowly oblong, slightly compressed, 1·5–4 cm. long, 4–14-flowered, breaking up at maturity beneath each lemma. Glumes (G_1, G_2, × 3) persistent, finely pointed; lower subulate, 7–12 mm. long, 1–3-nerved; upper narrowly lanceolate, 8–14 mm. long, 3-nerved. Lemmas (F, L, × 3) overlapping, later with the margins incurved, narrowly lanceolate or oblong-lanceolate in side view, 8–15 mm. long, pointed or slightly 2-toothed at the tip, keeled on the back, firm except for the membranous margins and tip, 7-nerved, minutely rough, with a fine straight or flexuous awn 2–8 mm. long from the tip. Paleas (P, × 3) shorter than the lemmas, with two rough keels. Anthers (FL, × 4) orange or reddish-orange, 5–7 mm. long. Grain (CE, CH, × 3) hairy at the top, tightly enclosed by the hardened lemma and palea. *Ch. no.* 2n = 42, 56.

A coarse fibrous grass of well-drained calcareous soils, abundant and often dominant on chalk and limestone downs, especially in S. England, also on roadside banks and verges, and sometimes on waste land; uncommon in Wales and N. England and rare in S. Scotland; local in Ireland. A variety (var. *villosus* Leight.) with softly hairy spikelets is often found among plants with hairless spikelets. Widespread in Europe, also in S.W. Asia and N.W. Africa; introduced into N. America. Flowering: June and July.

Awnless or Hungarian Brome, *Brōmus inermis* Leyss., a native of Europe and Asia, has been cultivated as a fodder plant in the British Isles. Being drought-resistant it persists on sandy and stony soils, and has become naturalized in a few widely scattered localities in England. It may be distinguished from *B. erectus* by its extensively creeping rhizomes, hairless leaves, and usually blunt awnless lemmas. *Ch. no.* 2n = 56. Flowering: June to August. *B. inermis* and *B. erectus* are sometimes placed in the genus *Zerna*.

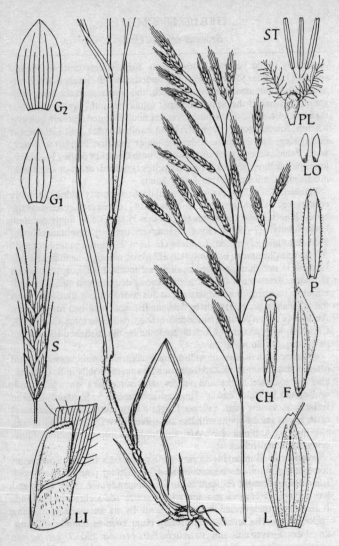

Bromus arvensis. Rare; arable and waste land.

FIELD BROME

Bromus arvensis L.

Annual, 25–90 cm. high. Culms loosely tufted or solitary, erect or spreading, slender to somewhat stout, unbranched, 2–5-noded, smooth. Leaves green; sheaths tubular, soon splitting, rounded on the back, the lower softly hairy, the upper hairless; ligules (LI, ×4) membranous, jagged, 2–4 mm. long; blades finely pointed, 5–20 cm. long, flat, 2–5 mm. wide, loosely hairy, rough. Panicles erect, or sometimes nodding, open and very loose, broadly ovate to elliptic, 8–25 cm. long, up to 20 cm. wide, green or purplish; branches clustered, eventually widely spreading, fine, unequal, rough, the longer bearing up to 8 spikelets; pedicels up to 3 cm. long.

Spikelets (S, × 2) loosely scattered, lanceolate to oblong, slightly compressed, 1–2 cm. long, 3–4 mm. wide, 4–10-flowered, breaking up at maturity beneath each lemma. Glumes (G₁, G₂, × 4) persistent, unequal, pointed, with membranous margins and tips; lower lanceolate, 4–6 mm. long, 3-nerved; upper narrowly ovate to elliptic, 6–8 mm. long, 5–7 nerved. Lemmas (F, L, × 4) overlapping, rounded on the back, elliptic or slightly obovate when opened out, pointed, slightly 2-toothed, 7–9 mm. long, 3–4 mm. wide, firm except for the membranous tips and margins, 7-nerved, minutely rough, with a fine straight rough awn 6–10 mm. long from near the tip. Paleas (P, × 4) nearly as long as the lemmas, the keels loosely fringed with short hairs. Anthers (ST, × 4) 3–4·5 mm. long. Grain (CH, × 4) hairy at the tip, tightly enclosed by the hardened lemma and palea. *Ch. no.* 2n = 14.

An introduced Brome of rather rare occurrence in cultivated fields, waste ground, and on rubbish dumps; sometimes persisting for several years on sandy soils in open situations. Cultivated for hay on the Continent on poor light soils. In the past its seeds may have been sown in the British Isles for the same purpose, since it has been found in fields of sainfoin, clovers, buckwheat, lupins, and rye-grasses. Throughout most of Europe and temperate Asia; introduced into N. America, etc. Flowering: June to August.

Several species belonging to the same group of *Bromus* as *B. arvensis* are occasionally introduced and found on rubbish tips, etc. They include *B. japonicus* Thunb., *B. squarrosus* L., *B. scoparius* L., and *B. briziformis* Fisch. & Mey. Some species, including the last, are cultivated on account of their ornamental panicles, which are dried and dyed with bright colours. The seven Bromes, from *B. arvensis* to *B. secalinus*, are sometimes separated as the genus *Serrafalcus* (see p. 83).

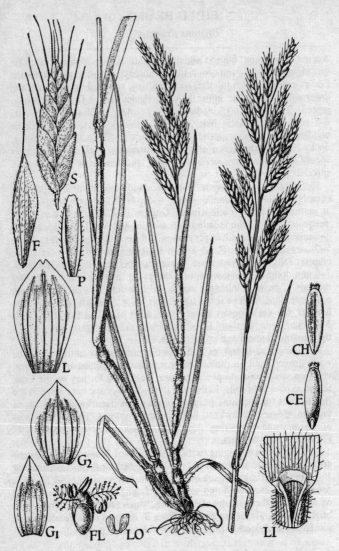

Bromus mollis. Very common; grassland, etc.

SOFT BROME OR LOP GRASS
Bromus mollis L.

Annual or biennial, 10–100 cm. high. Culms loosely tufted or solitary, erect or spreading, slender to relatively stout, 2–5-noded, short-hairy at the nodes. Leaves greyish-green; sheaths tubular, soon splitting, rounded on the back, softly hairy, or the upper hairless; ligules (LI, × 4) membranous, up to 2·5 mm. long, hairy, toothed; blades finely pointed, up to 20 cm. long, flat, 2–7 mm. wide, flaccid, softly short-hairy. Panicles at first erect and loose, afterwards contracted and nodding, 1·5–16 cm. long, up to 6 cm. wide, greyish-green or purplish; branches clustered, minutely hairy, bearing 1–5 spikelets; pedicels 2–10 mm. long.

Spikelets (S, × 2) narrowly ovate to oblong, slightly compressed, 12–22 mm. long, 3·5–6 mm. wide, 6–12-flowered, softly and shortly hairy, breaking up at maturity beneath each lemma. Glumes (G_1, G_2, × 3) persistent, pointed; lower ovate to oblong, 5–8 mm. long, 3–7-nerved; upper elliptic, 6–9 mm. long, 5–7-nerved. Lemmas (F, L, awn removed, × 3) closely overlapping, rounded on the back, obovate to elliptic, blunt, 8–11 mm. long, 4·5–5·5 mm. wide, with narrow membranous margins, prominently 7–9-nerved, with a fine rough awn 5–10 mm. long from just below the apex. Paleas (P, × 3) slightly shorter than the lemmas, the keels fringed with short stiff hairs. Anthers (FL, × 5) 0·2–2 mm. long. Grain (CE, CH, × 3) hairy at the top, tightly enclosed by the hardened lemma and palea. *Ch. no.* $2n = 28$.

The most widespread of all British species of *Bromus*, frequent on roadsides and waste ground, in meadows, hayfields, and on cultivated land, in all parts of the British Isles, but most common in the lowlands. Throughout Europe; in W. Asia; introduced into N. and S. America, Australia, etc. Flowering: May to July.

Bromus mollis belongs to a group of closely related species which, on account of the presence of hybrids, are difficult to distinguish. Var. *leiostachys* Hartm. has hairless spikelets. *B. lepidus* may be recognized by its smaller usually hairless lemmas. *B. thominii* Hard. (*B. hordeaceus* L.?), Lesser Soft Brome, is widespread in the lowlands of the British Isles, in hayfields, on roadsides, etc.; it differs from *B. mollis* in having usually hairless spikelets, with lemmas 6·5–8 mm. long. *B. ferronii* Mabille, Least Soft Brome, is of rare occurrence on cliffs of S. England, Wales, and the Channel Isles; it has stiffy erect panicles, densely hairy crowded spikelets, with lemmas 6·5–8 mm. long. *B. molliformis* Lloyd, of the Mediterranean Region, is rarely introduced; it differs from *B. mollis* by its narrower (shaggy-haired) 7–8 mm. long lemmas.

(*Bromus hordeaceus* subsp. *hordeaceus*)

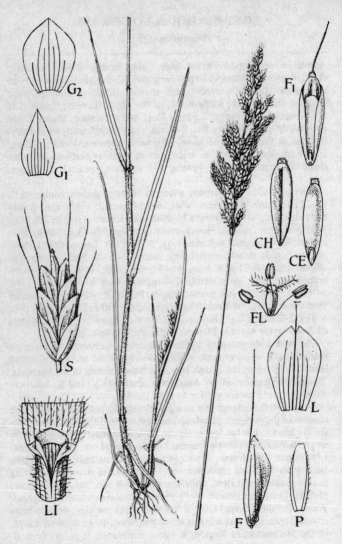

Bromus lepidus. Frequent; hayfields, roadsides, waste land.

SLENDER BROME
Bromus lepidus Holmb.

Annual or biennial, 10–90 cm. high. Culms loosely tufted or solitary, erect, or bent at the base, slender, 2–6-noded, minutely hairy or hairless. Leaves green; sheaths tubular, soon splitting, the lower softly hairy, the upper thinly hairy to hairless except for the hairy nodes; ligules (LI, × 5) membranous, up to 1 mm. long, too thed; blades finely pointed, 5–20 cm. long, flat, 2–5 mm. wide, softly hairy. Panicles erect and open when in flower, rather dense and nodding in fruit, bright green or tinged with purple, 2–10 cm. long, 1–4 cm. wide; branches clustered, minutely hairy, up to 4 cm. long, bearing 1–3 spikelets.

Spikelets (S, × 3) lanceolate to ovate or oblong, slightly compressed, 7–15 mm. long, 2·5–4 mm. wide, 3–11-flowered, breaking up at maturity beneath each lemma. Glumes (G_1, G_2, × 4) persistent, pointed; lower ovate to oblong, 4–5 mm. long, 3–7-nerved; upper ovate-elliptic to broadly elliptic, 5–6 mm. long, 5–7-nerved. Lemmas (F, L, × 4) closely overlapping at first, later with the lower margins incurved, rounded on the back, 5·5–6·5 mm. long, up to 3·5 mm. wide, obovate, angular above the middle, 2-toothed, pointed, 7-nerved, minutely and obscurely rough, firm except for the broad thin tips and margins, with a straight rough awn 3–7 mm. long from near the tip. Paleas (P, × 4) shorter than the lemmas and grains, the two keels fringed with short hairs. Anthers (FL, × 5) 0·8–2 mm. long. Grain (CE, CH, × 4) with its hairy top (F_1, × 4) visible at the tip of the lemma. *Ch. no.* 2n = 28.

Although this attractive little Brome was first noticed in Britain in 1836, nearly 100 years passed before it was recognized as a species distinct from *Bromus mollis*. It is now widespread in the areas of cultivated grassland throughout the British Isles, owing mainly to its seeds being mixed in the past with those of the two important fodder grasses, Italian and Perennial Rye-grass. Besides being present in sown hayfields and in weedy cornfields, it is of occasional to frequent occurrence on roadsides and waste land, especially in England. Also in Central and W. Europe from Scandinavia to Austria, Switzerland and France. Flowering: May to July.

The spikelets are usually hairless, but var. *micromollis* (Krosche) C. E. Hubbard has hairy spikelets. *Bromus mollis* may be readily distinguished from *B. lepidus* by its much larger spikelets and lemmas. *B. thominii* resembles the latter more closely, but has slightly larger lemmas (mostly 6·5–7·5 mm. long) and shorter grains, the tips of which are not visible at the apex of the lemma.

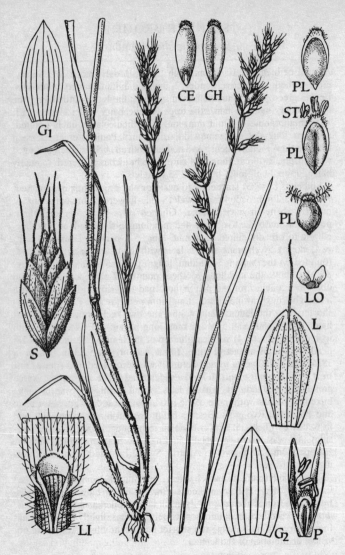

Bromus interruptus. Rare; arable land.

INTERRUPTED BROME
Bromus interruptus (Hack.) Druce

Annual or biennial, 20–100 cm. high. Culms loosely tufted or solitary, erect, slender to relatively stout, unbranched, 2–4 noded, minutely hairy. Leaves green; sheaths.tubular, soon splitting, rounded on the back, the lower softly hairy, the upper with shorter hairs; ligules (LI, × 4) membranous, 1–2 mm. long, toothed; blades pointed, 6–20 cm. long, flat, 2–6 mm. wide, softly hairy. Panicles stiffly erect, dense, oblong, usually interrupted, sometimes reduced to a single spikelet, 2–9 cm. long, up to 2 cm. wide, greyish-green; branches up to 1·5 cm. long.

Spikelets (S, × 3) stalkless or nearly so, in dense clusters, plump, broadly ovate to broadly oblong, 10–15 mm. long, 5–8 mm. wide, 5–11-flowered, softly hairy, slowly breaking up at maturity beneath each lemma. Glumes (G₁, G₂, × 4) persistent, unequal, blunt or abruptly pointed; lower oblong to elliptic, 5–7 mm. long, 3–7-nerved; upper ovate to broadly elliptic, 6–9 mm. long, 5–9-nerved. Lemmas (L, × 4) very closely overlapping, rounded on the back, obovate or elliptic-obovate, 7·5–9 mm. long, 5–5·5 mm. wide, minutely 2-toothed, moderately firm except for the narrow membranous margins, prominently 7–9-nerved, with a fine rough straight or flexuous awn 4–8 mm. long from near the tip. Paleas (P, × 4) shorter than the lemmas, split to the base between the slightly hairy keels. Anthers (ST, × 4) 1–1·5 mm. long. Ovary (PL, × 4) hairy at the top. Grain (CE, CH, × 3) tightly enclosed by the lemma and palea. *Ch. No.* 2n = 28.

A stiffly erect Brome of arable and waste land, recorded from scattered localities in S. and Central England, especially in the southern counties; at one time of fairly frequent occurrence and often locally abundant in fields of sainfoin, rye-grass, and clovers, its seeds being distributed with the seeds of these fodder plants; now very rare or extinct (-1972) in E. England. First collected in England in 1849; later named *B. mollis* var. *interruptus* Hack.; introduced into the Netherlands. Flowering: May to August.

A very distinct species, easily separated from all other species of *Bromus* by the split palea which is to be found in this divided state even when very young. The arrangement of the spikelets in small dense clusters of three gives the spike-like panicles the appearance of an ear of wheat, and provides another distinguishing characteristic. As with other annual Bromes, the small anthers may be frequently found enclosed by the lemma and palea at the hairy top of the grain, pollination taking place in the unopened floret.

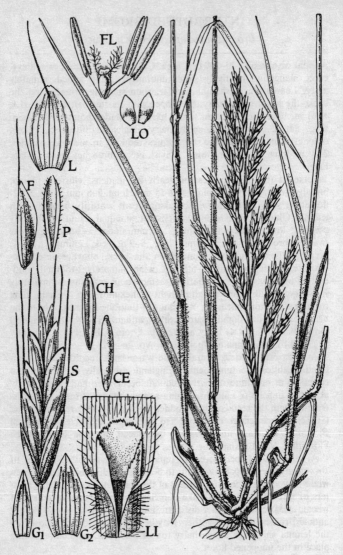

Bromus racemosus. Uncommon; meadows, arable land.

SMOOTH BROME
Bromus racemosus L.

Annual or biennial, 25–110 cm. high. Culms loosely tufted or solitary, erect or slightly spreading, slender to relatively stout, unbranched, 2–5-noded, smooth or minutely hairy. Leaves green; sheaths tubular, soon splitting, the lower loosely and softly hairy, the upper thinly hairy or hairless; ligules (LI, × 6) 1–3 mm. long, membranous, toothed; blades finely pointed, 5–20 cm. long, flat, 2–5 mm. wide, loosely and softly hairy. Panicles erect, rather stiff and open, finally somewhat contracted and nodding, 4–14 cm. long, 1·5–4 cm. wide, green or purplish: branches clustered, fine, rough, ascending, unequal, up to 6 cm. long, bearing 1–4 spikelets; pedicels up to 2·5 cm. long.

Spikelets (S, × 3) narrowly ovate to oblong, slightly compressed, 12–16 mm. long, 3·5–5 mm. wide, 4–8-flowered, breaking up at maturity beneath each lemma. Glumes (G_1, G_2, × 3) persistent, unequal, pointed; lower lanceolate-oblong, 4–6 mm. long, 3-nerved; upper ovate to elliptic, 4·5–7 mm. long, 5–7-nerved. Lemmas (F, L, × 3) overlapping, rounded on the back, broadly elliptic or slightly obovate, blunt, 6·5–8 mm. long, 4–5 mm. wide, minutely and obscurely rough, stiff, finely 7–9-nerved, with a fine straight rough awn 5–9 mm. long from near the tip. Paleas (P, × 3) slightly shorter than the lemmas, the keels fringed with short stiff hairs. Anthers (FL, × 6) mostly 2–3 mm. long. Grain (CE, CH, × 3) hairy at the tip, tightly enclosed by the hardened lemmas and paleas. *Ch. no.* 2n = 28.

This Brome is often confused with *B. commutatus*, so that its exact range is not known. It is recorded from various parts of the British Isles, but usually only from the lowlands. In S. and Central England it is frequent in the water-meadows of the Thames and other river valleys, occurring also in hayfields, on arable and waste land. In the rest of the British Isles it is apparently uncommon or rare, or perhaps even absent from Scotland. Scattered through Europe; introduced into N. America. Flowering: June and July.

Bromus racemosus and the species described on pp. 75–87 belong to the group which is occasionally separated as the genus *Serrafalcus*. Its species are all annuals or biennals; they differ from other annual Bromes in having lanceolate to ovate or oblong to broadly oblong spikelets, these narrowed in the upper part, broad glumes, with the lower glume 3–7-nerved and the upper 5–9-nerved. Several species have very small anthers, pollination taking place in the closed floret.

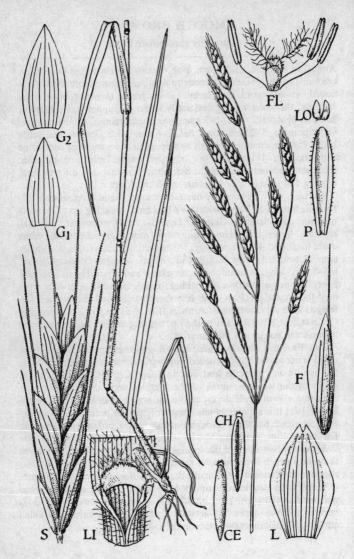

Bromus commutatus. Frequent; meadows, arable land.

MEADOW BROME

Bromus commutatus Schrad.

Annual or biennial, 40–120 cm. high. Culms loosely tufted or solitary, erect or spreading, slender to moderately stout, unbranched, 3–5-noded, smooth. Leaves green; sheaths tubular, splitting, the lower softly hairy, the upper thinly hairy or hairless; ligules (LI, × 3) 1–4 mm. long, membranous, becoming torn; blades finely pointed, up to 30 cm. long, flat, 3–9 mm. wide, loosely hairy, rough. Panicles loose, open or somewhat contracted, eventually drooping to one side, 6–25 cm. long, green or purplish; branches clustered, fine, unequal, up to 12 cm. long, rough or minutely hairy, bearing 1–4 spikelets; pedicels longer than the spikelets.

Spikelets (S, × 3) eventually nodding, lanceolate to oblong, 1·8–2·8 cm. long, 4·5–6 mm. wide, slightly compressed, 4–10-flowered, breaking up at maturity beneath each lemma. Glumes (G₁, G₂, × 3) persistent, slightly unequal, pointed; lower oblong-lanceolate, 5–7 mm. long, 3–5-nerved; upper elliptic, 6–9 mm. long, 5–9-nerved. Lemmas (F, L, awn removed, × 3) overlapping, rounded on the back, broadly elliptic or slightly obovate, blunt or slightly toothed, 8–11 mm. long, 5–6 mm. wide, firm except for the membranous margins, minutely rough, finely 7–11-nerved, with a fine straight rough awn 4–10 mm. long from just below the tip. Paleas (P, × 3) shorter than the lemmas, the keels loosely fringed with short stiff hairs. Anthers (FL, × 6) mostly 1·5–2 mm. long. Grain (CE, CH, × 3) hairy at the tip, tightly enclosed by the hardened lemma and palea. *Ch. no.* 2n = 28, 56.

Meadow Brome is widespread in the British Isles, but is most frequent on the moist soils of the lowlands; rare in Scotland, Wales, and Ireland; in England often abundant in water-meadows; also on cultivated and waste land, roadsides, hayfields, and rough grassland. Throughout Europe, N. Africa, W. Asia; introduced into N. America, etc. Called Hairy Chess in the United States. Flowering: May to July.

The spikelets are generally hairless, but in var. *pubens* Wats. they are softly hairy. *B. commutatus* has larger spikelets and lemmas and smaller anthers than the closely related *B. racemosus*. Both species differ from *B. mollis* in their looser and longer panicles, usually hairless spikelets, obscurely nerved and firmer lemmas, and mostly longer anthers.

None of the species of the *Serrafalcus* group (p. 83) of *Bromus* has any fodder value in the British Isles; they are generally regarded as weeds. All have attractive inflorescences which are useful, fresh or dried, for decorative purposes.

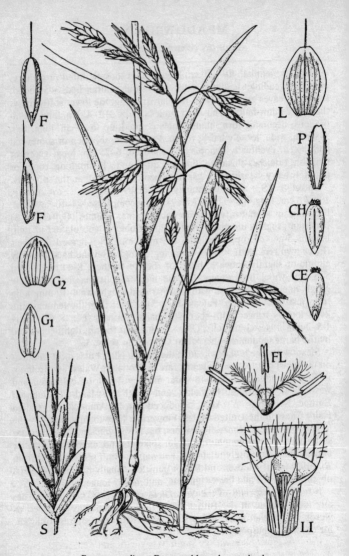

Bromus secalinus. Rare; arable and waste land.

RYE BROME
Bromus secalinus L.

Annual or biennial, 20–120 cm. high. Culms loosely tufted or solitary, erect, stiff, slender to somewhat stout, unbranched, 5–7-noded, smooth. Leaves green; sheaths tubular, soon splitting, rounded on the back, hairless, or the lower obscurely hairy; ligules (LI, × 4) 1–2 mm. long, membranous, toothed; blades pointed, 10–25 cm. long, flat, 4–10 mm. wide, loosely hairy, rough. Panicles erect or finally nodding, loose, open, or contracted, 5–20 cm. long, green, or purplish; branches clustered, fine, rough or minutely hairy, unequal, up to 8 cm. long, bearing 1–4 spikelets; pedicels up to 3 cm. long.

Spikelets (S, × 2) ovate to oblong, 1·2–2·4 cm. long, 4–7 mm. wide, slightly compressed, 4–11-flowered, very slowly breaking up at maturity beneath each lemma. Glumes (G_1, G_2, × 2) persistent, blunt, unequal, firm; lower ovate to oblong, 4–6 mm. long, 3–5-nerved; upper ovate to elliptic, 5–8 mm. long, 5–7-nerved. Lemmas (F, L, × 2) at first overlapping, finally with tightly incurved margins, rounded on the back, 7–9 mm. long, 4·5–5·5 mm. wide, broadly elliptic, blunt, 7-nerved, becoming tough and rigid except for the membranous margins, nearly smooth, with a fine straight rough awn up to 8 mm. long from near the tip, or awnless (var. *submuticus* Reichb.). Paleas (P, × 2) as long as the lemmas, the keels fringed with short stiff hairs. Anthers (FL, × 5) 1–2 mm. long. Grain (CE, CH, × 2) hairy at the tip, inrolled, tightly enclosed by the inrolled hardened lemma and palea. *Ch. no.* 2n = 28.

Rye Brome was no doubt introduced into the British Isles long ago with the seeds of cereals. In the past it has been very common, sometimes dominating fields of wheat. Now, with improved methods of freeing the grain of cereals from impurities, it is much less frequent and generally uncommon to rare. In England it may sometimes be found in fields of autumn-sown wheat, around stack-bottoms, and on waste ground; it is rare or now absent in most parts of Scotland, Wales, and Ireland. The most common form in England is var. *hirtus* (F. Schultz) A. & G., with softly and shortly hairy spikelets. Throughout Europe, N. Africa, and W. Asia; introduced into N. America, etc. Known also as Chess and Cheat. Flowering: June and July.

Bromus commutatus, *B. mollis*, *B. arvensis* and other species of the *Serrafalcus* group (p. 83) differ from *B. secalinus* in having softly and conspicuously hairy lower leaf-sheaths, and fragile mature spikelets, mostly with overlapping lemmas.

Bromus pseudosecalinus P. Smith of hayfields and roadsides occurs in various parts of England; it differs from *B. secalinus* in having pubescent lower sheaths, smaller spikelets and lemmas (5–6 mm. long).

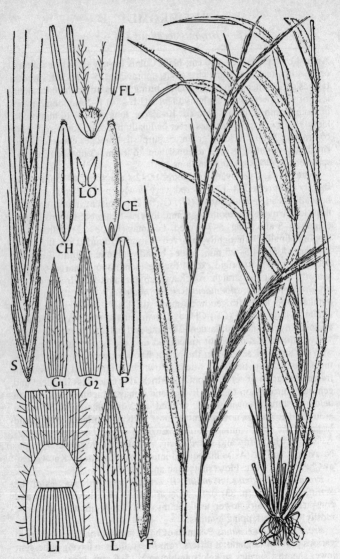

Brachypodium sylvaticum. Common; woods, hedgerows.

SLENDER or WOOD FALSE-BROME

Brachypodium sylvaticum (Huds.) Beauv.

A compactly tufted perennial, 30–90 cm. high. Culms erect or spread-ing, slender to moderately stout, unbranched, 4–5-noded, hairy at the nodes and often also towards them, otherwise smooth and hairless. Leaves green; sheaths rounded on the back or keeled upwards, loosely hairy with spreading or reflexed hairs, or the upper smooth, rarely all hairless; ligules (LI, × 3) blunt, 1–6 mm. long, membranous; blades narrowed to the sheath, finely pointed, up to 35 cm. long, flat, 4–12 mm. wide, erect or finally drooping, soft, mostly loosely hairy, rarely hairless and rough. Racemes spike-like, loose, erect or more often nodding, 6–20 cm. long, bearing 4–12 spikelets, green; axis slender; pedicels 0·5–2 mm. long.

Spikelets (S, × 3) cylindrical, lanceolate, or narrowly oblong, alter-nating in two rows on opposite sides of the axis, overlapping or up to their own length apart, 2–4 cm. (rarely more) long, 8–16-flowered, breaking up at maturity beneath each lemma. Glumes (G_1, G_2, × 4) persistent, unequal, rounded on the back, sharply pointed, firm, usually hairy; lower lanceolate, 6–8 mm. long, 5–7-nerved; upper lanceolate to narrowly oblong, 8–11 mm. long, 7–9-nerved. Lemmas (F, L, × 4) over-lapping, rounded on the back, oblong-lanceolate, pointed, 7–11 mm. long, tipped with a fine rough awn up to 12 mm. long, tough, 7-nerved, shortly and stiffly hairy, rarely only rough or quite smooth. Paleas (P, × 4) as long or nearly as long as the lemmas, narrowly oblong, blunt, with short-haired keels. Anthers (FL, × 5) 3·5–4 mm. long. Grain (CE, CH, × 4) hairy at the tip, tightly enclosed by the hardened lemma and palea. *Ch. no.* 2n = 18.

An ornamental grass, frequent in woods, copses, along hedgerows, and in other shady places throughout the British Isles; persisting in grass-land and along roadsides in areas originally woodland. Throughout Europe and temperate Asia, also in N.W. Africa. Flowering: July and August.

The species of *Brachypodium* are of no value agriculturally and are generally regarded as undesirable in grassland. They are somewhat intermediate in structure between *Bromus* and *Agropyron*, differing from both these genera in the form of the flower-head, the spikelets of *Bromus* being borne on long or short stalks in panicles, those of *Brachypodium* on very short stalks in spike-like racemes, whilst in *Agro-pyron* they are without stalks and form spikes. An annual of the Mediterranean Region, *B. distachyon* (L.) Beauv., with stiff, erect, few-spiculate racemes, is sometimes introduced.

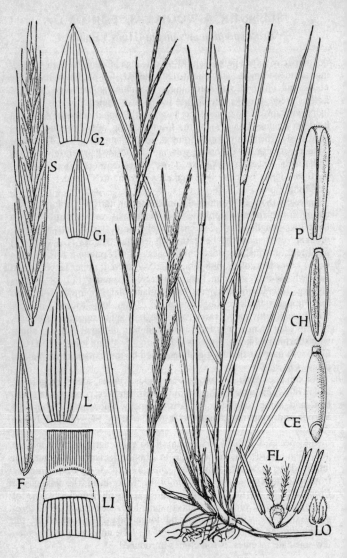

Brachypodium pinnatum. Locally common; grassland.

CHALK FALSE-BROME or TOR GRASS
Brachypodium pinnatum (L.) Beauv.

Perennial, 30–120 cm. high, forming loose to compact tufts, spreading by wiry scaly rhizomes. Culms usually erect, slender to somewhat stout, stiff, unbranched, 2–3-noded, smooth, usually hairless. Leaves green or yellowish-green; sheaths rounded on the back, hairless and smooth, or the lower shortly hairy; ligules (LI, × 4) blunt, up to 2 mm. long, membranous; blades finely pointed, up to 45 cm. long, rolled or flat, 2–6 mm. (rarely up to 10 mm.) wide, stiff to flaccid, erect, sparsely hairy, or hairless, rough. Racemes spike-like, erect, or sometimes nodding, 4–25 cm. long, bearing 3–15 spikelets, green or yellowish; axis slender; pedicels 1–2 mm. long.

Spikelets (S, × 3) cylindrical, lanceolate to narrowly oblong, straight or curved, alternating in two rows on opposite sides of the axis, overlapping, 2–4 cm. (rarely more) long, 8–22-flowered, usually solitary, very rarely in clusters of 2–3, breaking up at maturity beneath each lemma. Glumes (G$_1$, G$_2$, × 5) persistent, lanceolate to narrowly ovate, pointed, rounded on the back, firm, hairless; lower 3–5 mm. long, 3–6-nerved; upper 5–7 mm. long, 5–7-nerved. Lemmas (F, L, × 5) overlapping, rounded on the back, lanceolate-oblong, pointed, 6–10 mm. long, firm, 7-nerved, hairless and smooth, rarely short-hairy, tipped with a fine awn 1–5 mm. long. Paleas (P, × 5) as long as the lemmas, narrowly oblong, the two keels fringed with minute hairs. Anthers (FL, × 5) 3·5–4·5 mm. long. Grain (CE, CH, × 5) hairy at the apex, tightly enclosed by the hardened lemma and palea. *Ch. no.* 2n = 28.

A worthless grass of neglected open grassland on chalk and limestone; generally not grazed by cattle and consequently frequently abundant and spreading, sometimes dominating large areas. Widespread in S. England from Cornwall to Kent and northwards; uncommon to rare in East Anglia and N. England and occurring only in scattered localities; very rare in Scotland, Wales, and Ireland. Throughout the greater part of Europe, in S.W. Asia and N.W. Africa. Known also as Heath False-Brome. A variety with densely hairy spikelets (var. *pubescens* S. F. Gray) may be found growing with plants having hairless spikelets. Flowering: June to August.

Distinguished from *B. sylvaticum* by its form of growth, presence of rhizomes, usually hairless culms and leaf-sheaths, stiffer racemes and especially by the shorter-awned lemmas. In *Brachypodium* the lodicules are minutely ciliate whereas in the related genus *Bromus*, they are hairless.

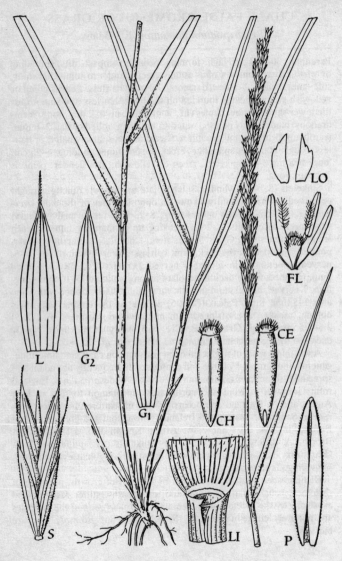

Agropyron donianum. Very rare; Scottish mountains.

DON'S TWITCH

Agropyron donianum F. B. White

A tufted perennial, 50–100 cm. high, without rhizomes. Culms erect or spreading, somewhat slender, sometimes slightly creeping at the base, about 4-noded, unbranched, smooth. Leaves green; sheaths rounded on the back, smooth, with short, pointed auricles (LI) at the top; ligules (LI, × 3) membranous, less than 1 mm. long; blades finely pointed, up to 30 cm. long, flat, 4–8 mm. wide, firm, loosely hairy or hairless above, hairless beneath, slightly rough. Spikes erect straight or slightly curved, 8–14 cm. long, compact, green; axis tough, minutely hairy along the angles.

Spikelets (S, × 2½) stalkless, in two rows alternating on opposite sides of the axis and with their broader sides appressed to it, mostly about half their length apart, 13–20 mm. long, 3–6-flowered, breaking up at maturity beneath each lemma. Glumes (G_1, G_2, × 4) persistent, nearly equal, narrowly oblong, finely pointed, 8–11 mm. long, prominently 3–6-nerved, rough on and between the nerves, the upper slightly wider than the lower. Lemmas (L, × 4) overlapping, rounded on the back, lanceolate-oblong, 10–12 mm. long, the tip narrowed into a straight rough awn up to 3 mm. long, rigid, 5-nerved, rough in the upper part. Paleas (P, × 4) about as long as the lemmas, minutely hairy on the keels. Anthers (FL, × 6) 2·5–3·5 mm. long. Grain (CE, CH, × 4) hairy at the top, tightly enclosed by the hardened lemma and palea.

This very rare species of a few Scottish mountains was discovered in 1810 on Ben Lawers in Perthshire by George Don, who named it *Triticum alpinum*, Since then it has been gathered on very few occasions, and for many years it has been regarded as a rather dubious species and often omitted from our floras, or treated as a variety of *A. caninum*. A valuable account of it published in 1950 stimulated successful searches for it in 1951. It is now known to occur in several localities in Caithness, Sutherland, Banff and Perthshire, at altitudes ranging from 75 to 210 m. in the first and 670 to 910 m. in the last county. It grows in rock-crevices, gullies, and on cliff-ledges, usually in the vicinity of water, and flowers in August and September. It may be distinguished from *A. caninum* by its very short awns. Varieties of *A. donianum* are found in Iceland and E. Greenland.

This species and *A. caninum* have been included in *Roegneria* on account of their tufted form of growth, absence of rhizomes, fragile mature spikelets and persistent glumes.

(*Elymus caninus* (L.) L.)

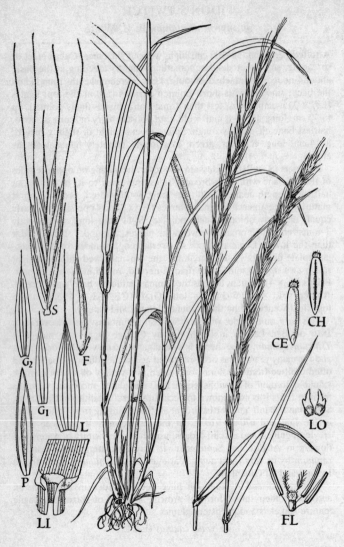

Agropyron caninum. Frequent; shady places.

94

BEARDED COUCH

Agropyron caninum (L.) Beauv.

A loosely tufted perennial, 30–110 cm. high, without rhizomes. Culms erect, or bent in the lower part, slender, unbranched, 2–5-noded, minutely hairy towards and at the nodes, or hairless and smooth. Leaves bright green; sheaths rounded on the back, hairless or the lower short-haired; ligules (LI, × 3) up to 1·5 mm. long, membranous; blades finely pointed, 10–30 cm. long, flat, 4–13 mm. wide, rather thin, rough, finely nerved, loosely hairy above, or hairless, Spikes curved or nodding, slender, 5–20 cm. long, green or tinged with purple; axis tough, rough or minutely hairy along the angles.

Spikelets (S, × 3) stalkless, alternating in two rows on opposite sides of the axis, with their broader sides appressed to it, lanceolate to oblong, 10–20 mm. long, 2–6-flowered, breaking up at maturity beneath each lemma. Glumes (G₁, G₂, × 3) persistent, equal or slightly unequal, lanceolate to narrowly oblong, 7–10 mm. long, rounded on the back, sharply pointed, sometimes short-awned from the tip, rigid, prominently 2–5-nerved, the nerves rough. Lemmas (F, L, × 3) overlapping, rounded on the back, lanceolate-oblong, 9–13 mm. long, rigid, 5-nerved, minutely hairy at the base, often with minute scattered hairs in the upper part, or smooth there, narrowed at the tip into a straight or flexuous awn 7–20 mm. long. Paleas (P, × 3) about as long as the lemmas, with two rough keels. Anthers (FL, × 4) 2–3 mm. long. Grain (CE, CH, × 3) hairy at the top, enclosed by the hardened lemma and palea. *Ch. no.* 2n = 28.

An attractive grass of shady places, locally common in woods and along hedgerows, widespread in England, Wales, and S. Scotland, rare in N. Scotland, uncommon in Ireland. Throughout most of Europe (except the extreme south) and in temperate Asia; introduced into N. America. Known also as Tufted Couch or Bearded Twitch. Flowering: June to August.

The plants are usually bright green, but in var. *glaucum* Lange, found in a few shaded places in S. England, the leaves, culms, and spikes are bluish-green, due to the presence of a white waxy covering. The closely related species, *A. donianum* F. B. White, of Perthshire, Sutherland Cailtiness and Banff, may be readily distinguished from *A. caninum* by its very short-awned lemmas. These two species have been placed in the genus *Roegneria*, whilst *Agropyron repens*, *A. junceiforme*, and *A. pungens* have been included in *Elytrigia*, this genus being separated from the other by the presence of rhizomes, spikelets mostly falling entire at maturity, larger anthers, and the deeply grooved grains.

(Elymus caninus (L.) L.)

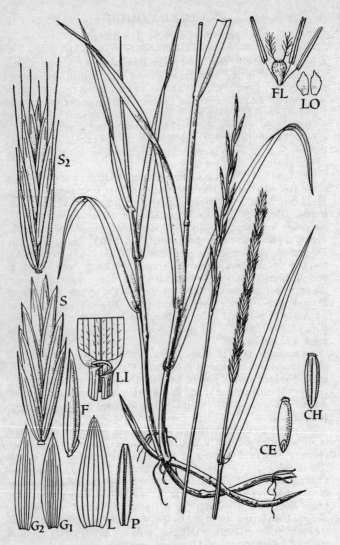

Agropyron repens. Very common; arable and waste land.

COUCH or TWITCH

Agropyron repens (L.) Beauv.

Perennial, 30–120 cm. high, forming tufts or large patches, spreading extensively by creeping wiry rhizomes. Culms erect, or bent below, slender to somewhat stout, 3–5-noded, smooth. Leaves dull green, rarely bluish- or greyish-green; sheaths rounded on the back, with short spreading auricles (LI) at the apex, hairless, or the lower loosely to closely hairy, smooth; ligules (LI, × 2) less than 1 mm. long, membranous; blades finely pointed, 6–30 cm. long, 3–10 mm. wide, flat, soft to rather stiff, smooth or rough beneath, usually loosely to sparsely hairy above, or hairless. Spikes erect, straight, slender, loose to compact, 5–20 (or 30) cm. long, green or less often bluish-green; axis tough, rough on the margins, hairless, rarely softly hairy.

Spikelets (S, × 3) oblong, elliptic, or wedge-shaped, 10–20 mm. long, 3–8-flowered, falling entire at maturity, stalkless, alternating in two rows on opposite sides of the axis, with the broader sides appressed to it, one-third to half their length apart. Glumes (G_1, G_2, × 3) similar, equal or nearly so, lanceolate to lanceolate-oblong, blunt or pointed, 7–12 mm. long, tough, 3–7-nerved, rough upwards on the keels. Lemmas (F, L, × 3) overlapping, lanceolate-oblong, blunt or pointed (sometimes sharply), keeled upwards, 8–13 mm. long, tough, 5-nerved. Paleas (P, × 3) nearly as long as the lemmas, with two rough keels. Anthers (FL, × 3) 3·5–6 mm. long. Grain (CE, CH, × 3) hairy at the top, tightly enclosed by the hard lemma and palea. *Ch. no.* 2n = 42.

A bad weed of cultivated land, being spread by seed but difficult to eradicate, as each piece of rhizome is capable of developing into a fresh plant. Also of field margins, roadsides, rough grassland, and waste land. Widespread in the British Isles, but common only in regions of arable farming. Distributed through most of Europe and temperate Asia; introduced into many temperate countries. Known also as Quick, Scutch, or Quack Grass. Flowering: end of June to August.

An exceedingly variable mainly self-sterile grass, the more prominent and frequent variants of which have been given varietal names. Plants with long-awned lemmas (awns up to 10 mm. long) are known as var. *aristatum* Baumg. (S_2, × 3). *Agropyron repens* crosses with the maritime, *A. junceiforme* and *A. pungens*, the hybrids being male-sterile. It may be separated from both these species by its thinner, mostly flat leaf-blades, with the very slender ribs more widely spaced and usually sparingly hairy. It also crosses with *Hordeum secalinum* (see p. 113). Var. *pubescens* (Doell.) Tzvelev has awned lemmas and hairy spike axis.

(*Elymus repens* (L.) Gould)

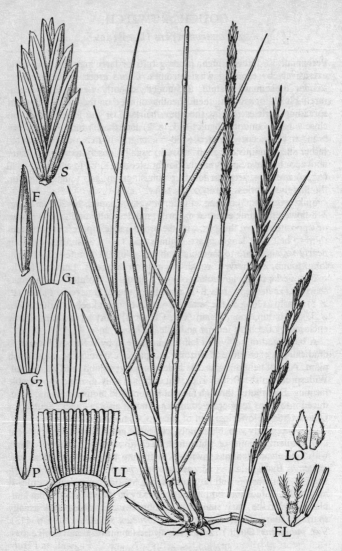

Agropyron pungens. Common; salt-marshes and dunes.

SEA COUCH
Agropyron pungens (Pers.) Roem. & Schult.

A bluish-grey or greyish-green perennial, 20–120 cm. high, forming tufts or large patches, spreading extensively by wiry rhizomes. Culms erect, or bent at the base, slender to stout, rigid, unbranched, 3–4-noded, smooth. Leaves hairless; sheaths rounded on the back, smooth, with short narrow auricles (LI) at the top; ligules (LI, × 4) less than 1 mm. long, membranous; blades with sharply pointed hard tips, 8–35 cm. long, flat, or often tightly inrolled, 2–6 mm. wide, stiff, smooth beneath, closely and prominently ribbed above, rough on the margins and on the ribs or the latter nearly smooth. Spikes erect, stiff, compact, 4–20 cm. long, slender to stout; axis tough, rough.

Spikelets (S, × 3) closely overlapping, one-fifth to half their length apart, singly and alternating in two rows on opposite sides of the axis, with their broader sides pressed against the flattened axis, falling entire or breaking up at maturity, oblong or elliptic-oblong, compressed, 10–20 mm. long, 3–10-flowered. Glumes (G_1, G_2, × 3) similar, equal or nearly so, lanceolate-oblong, pointed, keeled, 8–10 mm. long, tough and rigid, rough on the keels, prominently 4–7-nerved. Lemmas (F, L, × 3) closely overlapping, lanceolate-oblong, blunt or pointed, 7–11 mm. long, keeled upwards, tough, 5-nerved. Paleas (P, × 3) about as long as the lemmas, 2-keeled, with the keels rough. Anthers (FL, × 3) 5–7 mm. long. Grain minutely hairy at the top, enclosed by the hard lemma and palea. *Ch. no.* 2n = 42.

A stiff maritime couch-grass, also known as Sea Twitch occurring along the coasts of England and Wales from Northumberland, Yorkshire and Cumberland to Cornwall, and in a few places on those of the southern half of Eire; rare in Scotland; frequent on the margins of salt marshes and brackish creeks, in sandy or gravelly muds, and on shingle and consolidated sand-dunes, often over large areas. Also on the coasts of W. and S. Europe; introduced into N.E. America. Flowering: end of June to August.

A variable grass with numerous strains. In some the lemmas are very blunt, in others somewhat pointed, whilst they may bear at their tips minute or short mucros, or fine awns up to 10 mm. long, as in var. *setigerum* Dumort. Several hybrids (see pp. 97, 101) resulting from the crossing of *A. pungens* with *A. junceiforme* and *A. repens* grow with or near their parents; they are intermediate in structure and may be recognized by their sterile anthers.

A. maritimum (Koch & Ziz) Bouly de Lesdain (non Beauv., 1812) has been recorded from dunes on the coasts of S. and E. England and Holland; it is said to differ from *A. pungens* in having smooth-ribbed leaf-blades, and small few-flowered remote spikelets.

(*Elymus pungens* (Pers.) Melderis.)

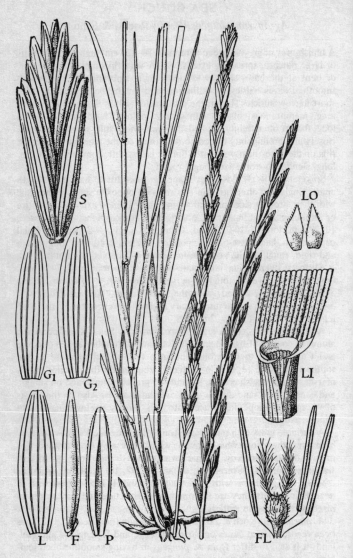

Agropyron × *obtusiusculum*. Uncommon; coastal dunes.

100

HYBRID SEA-COUCH
Agropyron × obtusiusculum Lange

Perennial, 20–100 cm. high, forming loose or compact tufts, spreading by long wiry rhizomes. Culms erect, spreading, or prostrate, slender to stout, rigid, 3–5-noded, smooth. Leaves bluish-green or greyish-green, hairless; sheaths rounded on the back, with narrow spreading auricles (LI) at the top; ligules (LI, × 5) less than 1 mm. long, membranous; blades narrowed to a hard point, 10–30 cm. long, flat or inrolled, 2–7 mm. wide, stiff, smooth beneath, usually rough on the closely and prominently ribbed upper surface. Spikes stiff, persistent, 6–22 cm. long, bluish-grey or greyish-green; axis tough, rough or smooth.

Spikelets (S, × 3) stalkless, alternating in two rows on opposite sides of the axis, with their broader sides pressed against the flattened part, solitary, persistent, about half their length or more apart, oblong to elliptic or wedge-shaped, 15–28 mm. long, 4–10-flowered. Glumes (G₁, G₂, × 3) similar, equal, or nearly so, oblong or lanceolate-oblong, usually blunt, 9–15 mm. long, keeled, tough, prominently 5–7-nerved, smooth or slightly rough on the keel. Lemmas (F, L, × 3) overlapping, oblong, blunt, with a small hard apical projection, 9–15 mm. long, rounded on the back below, keeled above, tough, smooth, 5-nerved. Paleas (P, × 3) about as long as the lemmas, with the keels rough or minutely hairy. Anthers (FL, × 6) sterile, not opening, 4–6·5 mm. long. *Ch. no.* 2n = 35.

This male-sterile hybrid, resulting from the crossing of *A. junceiforme* with *A. pungens*, grows here and there on the coasts of S. Eire, and of England from Cornwall to Yorkshire and Cumberland, as well as on those of W. Europe. In British Floras it has been usually named *Agropyron acutum* or *Triticum acutum*. Flowering: July and August.

It frequently occupies a zone in the fixed dunes intermediate between that of *A. junceiforme* on the loose sand and of *A. pungens* fringing the salt-marshes. By means of its far-creeping rhizomes it spreads in dry and wet sands and in shingle. The common forms of the hybrid are stiffly erect and as tall as *A. pungens*, whilst others are low and spreading and resemble *A. junceiforme*. Occasionally the lemmas are short-awned, probably from the cross with *A. pungens* var. *setigerum*. In Scotland, England, and N. Ireland, a somewhat similar male-sterile hybrid [*Agropyron × laxum* (Fries) Almq.], between *A. junceiforme* and *A. repens*, grows on the coast. It may usually be recognized by less prominent ribbing and by the short hairs on the upper surface of the leaf-blades.

(*Elymus pycnanthus × Elymus farctus* subsp. *boreali-atlanticus*)

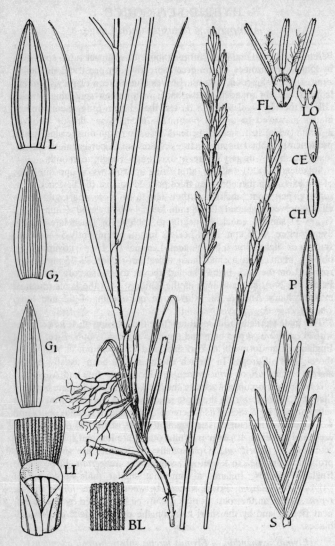

Agropyron junceiforme. Frequent; coastal dunes.

SAND COUCH

Agropyron junceiforme (A. & D. Löve) A. & D. Löve

A bluish-grey perennial, 20–60 cm. high, forming loose tufts or mats, spreading extensively by long slender wiry rhizomes. Culms erect, spreading or drooping, slender to somewhat stout, rather brittle, unbranched and few-noded above the base, smooth. Leaves bluish-grey; sheaths overlapping, rounded on the back, smooth; ligules (LI, × 5) truncate, 0·5–1 mm. long, membranous; blades finely pointed, spreading or usually drooping, 10–35 cm. long, 2–6 mm. wide, flat or often rolled, stiff to rather soft, smooth below, prominently ribbed above, with the ribs (BL) densely and minutely hairy; without auricles. Spikes stout, 4–20 cm. long, straight or curved; axis smooth, fragile, readily breaking just above each spikelet.

Spikelets (S, × 2) stalkless, alternating in two rows on opposite sides of the axis, with their broad sides appressed to it, breaking up at maturity beneath each lemma, oblong, elliptic, or wedge-shaped, 15–28 mm. long, 3–8-flowered, their own length or less apart. Glumes (G_1, G_2, × 2) similar, equal or slightly unequal, narrowly oblong, blunt, keeled or rounded on the back, 9–20 mm. long, very tough and rigid, prominently 7–11-nerved, smooth. Lemmas (L, × 2) overlapping, oblong or lanceolate-oblong, blunt or emarginate, with a very short hard apical mucro, rounded on the back below, keeled above, 11–20 mm. long, thick and rigid, 5-nerved, smooth. Paleas (P, × 2) shorter than the lemmas, with the two keels minutely hairy. Anthers (FL, × 2) 6–8 mm. long. Grain (CE, CH, × 2) minutely hairy at the top, enclosed by the hard lemma and palea. *Ch. no.* 2n = 28.

This coastal grass, being very tolerant of salt both in the soil and in sea-water, is able to grow nearer the sea than other British dune grasses. On sandy beaches it forms low dunes only a few feet high, backed by the higher dunes dominated by Marram Grass, or it may grow mixed with the latter and with Sand Fescue. It is of common occurrence on the sandy coasts of the British Isles and W. Europe, and has been introduced into N.E. America. Usually named *Agropyron junceum* (L.) Beauv. or *Triticum junceum* L. in our older Floras, a grass of sea shores in the eastern Mediterranean Region. Known also as Jointed Couch and Sand Twitch. Flowering: June to August.

Sand Couch hybridizes with *Agropyron pungens* and *A. repens*. It may be distinguished from both hybrids and species by the densely hairy ribs of the upper surface of the leaf-blades, those of the other Couch-grasses being only rough or sparingly hairy; its anthers also are fertile and its spikes brittle.

(*Elymus farctus* subsp. *boreali-atlanticus* (Simonet and Guinochet) Melderis.)

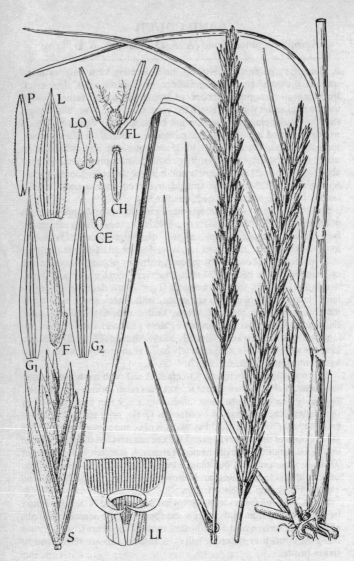

Elymus arenarius. Frequent; coastal dunes.

LYME GRASS
Elymus arenarius L.

A robust bluish-grey perennial, forming large tufts or masses, 60–200 cm. high, with long stout rhizomes. Culms erect or spreading, stout, unbranched, smooth. Leaves bluish-grey; sheaths smooth, with two narrow spreading auricles (LI) at the apex; ligules (LI, × 2) up to 1 mm. long, firmly membranous, minutely hairy; blades sharply pointed, up to 60 cm. or more long, flat or inrolled, 8–20 mm. wide, rigid, minutely rough above on the prominent nerves, smooth beneath. Spikes stout, compact, stiff, 15–35 cm. long, 1·2–2·5 cm. wide.

Spikelets (S, × 2) stalkless, usually in pairs, the pairs alternating on opposite sides of the axis, 2·0–3·2 cm. long, oblong or wedge-shaped, 3–6-flowered, breaking up at maturity beneath each lemma. Glumes (G_1, G_2, × 2) persistent, similar, narrowly lanceolate and finely pointed in side view, as long or nearly as long as the spikelet, keeled, usually rigid, hairy, especially on the keel, 3–5-nerved. Lemmas (F, L, × 2) decreasing in size upwards, the lowest 1·5–2·5 cm. long. lanceolate, pointed, tough, 7-nerved, densely hairy with short soft hairs. Paleas (P, × 2) as long as the lemmas , 2-keeled. Anthers (FL, × 2) 7–8 mm. long. Grain (CE, CH, × 2) tightly enclosed by the lemma and palea, 10 mm. long, hairy at the top, *Ch. no.* 2n = 56.

A robust grass of maritime sand-dunes, widespread along the coasts of Great Britain, most frequent and often locally abundant in the east and north; local in Ireland. Distributed along the shores of N. and N.W. Europe; introduced elsewhere. Hybrids with *Agropyron junceiforme* occur on the shores of the Baltic (× *Lemopyron bergrothii* (Lindb. f.) Tzvelev, × *Lemotrigia bergrothii* (Lindb. f.) Tzvelev, × *Elymotrigia bergrothii* (Lindb. f.) Hyland and × *Tritordeum bergrothii* Lindb. f.). Flowering: June to August.

An effective sand-binder, spreading by its extensively creeping rhizomes and by seeds, sometimes dominating large areas of dunes, or growing mixed with Marram and other sand grasses. It succeeds best in loose sand at the foot or on the seaward side of the dunes. Its presence in some districts is no doubt due to plantings made to prevent erosion. On account of its coloured leaves and spikes it is occasionally planted in garden beds and borders. It is usually propagated by division of the rootstock, small leafy pieces being planted 30 cm. or more apart when grown on sand-dunes. It withstands treading and flourishes at the front of dunes with *Agropyron junceiforme*.

In some districts no flowering spikes, or very few, are produced, owing to the presence of the stem smut fungus, *Ustilago hypodytes*, in the tissues of the plant. The culms, instead of bearing spikes, are covered with a dense layer of black fungus spores.

(*Leymus arenarius* (L.) Hochst.)

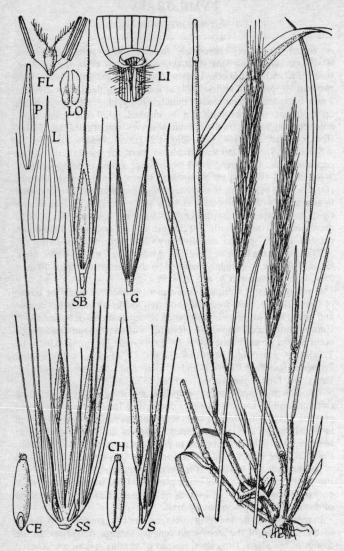

Hordelymus europaeus. Uncommon; woods.

WOOD BARLEY
Hordelymus europaeus (L.) Harz

A loosely tufted short-lived perennial, 40–120 cm. high. Culms erect, or bent below, slender to stout, 3–4-noded, hairy at the nodes, smooth. Leaves green; sheaths beset with spreading or reflexed hairs, or the upper hairless and smooth, with short spreading outgrowths (auricles) at the apex; ligules (LI, × 2) less than 1 mm. long, membranous; blades narrowed to a fine point, 10–30 cm. long, 5–14 mm. wide, flat, loosely to sparsely hairy, rough above and on the margins. Spike erect or nodding, bristly, dense, 5–10 cm. long, 7–12 mm. wide, green; axis persistent.

Spikelets (S, SB, × 3) usually in threes (SS, × 3) at each node of the axis, rarely in pairs, the trios alternating on opposite sides of the axis, usually 1- rarely 2-flowered (S), narrow, breaking up at maturity above the glumes. Glumes (G, × 3) persistent, erect, side by side in front of the lemma, similar, linear-lanceolate, narrowed into a fine straight rough awn (bristle) and including it 14–17 mm. long, flat, rigid. Lemmas (L, part of awn removed, × 3) lanceolate, 8–10 mm. long, narrowed into a fine rough awn (bristle) 1·5–2·5 cm. long, broadly rounded on the back (this outermost), becoming tough, 5-nerved, rough upwards. Paleas (P, × 3) narrow, as long as the lemmas, 2-keeled. Anthers (FL, × 3) 3–4 mm. long. Grain (CE, CH, × 3) about 7 mm. long, tightly enclosed by the hardened lemma and palea, hairy at the top. *Ch. no.* 2n = 28.

An attractive grass of woods and shady places, fairly widespread in England from Wiltshire to Kent and northwards to Northumberland and Westmorland, but generally uncommon; very rare in S. Scotland and N. Ireland, usually on calcareous soils. On the Chilterns it is sometimes locally quite abundant, especially in those beech-woods with undergrowth, and after a good seeding year. Scattered through Europe from Sweden southwards, also in S.W. Asia and N.W. Africa. Flowering: June to July.

Under cultivation in the open it succeeds on both sandy and heavy soils, seeding profusely, the seeds germinating in the autumn and flowering the following year. As it produces so few vegetative shoots, it rarely lasts more than two or three years.

This single species of *Hordelymus* has been usually treated as a member of *Hordeum* or *Elymus* in British Floras. From our species of the former it may be distinguished by the persistent axis of the spike, the way the spikelets break up at maturity, the persistent glumes and the bisexual lateral spikelets. From *Elymus arenarius* it is separated by its tufted habit, 1–2-flowered spikelets, and long-awned glumes and lemmas.

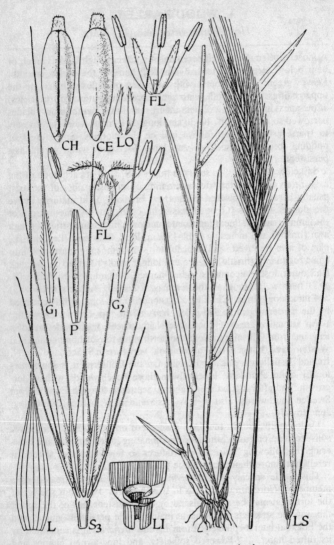

CH CE LO

FL

FL

G_1 G_2

P

L S_3 LI LS

Hordeum murinum. Common; waste land.

WALL BARLEY

Hordeum murinum L.

Annual, 6–60 cm. high. Culms loosely tufted or solitary, erect or spreading, slender to somewhat stout, 3–5-noded, smooth. Leaves light green; sheaths rounded on the back, the lower usually hairy, the upper smooth, slightly inflated; ligules (LI, × 2) membranous, up to 1 mm. long; blades finely pointed, with narrow spreading auricles (LI) at the base, 2–20 cm. long, 2–8 mm. wide, rather weak, loosely hairy or hairless, rough. Spikes erect or inclined, dense, compressed, bristly, 4–12 cm. long, 1–3 cm. wide, with the awns erect or slightly spreading, breaking up at maturity beneath each cluster of 3 spikelets, green or tinged with purple.

Spikelets (S_3, × 3) one-flowered, in threes, the middle one bisexual and stalkless, the two lateral (LS) male or barren, on short stalks, the three falling together. Lateral spikelets (LS, × 4): glumes bristle-like and long-awned, including the fine stiff awns 16–30 mm. long, slightly dissimilar, the upper very slightly wider near the base and fringed there with short hairs; lemma lanceolate, 7–11 mm. long, terminated by an awn 10–40 mm. long. Middle spikelet: glumes (G_1, G_2, × 3) in front of the lemma, bristle-like and long-awned, including the awn up to 26 mm. long, fringed with hairs in the lower part; lemma (L, × 3) lanceolate, 7–12 mm. long, broadly rounded on the back, 5-nerved, rough towards the tip, tipped with a stiff awn 18–50 mm. long; palea (P, × 3) as long as the lemma. Anthers (FL, × 8) $0 \cdot 7$–$1 \cdot 2$ mm. long. Grains (CE, CH, × 5) hairy at the top, tightly enclosed by the hardened lemma and palea, *Ch. no.* 2n = 28.

Wall Barley grows on waste ground, especially where the soils has been disturbed, on the margins of cultivated land, and on waysides, particularly by buildings and walls. It is widely distributed in the British Isles, but uncommon or rare in grassland and mountainous regions. Also throughout Europe and S.W. Asia. Flowering: end of May to August.

A closely related species, *H. leporinum* Link of the Mediterranean Region, is occasionally introduced into England and is naturalized in N. and S. America and Australia. It differs from *H. murinum* in having lateral spikelets which are longer and wider than the middle one. *H. glaucum* Steud. (*H. stebbinsii* Covas) of E. Mediterranean Region is also occasionally introduced.

The species of *Hordeum* may be recognized by their one-flowered spikelets being grouped in clusters of three, the trios alternating on opposite sides of the axis of the spike and usually falling together at maturity.

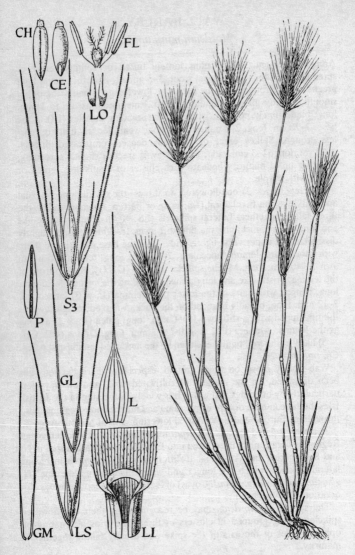

Hordeum marinum. Frequent; salt-marshes.

110

SEA BARLEY
Hordeum marinum Huds.

Annual, 10–40 cm. high. Culms loosely tufted or solitary, erect or spreading from a bent base, slender, stiff, unbranched, 3–4-noded, smooth. Leaves bluish-green; sheaths rounded on the back, smooth; ligules (LI, × 6) less than 1 mm. long, membranous; blades tapering to a fine point, often with small obscure auricles at the base, 1·5–8 cm. long, flat, 1–3·5 mm. wide, minutely hairy, or hairless. Spikes stiff, dense, oblong to ovate, 2–6 cm. long, 1·5–3 cm. wide, green or purplish, bristly, with the awns at first erect, later spreading, breaking up at maturity beneath each cluster of spikelets.

Spikelets (S_3, × 3) one-flowered, in threes alternating on opposite sides of the spike-axis, with the middle one bisexual and stalkless, the two lateral (LS) barren and on very short stalks, the three falling together. Lateral spikelets (LS, × 3): glumes (GL, × 3) dissimilar, rough, becoming very rigid, the lower bristle-like and long-awned, including the fine straight rough awn 8–26 mm. long, the upper broadly winged on one side, 4–6 mm. long, awned like the lower, the awn 10–22 mm. long; lemma lanceolate, 3–5 mm. long, tipped with a straight awn 3–5 mm. long. Middle spikelet: glumes (GM, × 3) similar, placed in front of the lemma, bristle-like throughout, including the fine straight awn 10–24 mm. long; lemma (L, × 3) narrowly ovate, 6–8 mm. long, rounded on the back, smooth, 5-nerved, tipped with an awn up to 24 mm. long; palea (P, × 3) narrow, as long as the lemma. Anthers (FL, × 6) 1·3–1·5 mm. long. Grain (CE, CH, × 3) hairy at the tip, tightly enclosed by the hardened lemma and palea. *Ch. no.* 2n = 14.

Sea Barley is to be found along the coasts of Great Britain from S. England and Wales to the south of Scotland. It is often locally abundant, especially in S. and E. England, on bare, slightly raised ground within and on the margins of salt-marshes, on grassy sea-banks, sea-walls, and waste ground. Also along the coasts of W. Europe and of the Mediterranean countries; introduced into N. America. Sometimes known as Squirrel-tail Barley or Grass. Flowering: June and July.

Mediterranean Barley, *H. hystrix* Roth (*H. gussonianum* Parl.), of the Mediterranean Region, occurs occasionally on waste ground and rubbish-dumps, and rarely as a weed in cultivated places. It is very similar to *H. marinum* but may be distinguished by both glumes of its lateral spikelets being bristle-like, *Ch. no.* 2n = 14.

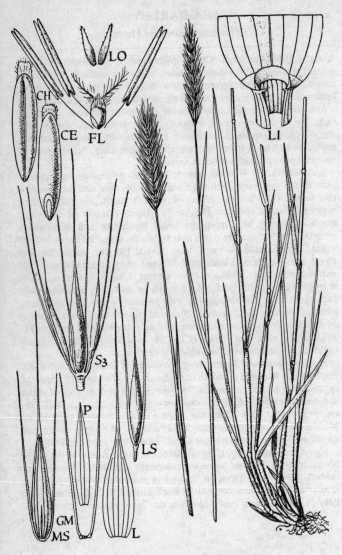

Hordeum secalinum. Common; grassland.

MEADOW BARLEY

Hordeum secalinum Schreb.

A tufted perennial, 20–80 cm. high. Culms erect, or bent at the base, slender, 3–5-noded, smooth. Leaves green or greyish-green; sheaths rounded on the back, the lower softly hairy, the upper hairless, smooth; ligules (LI, × 6) less than 1 mm. long, membranous; blades finely pointed, with very short spreading auricles at the base, up to 15 cm. long, 2–6 mm. wide, loosely short-hairy, or hairless, rough or smoooth beneath. Spikes erect or inclined, dense, 2–8 cm. long, 0·7–1·5 cm. wide, with the awns erect or slightly spreading, breaking up at maturity beneath each cluster of spikelets.

Spikelets (S_3, × 3) one-flowered, in threes alternating on opposite sides of the spike-axis, the middle one (MS) bisexual and stalkless, the two lateral (LS) male or barren and often much reduced in size, on very short stalks, the three falling together. Lateral spikelets (LS, × 3): glumes similar, bristle-like and long-awned, including the fine rough awn up to 14 mm. long; lemma very narrow to lanceolate, 4–6 mm. long, tipped with a fine awn up to 3 mm. long, minutely hairy or rough in the upper part. Middle spikelet (MS, × 3): glumes (GM, × 3) like those of the lateral spikelets, placed in front of the lemma; lemma (L, × 3) broadly lanceolate, 6–9 mm. long, 5-nerved, smooth on the back, tipped with a fine awn 6–12 mm. long; palea (P, × 3), as long as the lemma; anthers (FL, × 6) 3–4 mm. long. Grains (CE, CH, × 4) hairy at the tip, tightly enclosed in the hardened lemma and palea. *Ch. no.* 2n = 28.

A rather stiff grass of lowland coastal and inland meadows and pastures, mostly on moist heavy soils, frequent and often locally abundant in the southern part of England, less common to rare in the north and west, Wales, Ireland, and Scotland. Also throughout W. and S. Europe, and in N.W. Africa. The name *Hordeum nodosum* L. has been misapplied to this grass. Flowering: June and July.

A rare male-sterile hybrid with *Agropyron repens* [× *Agrohordeum langei* (K. Richt.) Camus] has been found near Bristol. Fox-tail Barley, *H. jubatum* L., of N. America, is sometimes cultivated in gardens on account of its ornamental spikes, the fine silky awns of which are up to 6 cm. long; it also occurs occasionally on waste ground and rubbish tips. The two cultivated Barleys, *H. vulgare* L. (p. 425) and *H. distichon* L. (p. 426), are extensively cultivated in the British Isles for their grain which is used as food for stock or for malting. They may be recognized by the persistent axes of their spikes.

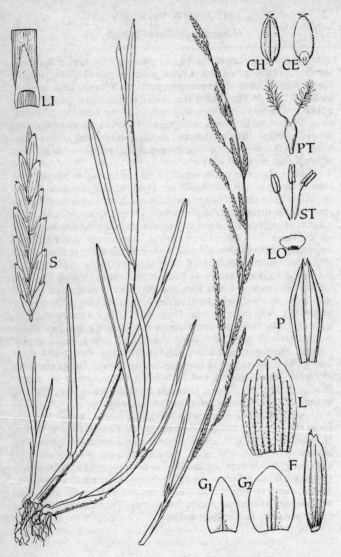

Glyceria declinata. Frequent; wet places.

114

GLAUCOUS SWEET-GRASS
Glyceria declinata Bréb.

Perennial, usually loosely tufted, 10–45 cm. high. Culms erect, or ascending from a curved or bent base, or prostrate, 1–3-noded, smooth. Leaves greyish-green or tinged with purple, hairless; sheaths keeled, entire, usually smooth; ligules (LI, × 2) 4–9 mm. long, membranous; blades equally wide throughout, abruptly pointed or blunt, at first folded, becoming flat, 3–18 cm. long, 1·5–8 mm. wide, smooth except for the rough margins, often rather stiff. Panicles linear to lanceolate, straight or curved, often one-sided, sparingly branched, 4–38 cm. long; axis smooth; branches solitary or in pairs or threes, appressed to or spreading on one side of the axis, smooth; pedicels 1·5–4 mm. long.

Spikelets (S, × 3) narrowly oblong, slightly compressed, 1·3–2·5 cm. long, 1·5–2 mm. wide, 8–15-flowered, breaking up at maturity beneath each lemma, green, or purplish. Glumes (G_1, G_2, × 6) persistent, ovate to oblong, blunt, membranous, usually 1-nerved, smooth; lower 1·5–2·5 mm. long; upper 2·5–3 mm. long. Lemmas (F, L, × 6) overlapping, much exceeding the glumes, broadly elliptic-oblong, usually with a broad 3-lobed or 3–5-toothed tip, 4–5 mm. long, becoming firm except for the thin whitish apex, 7-nerved, minutely rough. Paleas (P, × 6) narrowly elliptic, narrowed into a sharply 2-toothed tip, this usually slightly projecting from the tip of the lemma, with the two keels narrowly winged. Anthers (ST, × 6) 0·8–1 mm. long, purple or yellow. Grain (CE, CH, × 6) chestnut brown, 1·5–2·3 mm. long, enclosed by the hardened lemma and palea. Ch. no. 2n = 20.

Widely distributed in the British Isles, probably, occurring in most counties, although its exact range is not yet known, owing to confusion in the past with *G. fluitans*; on muddy or dried-up margins and in the shallow water of ponds, ditches and streams, moderately common; less frequent than *G. fluitans*. Grazed by cattle with other aquatic grasses. Throughout W. and Central Europe, from S. Norway and Sweden to S. Spain and Corsica; Madeira; also in the United States. Known also as Small Flote-grass and Small Sweet-Grass. Flowering: June to September.

Distinguished from other British species of *Glyceria* by the 3-toothed or 3–5-lobed tips of the lemmas and by the sharply 2-toothed tips of the paleas. A rather rare hybrid from Hertfordshire (ex Stace) between *G. declinata* and *G. fluitans* may be recognized by its persistent spikelets, 5–5·5 mm. long blunt lemmas, and the 0·5–1·8 mm. long sterile anthers. The species of *Glyceria* may be separated from *Poa* and *Puccinellia* by the very short truncate-joined lodicules (LO) and by the fine line-like hilum of the grain (CH).

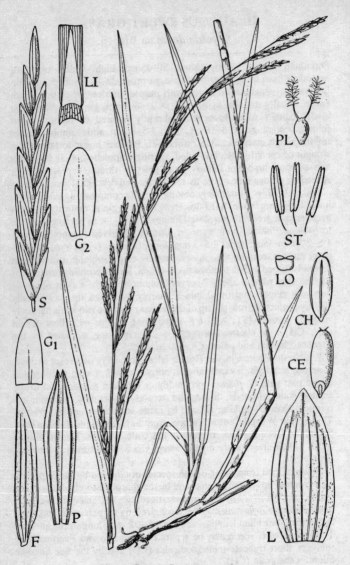

Glyceria fluitans. Common; wet places.

FLOATING SWEET-GRASS
Glyceria fluitans (L.) R. Br.

Perennial, up to 1 m. high, loosely tufted or forming loose masses in shallow water. Culms erect or spreading, sometimes with a prostrate or floating base, few-noded, slender to rather stout, smooth. Leaves green, or with the sheaths purple, hairless; sheaths tubular, smooth; ligules (LI, × 1½) lanceolate-oblong, 5–15 mm. long, membranous; blades pointed, 5–25 cm. long, 3–10 mm. wide, folded or flat, smooth except for the rough margins. Panicles open in flower, afterwards contracted and narrow, erect or curved and nodding, 10–50 cm. long, sparingly branched in the lower part; main-axis smooth; branches usually in pairs or solitary, the longer of a pair bearing 1–4 spikelets, the shorter with 1 spikelet, appressed to the axis after flowering; pedicels 1–4 mm. long.

Spikelets (S, × 3) narrowly oblong, 18–35 mm. long, 2–3·5 mm. wide, 8–16-flowered, green or purplish, breaking up at maturity beneath the lemmas. Glumes (G_1, G_2, × 6) persistent, elliptic-oblong or oblong, blunt, 1–3-nerved, thin; lower 2–3 mm., upper 3–5 mm. long. Lemmas (F, L, × 6) rounded on the back, at first overlapping, later with incurved margins, elliptic-oblong or oblong, somewhat blunt or pointed, entire, 6–7·5 mm. long, 7-nerved, firm except for the thin whitish apex, minutely rough. Paleas (P, × 6) sharply 2-toothed, with the teeth reaching the tip of the lemmas or usually shortly projecting. Anthers (ST, × 6) 2–3 mm. long. Grain (CE, CH, × 6) 2–3 mm. long, dark brown, enclosed by the hardened lemma and palea. *Ch. no.* 2n = 40.

A succulent aquatic grass, distributed throughout the British Isles, probably occurring in every county; in shallow water of ponds and lake margins, in ditches, sluggish streams, and river-margins; often abundant and sometimes dominating such habitats. Widespread in Europe, especially in the west, also in N.E. America. Sometimes called Flotegrass or Manna-grass. Flowering: end of May to August.

Glyceria declinata and *G. plicata* may be separated from *G. fluitans* by their shorter lemmas (4–5 mm.) and smaller anthers (0·8–1·5 mm.). Both species hybridize with *G. fluitans*, the progeny being sterile. The hybrid between *G. fluitans* and *G. declinata* is rare, but that between *G. fluitans* and *G. plicata* is widespread in Britain and often abundant; an account of it is given under *G × pedicellata* (p. 119).

Floating Sweet-grass is eagerly grazed by cattle on account of its palatable succulent foliage.

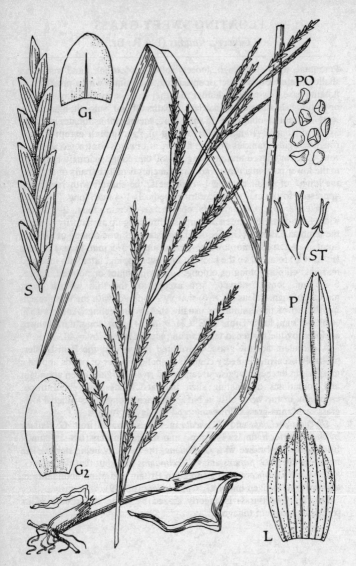

Glyceria × *pedicellata*. Frequent; wet places.

HYBRID SWEET-GRASS
Glyceria × *pedicellata* Towns.

Perennial, up to 1 m. high, sometimes in large patches, and with long floating runners. Culms ascending from an extensively creeping branched base, slender to rather stout, fleshy, smooth. Leaves green, hairless; sheaths often minutely rough towards the blades, or quite smooth; ligules oblong, membranous, whitish, up to 10 mm. long; blades abruptly pointed or rather blunt, up to 35 cm. long, folded or flat, 5–12 mm. wide, rough on the nerves beneath and sometimes above, or smooth except for the rough margins. Panicles lanceolate to oblong, loose, 10–50 cm. long; branches erect or finally spreading, slender, mostly in pairs or threes in the lower part of the panicle, singly above or sometimes throughout, unequal, the longer up to 11 cm. long, and bearing up to 9 spikelets, the shorter branches with 1 or 2 spikelets, smooth; pedicels 1–6 mm. long.

Spikelets (S, × 3) linear-oblong, becoming slightly compressed, 1·5–3·5 cm. long, 9–16-flowered, green, rarely purplish, more or less persistent. Glumes (G_1, G_2, × 6) broadly oblong to broadly elliptic, blunt, very thin, whitish, 1-nerved; lower 2–3 mm. long; upper 3–4·5 mm. long. Lemmas (L, × 6) overlapping, rounded on the back, elliptic-oblong, very blunt, 4–6 (mostly 5–5·5) mm. long, firm except for the whitish membranous apex, prominently 7-nerved, minutely rough. Paleas (P, × 6) as long as the lemmas, oblong, shortly 2-toothed, with the keels narrowly winged in the upper part. Anthers (ST, × 6) pale yellow, 1–1·8 mm. long, remaining closed, with imperfect pollen (PO). *Ch. no.* 2n = 40.

This male-sterile hybrid is the offspring of the cross between *G. fluitans* and *G. plicata*. It is widely distributed in England, being recorded from many localities between Cornwall and Kent and northwards to Northumberland, but is most frequent in the south. It is known also from scattered localities in Scotland and Ireland and no doubt occurs in Wales. Also in W. Europe. The hybrid may grow with one or both parents, or more often alone, in shallow ponds, streams, ditches, and in swampy depressions in pastures. Flowering: June to August.

Hybrid Sweet-grass may be recognized by its persistent spikelets (those of the species readily breaking up at maturity for the dispersal of the seed) and by the sterile anthers. Its lemmas and anthers are smaller than those of *G. fluitans* and mostly slightly longer than those of *G. plicata*. It is a vigorous hybrid, its luxuriant succulent growth being much relished by cattle.

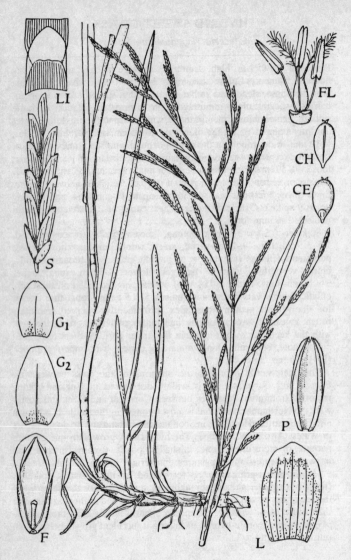

Glyceria plicata. Frequent; wet places.

PLICATE SWEET-GRASS
Glyceria plicata Fries

Perennial, 30–75 cm. high, forming tufts or loose patches. Culms ascending from a prostrate base, rooting at the nodes, branched in the basal portion, unbranched above, slender to relatively stout, spongy, smooth. Leaves green or greyish green; sheaths entire, keeled, rough or minutely hairy; ligules (LI, × 2) oblong, membranous, whitish, 2–8 mm. long; blades pointed, 5–30 cm. long, folded or flat, 3–14 mm. wide, rough on both sides, or nearly smooth above. Panicles commonly rather broad, lanceolate to oblong, or broadly ovate, loose, 10–45 cm. long; branches finally widely spreading, the lower in clusters of 2–5, with one branch longer than the rest and up to 12 cm. long, the others shorter and with one to few spikelets, slender; pedicels 1–6 mm. long.

Spikelets (S, × 3) linear-oblong, at first cylindrical, later slightly compressed, 10–25 mm. long, 1·5–2 mm. wide, 7–16-flowered, green or purplish, breaking up at maturity beneath each lemma. Glumes (G_1, G_2, × 6) persistent, oblong to broadly elliptic, very blunt, membranous, 1-nerved; lower 1·5–2·5 mm. long; upper 2·5–4 mm. long. Lemmas (F, L × 6) overlapping, later with incurved margins, rounded on the back, broadly elliptic to broadly obovate-oblong, very blunt or very slightly 3-lobed, 3·5–5 mm. long, prominently 7-nerved, firm except for the broad thin whitish tip, minutely rough. Paleas (P, × 6) oblong, very blunt, as long as or usually shorter than the lemmas, narrowly winged on the two keels. Anthers (FL, × 8) 1–1·5 mm. long. Grain (CE, CH, × 6) about 2 mm. long, enclosed by the hardened lemma and palea. *Ch. no.* 2n = 40.

This species of Sweet-grass is generally distributed throughout England, and extends to S.E. and W. Scotland; it occurs also in Wales and in widely scattered localities in Ireland; in ponds, ditches, streams, and swampy places; usually less frequent than *G. fluitans*. Widespread in Europe; also in W. Asia and N. Africa. Flowering: June to August.

As in other species of *Glyceria*, its luscious foliage is eagerly grazed by cattle, whilst its seeds are eaten by water-fowl. It may be distinguished from *G. fluitans* by its rough or minutely hairy leaf-sheaths, usually much-branched wider panicles, very blunt shorter lemmas and the smaller anthers. *G. maxima* is much taller and stouter, with longer leaf-blades, wider spikelets, and smaller lemmas.

For the hybrid, *G. fluitans* × *plicata*, see *G.* × *pedicellata* (p. 119).

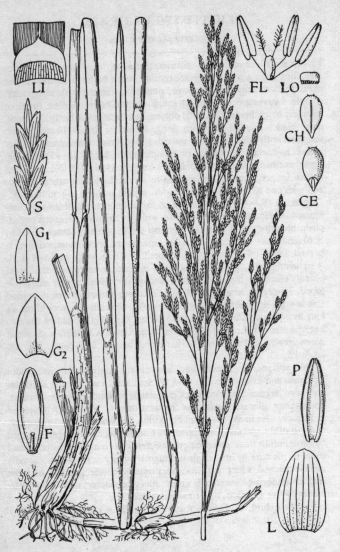

Glyceria maxima. Common; wet places.

122

REED SWEET-GRASS
Glyceria maxima (Hartm.) Holmb.

A stout leafy perennial, 90–250 cm. high, with numerous vegetative shoots, spreading by stout rhizomes and covering large areas. Culms erect, stout to robust, smooth or rough towards the panicle. Leaves with cross-nerves, green, hairless; sheaths entire, later splitting, keeled upwards, rough towards the blade or smooth; ligules (LI, × 1) 3–6 mm. long, blunt, but generally with a central point, firmly membranous; blades abruptly pointed, 30–60 cm. long, 7–20 mm. wide, rough on the margins and sometimes beneath. Panicles open and loose or becoming contracted and rather dense, broadly ovate to oblong, 15–45 cm. long, much-branched; branches clustered, very slender, rough, the lower up to 20 cm. or more long; pedicels 1–10 mm. long.

Spikelets (S, × 3) narrowly oblong or oblong, slightly compressed, 5–12 mm. long, 2–3·5 mm. wide, closely 4–10-flowered, green, or tinged with yellow or purple, slowly breaking up at maturity beneath each lemma. Glumes (G_1, G_2, × 6) persistent, broadly ovate to oblong or elliptic, membranous, 1-nerved; lower 2–3 mm. long; upper 3–4 mm. long. Lemmas (F, L, × 6) overlapping, rounded on the back, elliptic to ovate-elliptic, very blunt, 3–4 mm. long, firm except for the membranous apex, prominently 7-nerved, minutely rough on the nerves. Paleas (P, × 6) about as long as the lemmas, oblong, with two rough keels. Anthers (FL, × 6) 1·5–2 mm. long. Grain (CE, CH, × 6) 1·5–2 mm. long, dark brown, enclosed by the hardened lemma and palea. *Ch. no.* 2n = 60.

A luxuriant aquatic grass, common to very abundant in the lowlands of the British Isles, uncommon to rare in S.W. England, Wales, and N. Scotland; on the banks of slow-running rivers and canals. in large ponds and lakes, and in marshy areas subject to flooding during the winter; forming extensive pure stands as in the Fens and Broads; growing in deeper water (up to 0·7 m.) than the other species of *Glyceria*. Throughout most of Europe and temperate Asia; introduced into Australia, New Zealand, and N. America. Also called Reed Meadow-grass, Reed-grass, or Reed. Flowering: June to August.

A nutritious fodder plant, readily eaten by cattle and on this account worth encouraging in water meadows too swampy for other grasses. It is also of value on river banks for the prevention of erosion. Var. *variegata*, with the leaves striped green and pale yellow, is useful for planting on the margins of ornamental pools and streams.

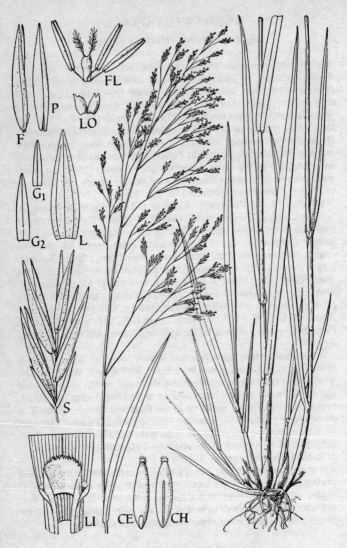

Festuca altissima, Rare; shaded places.

124

REED FESCUE or WOOD FESCUE
Festuca altissima All.

A compactly tufted perennial, 50–120 cm. high. Culms erect, slender to moderately stout, unbranched, 3–4 noded, smooth, clothed at the base with bladeless sheaths. Leaves hairless, green; sheaths smooth, or rough upwards, rounded on the back, without auricles; ligules (LI, × 4) thinly membranous, up to 5 mm. long, becoming torn; blades gradually narrowed to a fine point, up to 60 cm. long, flat, 4–14 mm. wide, thin to firm, finely nerved, minutely rough on both sides or only on the margins. Panicles loose, open, nodding, 10–18 cm. long, up to 12 cm. wide, green; branches usually in pairs, fine, spreading, smooth or slightly rough; pedicels very unequal, 1·5–15 mm. long.

Spikelets (S, × 6) oblong or wedge-shaped, 5–8 mm. long, 2–5-flowered, breaking up at maturity above the glumes and between the lemmas. Glumes (G_1, G_2, × 6) persistent, very narrow, shorter than the lowest lemma, slightly unequal, finely pointed, 1-nerved, smooth; lower narrowly lanceolate, 2–3 mm. long; upper narrowly oblong, 3–4 mm. long. Lemmas (F, L, × 6) lanceolate, finely pointed, 4–6 mm. long, rounded on the back below, keeled in the upper part, firmly membranous, 3-nerved, minutely rough. Paleas (P, × 6) about as long as the lemmas, with two rough keels. Anthers (FL, × 6) 2·5–3 mm. long. Grain (CE, CH, × 6) hairy at the top, enclosed by the hardened lemma and palea. *Ch. no.* 2n = 14, 42.

Reed Fescue is rather sparsely distributed in the British Isles, being confined almost to the west and north, except for outliers in Kent, Sussex, and Buckinghamshire. It occurs in scattered localities from Gloucestershire and S. and Central Wales northwards through Derbyshire to Cumberland and Durham as well as in many parts of Scotland and Ireland; in moist wooded valleys, and on rocky slopes, wood margins, and stream sides. Also here and there throughout Europe and in S.W. Asia. In the past usually named *F. sylvatica* Vill. Flowering: end of May to July.

A very distinct species of *Festuca* readily separated from other members of the genus by its wide flat leaf-blades, relatively long membranous ligules, awnless spikelets, and 3-nerved awnless lemmas. The genus *Festuca* is now restricted to perennial grasses, with panicles of 2- to many-flowered spikelets, the 1–3-nerved glumes of which are equal or slightly unequal and shorter than the lowest lemma, the lemmas rounded on the back, usually 5–7-nerved, narrowed upwards and frequently tipped with a straight awn, and each grain with a very narrow long hilum.

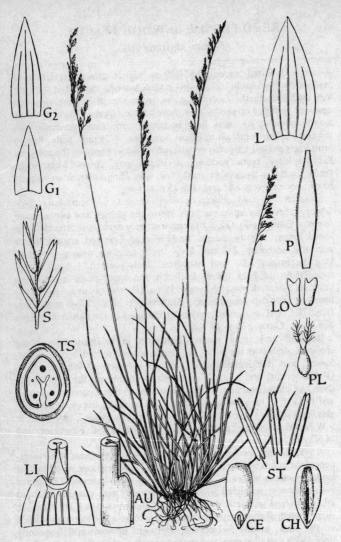

Festuca tenuifolia. Frequent; acidic grassland.

FINE-LEAVED SHEEP'S FESCUE
Festuca tenuifolia Sibth.

A densely tufted fine-leaved perennial, 10–45 cm. high, without rhizomes. Culms erect, or slightly bent at the base, very slender, stiff, 1–3-noded, smooth, or rough near the panicle. Leaves hairless, bright to dark green; sheaths rounded on the back, open to the base (TS), smooth or roughish, with small rounded auricles (AU) at the apex; ligules (LI, × 15) extremely short, membranous; blades hairlike, blunt or finely pointed, 3–25 cm. long, tightly infolded (TS), 0·2–0·4 mm. in diameter, straight or flexuous, mostly 5-nerved, smooth or rough. Panicles erect, contracted and rather dense, linear to lanceolate or narrowly oblong, 2–10 cm. long, yellowish-green, green, or purplish; axis minutely rough; branches erect or slightly spreading, short; pedicels 1–2 mm. long.

Spikelets (S, × 6) oblong or elliptic, 3–7 mm. long, 3–8-flowered, breaking up at maturity beneath the lemmas. Glumes (G, G_2, × 12) persistent, slightly unequal, lanceolate, pointed, firm; lower 1·5–2·5 mm. long, 1-nerved; upper 2·5–3·5 mm. long, 3-nerved. Lemmas (L, × 12) at first overlapping, later loose, rounded on the back, or keeled only near the tip, 2·5–3·5 mm. long, lanceolate or narrowly oblong-lanceolate in side view, finely pointed, very rarely awned, firm, 5-nerved, minutely rough near the tips. Paleas (P, × 12) as long as the lemmas, minutely rough upwards on the two keels. Anthers (ST, × 12) 1–2 mm. long. Grain (CE, CH, × 12) tightly enclosed by the hardened lemma and palea. *Ch. no.* 2n = 14.

Widespread in the British Isles, but less common than *F. ovina*; on heaths, moorland, parkland, hill-grassland and in open woodland; on acid sandy, gravelly, or peaty soils, and in dry or damp places. Scattered throughout Europe; introduced into N.E. America where it is known as Hair Fescue, also in New Zealand. Flowering: May and June.

A variant with minutely hairy lemmas is var. *hirtula* (Hack. ex Travis) Howarth. *Festuca ovina* may be distinguished from *F. tenuifolia* by its short-awned longer lemmas and relatively thicker leaf-blades. *Festuca rubra* differs from both kinds of Sheep's Fescue in having larger spikelets and in the margins of the young leaf-sheaths being united.

Fine-leaved Sheep's Fescue has been used as a lawn grass; it forms a close dark green turf which is fairly drought-resistant and withstands close cutting. It has also been sown in woodlands where it persists in moderate shade, but it forms isolated tufts only and not a continuous cover, sometimes proliferous in Scotland.

Hybrids with *F. ovina* have been recorded, with *ch. no.* 2n = 21.

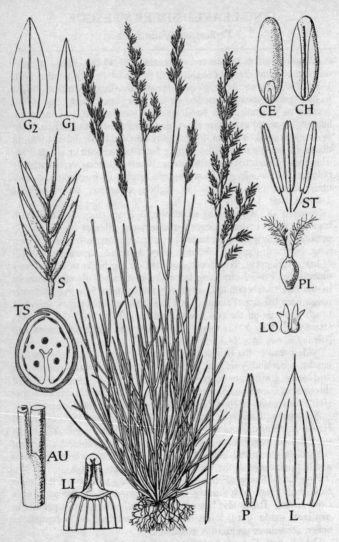

Festuca ovina. Common; grassland.

SHEEP'S FESCUE
Festuca ovina L.

A densely tufted perennial, 5–60 cm. high, without rhizomes. Culms erect or spreading, very slender, stiff, 1–2-noded, angular and rough near the panicle, or smooth; young shoots growing up within the leaf-sheaths. Leaves green or greyish-green, hairless; sheaths open (TS), rounded on the back, smooth, tipped with rounded auricles (AU); ligules (LI, × 10) extremely short; blades hair- or bristle-like, with a blunt tip, 3–25 cm. long, tightly infolded (TS), 0·3–0·6 mm. wide, firm, rough near the tip or all over, 5–7-nerved. Panicles erect, lanceolate or narrowly oblong, 3–12 cm. long, open in flower, later rather dense, somewhat one-sided, green or purplish; axis angular, rough; branches erect or slightly spreading; pedicels 1–3 mm. long.

Spikelets (S, × 4) elliptic to oblong, 5–10 mm. long, 3–9-flowered, breaking up at maturity beneath each lemma. Glumes (G_1, G_2, × 8) persistent, slightly unequal, pointed, firm; lower lanceolate, 2–3 mm. long, 1-nerved; upper oblong, 3–4 mm. long, 3-nerved; Lemmas (L, × 8) at first overlapping, later loose, rounded on back, lanceolate or narrowly oblong-lanceolate in side view, finely pointed, 3·5–5 mm. long, tipped with a fine awn 0·5–1·5 mm. long, firm, 5-nerved, rough near the tip. Paleas (P, × 8) as long as the lemmas, with the two keels rough upwards. Anthers (ST, × 8) 2–2·5 mm. long. Grain (CE, CH, × 8) enclosed by the hardened lemma and palea. *Ch. no.* 2n = 28.

Sheep's Fescue is widely distributed in the British Isles, being found in every county, usually on rather poor, well-drained shallow soils, both acidic and basic, in open situations on heaths, moors, and especially in hill and mountain grassland where it is often very abundant and frequently the dominant grass; from near sea-level to over 1220 m. Widespread in the northern temperate zone. Flowering: May to July.

It is very hardy, drought-resistant, and withstands close cutting and heavy grazing. Although its yield of foliage is low, being nutritious it provides valuable food for sheep on the upland grasslands where the more luscious herbage plants do not flourish. It is also useful as a lawn grass, but seed may be difficult to obtain.

The lemmas are clothed with very short hairs in var. *hispidula* (Hack.) Hack. *F. vivipara* (L.) Sm. (*F. ovina* var. *vivipara* L.) Viviparous Fescue, of Wales, the Lake District, Ireland, Scotland, and N. Europe, is very similar in habit to *F. ovina* and *F. tenuifolia*, but the spikelets are sometimes partly proliferous and partly sexual. *Ch. no.* 2n = 21, 28, 42, 49. (A. J. Wilmot in M. S. Campbell, *Flora of Uig* recognizes seven sub-species.)

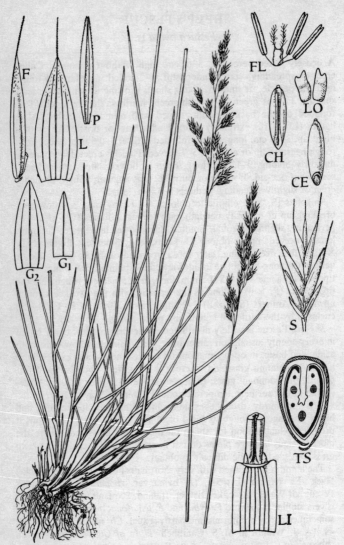

Festuca longifolia. Uncommon; dry grassland.

130

HARD FESCUE
Festuca longifolia Thuill.

A densely tufted perennial, 15–70 cm. high, without rhizomes. Culms erect, or slightly bent at the base, slender, stiff, 1–2-noded, rough near the panicle or smooth; young shoots growing up within the leaf-sheaths. Leaves greyish-green or slightly bluish-green, hairless or nearly so; sheaths open to the base (TS), smooth; ligules (LI, × 6) extremely short; blades sharply pointed, the basal 5–30 cm. long, straight or curved, tightly infolded, 0·5–1 mm. wide in side view, bluntly keeled, stiff, mostly 7-nerved (TS), very rough to almost smooth. Panicles erect, linear to lanceolate or narrowly oblong, one-sided, loose or becoming contracted, 2–12 cm. long, purplish, reddish or greenish; axis and branches angular, rough, the latter erect or slightly spreading; pedicels 1–4 mm. long.

Spikelets (S, × 3) oblong or elliptic, 6–10 mm. long, loosely 4–9-flowered, breaking up at maturity beneath each lemma. Glumes (G_1, G_2, × 6) persistent, slightly unequal, finely pointed, firm; lower lanceolate, 2·5–3·5 mm. long, 1-nerved; upper oblong-lanceolate, 3·5–5 mm. long, 3-nerved. Lemmas (F, L, × 6) at first overlapping, later with the margins inrolled, rounded on the back, narrowly oblong-lanceolate in side view, 4–5·5 mm. long, narrowed at the tip into a fine rough awn up to 4 mm. long, firm, finely 5-nerved, minutely rough on the upper part. Paleas (P, × 6) about as long as the lemmas, with the two keels rough above. Anthers (FL, × 6) 2–3 mm. long. Grain (CE, CH, × 6) tightly enclosed between the hardened lemma and palea. *Ch. no.* 2n = 42.

A drought-resistant Fescue, probably introduced into Britain during the 19th century by seed imported from Germany; sown on road verges, railway banks, in parks and sports-grounds, and as a lawn grass. Now naturalized on well-drained stony and sandy soils, especially in S. and Central England, but generally uncommon to rare. Widespread in Europe; introduced into N. America. The name *F. duriuscula* L. has been applied erroneously to this grass. In var. *villosa* (Schrad.) the spikelets are densely hairy. Flowering: May and June.

Blue or Grey Fescue, *F. glauca* Lam. of the Channel Isles, Central and S.W. Europe, is very similar to *F. longifolia*. It is cultivated in gardens as a border, edging, or rock plant, on account of its dense bluish-white tufts of smooth cylindrical leaves. *F. glauca* var. *caesia* (Sm.), of some East Anglian heaths, is a rare variety, with leaves of equal length but less bluish-grey and slightly more slender than typical *F. glauca*. In both *F. longifolia* and *F. glauca* the leaf-blades are slightly thicker than those of *F. ovina* and the awns are longer.

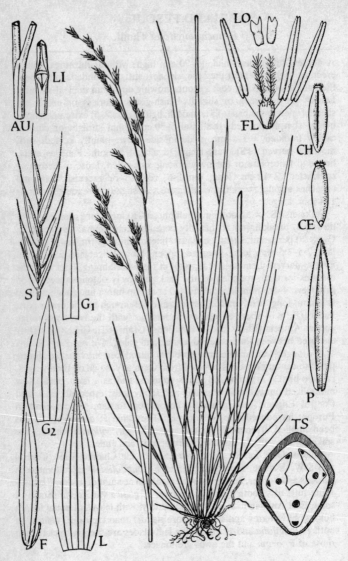

Festuca heterophylla. Rare; woods.

VARIOUS-LEAVED FESCUE
Festuca heterophylla Lam.

A densely tufted perennial, 60–120 cm. high, very leafy at the base, without rhizomes. Culms erect, or slightly bent at the base, moderately slender, 2–3-noded, smooth; young shoots growing up within the old leaf-sheaths. Leaves green; sheaths entire (TS) when young, smooth, rounded on the back, slightly auricled (AU); ligules (LI, × 6) extremely short; blades of two kinds, the basal very fine, thread-like, up to 60 cm. long, infolded, 0·3–0·5 mm. wide, 3-nerved and 3-angled (TS), rough on the margins or smooth, rather weak, the culm-blades conspicuously broader, up to 25 cm. long, flat, 2–4 mm. wide, short-hairy on the nerves above. Panicles loose, open or contracted, nodding, 6–18 cm. long, one-sided, green; axis and branches angular, rough, the latter paired or solitary; pedicels 2–4 mm. long.

Spikelets (S, × 3) lanceolate to oblong, 7–14 mm. long, loosely 3–9-flowered, breaking up at maturity beneath the lemmas. Glumes (G_1, G_2, × 6) persistent, slightly unequal, finely pointed, rough upwards on the keels; lower narrowly lanceolate, 3–5·5 mm. long, 1-nerved; upper oblong-lanceolate, 4–6·5 mm. long, 3-nerved. Lemmas (F, L, × 6) at first overlapping, finally loose, with the margins incurved, rounded on the back, 5–8 mm. long, lanceolate to narrowly oblong-lanceolate in side view, narrowed into a fine straight rough awn 1·5–6 mm. long, firm except for the narrow membranous margins, finely 5-nerved minutely rough in the upper part. Paleas (P, × 6) as long as the lemmas, minutely rough on the keels upwards. Anthers (FL, × 6) 2·5–4·5 mm. long. Grain (CE, CH, × 6) minutely hairy at the top, enclosed by the hardened lemma and palea. *Ch. no.* 2n = 28, 42.

It is very probable that this grass was introduced into the British Isles as a fodder plant in the early part of the 19th century, and sown in woodlands with other exotic grasses, such as *Poa chaixii*. It is of rare occurrence, but is now thoroughly established and occasionally locally abundant in a few woods and wood margins on dry sandy or gravelly soils, especially in S. England; it is also naturalized as far north as Northumberland and in several places in Scotland. Thinly distributed through Central and S. Europe, and in S.W. Asia. Flowering: June and July.

Distinguished from *F. rubra* by its dense tufts, absence of rhizomes, finer basal leaf-blades, and the hairy top of the ovary (FL), and from *F. ovina* by its longer 3-angled basal leaf-blades, closed leaf-sheaths (TS), wider flat culm-blades, larger spikelets, and longer lemmas.

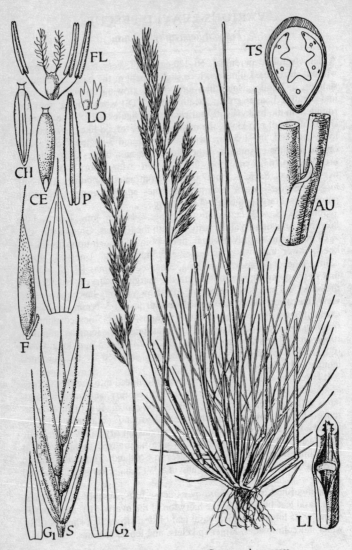

FL LO CH CE P L F G₁ S G₂ TS AU LI

Festuca rubra subsp. *commutata*. Common; lawn grass.

CHEWINGS FESCUE

Festuca rubra L. subsp. *commutata* Gaud.

A densely-tufted perennial, 20–90 cm. high, without rhizomes. Culms erect, or slightly bent at base, slender to relatively stout, 1–3-noded, smooth; young shoots mostly growing up within or sometimes outside the old leaf-sheaths. Leaves green, hairless; sheaths tubular (TS), soon splitting, smooth; ligules (AU, LI, × 8) extremely short; blades slightly pointed, bristle-like, the basal 5–45 cm. long, tightly infolded (TS), to 7-ribbed, 0·6–1 mm. wide, stiff to rigid, bluntly keeled, smooth, or rough near the tip. Panicles erect, linear to lanceolate, contracted after flowering, 3–20 cm. long, purplish, reddish, green.

Spikelets (S, × 6), oblong, 6–12 mm long, 3–9-flowered, glabrous to densely-pubescent in the same clump, breaking up at maturity beneath each lemma. Glumes (G$_1$, G$_2$, × 6) persistent, pointed, firm; lower narrowly lanceolate, 2–4 mm. long, 1-nerved; upper oblong-lanceolate, 3–6 mm. long, 3-nerved. Lemmas (F,L, × 6) at first overlapping, later with the margins incurved, rounded on the back, narrowly lanceolate or oblong-lanceolate in side view, lower 5–6·5 mm. long, the tip narrowed into a fine awn 1–4 mm. long, firm, finely 5-nerved, glabrous or rarely hairy. Paleas (P, × 6) as long as the lemmas, with the two keels rough about the middle. Anthers (FL, × 6) 2–3 mm. long. Grain (CE, CH, × 6) tightly enclosed by the hardened lemma and palea. *Ch. no.* 2n = 42.

The name Chewings Fescue is from a Mr. Chewing who first sold its seed in New Zealand, whence many hundreds of tons were exported annually to the United Kingdom. Subsequently, seed was imported from the United States and the continent. It has been sown for the formation of lawns either alone or in combination with Common Bent and Red Fescue, with which it blends to form a fine turf particularly suited for drier soils due to its drought resistance. Flowering: June.

This grass is now widely distributed in the British Isles occurring naturally, particularly in the south, on well-drained chalky, gravelly, or sandy soils, in open grassland, road verges and waste ground. Found in most parts of Europe. Distinguished from *Festuca rubra* subspecies by the absence of rhizomes and from *Festuca ovina* by its thicker leaf-blades, tubular leaf-sheaths, smooth culms and longer-awned lemmas. A tentative key to the subspecies of *Festuca rubra* is shown on pages 373–4.

(*Festuca nigrescens* Lam.)

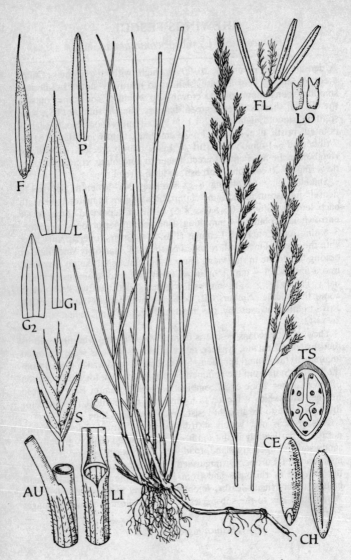

Festuca rubra subsp. *rubra*. Very common; grassland.

STRONG CREEPING RED FESCUE

Festuca rubra L. subsp. *rubra*

Perennial, 22–100 cm. high, with relatively long to very long slender. scaly creeping rhizomes, forming dense or loosely-tufted patches. Culms erect or curved towards the base, slender to relatively stout, 2–3-noded, smooth; young shoots mostly growing up outside the leaf-sheaths. Leaf-sheaths tubular (TS), entire, soon splitting, rounded on the back, basal outer leaf-sheaths densely covered with downward-pointing hairs, lowest sheath purple. Rounded auricles (AU); ligules very short (LI, × 8); blades abruptly pointed or blunt, bristle-like, tightly infolded, green, the basal blade to 50 cm. long, when folded 0·3–0·5 mm. wide. Culm blades 7–11-ribbed and minutely hairy above, densely hairy on the ribs. Panicles 5–19 cm., inclined or erect, contracted, lowest branches paired.

Spikelets (S, × 3) lanceolate to oblong, to 15 mm. long, green, glabrous, 4–10-flowered. Glumes (G_1, G_2, × 6) persistent, pointed, oblong-lanceolate, sparsely hairy or glabrous, minutely rough near the tip; upper glume 3–4·5 mm. long. Lemmas 4·5–5·5 (rarely to 6) mm. long, usually awned. Awns 0·5–3 mm. long. Anthers 2–3 mm. long (FI, × 6). *Ch. no.* 2n = 56.

Strong Creeping Red Fescue is widespread in the British Isles and almost throughout Europe. Native and abundant in short grassland, on dunes, moors and mountain slopes, in mixed woodland, hedgerows and waste land.

There are numerous variants of *Festuca rubra* and a tentative key to certain subspecies, first published in the *Flora of Moray, Nairn and East-Inverness*, is included on pages 373–80 together with brief descriptions of the subspecies *litoralis, pruinosa, arenaria* and *megastachys*.

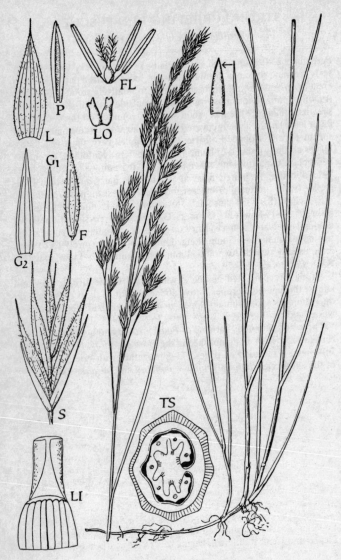

Festuca juncifolia. Rare; sand-dunes.

138

RUSH-LEAVED FESCUE
Festuca juncifolia St.-Amans

A bluish-green perennial, 20–90 cm. high, with slender extensively creeping rhizomes and scattered shoots and culms. Culms erect or spreading, rather stout, about 2-noded towards the base, ribbed near the panicle, smooth. Leaf-sheaths tubular (TS), smooth, hairless, rounded on the back, the basal purplish; ligules (LI, × 6) membranous, of the basal leaves extremely short, of the culm leaves 0·5–4 mm. long; blades very narrow, with a hard sharply pointed tip, up to 30 cm. long, tightly inrolled (TS) and 1–1·5 mm. wide, or opening out and up to 5 mm. wide, tough, smooth beneath, prominently 5–9-ribbed above, with the ribs densely and minutely hairy. Panicles erect or inclined, lanceolate, 8–20 cm. long, loose becoming contracted and rather dense before and after flowering, greyish-green or tinged with purple; branches angular, rough or minutely hairy, in pairs or solitary, the longer bare towards the base; pedicels stout, mostly 2–4 mm. long.

Spikelets (S, × 3) elliptic or oblong, 10–18 mm. long, compressed, 4–12-flowered, breaking up at maturity beneath each lemma. Glumes (G_1, G_2, × 3) persistent, narrowly lanceolate, finely pointed, slightly unequal, firm, rough near the tip; lower 6–8 mm. long, 1–3-nerved; upper 8–10 mm. long, 3-nerved. Lemmas (F, L, × 3) overlapping, rounded on the back, 7–10 mm. long, narrowly lanceolate in side view, very finely pointed, or narrowed into a rough awn up to 3 mm. long, usually softly and densely hairy, firm, finely 5-nerved. Paleas (P, × 3) shorter than the lemmas, with minutely rough keels. Anthers (FL, × 3) 4–5 mm. long. *Ch. no.* 2n = 56 (ex Stace).

A rare coastal grass of S. and E. England and S.E. Scotland; on sand-dunes where it is often associated with Marram Grass, also on sandy shingles and muddy creek-banks; recorded from N. and S. Devon, Dorset, Kent, Suffolk, Norfolk, Lincoln, Durham, Fife, and Angus. Also on coasts of W. Europe from Holland to N. Spain. Sometimes known as *F. dumetorum* L. Flowering: June and July.

It closely resembles some maritime varieties of *Festuca rubra*, especially subsp. *arenaria* (Osbeck) Syme, which also grows on sand-dunes and has a similar loose form of growth. It may be separated from that variety by its longer lemmas and anthers, and by the stiffer thicker leaf-blades which have a continuous layer of fibres (sclerenchyma) just within the lower surface (TS).

Festuca juncifolia var. *glabrata* (Lebel) (*F. arenaria* var. *glabrata* Lebel) is of rare occurrence on some dunes in Northumberland, Norfolk, Devon and Kent; it differs in having hairless or nearly hairless spikelets.

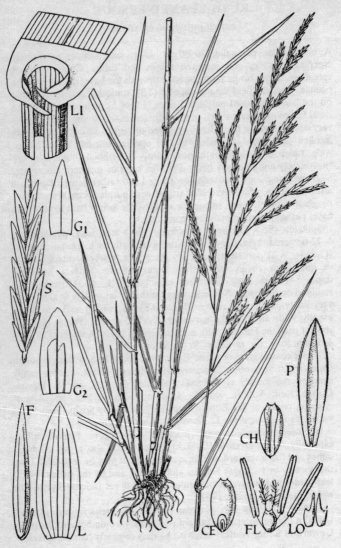

Festuca pratensis. Common; grassland.

MEADOW FESCUE
Festuca pratensis Huds.

A loosely tufted perennial, 30–120 cm. high, forming large tussocks when growing alone. Culms erect or spreading, moderately slender to stout, unbranched, 2–4-noded, smooth. Leaves bright green, hairless; sheaths rounded on the back, smooth, bearing narrow spreading hairless auricles (LI) at the apex; ligules (LI, × 4) about 1 mm. long, membranous; blades tapering to a fine tip, up to 45 cm. long, flat, 3–8 mm. wide, glossy below, rough on the margins and sometimes above. Panicles loose, erect or more often nodding, lanceolate to ovate, more or less one-sided, 10–35 cm. long, green or purplish; axis rough in upper part; branches usually in pairs, unequal, slender, angular, rough, the shorter usually bearing 1 or 2 spikelets, the longer several; pedicels up to 5 mm. long.

Spikelets (S, × 3) cylindrical, becoming lanceolate or narrowly oblong, 10–20 mm. long, 5–14-flowered, breaking up at maturity beneath each lemma. Glumes (G_1, G_2, × 6) persistent, narrowly lanceolate to oblong, slightly unequal, firm except for the membranous tips and margins; lower 2–4 mm. long, 1-nerved; upper 3–5 mm. long, 1–3-nerved. Lemmas (F, L, × 6) overlapping, narrowly oblong or lanceolate-oblong in side view, pointed, usually awnless, 6–7 mm. long, rounded on the back, firm except for the membranous margins and tip, 5-nerved, smooth or minutely rough near the tip. Paleas (P, × 6) as long as the lemmas, with rough keels. Anthers (FL, × 5) 3–4 mm. long. Grain (CE, CH, × 6) tightly enclosed by hardened lemma and palea. *Ch. no.* 2n = 14.

A valuable grazing and hay grass for rich moist soils, widespread in the British Isles, but most common in England, rare in N. Scotland; often abundant in water-meadows, in low-lying grassland, old pastures and on roadsides, especially on loamy or heavy soils. Throughout Europe, also in S.W. Asia; introduced into N. America, etc. Sometimes named *F. elatior* L. Flowering: June to August.

It most closely resembles *F. arundinacea*, which differs in having minute hairs on the auricles at the junction of leaf-sheath and blade, and in bearing 3 or more spikelets on the shorter of each pair of panicle-branches. The hybrid, × *Festulolium loliaceum*, between *Festuca pratensis* and *Lolium perenne*, is described on p. 147. *Festuca pratensis* also hybridizes with *F. arundinacea* and *F. gigantea*, the progeny of both crosses, *F.* × *aschersoniana* Dörfl. and *F.* × *schlickumii* Grantz. respectively, being sterile and intermediate in structure between their parents.

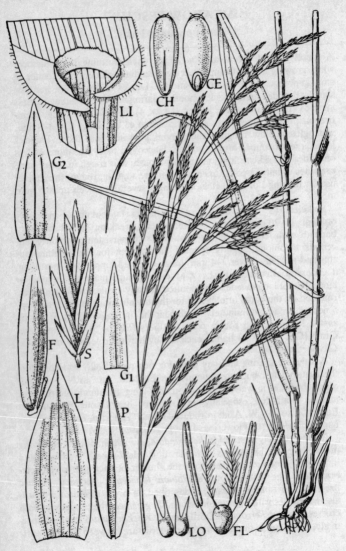

Festuca arundinacea. Common; grassland.

TALL FESCUE
Festuca arundinacea Schreb.

A tufted perennial, 45–200 cm. high, without rhizomes, sometimes forming large dense tussocks. Culms mostly erect, usually stout to robust, unbranched, 2–5-noded, rough towards the panicle or smooth. Leaves green; sheaths rounded on the back, smooth or rough, with small narrow spreading auricles (LI) at the apex, minutely hairy on the auricles and at the junction with the blade; ligules (LI, × 4) up to 2 mm. long, membranous; blades long-tapering to a fine tip, 10–60 cm. long, flat, 3–12 mm. wide, stiff, rough, or smooth only below. Panicles erect or nodding, lanceolate to ovate, loose and open, or contracted, 10–50 cm. long, green or purplish; axis and branches rough, the latter angular, spreading, bare and undivided in the lower part, usually in pairs, with the shorter one bearing 3 or more spikelets; pedicels up to 8 mm. long.

Spikelets (S, × 3) elliptic to oblong, 10–18 mm. long, closely 3–10-flowered, breaking up beneath each lemma at maturity. Glumes (G_1, G_2, × 6) persistent, slightly unequal to equal, pointed; lower narrowly lanceolate, 3–6 mm. long, 1-nerved; upper laceolate to lanceolate-oblong, 4·5–7 mm. long, 3-nerved. Lemmas (F, L, × 6) overlapping, or later with their margins incurved, lanceolate or oblong-lanceolate in side view, pointed to blunt, 6–9 mm. long, broadly rounded on the back, awnless, or with the middle nerve continued as a fine rough awn 1–4 mm. long, firm except for the membranous upper margins, 5-nerved, rough especially on the nerves. Paleas (P, × 6) as long as the lemmas, with rough keels. Anthers (FL, × 6) 3–4 mm. long. Grain (CE, CH, × 6) tightly enclosed by the lemma and palea. *Ch. no.* 2n = 42.

A variable grass, distributed throughout the British Isles. The different native strains occupy distinct habitats, the taller robust kinds growing on heavy soils in low-lying meadows and by the sides of rivers and streams, whilst the shorter types are found in grazed pastures, and on drier calcareous and sandy soils in rough hill and downs grassland. Throughout Europe, N.W. Africa, and temperate Asia; introduced into N. America, etc. Sometimes named *F. elatior* L. Flowering: June to August.

Strains of Tall Fescue have been used to some extent as pasture grasses in parts of the British Isles, but they are mostly coarser and less palatable than Meadow Fescue (*F. pratensis*). This species forms male-sterile hybrids with *Lolium perenne*. Such hybrids resemble *F. arundinacea*, and may be recognized by minute hairs on the auricles, and almost stalkless spikelets (see p. 147).

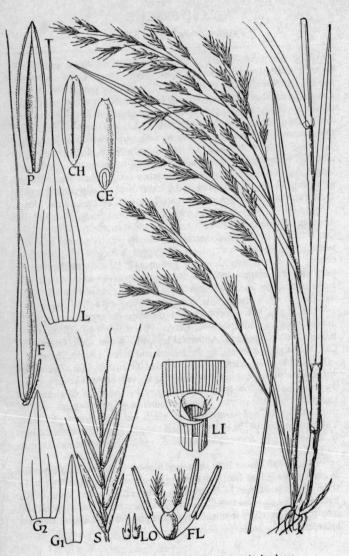

Festuca gigantea. Common; woods and other shady places.

GIANT FESCUE
Festuca gigantea (L.) Vill.

A loosely tufted hairless perennial, 45–150 cm. high, without rhizomes. Culms erect or spreading, usually stout, unbranched, 2–5-noded, with the nodes deep purple, smooth. Leaves bright green, hairless; sheaths rounded on the back, smooth, or the lower rough, with prominent spreading narrow auricles (LI) at the apex; ligules (LI, × 1½) up to 2·5 mm. long, membranous; blades long-tapering to a fine tip, up to 60 cm. long, flat, 6–18 mm. wide, usually drooping, smooth and glossy beneath, rough on the margins and sometimes also above. Panicles nodding, lanceolate to ovate, loose, 10–50 cm. long, green; axis and branches angular, rough, the latter spreading, flexuous, usually in pairs, bare for some distance at the base, unequal, the shorter one with several spikelets; pedicels 1·5–6 mm. long.

Spikelets (S, × 3) lanceolate to narrowly oblong, 8–20 mm. long, loosely 3–10-flowered, readily breaking up at maturity beneath each lemma. Glumes (G_1, G_2, × 6) persistent, slightly unequal, finely pointed, firm except for the broad membranous margins; lower narrowly lanceolate, 4–7 mm. long, 1–3-nerved; upper lanceolate, 5–8 mm. long, 3-nerved. Lemmas (F, L, × 6) at first overlapping, later with the margins incurved, broadly rounded on the back, lanceolate in side view, 6–9 mm. long, narrowed at the tip into a straight or flexuous hair-like rough awn 10–18 mm. long, firm except for the membranous upper margins, minutely rough, 5-nerved. Paleas (P, × 6) as long as the lemmas, with minutely rough keels. Anthers (FL, × 6) 2·5–3 mm. long. Grain (CE, CH, × 6) tightly enclosed by the lemma and palea. *Ch. no.* 2n = 42.

A common grass of damp open woodlands and shady places throughout the British Isles, frequently growing with *Bromus ramosus* and *Brachypodium sylvaticum*. Widely distributed in Europe and temperate Asia; introduced into N. America. Known also as Giant or Tall Brome. Flowering: July, August.

Giant Fescue may be separated from all British species of *Festuca* by its long awns. If forms hybrids with *F. pratensis*, *F. arundinacea*, and *Lolium perenne*. All the hybrids have awned lemmas and are male-sterile, their anthers remaining closed. The crosses with *F. pratensis* and *F. arundinacea*, *F.* × *schlickumii* Grantz. and *F.* × *gigas* Holmb. (mainly from Scottish localities) respectively, are intermediate in the structure of their spikelets and panicles between their parents, the first hybrid having hairless and the second minutely hairy auricles. The cross with *Lolium perenne* bears *Lolium*-like racemes. All the hybrids are rare.

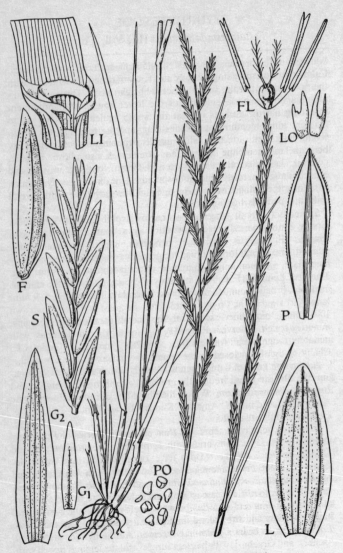

× *Festulolium loliaceum*. Uncommon; grassland.

HYBRID FESCUE

× *Festulolium loliaceum* (Huds.) P. Fourn.

A loosely tufted perennial, 30–120 cm. high. Culms erect, or spreading, slender to moderately stout, 2–4-noded, smooth. Leaves green, hairless; sheaths rounded on the back, smooth; ligules (LI, × 4) up to 1 mm. long, membranous; blades finely pointed, up to 35 cm. long and 7 mm. wide, rough on the margins and towards the tip, or nearly smooth, glossy beneath, with small auricles (LI) at the base. Racemes or spikes erect, slender, 10–30 cm. long, usually unbranched, or if branched then with the branches resembling the spikes or racemes; axis smooth or rough.

Spikelets (S, × 3) on stalks 0·5–15 mm. long, or stalkless, mostly persistent, sterile, narrowly oblong, 10–30 mm. long, 5–15-flowered, erect or slightly spreading, overlapping or their own length or more apart, alternating in two rows on opposite sides of the axis. Glumes (G_1, G_2, × 6) pointed, smooth; lower adjacent to the axis, 1·5–6 mm. long, 0–3-nerved; upper lanceolate or narrowly oblong, 8–12 mm. long, 5-nerved. Lemmas (F, L, × 6) overlapping, rounded on the back, lanceolate-oblong to elliptic, 6–10 mm. long, firm except for the thin tips and margins, 5-nerved, smooth, or minutely rough near the tip. Paleas (P, × 6) about as long as the lemmas, minutely rough on the two keels. Anthers (FL, × 6) 2·5–4 mm. long, with imperfect pollen (PO). *Ch. no.* 2n = 14, 21.

This sterile intergeneric hybrid, the product of the crossing of *Festuca pratensis* and *Lolium perenne*, may be found in old pastures and meadows, water-meadows, and on roadsides through old grassland, usually on rich heavy soils, sometimes with both parents, or with the *Festuca* absent. Recorded from most lowland districts of England from Northumberland southwards; also in S. Wales and Ireland, and in W. Europe from Sweden to France, Italy, and Austria. Flowering: June to August.

Four more sterile anther hybrids between species of *Festuca* and *Lolium* have been collected on a few occasions in Britain and in other parts of W. Europe. They are: *Festuca arundinacea* × *Lolium perenne* [× *Festulolium holmbergii* (Dörfl.) P. Fourn.], which may be distinguished from × *Festulolium loliaceum* by its minutely hairy auricles; *Festuca arundinacea* × *Lolium multiflorum*, which also has hairy auricles, but differs from the last in the lemmas bearing awns up to 5 mm. long; *Festuca pratensis* × *Lolium multiflorum* [× *Festulolium braunii* (K. Richt.) A. Camus], with hairless auricles and short-awned lemmas; *Festuca gigantea* × *Lolium perenne* [× *Festulolium brinkmannii* (A. Br.) Aschers. and Graebn.], with hairless auricles and the lemmas tipped with fine awns up to 20 mm. long (Isle of Wight).

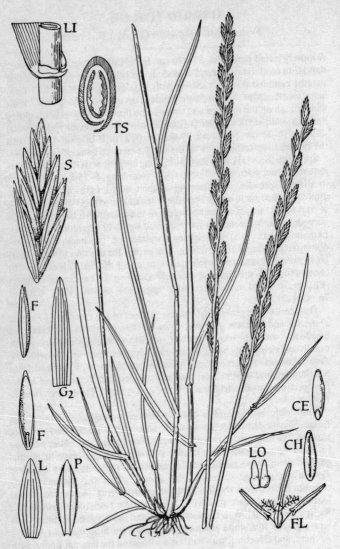

Lolium perenne. Very common; grassland.

PERENNIAL RYE-GRASS
Lolium perenne L.

A loosely to densely tufted perennial, 10–90 cm. high. Culms erect or spreading, slender, 2–4-noded, smooth. Leaves green, hairless; sheaths smooth, the basal usually pinkish when young; ligules (LI, × 2) up to 2 mm. long, membranous; blades pointed or blunt, folded when young (TS), 3–20 cm. long, 2–6 mm. wide, with small narrow projections (auricles) at the base (LI), smooth and glossy below, smooth or slightly rough above. Spikes straight or slightly curved, stiff, slender to somewhat stout, flattened, 4–30 cm. long, green or purplish; axis smooth.

Spikelets (S, × 3) stalkless, alternating on opposite sides of the axis, spaced, or less than their own length apart, their edges fitting into hollows in the axis, oblong to elliptic, 7–20 mm. long, 4–14-flowered, breaking up at maturity beneath the lemmas. Lower glume present only in the terminal spikelet, similar to the upper; upper glume (G_2, × 3) external, persistent, usually shorter than the spikelet, narrowly lanceolate to oblong-lanceolate, blunt, rounded on the back, 5–7-nerved, smooth. Lemmas (F, L, × 3) overlapping, oblong or ovate-oblong, blunt or slightly pointed, 5–7 mm. long, rounded on the back, awnless, firm below, thin at the tips, 5-nerved, smooth. Paleas (P, × 3) as long as the lemmas, the two keels minutely rough. Anthers (FL, × 3) 3–4 mm. long. Grain (CE, CH, × 3) tightly enclosed by the hardened lemma and palea. *Ch. no.* 2n = 14, 28.

A valuable grazing and hay grass, prominent in old pastures and meadows, especially on rich heavy soils of the lowlands, also on roadsides and waste land. Extensively sown in most parts of the British Isles for the formation of new pastures, with other grasses and White and Red Clovers. Widespread in Europe, temperate Asia, and N. Africa; introduced into N. and S. America, Australia, and New Zealand. Known also as Ryegrass, Ray Grass or Eavers. Flowering: May to August.

Perennial Rye-Grass has been cultivated in England for about 300 years. During this time numerous strains have been selected, ranging from short-lived stemmy types to the very persistent leafy varieties derived from old grasslands. The latter strains are most desirable pasture plants, giving heavy yields of highly nutritious and very palatable grazing over a long period.

Lolium perenne hybridizes with other species of *Lolium* and with species of *Festuca* (see p. 147). It is very variable in structure, especially so far as its spikes are concerned, these sometimes being loosely branched, or shortened and much congested.

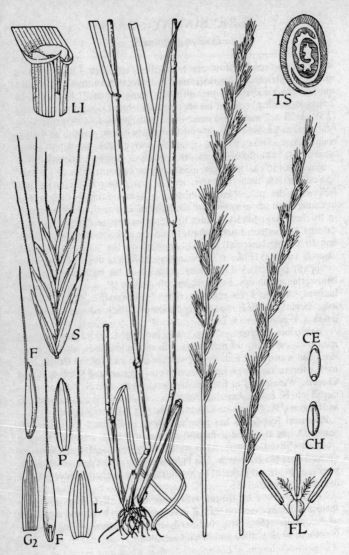

Lolium multiflorum. Common; hayfields.

ITALIAN RYE-GRASS
Lolium multiflorum Lam.

Annual or biennial, 30–100 cm. high. Culms tufted or solitary, erect or spreading, slender to somewhat stout, unbranched, or branched towards the base, 2–5-noded, smooth, or rough towards the spike. Leaves green, hairless; sheaths rounded on the back, smooth or rough; ligules (LI, × 2) about 1–2 mm. long, membranous; blades finely pointed, rolled in the young shoots (TS), 6–25 cm. long, up to 10 mm. wide, glossy and smooth below, smooth or rough above, with narrow spreading auricles at the base (LI). Spikes slender to rather stout, erect or nodding, compressed, 10–30 cm. long, green or purplish; axis mostly rough.

Spikelets (S, × 3) stalkless, alternate and singly in two rows on opposite sides of the axis, with their edges in hollows, oblong, compressed, awned, overlapping or their own length or more apart, 8–25 mm. long, 5–15-flowered, breaking up at maturity beneath each lemma. Lower glume present only in the terminal spikelet, similar to the upper; upper glume (G_2, × 3) persistent, varying in length but much shorter than the spikelet, narrowly oblong or lanceolate-oblong, blunt or pointed, 4–7-nerved, smooth. Lemmas (F, L, × 3) overlapping, oblong or lanceolate-oblong, blunt or minutely 2-toothed, rounded on the back, 5–8 mm. long, firm except for the thin margins and tip, 5-nerved, smooth or minutely rough, with the fine straight awn up to 10 mm. long from near the tip. Paleas (P, × 3) as long as the lemmas, with two minutely rough keels. Anthers (FL, × 3) 3–4·5 mm. long. Grain (CE, CH, × 3) tightly enclosed by the hardened lemma and palea. *Ch. no.* 2n = 14, 28.

A valuable fodder plant introduced into Britain about 1830, now much sown for hay or grazing in most parts of the British Isles; frequent as an escape from cultivation, naturalized on roadsides, field margins, and waste ground. A native of Central and S. Europe, N.W. Africa, and S.W. Asia; introduced into most temperate countries; in the past often named *L. italicum* A. Br. Flowering: June to August.

Lolium multiflorum readily hybridizes with *L. perenne*, the progeny of such crosses, *L.* × *hybridum* Hausskn., being often found where the two species are cultivated. The hybrids have awned or awnless lemmas, leaf-blades rolled in the young shoot, and may be annuals or short-lived perennials. One such hybrid, raised in New Zealand, is grown in the British Isles as Short Rotation Rye-grass. Like Italian Rye-grass, it makes rapid leafy growth, but persists for two to four years. *L. multiflorum* crosses with *Festuca arundinacea* and *F. pratensis* (see p. 147). *Lolium multiflorum* × *Lolium temulentum* has a long glume.

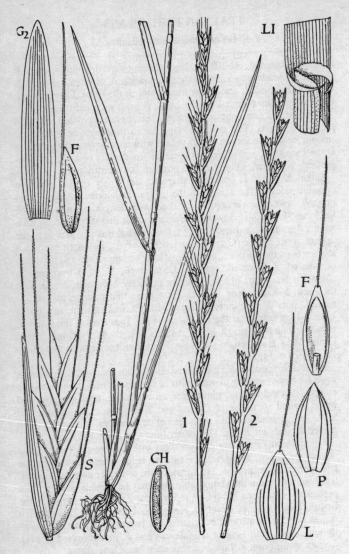

Lolium temulentum. Rare; arable and waste ground.

DARNEL

Lolium temulentum L. (Figure 1)
var. *arvense* Lilj. (Figure 2)

A stiff annual, 30–90 cm. high. Culms tufted or solitary, erect, or slightly spreading, slender to moderately stout, 2–4-noded, rough towards the spike, or smooth. Leaves hairless, green; sheaths rounded on the back, smooth or rough; ligules (LI, × 2) blunt, up to 2 mm. long, membranous; blades with narrow spreading auricles (LI) at the base, narrowed to a fine hard point, 6–40 cm. long, flat, 3–13 mm. wide, firm, rough, or smooth except for the margins. Spikes erect, 10–30 cm. long, 5–12 mm. wide, rigid, green; axis stout, rough or smooth on the back.

Spikelets (S, × 3) about their own length or more apart, with one edge against the axis, oblong, 12–26 mm. long, 4–6 mm. wide, 4–10-flowered, breaking up at maturity beneath each floret (F), the latter plump. Lower glume usually suppressed, except in the terminal spikelet; upper glume (G_2, × 3) usually extending to the tip of or exceeding the uppermost lemma, narrow, blunt, rigid, flat, smooth or rough, 7–9-nerved. Lemmas (F, L, × 3) elliptic to ovate, blunt, 6–8 mm. long, rounded on the back, becoming tumid and hard, smooth, 5–9-nerved, awned from near the apex, the awn straight, rough, up to 2 cm. long. Paleas (P, × 3) as long as the lemmas, 2-keeled. Anthers about 2·5 mm. long. Grain (CH, × 3) tightly enclosed by and more or less adhering to the hardened lemma and palea. *Ch. no.* 2n = 14.

At one time a common weed of arable land, but now usually restricted to waste land and rubbish dumps; of occasional to rare occurrence in the British Isles. Native of the Mediterranean Region, now widespread in temperate countries. Known also as Bearded Rye-grass. Flowering: June to August.

A variable grass, some forms being exceedingly rough and others quite smooth. The lemmas may be awned (1 in Fig.) as described above, or without awns (2 in fig.) as in the var. *arvense* Lilj. (*L. arvense* With.). The grains sometimes contain the mycelium of a fungus. They also have the reputation of being poisonous.

Lolium remotum Schrank of Central Europe, in the past a weed of flax, but now only of rare occurrence on rubbish-tips, is a slender annual resembling *L. temulentum* but with smaller spikelets (8–11 mm.) and smaller awnless lemmas (4–5 mm.). *L. persicum* Boiss. & Hoh., of Persia, has been introduced in wheat from N. America. It is an annual, with spikelets up to 2 cm. long, and narrow long-awned lemmas (9–10 mm. long). *L. rigidum* Gaud., of the Mediterranean Region, is sometimes introduced; it is an annual, with awnless lemmas.

153

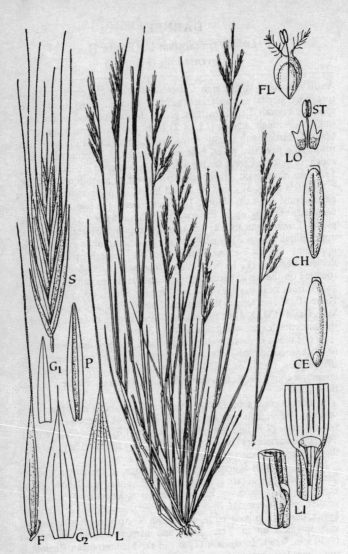

Vulpia bromoides. Common; poor grassland.

SQUIRREL-TAIL FESCUE
Vulpia bromoides (L.) S. F. Gray

Annual, 5–60 cm. high. Culms loosely tufted or solitary, erect, or ascending from a bent or prostrate base, very slender, rather stiff, often branched in the lower part, 2–4-noded, smooth. Leaves green; sheaths smooth, rounded on the back; ligules (LI, × 6) membranous, up to 0·5 mm. long; blades finely pointed, 1–14 cm. long, flat or rolled, 0·5–3 mm. wide, flaccid to rather stiff, rough near the tip and on the margins, minutely hairy above. Panicles long-exserted from the uppermost sheath, erect or slightly nodding, lanceolate to narrowly oblong, rather loose to compact, one-sided, 1–10 cm. long, sometimes reduced to a single spikelet, green or purplish; axis angular, scaberulous; branches erect or slightly spreading; pedicels thickened, 1–4 mm. long.

Spikelets (S, × 5) oblong or wedge-shaped, 7–14 mm. long (excluding the awns), 5–10-flowered, breaking up between the lemmas. Glumes (G_1, G_2, × 6) persistent, finely pointed; lower half to three-fourths the length of the upper, 3–6 mm. long, subulate-lanceolate, 1-nerved; upper lanceolate or oblong-lanceolate, 6–10 mm. long, 3-nerved. Lemmas (F, L, × 6) at first overlapping, rounded on the back, with the margins finally incurved, linear-lanceolate in side view, 5–9 mm. long, narrowed into a fine rough awn up to 13 mm. long, firm, finely 5-nerved, rough. Paleas (P, × 6) about as long as the lemmas, rough on the two keels. Anther (FL, ST, × 10) usually 1, 0·3–0·6 mm. long. Grain (CE, CH, × 6) tightly enclosed by the lemma and palea. *Ch. no.* 2n = 14.

A slender grass of dry places, frequent throughout the British Isles; on heaths, hill grassland, roadsides, often abundant and forming pure masses on open sandy or stony ground and on waste land, occasional in open woodland and as a weed of cultivated land; from sea-level to nearly 610 m. Distributed through much of Europe and the Mediterranean Region; on the high mountains of tropical Africa; introduced to N. and S. America, S. Africa, etc. Known also as Barren Fescue. A rare hybrid with *Festuca rubra* has been found in Sussex and Suffolk. Flowering: May to July.

The closely related *Vulpia myuros* may be distinguished by its longer nodding or curved panicles which are enclosed at the base in or only shortly exserted from the leaf-sheaths, by the more unequal glumes, and the usually 1-nerved upper glume. In these, as well as in other species of *Vulpia*, the flower usually has only a single very small stamen which may remain enclosed between the lemma and palea at the top of the mature grain.

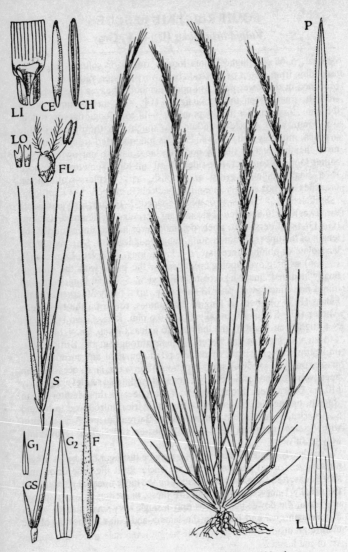

Vulpia myuros. Uncommon; waste and cultivated land.

RAT'S-TAIL FESCUE
Vulpia myuros (L.) C. C. Gmel.

Annual, 10–70 cm. high. Culms tufted or solitary, erect, or ascending from a bent base, slender to very slender, often branched towards the base, 2–3-noded, smooth, usually sheathed up to the base of the panicle or with this shortly exserted. Leaves green; sheaths smooth, rounded on the back; ligules (LI, × 6) up to 1 mm. long, membranous; blades finely pointed, 2–15 cm. long, inrolled or opening out and 0·5–3 mm. wide, flaccid to firm, smooth beneath, rough on the margins, short-hairy above. Panicles linear, contracted, lax to rather dense, usually curved or nodding, sometimes raceme-like in the upper part, 5–30 cm. long, green or purplish; axis angular, rough; branches mostly appressed to the axis; pedicels thickened, 1–3 mm. long.

Spikelets (S, × 3) oblong or wedge-shaped, 7–10 mm. long (excluding the awns), 3–7-flowered, readily breaking up at maturity beneath each lemma. Glumes (GS, G_1, G_2, × 6) persistent, very unequal, shorter than the adjacent lemmas, finely pointed; lower one-sixth to half the length of the upper, linear-lanceolate, 1–3·5 mm. long, 1-nerved; upper subulate-lanceolate, 3–8 mm. long, 1–3-nerved. Lemmas (F, L, × 6) at first overlapping, at length with the margins incurved, rounded on the back, linear-lanceolate in side view, 5–7 mm. long, narrowed into a fine straight rough awn up to 15 mm. long, firm, finely 5-nerved, rough. Paleas (P, × 6) about as long as the lemmas, with two rough keels. Anthers (FL, × 14) 1–2, 0·3–0·6 (rarely more) mm. long. Grain (CE, CH, × 6) tightly enclosed by the hardened lemma and palea, *Ch. no.* 2n = 14, 42.

This slender weedy grass is much less common and far less widely distributed than *V. bromoides*. It is more frequent and probably native in S. England, Wales, and S. Ireland, but comparatively rare and introduced in N. England and Scotland; on waste and cultivated ground, roadsides, dry sandy or gravelly places, and occasionally as a weed in sown hayfields. Also in Central and S. Europe, Mediterranean Region; naturalized in N. and S. America, Australia, S. Africa, etc. A rare hybrid with *Festuca rubra* has been found in Merioneth. Flowering: May to July.

Vulpia megalura (Nutt.) Rydb. (*Festuca megalura* Nutt.), Fox-tail Fescue, of N. and S. America, has been found in S. England as a weed on cultivated land, where it has been introduced, probably with seeds of other plants, or with wool, etc. It is somewhat similar to *V. myuros*, but may be distinguished by the fine hairs on the margins of the upper part of the lemmas.

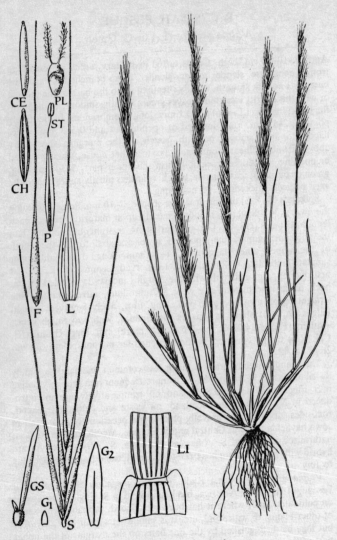

CE

PL

ST

CH

P

L

F

G₂

LI

GS

G₁

S

Vulpia ambigua. Rare; sandy places.

BEARDED FESCUE
Vulpia ambigua (Le Gall) A. G. More

A loosely tufted annual, 5–30 cm. high. Culms erect, or bent at the base and spreading, very slender, sometimes branched in the lower part, 1–2-noded, sheathed up to the panicle, or with this shortly exserted. Leaves green or reddish; sheaths smooth, rounded on the back; ligules (LI, × 7) extremely short, membranous; blades with a fine blunt or pointed tip, 1–10 cm. long, inrolled or opening out and up to 2 mm. wide, rough on the margins, minutely hairy on the upper surface. Panicles erect, very narrow, linear or lanceolate, contracted, green, purplish or reddish, one-sided, 3–13 cm. long, sparingly branched, raceme-like in the upper part or throughout; axis angular; branches short, erect; pedicels swollen, up to 1 mm. long.

Spikelets (S, × 6) overlapping, narrowly oblong or wedge-shaped, 5–7 mm. long (excluding the awns), loosely 3–7-flowered, breaking up at maturity beneath each fertile lemma (lower 1–3 fertile, upper 3–7 male or sterile). Glumes (GS, G_1, G_2, × 10) persistent, very unequal, much shorter than the lowest lemma, membranous; lower ovate or oblong, 0·2–1 mm. long, nerveless; upper linear-lanceolate 1·5–3 mm. long, 1-nerved. Lemmas (F, L, × 6) at first overlapping, later with the margins incurved, 4–5 mm. long, narrowly lanceolate in side view (F), firm, finely 3–5-nerved, rough, narrowed upwards into a fine straight rough awn up to 10 mm. long. Paleas (P, × 6) nearly as long as the lemmas, 2-keeled, with the keels rough. Anther (ST, × 10) 1, 0·3–0·4 mm. long. Grain (CE, CH, × 6) tightly enclosed by the hardened lemma and palea. *Ch. no.* 2n = 28.

A slender stiff grass of S.W. Europe, found on coastal sands and sandy heaths in Devon, Somerset, Dorset, Hampshire, Sussex, Kent, Suffolk, and the Channel Isles, and on sandy heaths and warrens in W. and E. Norfolk and W. Suffolk; generally rather rare, but occasionally locally very abundant in disturbed soil on roadsides, tracks, and burrows in some parts of Breckland. Known also as Purple Fescue. Flowering: May and June.

Vulpia myuros is similar to *V. ambigua* but has mostly taller culms, usually longer nodding panicles, larger spikelets and lemmas, and less unequal glumes. *V. bromoides* may be distinguished from *V. ambigua* by its looser panicles, larger spikelets, longer lemmas, and slightly unequal glumes.

Vulpia ciliata Dum. (*Festuca ciliata* Danth., *F. danthonii* A. G.) of the Mediterranean Region, occurs occasionally on rubbish tips and on waste ground at ports. It differs from *V. ambigua* in having loosely hairy, slightly longer lemmas.

(*Vulpia ciliata* subsp. *ambigua* (Le Gall) Stace & Auquier)

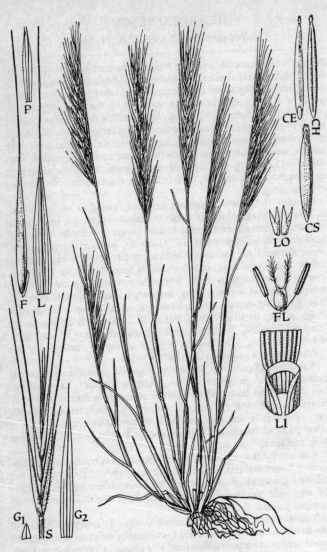

Vulpia membranacea. Local; coastal dunes.

160

DUNE FESCUE
Vulpia membranacea (L.) Dum.

Annual, 10–60 cm. high. Culms loosely tufted or solitary, erect or spreading, slender, usually unbranched, 2–3-noded, smooth. Leaves green; sheaths mostly overlapping, smooth, rounded on the back; ligules (LI, × 6) extremely short, membranous; blades with blunt tips, 1–10 cm. long, inrolled or opening out and up to 3 mm. wide, stiff to rather weak, smooth beneath, minutely hairy above on the prominent ribs. Panicles erect, stiff, narrowly oblong, dense, 2–12 cm. long, one-sided, green or purplish, branched in the lower part or raceme-like throughout; axis rough; branches and pedicels erect, the latter thickened upwards, 3–7 mm. long, rough.

Spikelets (S, × 2) closely overlapping, narrowly oblong or wedge-shaped, 12–16 mm. long (excluding the awns), loosely 2–3-flowered and with 3–4 sterile lemmas at the apex, breaking up at maturity, or falling with the pedicel attached. Glumes (G_1, G_2, × 3) very unequal; lower 0·2–1·6 mm. long; upper narrowly lanceolate, keeled, 10–14 mm. long, tipped with an awn 4–6 mm. long, rough, firm except for the membranous margins, 3-nerved. Fertile lemmas (F, L, × 3) narrowly lanceolate in side view, keeled, 8–16 mm. long, narrowed into a fine straight rough awn up to 25 mm. long, firm, rough, finely 3–5-nerved. Sterile lemmas much smaller and narrower than the fertile. Paleas (P, × 3) with two rough keels. Anthers (FL, × 10) 1–3, 0·8–1·5 mm. long. Grain (CE, CH, CS, × 4) hairy at the tip, tightly enclosed by the lemma and palea. *Ch. no.* 2n = 14, 42.

A local grass of sand dunes, sparsely distributed along the coast of England and Wales from Cornwall to Kent and northwards to Norfolk and Lancashire; rare in Scotland (Angus); also on the east coast of Eire from the Boyne southwards to Wexford; frequent in the Channel Isles. Widespread in the Mediterranean Region, extending to W. Europe. Introduced into Australia. Flowering: end of May and June.

Vulpia membranacea may be easily separated from the other species of *Vulpia* by its larger spikelets, extremely unequal glumes, larger upper glume, lemmas and awns, and by the presence of several sterile lemmas at the tip of the spikelet.

The genus *Vulpia* is often included in *Festuca*, from which its species differ in all being annuals, with conspicuously unequal glumes and very narrow long-awned lemmas.

A mostly male-sterile hybrid (*ch. no.* 2n = 35, 42), intermediate between *Vulpia membranacea* and *Festuca rubra*, has been found on the sand-dunes of Guernsey, Kent, Sussex, Devon, Cornwall, Somerset, Merioneth, Anglesey, and Lancashire.

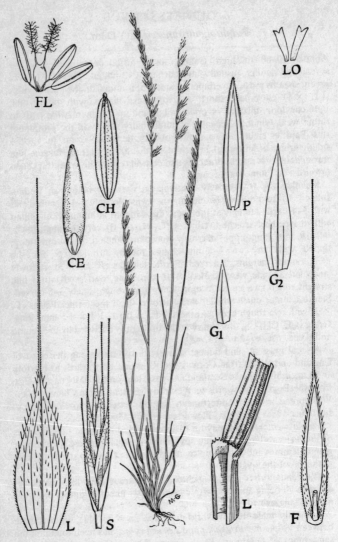

Nardurus maritimus. Uncommon; grassland and waste ground.

162

MATGRASS FESCUE
Nardurus maritimus (L.) Murbeck

Annual, green or suffused with purple, 5–35 cm. high. Culms erect or spreading, solitary or loosely tufted, very slender, sometimes branched in the lower part, few-noded towards the base. Leaf-sheaths very narrow, minutely hairy or hairless; ligules (LI, × 10) blunt, up to 1 mm. long, membranous; blades very narrow, blunt or pointed, 0·5–8 cm. long, flat or rolled, 0·2–0·5 mm. wide, minutely hairy above, hairless or nearly so beneath, flaccid. Inflorescence a solitary erect or slightly nodding spike-like raceme, slender, 1·5–10 cm. long, 2–3 mm. wide, one-sided, green or purplish; axis very slender, minutely rough; pedicels 0·8–1·5 mm. long.

Spikelets (S, × 5) lanceolate-oblong to oblong, compressed, 4–7 mm. long, 2–6-flowered, alternating on one side of the main axis and slightly overlapping, breaking up at maturity beneath the lemmas. Glumes (G₁, G₂, × 10) lanceolate, pointed, unequal, shorter than the lemmas, keeled, firm; lower 1–2 mm. long, 1-nerved; upper 2·5–4 mm. long, 3-nerved. Lemmas (F, L, × 10) lanceolate in side view, pointed, 3–4 mm. long, rounded on the back, 5-nerved, becoming hardened, minutely and stiffly hairy in the upper part or all over, or hairless, tipped with a fine straight rough awn 1–6 mm. long. Paleas (P, × 10) as long as the lemmas, narrowly oblong, minutely rough on the keels. Anthers (FL, × 10) 3, 0·7–1·3 mm. long. Grain (CE, CH, × 10) 2·5–3 mm. long, tightly embraced by the firm lemma and palea. *Ch. no.* 2n = 14.

This very slender little grass was only recorded from a few widely separated localities in S., Central, and E. England between 1903 and 1949, but since then it has been found in many places; it is now known to occur here and there from S. Devon to Kent and northwards to Derbyshire, Rutland, Lincolnshire, and W. Norfolk; in dry places in thin grassland, in disturbed soil or even on bare chalk; mostly on chalk or limestone; also on waste ground, tips, and railway tracks; widespread in the Mediterranean Region. Flowering: May to July.

Nardurus maritimus has the appearance of being a native grass, overlooked on account of its slender culms and leaves, rather than a recent introduction. It is somewhat variable, particularly in the degree of hairiness of the spikelets, ranging from almost hairless to closely and softly hairy (subvar. *villosus* Maire). It resembles species of *Vulpia*, from which it may be separated, by its one-sided spike-like racemes, slightly unequal glumes, smaller lemmas and 3 stamens.

(*Vulpia unilateralis* (L.) Stace)

163

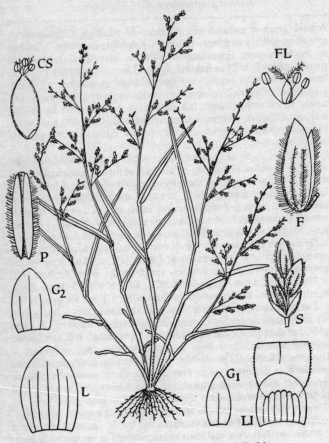

Poa infirma. Rare; Cornwall, Channel and Scilly Isles.

EARLY MEADOW-GRASS
Poa infirma H.B.K.

A loosely tufted yellowish-green annual, 1–25 cm. high. Culms erect, spreading or prostrate, very slender, usually branched near the base, 1–3-noded, smooth. Leaves green, hairless; sheaths keeled, smooth, thin; ligules (LI, × 5) membranous, up to 3 mm. long; blades with an abruptly pointed or blunt tip, 0·5–8 cm. long, folded or opening out, 1–4 mm. wide, thin, minutely rough on the margins. Panicles lanceolate to ovate, 0·5–10 cm. long, loose, pale green; branches in pairs or solitary, spreading, very fine, smooth, bare and undivided in the lower part; pedicels 0·3–3 mm. long.

Spikelets (S, × 6) ovate or oblong, compressed, 2–4 mm. long, 2–4-flowered, readily breaking up at maturity beneath each lemma. Glumes (G_1, G_2, × 10) persistent, keeled, blunt, thinly membranous; lower ovate, 1–1·5 mm. long, 1-nerved; upper elliptic or oblong, 1·3–2·5 mm. long, 1–3-nerved. Lemmas (F, L, × 10) oblong and blunt in side view, 2–2·5 mm. long, keeled, membranous, with very thin tips and margins, 5-nerved, densely hairy with short silky hairs up to or beyond the middle. Paleas (P, × 10) as long as the lemmas, with the two keels densely hairy. Anthers (FL, × 10) 0·2–0·5 mm. long, often found at the tip of the grain (CS). Grain (CS, × 10) tightly embraced by the thin lemma and palea. *Ch. no.* 2n = 14.

This dwarf annual *Poa* was first collected in the British Isles in W. Cornwall in 1876 by W. Curnow, a well-known Cornish botanist. It was not observed again until 1950, when it was found at the Lizard and in the Scilly Isles. In these islands it is said to be widely distributed, often abundant on waste ground, roadsides, tracks, and cliff paths. Also in the Channel Isles, where it is common in sandy places, by paths, and in short grass-turf. Widespread in the Mediterranean Region, from the Canary Islands eastwards through S. Europe and N. Africa to N.W. India; introduced into S. America. Flowering: March to May.

Very similar to *Poa annua* L., but distinguished by the smaller glumes, lemmas, and anthers. A hybrid with *P. annua*, having 2n = 21 chromosomes, has been found in Guernsey.

In the genus *Poa* the spikelets, borne in panicles, are 2–10-flowered, compressed, with keeled glumes and lemmas, the latter exceeding the glumes, awnless, 5-nerved, thin-tipped and margined, often hairy on the nerves and with fine curled hairs at the base; the leaf-blades are folded about the middle nerve when young and have a hooded tip, whilst the sheaths are keeled.

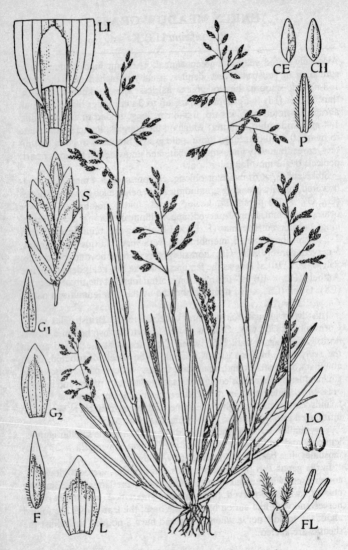

Poa annua. Very common; arable and waste land.

ANNUAL MEADOW-GRASS
Poa annua L.

A loosely to compactly tufted annual or short-lived perennial, 3–30 cm. high. Culms erect, spreading, or prostrate, sometimes with a creeping base and rooting at the nodes, very slender, weak, unbranched, or branched towards the base, 2–4-noded, smooth. Leaves green, hairless; sheaths compressed, keeled, smooth; ligules (LI, × 5) thinly membranous, 2–5 mm. long; blades with abruptly pointed or blunt hooded tips, 1–14 cm. long, folded or opening out and 1–5 mm. wide, weak, often crinkled when young, minutely rough only on the margins. Panicles ovate or triangular, open and loose, or somewhat dense, 1–12 cm. long, pale to bright green, reddish or purplish; branches mostly paired or solitary, spreading, smooth, bare and undivided in the lower part; pedicels 0·3–4 mm. long.

Spikelets (S, × 6) ovate or oblong, 3–10 mm. long, 3–10-flowered, readily breaking up beneath each lemma at maturity. Glumes (G_1, G_2, × 6) persistent, pointed, keeled; lower lanceolate to ovate, 1·5–3 mm. long, 1-nerved; upper elliptic or oblong, 2–4 mm. long, 3-nerved. Lemmas (F, L, × 6) overlapping, semi-elliptic or oblong and rather blunt in side view, 2·5–4 mm. long, keeled, 5-nerved, membranous and with broad delicate tips and margins, sparsely to densely hairy on the nerves below the middle, or hairless. Paleas (P, × 6) slightly shorter than the lemmas, with hairy or rarely hairless keels. Anthers (FL, × 10) 0·7–1·3 mm. long. Grain (CE, CH, × 3) enclosed by the lemma and palea. *Ch. no.* 2n = 28.

A rather variable grass, distributed throughout the British Isles in a great variety of situations, but most common on cultivated and waste land; frequent in short thin grassland, on paths and roadsides; in damp as well as dry places; in the open and in partial shade; on a wide range of soil types, from sands to clays; from near sea-level to high elevations on mountains. Widespread in temperate regions; occurring on mountains in the tropics. Known also as Annual Poa or Annual Blue-grass. Flowering throughout the year.

Although not an ideal lawn grass, it is often abundant in shaded and in closely mown turf, where it provides a fine green sward except under dry conditions. This is due to its seeding throughout the year and to the continuous replacement of dying plants by new ones from seed. The short-lived perennial races, var. *reptans* Hausskn. and var. *aquatica* Aschers., are found usually in loose sandy soils, or under moist conditions respectively.

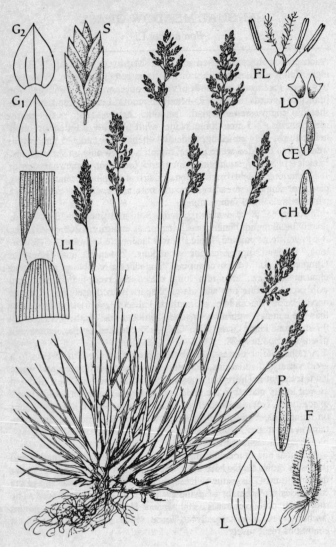

Poa bulbosa. Rare; coastal sands.

BULBOUS MEADOW-GRASS
Poa bulbosa L.

A tufted bulbous-based perennial, 5–40 cm. high. Culms erect or spreading, very slender, unbranched, 2–4-noded, smooth. Leaves hairless; sheaths smooth, purplish or the upper green, the inner basal ones enlarged and fleshy, forming a bulbous pear-shaped thickening at the base of the vegetative shoot, the outer basal sheaths membranous; ligules (LI, × 6) up to 4 mm. long, whitish-membranous; blades very narrow, abruptly pointed, the basal 1–10 cm. long, folded, or opening out and 1–2 mm. wide, firm to soft, green or greyish-green, minutely rough on the margins, otherwise smooth, soon drying and breaking up. Panicles erect, ovate or oblong, contracted and moderately dense, 2–6 cm. long, 1–2·5 cm. wide; branches ascending, hair-like, minutely rough; pedicels 0·3–3 mm. long.

Spikelets (S, × 6) ovate to broadly oblong, compressed, 3–5 mm. long, 3–6-flowered, variegated with green, purple, gold, and white, breaking up at maturity beneath each lemma. Glumes (G_1, G_2 × 6) persistent, keeled, finely pointed, equal, 2–3 mm. long, rough on the keels, with broad membranous margins; lower ovate, 1–3-nerved; upper broader, 3-nerved. Lemmas (F, L, × 6) closely overlapping, lanceolate to lanceolate-oblong in side view, pointed, 2·5–3·5 mm. long, keeled, membranous, finely 5-nerved, with a dense fringe of short white hairs on the keel and marginal nerves, and with fine crinkled long hairs at the base. Paleas (P, × 6) nearly as long as the lemmas, minutely hairy on the keels. Anthers (FL, × 6) 1–1·5 mm. long. Grain (CE, CH, × 6) tightly enclosed between the lemma and palea. *Ch. no.* 2n = 28, 35, 45.

A dwarf grass of open sandy and grassy places on the coast of S. and E. England from Cornwall to W. Norfolk and Lincolnshire, and in S. Scotland, of local occurrence and generally rare; introduced in a few places inland. Widespread in the Mediterranean Region, extending up the coast of W. Europe; introduced into N. America, Australia, etc. Flowering: March to May.

The leaves and culms soon wither, leaving the bulbous bases. These contain food reserves and may become detached and blown about by the wind, each forming the basis of a new plant. A proliferous variant (var. *vivipara* Koel.), in which the upper part of the spikelet is replaced by a miniature plant, is occasionally cultivated in gardens and appears to be wild in Glamorgan. The bulbils have been occasionally introduced with the seeds of Lucerne from France.

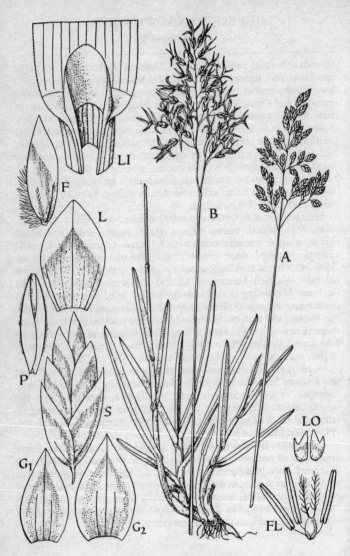

Poa alpina. Rare; mountains.

ALPINE MEADOW-GRASS
Poa alpina L. (Figure A)

A tufted perennial, 5–40 cm. high, thickened at the base with old leaf-sheaths, without rhizomes. Culms erect, or spreading from a bent base, slender, unbranched, 1–2-noded below the middle or towards the base, smooth. Leaves mostly basal, hairless, green; sheaths smooth, rounded on the back, the lower with membranous margins; ligules (LI, × 6) blunt or pointed, up to 6 mm. long, membranous; blades blunt or abruptly pointed, 2–12 cm. long, folded about the middle nerve, or flat and 2–5 mm. wide, minutely rough on the margins, or nearly smooth. Panicles ovate, erect or nodding, open, moderately loose to dense, 3–7 cm. long, up to 7 cm. wide, purplish or green; axis smooth; branches mostly in pairs, spreading, minutely rough; pedicels 0·5–2 mm. long.

Spikelets (S, × 6) crowded towards the ends of the branches, ovate to oblong, compressed, 4–7 mm. long, 2–5-flowered, breaking up at maturity beneath each lemma. Glumes (G_1, G_2, × 6) persistent, equal or slightly unequal, keeled, ovate to elliptic, pointed, rough on the keels towards the tips, with broad whitish-membranous margins; lower 2·5–4 mm. long, 1–3-nerved; upper 3–4·5 mm. long, 3-nerved. Lemmas (F, L, × 6) closely overlapping, oblong or narrowly elliptic-oblong in side view, pointed, 3·5–5 mm. long, keeled, finely 5-nerved, with a dense fringe of fine white hairs along the keel and marginal nerves below the middle, and with shorter hairs on the inner nerves, with a broad membranous apex. Paleas (P, × 6) as long as the lemmas, with minutely hairy keels. Anthers (FL, × 6) 1·5–2·5 mm. long, *Ch. no.* 2n = 14, 21, 35, 42, etc.

A rare grass of rocky and stony places on the upper slopes of the mountains of N. Wales (Merioneth and Caernarvon), N.W. Yorkshire, Lake District, Scottish Highlands, and Eire (Kerry and Sligo); from 300 to 1220 m. Also throughout the Arctic and at high elevations in temperate Europe, Asia, and N. America. Called Alpine Poa and in N. America Alpine Blue-grass. Flowering: July and August.

The spikelets are usually proliferous (B in fig.) in the British Isles, the upper part of each spikelet being replaced by a miniature plant (var. *vivipara* L.). As these plantlets develop, the panicles become heavier and bend until they touch the ground, where, if in contact with soil, each plantlet roots and may eventually become a separate plant. A hybrid, *P. × jemtlandica* (Almq.) K. Richt., between *P. alpina* and *P. flexuosa* is found on a few Scottish mountains (see p. 173).

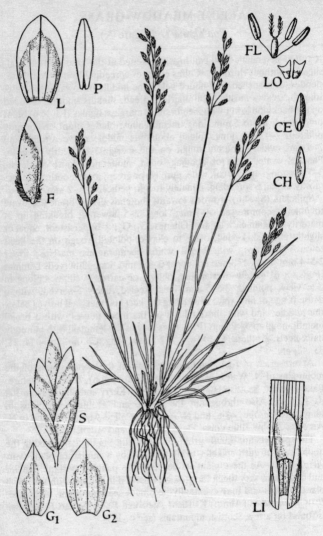

Poa flexuosa. Very rare; Scottish mountains.

WAVY MEADOW-GRASS

Poa flexuosa Sm.

A tufted perennial, 6–25 cm. high, without rhizomes. Culms erect or slightly spreading, very slender, unbranched, 1–2-noded towards the base, smooth. Leaves green, hairless; sheaths smooth, narrow; ligules (LI, × 6) whitish-membranous, up to 4 mm. long; blades narrow, with a slender slightly hooded pointed tip, 2–6 cm. long, folded or opening out and 1–2 mm. wide, minutely rough on the margins and above towards the tip, smooth below. Panicles erect, loose, lanceolate to narrowly ovate, 1–5 cm. long, 1–2 cm. wide; axis smooth; branches usually in pairs, very fine, smooth, bearing few spikelets, flexuous; pedicels 1–5 mm. long.

Spikelets (S, × 6) ovate to elliptic, compressed, 4–5·5 mm. long, 2–4-flowered, variegated with purple, green, gold and white, breaking up beneath each lemma at maturity. Glumes (G_1, G_2, × 6) persistent, slightly unequal to almost equal, keeled, minutely rough on the keels towards the tips, pointed, with broad membranous margins; lower ovate, 2·5–3·5 mm. long, 1–3-nerved; upper oblong-elliptic, 3–4 mm. long, 3-nerved, Lemmas (F, L, × 6) closely overlapping, oblong and abruptly pointed or blunt in side view, 3–4 mm. long, keeled, with a fringe of short hairs along the keel and marginal nerves in the lower third, and with a few crinkled hairs at the base, rough on the keel, finely 5-nerved, membranous in the upper part. Paleas (P, × 6) about three-fourths the length of the lemmas, with minutely rough keels. Anthers (Fl, × 6) 0·8–1·2 mm. long. Grain (CE, CH, × 6) enclosed by the lemma and palea. *Ch. no.* 2n = 42.

A very rare grass, found among stones on a few Scottish mountains (Ben Nevis, Cairntoul, Cairngorm, and Lochnagar), from 760 to 1100 m. Also in Norway, Sweden, and Iceland. In the past included with the Central and S. European grasses, *Poa laxa* Haenke and *P. minor* Gaud., or separated as *P. laxa* var. *scotica* Druce. Sometimes called Wavy Poa. Flowering: July and August.

Poa × jemtlandica (Almq.) K. Richt., (*ch. no.* 2n = 37), is a very rare hybrid, the product of the crossing of *P. alpina* and *P. flexuosa*. It grows at high elevations on the stony slopes of Ben Nevis, Cairntoul, Lochnagar, and perhaps on other Scottish mountains, as well as in Scandinavia. It differs from *P. flexuosa* in its spikelets being proliferous, and from *P. alpina* by its more slender rootstock and long-tapering pointed leaf-blades.

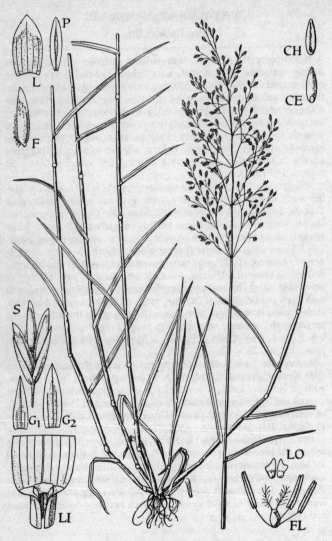

Poa nemoralis. Common; woods.

WOOD MEADOW-GRASS
Poa nemoralis L.

A loosely tufted perennial, 15–90 cm. high, without rhizomes. Culms erect or spreading, slender, 3–5-noded, smooth. Leaves green, hairless; sheaths smooth; ligules (LI, × 6) up to 0·5 mm. long, membranous; blades finely to abruptly pointed, 5–12 cm. (rarely more) long, flat, 1–3 mm. wide, usually weak, minutely rough or nearly smooth. Panicles usually nodding, lanceolate to ovate or oblong, very lax and open, or sometimes contracted, 3–20 cm. long, greenish or purplish; branches clustered, hair-like, flexuous, spreading, bare and undivided in the lower part, minutely rough; pedicels 0·5–6 mm. long.

Spikelets (S, × 6) lanceolate to ovate or oblong, compressed, 3–6 mm. long, 1–5-flowered, breaking up at maturity beneath each lemma. Glumes (G_1, G_2, × 6) persistent, equal or slightly unequal, finely pointed, 3-nerved, membranous, rough on the keels; lower lanceolate, 2–3 mm. long; upper lanceolate to ovate or oblong, 2·5–3·5 mm. long. Lemmas (F, L, × 6) overlapping, narrowly oblong to lanceolate-oblong in side view, blunt or slightly pointed, mostly 2·6–3·6 mm. long, keeled, finely 5-nerved, with delicate tips and margins, the keel and marginal nerves fringed with fine hairs up to the middle, with or without a few long hairs at the base. Paleas (P, × 6) about as long as the lemmas, with minutely rough keels. Anthers (FL, × 6) 1·3–2 mm. long. Grain (CE, CH, × 6) enclosed in the hardened lemma and palea. *Ch. no.* 2n = 28, 42, 56.

A rather delicate grass of shady places, in most parts of the British Isles, often locally abundant in woods and hedgerows on sandy to heavy soils. Widespread in Europe and temperate Asia; and in N.E. America. Known also as Wood Blue-grass or Wood Poa. Flowering: June and July.

A very variable species of which a large number of varieties have been recognized. In some cases the differences are due to the degree of shade and moisture, plants from deep shade being weakly developed and often with 1–2-flowered spikelets, whilst others from moist slightly shaded places are more robust, with larger 3–5-flowered spikelets. Plants are occasionally found in open dry situations, especially on walls; these have stiff erect culms and panicles. Mountain forms usually have loose panicles with fewer and larger spikelets, and longer glumes and lemmas (3·5–4 mm.).

In the past the seeds of this grass were sown in woods and woodland glades for ornament and cover, and also for forming lawns in shaded places, but it is useless for the latter purpose.

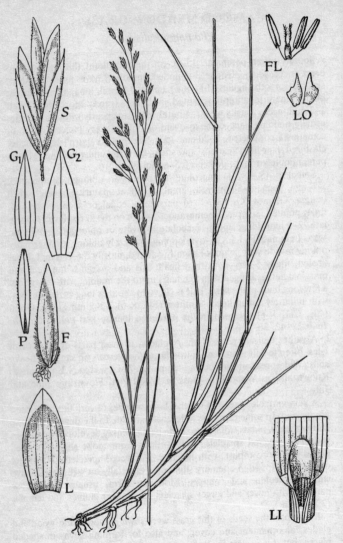

Poa balfouri. Rare; mountains.

BALFOUR'S MEADOW-GRASS
Poa balfouri Parn.

A loosely tufted perennial, 15–40 cm. high, without rhizomes. Culms erect, or ascending from a bent or short prostrate base, slender, unbranched, 2–3-noded in the lowest third, smooth, or minutely rough near the panicle. Leaves hairless, greyish-green; sheaths smooth, the lower slightly keeled; ligules (LI, × 6) membranous, whitish, blunt, the uppermost 1–3 mm. long; blades with an abruptly pointed hooded tip, 3–8 cm. long, folded or opening out and 2–3 mm. wide, rather weak, minutely rough on the margins. Panicles loose, inclined or usually nodding, narrow and more or less contracted, 4–10 cm. long, sparingly branched; branches in clusters of 2–4, slender, erect or slightly spreading, rough, naked towards the base, bearing 1–5 spikelets; pedicels 1–8 mm. long.

Spikelets (S, × 6) narrowly ovate to elliptic or oblong, compressed, 5–7 mm. long, 2–4-flowered, greyish-green, often variegated with purple and yellow, breaking up at maturity beneath each lemma. Glumes (G_1, G_2, × 6) persistent, finely pointed, unequal, keeled, 3-nerved, minutely rough on the keels towards the tip; lower lanceolate, 3–4 mm. long; upper ovate or oblong-ovate, 3·5–5 mm. long. Lemmas (F, L, × 6) overlapping, keeled, oblong and rather blunt in side view, 3·5–4·5 mm. long, finely 5-nerved, firm except for the membranous tip and margins, thinly hairy below the middle on the keel and marginal nerves. Paleas (P, × 6) as long as the lemmas, rough or minutely hairy on the keels. Anthers (FL, × 6) 1·5–2 mm. long, *Ch. no.* 2n = 42.

A rare imperfectly known mountain grass of N. Wales (Caernarvon), W. Yorkshire (Ingleborough), the Lake District, and of scattered localities in Sotland from Dumfries to E. and W. Ross; on rocky slopes and ledges, cliffs, and in wet gullies, from 300 to 910 m. Also in Iceland and Scandinavia. Flowering: July and August.

In its form of growth *P. balfouri* is very similar to the mountain variety of *P. nemoralis* with rather large spikelets, differing mainly in its longer conspicuous ligules. It is also very closely related to *P. glauca*, which, however, has stiffer culms, firmer leaf-blades, stiffly erect and usually open panicles, broader glumes and more hairy lemmas, characteristics which it maintains under cultivation.

(*Poa glauca* Vahl)

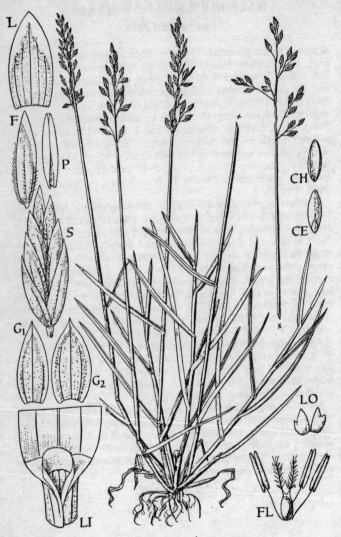

Poa glauca. Very rare; mountains.

178

GLAUCOUS MEADOW-GRASS

Poa glauca Vahl

A tufted bluish-grey perennial, covered with a whitish wax, 10–40 cm. high, without rhizomes. Culms mostly erect, stiff, slender, up to 3-noded below the middle, smooth. Leaves hairless; sheaths mostly overlapping, rounded on the back or slightly keeled, smooth; ligules (LI, × 6) membranous, blunt, the upper 1–2·5 mm. long; blades with an abruptly pointed hooded tip, 2–8 cm. long, folded or opening out and 2–4 mm. wide, stiff, spreading, smooth or nearly so. Panicles stiffly erect, lanceolate to ovate, open or contracted, 2–10 cm. long, up to 4 cm. wide, usually variegated with purple; branches mostly in pairs or threes, angular, stiff, rough, more or less spreading, bare and undivided in the lower part; pedicels 0·5–4 mm. long.

Spikelets (S, × 6) ovate to oblong, compressed, 4–6 mm. long, 3–6-flowered, breaking up at maturity beneath each lemma. Glumes (G_1, G_2, × 6) persistent, equal or nearly so, ovate to elliptic, 3–4·5 mm. long, pointed, keeled, 3-nerved, minutely rough on the keels in the upper part. Lemmas (F, L, × 6) overlapping, oblong and rather blunt in side view, 3–4 mm. long, keeled, densely silkily hairy on the keels and marginal nerves up to the middle, sometimes with shorter hairs on the intermediate nerves, finely 5-nerved, firm and with broad membranous tip and margins. Paleas (P, × 6) about as long as the lemmas, with the keels minutely hairy or rough. Anthers (FL, × 6) 1·5–2 mm. long. Grain (CE, CH, × 6) enclosed by the lemma and palea. *Ch. no.* 2n = 42, 56, etc.

The British records of this attractive mountain grass are not very reliable owing to its being confused with *P. balfouri* and *P. nemoralis*. It is apparently very rare on the higher Scottish mountains of Perth, Angus, and W. Ross, etc., on damp rocky slopes and ledges, from 610 to 910 m. It is also recorded from N. Wales (Snowdon), N.W. England and from other parts of Scotland, but some of these records probably refer to *Poa balfouri* or to the mountain variants of *P. nemoralis*. Widespread in northern cold regions. Flowering: July and August.

This is one of the few Scottish mountain grasses which survive the winters of S. England, where, on account of the bluish-white bloom on the leaves, stems, and panicles, it is occasionally cultivated as a decorative plant. This characteristic waxy covering distinguishes it from *Poa balfouri* and *P. nemoralis*. From these two grasses it may also be separated by its broader glumes, more densely hairy lemmas, stiffer culms and panicles.

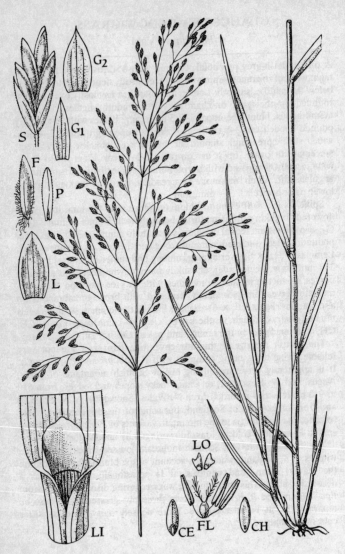

Poa palustris. Rare; wet places.

SWAMP MEADOW-GRASS
Poa palustris L.

A short-lived loosely tufted perennial, 30–150 cm. high, without rhizomes. Culms erect or spreading, sometimes bent and rooting at the base, slender to relatively stout, usually unbranched, 3–4-noded, smooth. Leaves green, hairless; sheaths smooth, the lower slightly keeled; ligules (LI, × 6) oblong, 2–5 mm. long, membranous; blades pointed, up to 20 cm. long, flat, 2–4 mm. wide, usually flaccid, rough. Panicles ovate to oblong, open and loose, erect or mostly nodding, 10–30 cm. long, up to 15 cm. wide, yellowish-green or purplish; branches mostly in distant clusters of 3–6, spreading, fine, flexuous, rough, bare and undivided in the lower part, loosely divided above; pedicels 1–5 mm. long.

Spikelets (S, × 6) ovate to oblong, compressed, 3–5 mm. long, 2–5-flowered, breaking up at maturity beneath each lemma. Glumes (G_1, G_2, × 6) persistent, equal or slightly unequal, finely pointed, keeled, rough on the keels; lower lanceolate, 2–3 mm. long, 1–3-nerved; upper narrowly ovate or elliptic, 2·5–3 mm. long, 3-nerved. Lemmas (F, L, × 6) overlapping, narrowly oblong and rather blunt in side view, 2·5–3 mm. long, keeled, usually with golden or brownish tips, finely 5-nerved, firm except for the membranous tip and margins, the keels and marginal nerves fringed below the middle with short white hairs, also with longer crinkled hairs at the base. Paleas (P, × 6) about as long as the lemmas, with two rough keels. Anthers (FL, × 6) 1·3–1·5 mm. long. Grain (CE, CH, × 6) tightly enclosed by the hardened lemma and palea. *Ch. no.* 2n = 28, 42.

Although this grass is widespread in Europe, temperate Asia, and N. America, its occurrence in the British Isles may be due entirely to its past cultivation here as a fodder grass. It was introduced for this purpose about 1814 and on several occasions since, but apparently it is not so useful here as a grazing or hay plant as in N. America, where it is known as Fowl Blue-grass. In the lowland districts of the British Isles it is now established in a few widely scattered localities on river and pond margins, in fens of East Anglia, and in marshy places; occasionally it occurs also on waste ground and rubbish dumps. Flowering: June and July.

Poa palustris may be distinguished from *P. nemoralis* by its much longer ligules, from *P. trivialis* by its smooth leaf-sheaths, blunt ligules and obscurely nerved bronze-tipped lemmas, and from *P. pratensis* by its longer ligules and the absence of rhizomes.

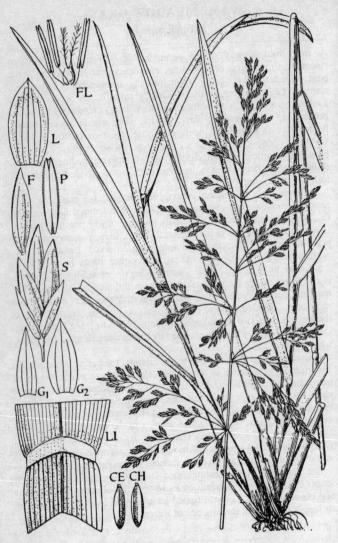

Poa chaixii. Rare; woods.

BROAD-LEAVED MEADOW-GRASS
Poa chaixii Vill.

A compactly tufted perennial, 60–130 cm. high. Culms erect, or bent at the base, moderately stout, 2–3-noded, rough near the panicle, or smooth; vegetative shoots strongly flattened. Leaves bright green; sheaths compressed and sharply keeled, prominently nerved, usually minutely rough on the nerves; ligules (LI, × 4) membranous, up to 1·5 mm. long; blades abruptly sharply pointed, up to 50 cm. long, at first folded and hooded at the tip, afterwards flat and 5–10 mm. wide, firm, rough below on the projecting mid-rib and on the margins or only on the latter, finely nerved and also with numerous cross-nerves. Panicles erect or slightly nodding, open and loose, ovate to ovate-oblong, 10–25 cm. long, 5–12 cm. wide, green; axis minutely rough, or smooth below; branches in clusters of up to 7, very fine, spreading or the lower drooping, flexuous, bare and undivided towards the base, rough, pedicels 0·5–3 mm. long.

Spikelets (S, × 6) ovate to oblong, compressed 4–6·5 mm. long, loosely 2–3–4-flowered, breaking up at maturity beneath each lemma. Glumes (G_1, G_2, × 6) persistent, unequal, pointed, firm, rough upwards on the keels; lower lanceolate, 2–3·5 mm. long, 1–3-nerved; upper ovate-elliptic, 3–4 mm. long, 3-nerved. Lemmas (F, L, × 6) at first overlapping, 3·5–4 mm. long, lanceolate-oblong in side view, abruptly pointed, keeled, minutely rough, hairless, finely 5-nerved, firm. Paleas (P, × 6) as long as the lemmas, with two rough keels. Anthers (FL, × 6) 2–2·8 mm. long. Grain (CE, CH, × 6) tightly enclosed by the hardened lemma and palea. *Ch. no.* 2n = 14.

An ornamental broad-leaved grass, introduced into the United Kingdom over a century ago and sown with other grasses to improve the undergrowth in the open parts of woodlands on many large estates. It became naturalized and has persisted to the present day in widely scattered localities in England and Scotland. It thrives in humus on well-drained moist soils, on the margins of woods, in woodland glades, and wherever the shade is not too dense. Distributed from Scandinavia to France and Italy and eastwards to S.W. Asia; introduced into N. America. Known also as Chaix's Meadow-grass. Flowering: May to July.

Distinguished from the other species of *Poa* by its tufted form of growth, strongly flattened shoots and especially by its broader leaf-blades and minutely rough hairless lemmas. Its unusual leaves, fanlike shoots, and decorative inflorescenes make it an attractive ornamental grass. Hybrid with *Poa nemoralis* is intermediate, with hairless scabrous lemmas, inner nerves less prominent, more pointed leaves, narrower panicle, 2-flowered spikelets and sterile stamens.

183

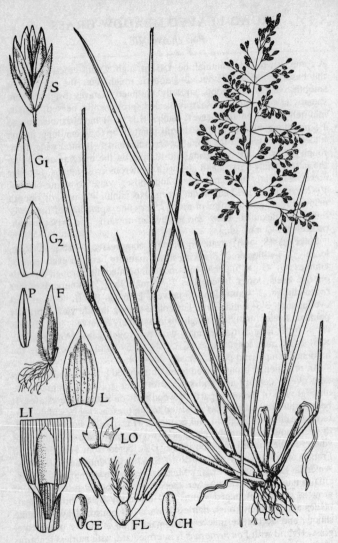

Poa trivialis. Very common; grassland, etc.

ROUGH MEADOW-GRASS
Poa trivialis L.

A loosely tufted perennial, 20–100 cm. high, with creeping leafy stolons. Culms erect, or usually spreading from a decumbent base, slender to somewhat stout, 3–5-noded, smooth. Leaves green or purplish, hairless; sheaths usually rough, rarely smooth, keeled; ligules (LI, × 4) pointed, 4–10 mm. long, membranous; blades abruptly and sharply pointed, 3–20 cm. long folded at first, afterwards flat, 1·5–6 mm. wide, flaccid or firm, minutely rough, or nearly smooth, glossy below. Panicles ovate to oblong, erect or nodding, open and very loose, or contracted and rather dense, 3–20 cm. long, up to 15 cm. wide, purplish, reddish, or green; branches mostly in clusters of 3–7, fine, spreading, bare and undivided in the lower part, rough; pedicels 0·3–2 mm. long.

Spikelets (S, × 6) ovate to elliptic or oblong, compressed, mostly 3–4 mm. long, 2–4-flowered, breaking up at maturity beneath each lemma. Glumes (G$_1$, G$_2$, × 6) persistent, finely pointed, slightly unequal, with minutely rough keels; lower lanceolate, 2–3 mm. long, 1-nerved; upper ovate, 2·5–3·5 mm. long, 3-nerved. Lemmas (F, L, × 6) overlapping at first, later with incurved margins, narrowly oblong and pointed in side view, 2·5–3·5 mm. long, keeled, with short hairs on the keel up to about the middle and long crinkled hairs at the base, the rest usually hairless, distinctly 5-nerved, with membranous tips and margins. Paleas (P, × 6) nearly as long as the lemmas, with two minutely rough keels. Anthers (FL, × 6) 1·5–2 mm. long. Grain (CE, CH, × 6) tightly enclosed by the hardened lemma and palea. *Ch. no.* 2n = 14.

Rough Meadow-grass is very common in meadows and pastures of the lowlands, especially on rich moist soils, but it is also frequent on waste and cultivated land, on pond and stream margins, and it occurs sometimes in partial shade. Widely distributed in the British Isles, being recorded from every county; also throughout Europe, temperate Asia, N. Africa, introduced to N. and S. America, Australia, etc. Known also as Rough-stalked Meadow-grass and in N. America as Rough Blue-grass. Flowering: June and July.

From other species of *Poa* it may be readily recognized by its usually rough sheaths and the longer, pointed ligules. Its seeds are included in mixtures for permanent pastures, especially those on wet heavy soils, where it makes low vigorous growth, which remains green in winter, is very palatable to stock, and useful for hay. Its seeds are sometimes included in mixtures for coarse lawns on heavy soils.

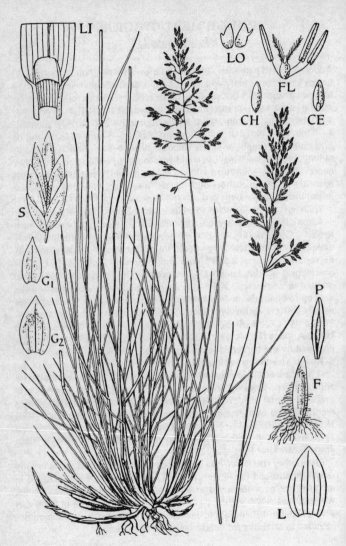

Poa angustifolia. Frequent; dry grassland.

NARROW-LEAVED MEADOW-GRASS
Poa angustifolia L.

Perennial, forming small compact tufts, 20–60 cm. high, spreading by slender wiry rhizomes. Culms erect, slender, stiff, about 2-noded below the middle, smooth. Leaves green; sheaths smooth or the lower minutely rough, the basal keeled; ligules (LI, × 7) membranous, the lower extremely short, the upper up to 1 mm. long; blades abruptly pointed or blunt, the basal bristle-like, 3–30 cm. long, folded about the midrib and bluntly keeled, or opening out and 1–2 mm. wide, those of the culm sometimes wider, smooth, or slightly rough near the tip, hairless or minutely hairy above. Panicles erect or nodding, lanceolate to ovate, loose or contracted, 3–14 cm. long, up to 9 cm. wide, purplish or green; branches hair-like, spreading, mostly in clusters of 3–5, unequal, minutely rough, bare in the lower part; pedicels 0·3–2 mm. long.

Spikelets (S, × 6) ovate to oblong, 2·5–5 mm. long, 2–5-flowered, compressed, breaking up at maturity beneath each lemma. Glumes (G_1, G_2, × 6) persistent, pointed, minutely rough on the keels; lower narrowly ovate, 1·5–2·5 mm. long, 1-nerved; upper ovate or elliptic, 2–3 mm. long, 3-nerved. Lemmas (F, L, × 6) overlapping, narrowly oblong in side view, with a blunt or slightly pointed tip, 2–3 mm. (rarely more) long, keeled, with a fringe of short white hairs on the keel and marginal nerves below the middle, with longer crinkled hairs at the base, with membranous tip and margins, finely 5-nerved. Paleas (P, × 6) as long as the lemmas, with minutely rough keels. Anthers (FL, × 6) 1·5–2 mm. long. Grain (CE, CH, × 6) tightly enclosed by the hardened lemma and palea. *Ch. no.* 2n = 51–66.

This slender-leaved meadow-grass is found in rough hill-grassland, especially on chalky and limestone soils, frequently growing among the tufts of *Bromus erectus* and other grasses, or in poor thin grassland on sandy and gravelly soils. It is of common occurrence in England, especially in the south, and rare in Scotland, but its precise area of distribution is not yet known. Widespread in Europe, also in S.W. Asia. Flowering: April to June.

It is usually regarded as a variety or subspecies of the common Meadow-grass, *Poa pratensis*, from which it may be distinguished by its narrower and mostly stiffer lower leaf-blades and usually smaller spikelets. In habit and in its narrow leaf-blades it strongly resembles *Festuca rubra*, which, however, has awned lemmas.

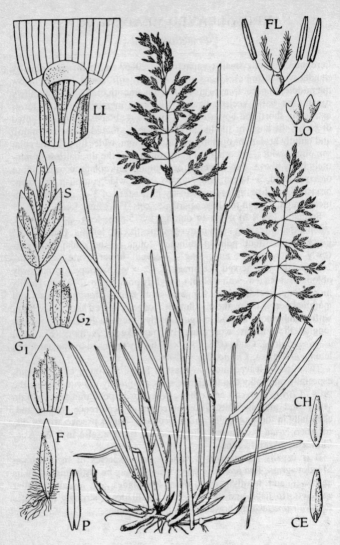

Poa pratensis. Very common; grassland.

SMOOTH MEADOW GRASS
Poa pratensis L.

A very variable perennial, 10–90 cm. high, with creeping slender rhizomes, forming loose to compact tufts or turf. Culms erect, or bent below, slender to relatively stout, cylindrical, 2–4-noded, smooth. Leaves green or greyish-green; sheaths smooth, the lower compressed and keeled, hairless or minutely hairy; ligules (LI, × 6) membranous, the lower very short, the upper 1–3 mm. long; blades with an abruptly pointed or blunt hooded tip, from very short up to 30 cm. long, folded or opening out and 2–4 (rarely to 6) mm. wide, rough or almost smooth. Panicles ovate to pyramidal or oblong, erect or nodding, loose and open to contracted and rather dense, 2–20 cm. long, 1–12 cm. wide, purplish, green, or greyish; branches mostly in clusters of 3–5, spreading, unequal, hair-like, flexuous, minutely rough; pedicels 0·2–2 mm. long.

Spikelets (S, × 6) ovate to oblong, compressed, 4–6 mm. long, 2–5-flowered, breaking up at maturity beneath each lemma. Glumes (G₁, G₂, × 6) persistent, pointed, unequal, rough on the keels; lower ovate, 2–3·5 mm. long, 1–3-nerved; upper ovate to elliptic, 2·5–4 mm. long, 3-nerved. Lemmas (F, L, × 6) overlapping, oblong or ovate-oblong in side view, blunt or slightly pointed, 3–4 mm. long, thinly to densely hairy on the keel and marginal nerves up to about the middle, with long fine crinkled hairs at the base, finely 5-nerved, with thin tips and margins. Paleas (P, × 6) about as long as the lemmas, with two rough keels. Anthers (FL, × 6) 1·5–2 mm. long. Grain (CE, CH, × 6) tightly enclosed by the hardened lemma and palea. *Ch. no.* 2n = 50–124.

Meadow Grass is widespread in the British Isles, occurring in a great variety of habitats from near sea-level to several thousand feet above. It is often common in old meadows and pastures, and especially frequent on roadsides; also on cultivated and waste land, on walls, and in shaded places; mainly on well-drained sandy, gravelly, and loamy soils. Throughout Europe, in temperate Asia; introduced into N. America, etc. Also called Smooth-stalked Meadow-grass, and in N. America, Kentucky Blue-grass. Flowering: May to early July.

In *Poa pratensis* are included numerous races and strains. Some are sexual, others apomictic, that is, they produce viable seed without fertilization. It is an important hay and pasture grass, especially on the Continent and in N. America, but in the British Isles it has been used mainly for sowing on banks, roadsides, or mixed with other grasses in sports-fields.

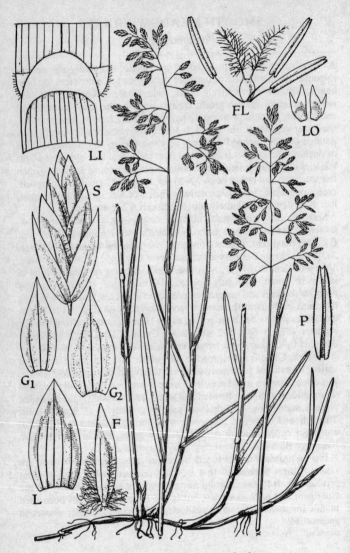

Poa subcaerulea. Rare; damp or sandy places.

SPREADING MEADOW-GRASS
Poa subcaerulea Sm.

Perennial, 10–40 cm. high, with scattered solitary vegetative shoots and culms, or small tufts, arising from slender extensively creeping rihzomes. Culms erect or ascending from a bent base, slender, 1–2-noded, smooth. Leaves green or whitish-green; sheaths smooth, the basal compressed and keeled, often fringed with minute hairs at the junction with the blade; ligules (LI, × 6) up to 2 mm. long, membranous; blades with a blunt or slightly pointed hooded tip, smooth, or slightly rough at the tip, the lower 3–15 cm. long, folded or opening out, 1·5–4 mm. wide, the upper much shorter. Panicles ovate, loose and open, erect or nodding, 2–8 cm. long, 2–6 cm. wide, green, purplish, or whitish; branches mostly in pairs or three, sometimes up to five, spreading, bare near the base, smooth, or rough near the tips; pedicels 0·5–3·5 mm. long.

Spikelets (S, × 6) ovate to elliptic, 4–7 mm. long, 2–4-flowered, compressed, breaking up at maturity beneath each lemma. Glumes (G$_1$, G$_2$, × 6) persistent, tapering to a finely pointed tip, slightly unequal, rough on the keels, usually 3-nerved, with membranous margins; lower narrowly ovate, 3–4·5 mm. long; upper ovate, 3–5 mm. long. Lemmas (F, L, × 6) overlapping, oblong and abruptly pointed in side view, 3–5 mm. long, the keel and marginal nerves fringed up to about the middle with soft short hairs, with longer crinkled hairs at the base, firm except for the membranous margins, finely 5-nerved. Paleas (P, × 6) nearly as long as the lemmas, with rough keels. Anthers (FL, × 6) 1·5–3 mm. long. Grain tightly enclosed by the hardened lemma and palea. *Ch. no.* 2n = 54–147.

This kind of Meadow-grass grows in marshy pastures and meadows, on stream and river-sides, damp coastal sands, and on moist hill and mountain slopes up to 610 m. or more in England and Wales, and the Scottish Highlands. It is most frequent in the northern part of the British Isles, especially Scotland, becoming less common southwards, especially in the south of England. Also in N.W. Europe. Flowering: June and July.

Poa subcaerulea and *P. angustifolia* are generally included in the variable *Poa pratensis*, either as subspecies or varieties, but each is sufficiently distinct to be regarded as a separate species. Whilst *P. angustifolia* and *P. pratensis* develop compact tufts of shoots and culms, *P. subcaerulea* has a more extensive system of rhizomes which give rise to scattered shoots and culms. It also differs from those species in possessing rather sharply pointed glumes.

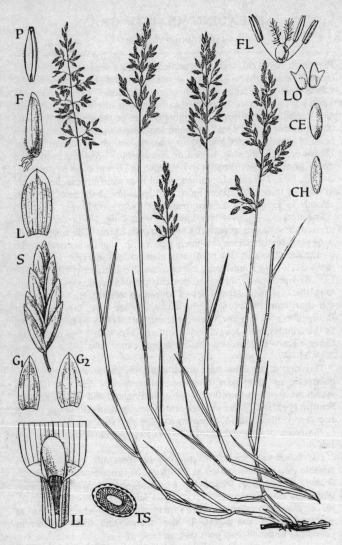

Poa compressa. Frequent; dry soils.

FLATTENED MEADOW-GRASS

Poa compressa L.

A stiff perennial, 10–60 cm. high, spreading by wiry rhizomes. Culms in loose tufts or scattered erect, or bent and ascending, slender, flattened (TS), wiry, 4–6-noded, smooth. Leaves bluish- or greyish-green, hairless; sheaths compressed, keeled, smooth; ligules (LI, × 6) blunt, 0·5–3 mm. long, membranous; blades abruptly pointed or blunt, 2–12 cm. long, folded, or opening out and 1–4 mm. wide, usually stiff, more or less rough, or smooth below. Panicles stiff, narrowly oblong to ovate, contracted and dense, or open and moderately loose, 1·5–10 cm. long, 0·5–3 cm. wide, green, yellowish-green or purplish; branches paired or clustered, angular, slightly rough, with spikelets to the base, or the longer ones bare there; pedicels 0·3–2 mm. long.

Spikelets (S, × 6) densely clustered, ovate, elliptic or oblong, compressed, 3–8 mm. long, 3–10-flowered, breaking up at maturity beneath each lemma. Glumes (G_1, G_2, × 6) persistent, ovate, oblong, or elliptic, pointed, equal or slightly unequal, 2–3 mm. long, firm except for the membranous margins, 3-nerved, rough on the keels. Lemmas (F, L, × 6) at first overlapping, later with inflexed margins, narrowly oblong and blunt in side view, 2·5–3 mm. long, firm except for the membranous tips, obscurely 5-nerved, softly hairy on the keel and marginal nerves below the middle or only near the base, sometimes also with long crinkled hairs at the base, or quite hairless. Paleas (P, × 6) nearly as long as the lemmas, with two rough keels. Anthers (FL, × 6) 1·3–1·5 mm. long. Grain (CE, CH, × 6) tightly enclosed by the hardened lemma and palea. *Ch. no.* 2n = 42, 56, etc.

Widespread in the British Isles except in N. Scotland, Ireland, and Wales; in some districts of frequent occurrence, in others uncommon to rare; in poor thin grassland, on dry banks, and on waste ground, mostly on shallow well-drained soils, commonly found on old walls and ruins. Also throughout the greater part of Europe and in S.W. Asia; introduced into N. America where it is known as Canada Blue-grass. Flowering: June to August.

Resembling *Poa pratensis* in having creeping rhizomes, but easily recognized by its distinctly flattened culms, and the obscure side nerves of the lemmas. In N. America, it has some value as a pasture grass on poor dry soils, but in Britain there are more desirable fodder grasses for such situations.

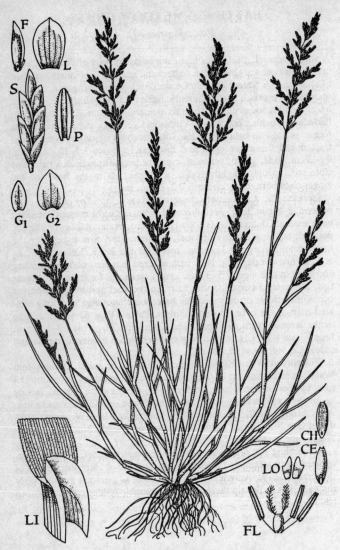

Puccinellia fasciculata. Uncommon; salt-marshes.

BORRER'S SALT-MARSH-GRASS

Puccinellia fasciculata (Torr.) Bicknell

A loosely to densely tufted perennial, 6–60 cm. high. Culms erect or spreading, slender to relatively stout, unbranched, 1–3-noded, smooth. Leaves greyish-green, hairless; sheaths rounded on the back, smooth; ligules (LI, × 5) very blunt, 1–2·5 mm. long, membranous; blades hooded at the blunt or slightly pointed tip, 2–16 cm. long, flat or folded upwards, 1·5–5 mm. wide, firm, rough above, smooth beneath. Panicles erect, 2·5–18 cm. long, lanceolate to narrowly oblong or ovate, contracted and dense or loose and open, unilateral, greyish-green or tinged with purple; branches stiff, rough, crowded with spikelets to the base, or the longer rarely bare there; pedicels extremely short.

Spikelets (S, × 6) densely clustered, oblong, 4–6 mm. long, 3–8-flowered, breaking up at maturity beneath each lemma. Glumes (G_1, G_2, × 6) persistent, rounded on the back, green and firm except for the white membranous margins and tips, unequal, ovate to elliptic, mostly blunt; lower 1–1·5 mm. long, 1-nerved; upper 1·5–1·8 mm. long, 3-nerved. Lemmas (F, L, × 6) exceeding the glumes, overlapping, elliptic, blunt, 1·8–2·3 mm. long, green and firm except for the white membranous margins and tips, minutely hairy at the base, 5-nerved, the middle nerve usually minutely projecting at the tip. Paleas (P, × 6) as long as the lemmas, oblong, 2-keeled, the keels minutely hairy. Anthers (FL, × 12) 0·6–1 mm. long. Grains (CE, CH, × 6) about 1·5 mm. long, enclosed between the hardened lemma and palea (F). *Ch. no.* 2n = 28 (Jones and Newton).

A rather uncommon or rare grass of coastal mud flats and salt-marshes in S. England from Norfolk to Cornwall, in Glamorgan, and of Dublin, Waterford, and Wexford in Eire; scattered over bare mud, firm sand, and shingle, and in bare places in and near *Puccinellia maritima* salt-marshes. Also on the coasts of W. Europe from Sweden southwards, the western Mediterranean, S. Africa, and N. America. Flowering: June to September.

The species of *Puccinellia* have been included in the genera *Festuca*, *Glyceria*, and *Poa*. From the first they may be distinguished by the blunt thin-margined broader tips of the lemmas and the minute basal hilum; from the third by the lemmas being rounded (not keeled) on the back; and from *Glyceria*, in which they have been usually classified in British Floras, by the free margins of the leaf-sheaths, the smooth lemmas, and the minute hilum of the grain.

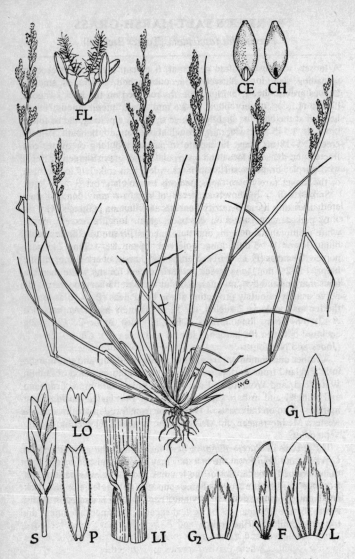

Puccinellia capillaris. Uncommon; coasts of N. and N.E. Scotland.

NORTHERN SALT-MARSH-GRASS

Puccinellia capillaris (Liljebl.) Jansen

A loosely to compactly tufted perennial. Culms prostrate, spreading or erect, 6–40 cm. long, slender, 2–4-noded, smooth. Leaves greyish-green, hairless; sheaths smooth, rounded on the back; ligules (LI, × 3) 0·5–3 mm. long, membranous; blades with an abruptly pointed or blunt tip, 2–12 cm. long, flat or rolled, 1–2 mm. wide opened out, minutely rough above. Panicles linear to lanceolate or ovate, loose below, or contracted and rather dense throughout, 2–12 cm. long, 0·5–4 cm. wide at the base, greenish; branches erect or the lower spreading, 2–3 (−5) together, rough; pedicels short, rough.

Spikelets (S, × 5) narrowly oblong to oblong, 3·5–9 mm. long, 1·5–2 mm. wide, 2–8-flowered, breaking up at maturity beneath each lemma. Glumes (G_1, G_2, × 10) persistent, blunt or pointed, ovate to elliptic or oblong, unequal; lower 1–2 mm. long, 1-nerved; upper 1·6–2·8 mm. long, 3-nerved. Lemmas (F, L, × 10) rounded on the back, oblong in side view, oblong to elliptic opened out, very blunt, 2–3 mm. long, minutely hairy at the base and on the nerves near the base, the nerves not reaching the yellowish, purplish or greenish membranous tips. Paleas (P, × 10) as long as or slightly shorter than the lemmas, narrowly oblong, minutely hairy on the two keels. Anthers (FL, × 10) 0·5–1·2 mm. long. Grain (CE, CH, × 10) 1·2–1·8 mm. long, enclosed by the hardened lemma and palea. *Ch. no.* 2n = 42. (2n = 28, Caithness, det. K. Jones 1968).

A slender mostly prostrate grass, sparingly distributed along the coasts of N. and E. Scotland; recorded from the Shetland and Orkney Islands, Sutherland, Caithness, Banff and Fife; in well-drained places, often on cliffs, in rock-crevices and among stones, and in sandy soils between rocks near the sea. Also from Scandinavia southwards to Holland, where it has been incorrectly named *Puccinellia retroflexa* (Curt.) Holmb., a synonym of *P. distans*; and in N.E. America and Iceland. Flowering: June to August.

In the past this grass was named *Puccinellia distans* var. *prostrata* (Beeby) Druce (*Glyceria distans* var. *prostrata* Beeby). *P. distans* may be distinguished by its mostly longer culms, wider leaf-blades, broader very loose panicles, with branches in clusters, bare for up to half their length and becoming deflexed at maturity; it has also somewhat broader and shorter lemmas.

Hybrids between *P. capillaris* and *P. maritima* have been recorded from Scandinavia and named *P.* × *mixta* Holmb.; they may occur in Scottish localities where the two species grow together.

(*Puccinellia distans* subsp. *borealis* (Holmberg) W. E. Hughes.)

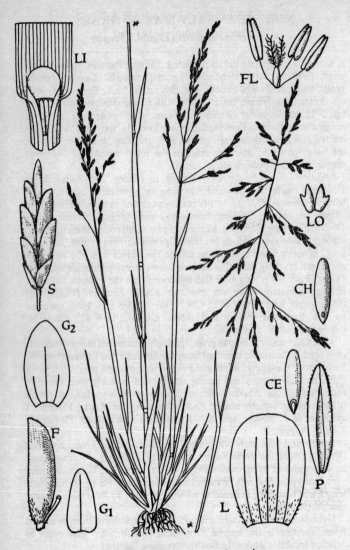

Puccinellia distans. Frequent; salt-marshes.

REFLEXED SALT-MARSH-GRASS
Puccinellia distans (L.) Parl.

A tufted perennial, 10–60 cm. high. Culms erect, spreading, or prostrate, slender, 2–4-noded, smooth. Leaves greyish- or whitish-green,
hairless; sheaths rounded on the back, smooth; ligules (LI, × 6)
1–2 mm. long, membranous; blades with an abruptly pointed or blunt
hooded tip, 2–10 cm. long, flat or rolled, 1·5–4 mm. wide, rough above.
Panicles narrowly to broadly ovate or triangular, usually very loose and
open, symmetrical, 3–18 cm. long, up to 14 cm. wide; branches clustered, bare for up to half their length, finally deflexed, stiff, rough;
pedicels very short.

Spikelets (S, × 6) narrowly oblong, 3–7 mm. long, 3–9-flowered,
breaking up at maturity beneath each lemma, greenish or purplish, variegated with white or yellow. Glumes (G_1, G_2, × 12) persistent, blunt,
ovate to elliptic, unequal; lower 1–1·5 mm. long, 1-nerved; upper
1·5–2 mm. long, 3-nerved. Lemmas (F, L, × 12) overlapping, rounded
on the back, 2–2·5 mm. long, broadly oblong-elliptic, very blunt, minutely hairy at the base, 5-nerved, the nerves not reaching the broad white
or yellowish membranous tips. Paleas (P, × 12) about as long as the
lemmas, the two keels minutely hairy. Anthers (FL, × 12) 0·8–1 mm.
long. Grain (CE, CH, × 12) 1·5 mm. long, enclosed between the
hardened lemma and palea. *Ch. no.* 2n = 28, 42.

Widely distributed around the shores of the British Isles, but rare in
N. Scotland and Ireland; on mud in the higher parts of salt-marshes, or
on sandy or gravelly soils, and among rocks; locally common, especially
in the east and south; also occasionally in river-meadows, on waste land,
rubbish tips, etc., both near the sea and inland. In most parts of Europe,
temperate Asia, N.W. Africa, and N. America. Known also as Reflexed
Poa or Reflexed Meadow-grass. Flowering: June and July.

Some forms of this grass are decidedly perennial, with numerous
vegetative shoots, whilst others have the appearance of short-lived perennials or annuals. Hybrids between *P. distans* and *P. maritima* (*P. ×
hybrida* Holmb.), and between *P. distans* and *P. rupestris* [*P. ×
pannonica* (Hack.) Holmb.] have been recorded.

Puccinellia pseudodistans (Crép.) J. & W., Greater Salt-Marsh-Grass,
a S.W. European grass, intermediate in structure between *P. distans* and
P. fasciculata, has been found in wet muddy places on the higher parts
of salt-marshes in S.E. England. Its panicles are asymmetrical, with the
longer branches bare at the base, and spreading, but not deflexed, and
the middle nerve of the lemma minutely projecting at the tip. *Ch. no.*
2n = 28.

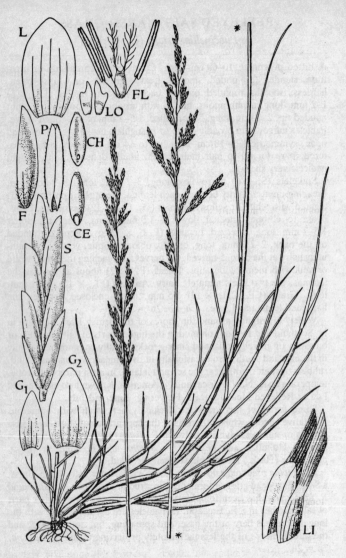

Puccinellia maritima. Very common; salt-marshes.

COMMON SALT-MARSH-GRASS

Puccinellia maritima (Huds.) Parl.

Perennial, 10–80 cm. high, densely tufted or loose and spreading, often with creeping stolons, usually rooting at the nodes and forming a compact turf. Culms erect, spreading or prostrate, slender to moderately stout, 2–4-noded, smooth. Leaves greyish-green or dark green, hairless; sheaths rounded on the back, smooth; ligules (LI, × 6) blunt, 1–3 mm. long, membranous; blades narrow, with a blunt or abruptly pointed slender hooded tip, 2–20 cm. (rarely more) long, folded or inrolled, or opening out and 1–3 mm. wide, smooth beneath, rough on the nerves above. Panicles erect, stiff, linear to ovate, 2–25 cm. long, usually finally contracted, rather dense and 0·4–2·5 cm. wide, or open and up to 8 cm. wide, green or mostly purple; branches usually erect after flowering, sometimes permanently spreading, stiff, rough; pedicels very short.

Spikelets (S, × 6) narrowly oblong, more or less cylindrical, 5–13 mm. long, 3–10-flowered, breaking up at maturity beneath each lemma. Glumes (G_1, G_2, × 6) persistent, lanceolate to ovate, unequal; lower 1·5–3·5 mm. long, 1–3-nerved; upper 2–4 mm. long, 3-nerved. Lemmas (F, L, × 6) much exceeding the glumes, overlapping, rounded on the back, elliptic to broadly oblong, rather blunt or slightly pointed, 3–5 mm. long, firm except for the white membranous tips and margins, silky-hairy towards the base, 5-nerved. Paleas (P, × 6) as long as the lemmas, with the two keels minutely hairy. Anthers (FL, × 6) 2–3 mm. long. Grain (CE, CH, × 6) 1·5–3 mm. long, enclosed between the hardened lemma and palea (F). *Ch. no.* 2n = 49, mostly 56, 63, 70, etc.

A rather variable vigorous coastal grass, distributed round the shores of the British Isles, but most abundant in the east and south; the main constituent of grassy salt-marshes or saltings, covering extensive areas of mud flats, rarely also on sand, shingle, and among rocks; inland in brakish areas in Worcestershire and Staffordshire. Widespread along the shores of W. Europe and in N.E. America. Known also as Sea Poa or Sea Meadow-grass. Flowering: June and July.

Caespitose growth related to daylength of less than 12 hours, stoloniferous growth and long stems related to daylength of about 16 hours (Weike 1979).

This shallow-rooted grass colonizes bare coastal mud, spreading by its long runners to form a continuous turf, broken only by drainage gullies. Its leaves and stems act as a filter, collecting silt and debris as the tides advance and recede, thus raising the level of the marsh. It differs from other British species of the genus in being stoloniferous, and in having longer spikelets, lemmas, and anthers. It is probably apomictic. Hybrids with other species of *Puccinellia* have been recorded (see pp. 199, 203).

Puccinellia rupestris. Uncommon; salt-marshes.

STIFF SALT-MARSH-GRASS
Puccinellia rupestris (With.) Fern. & Weath.

A loosely to densely tufted annual or biennial, 4–40 cm. high. Culms spreading or prostrate, slender to relatively stout, unbranched, 1–3-noded below the middle, smooth. Leaves greyish-green, hairless; sheaths rounded on the back, smooth; ligules (LI, × 6) very blunt to pointed, 1–2·5 mm. long, membranous; blades hooded at the blunt or slightly pointed tip, 1–10 cm. long, 2–6 mm. wide, firm, rough above, smooth beneath. Panicles ovate to oblong, stiff, dense to somewhat loose, one-sided, 2–8 cm. long, 1–4:5 cm. wide; branches stiff, spreading, slightly rough; pedicels extremely short.

Spikelets (S, × 6) close together on one side of the branches, narrowly oblong, 5–9 mm. long, 3–5-flowered, breaking up at maturity beneath each lemma. Glumes (G_1, G_2, × 6) persistent, green and firm except for the whitish membranous tips and margins, ovate to elliptic, blunt, unequal; lower 1·5–2·5 mm. long, 1–3-nerved; upper 2·5–3 mm. long, 3-nerved. Lemmas (F, L, × 6) exceeding the glumes, overlapping, rounded on the back, broadly elliptic, blunt, 3–4 mm. long, firm and green except for the white membranous tips and margins, minutely hairy at the base, 5-nerved, the middle nerve sometimes minutely projecting at the tip. Paleas (P, × 6) as long as the lemmas, narrowly oblong, 2-keeled, the keels minutely hairy. Anthers (FL, × 12) about 1 mm. long. Grain (CE, CH, × 12) about 2 mm. long, enclosed between the hardened lemma and palea (F). *Ch. no.* 2n = 42 (Jones and Newton).

A rather stiff grass of the coasts of England and Wales, sometimes locally abundant, especially in the south and south-east, but generally uncommon; on the margins of and in muddy salt-marshes, and on sandy mud- or sandy shingle-banks, etc.; introduced elsewhere. Also on the coasts of W. Europe from Norway to Spain; introduced into N. America. Flowering: May to August.

A male-sterile hybrid (*P.* × *pannonica* (Hack.) Holmb.] between this species and *P. distans* has been found at several places on the coast from Norfolk to Devon; it is a perennial, with somewhat similar but looser panicles than those of *P. rupestris*, very short pedicels, with lemmas 2–3·3 mm. long, and imperfect anthers. A sterile hybrid between *P. rupestris* and *P. maritima* (*P.* × *krusemanniana* Jans. & Wacht.), has been collected in Sussex; in this the panicles are looser and larger than those of *P. rupestris*, the spikelets up to 12 mm. long, the lemmas 4–4:5 mm. long, with 2 mm. long imperfect anthers.

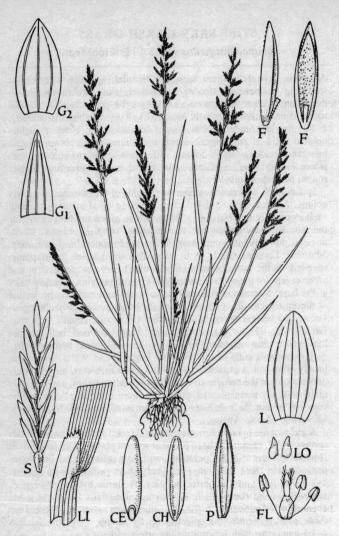

Catapodium rigidum. Common; dry open places.

FERN GRASS
Catapodium rigidum (L.) C. E. Hubbard

A glabrous annual, 2–30 cm. high. Culms tufted or solitary, erect or spreading, very slender, often rigid, 2–5-noded, smooth. Leaves green or purplish, hairless; sheaths smooth; ligules (LI, × 6) blunt, 1–3 mm. long, membranous; blades finely pointed, 1–10 cm. long, inrolled or flat, 0·5–2 mm. wide, finely nerved, minutely rough on the nerves. Panicles linear to ovate in outline, one-sided, stiff, rather dense to somewhat loose, 1–8 cm. long, up to 2·5 cm. wide at the base, branched in the lower part and unbranched above, or in weak plants with the branches reduced to solitary spikelets, green or purplish; main-axis and branches rigid, 3-angled, smooth, the latter up to 2 cm. long; pedicels up to 1·5 mm. long.

Spikelets (S, × 6) overlapping, appressed to one side of the axis and branches, narrowly oblong, 3·5–7 mm. long, 1–1·5 mm. wide, 3–10-flowered, slowly breaking up at maturity beneath each lemma. Glumes (G_1, G_2, × 12) persistent, slightly unequal, pointed, up to 2 mm. long; lower lanceolate, 1–3-nerved; upper elliptic, 3-nerved. Lemmas (F, L, × 12) overlapping at first, becoming spaced, much exceeding the glumes, narrowly oblong in side view, blunt, rounded on the back, 2–2·5 mm. long, nearly smooth, 5-nerved, tough except for the narrow thin margins. Paleas (P, × 12) almost as long as the lemmas, with the keels minutely rough. Anthers (FL, × 12) about 0·3 mm. long. Grain (CE, CH, × 12) narrowly oblong, tightly enclosed between the hardened lemma and palea. *Ch. no.* 2n = 14.

A small stiff grass of well-drained habitats, scattered throughout the British Isles, but most frequent on calcareous soils in England, especially in the south; on dry banks, walls, stony, rocky, and sandy places, sometimes in thin short grassland on shallow soils. Distributed through W. and S. Europe, N. Africa, and W. Asia; introduced into N. and S. America, S. Africa, and Australia. Sometimes called Hard Poa or Hard Meadow-grass. Flowering: May to July.

Plants from the Channel and Scilly Isles, S. Ireland and the Mediterranean Region, etc., with taller culms of 18–38 cm., longer leaves of 6–13 cm., larger and looser panicles of 6–13 cm. and longer lemmas, have been named *Catapodium rigidum* var. *majus* (C. Presl) Lousley. In contrast, *Catapodium rigidum* subsp. *rigidum* has panicles of 3·5–4 cm. culms of 3–12 cm. and leaves of 2·5–4 cm.

Catapodium rigidum is often placed in the genus *Scleropoa*, but the two genera cannot be distinguished satisfactorily, and the latter is therefore included in the former. It is also sometimes referred to the genus *Festuca*, all species of which are, however, perennials, with pointed or usually awned lemmas, and grains of a different structure.

(*Desmazeria rigida* (L.) Tutin)

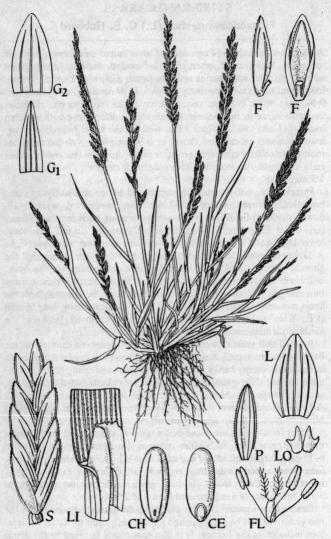

Catapodium marinum. Frequent; coastal sands and shingle.

STIFF SAND-GRASS
Catapodium marinum (L.) C. E. Hubbard

Annual, 3–20 cm. high. Culms tufted or solitary, erect, spreading, or prostrate, slender, rigid, often branched towards the base, few-noded, smooth. Leaves hairless; sheaths smooth; ligules (LI, × 6) blunt, 0·5–3 mm. long, membranous; blades narrowed to a fine blunt tip, 1–10 cm. long, 1–3·5 mm. wide, flat or rolled, dark green, minutely rough above, smooth beneath. Panicles spike-like, narrow, 0·5–7 cm. long, 4–12 mm. wide, rigid, branched in the lower part, with the branches erect, up to 1 cm. long, and bearing up to 4 spikelets, or unbranched and forming a raceme, green, or purplish; axis flattened on the back, angular in front; pedicels extremely short.

Spikelets (S, × 6) in two rows on one side of the axis, touching or overlapping, lanceolate-oblong to oblong, slightly compressed, 4–9 mm. long, 4–12-flowered, slowly breaking up at maturity beneath each lemma. Glumes (G_1, G_2, × 6) persistent, equal or nearly so, 2–3·5 mm. long; lower lanceolate, 1–3-nerved; upper ovate or oblong, 3-nerved. Lemmas (F, L, × 6) exceeding the glumes, overlapping, narrowly elliptic or oblong-elliptic in side view, blunt, 2·5–3·8 mm. long, rounded on the back below, keeled above, nearly smooth, tough except for the narrow membranous margins, 5-nerved. Paleas (P, × 6) a little shorter than the lemmas, with the two keels minutely hairy. Anthers (FL, × 6) 0:5–1 mm. long. Grain (CE, CH, × 12) shorter than the palea, tightly enclosed between it and the hardened lemma. *Ch. no.* 2n = 14.

A stiff dwarf grass occurring here and there on the coasts round the British Isles; on sands, shingle, and in rocky places, sometimes rather sparse, but occasionally very abundant in open situations or amongst Marram and other coastal grasses. Widespread on the shores of the Mediterranean from Spain to Cyprus, in N.W. Africa, the Azores, extending northwards along the coast to Holland. Known also as Darnel Meadow-grass or Darnel Poa. Flowering: May to July.

The species of *Catapodium* were at one time included in the genus *Poa*, from which they are separated by their lemmas being rounded on the back below and quite hairless, whereas in species of *Poa* the lemmas are distinctly compressed and keeled, and usually hairy in the lower part. *Catapodium rigidum* sometimes grows with *C. marinum*; it may be recognized by its usually looser and wider panicles, longer pedicels, thinner leaves, narrower lemmas, and smaller anthers. A male-sterile hybrid between the two species has been found in Merioneth.

(*Desmazeria marina* (L.) Druce)

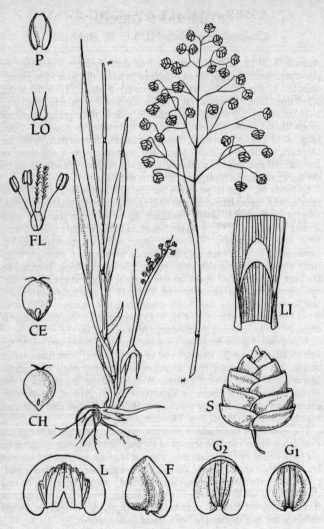

Briza minor. Rare; local, arable land.

LESSER OR SMALL QUAKING-GRASS
Briza minor L.

A loosely tufted annual, 10–60 cm. high. Culms erect, or slightly bent at the base, slender, round, 2–4-noded, smooth. Leaves green, hairless; sheaths round, smooth; ligules (LI, × 2) blunt, 3–6 mm. long, membranous; blades narrowly lanceolate, finely pointed, 3–14 cm. long, 3–9 mm. wide, flat, finely nerved, minutely rough above and on the margins. Panicles loose, obovate, 4–20 cm. long, 2–10 cm. wide; branches finely divided, minutely rough, with curved hair-like pedicels 4–12 mm. long.

Spikelets (S, × 5) nodding, orbicular to triangular-ovate, 3–5 mm. long and wide or wider, 4–8-flowered, shining, green, or tinged with purple. Glumes (G_1, G_2, × 5) persistent, horizontally spreading, hooded at the apex, 2–3·5 mm. long, firmly membranous, 3–5-nerved. Lemmas (F, L, × 5) closely overlapping, similar to the glumes, very broad, cordate at the base, rounded at the top and on the back, deeply concave, becoming hardened and shining in the centre but with broad white membranous margins, hairless, 7–9-nerved. Paleas (P, × 5) shorter than the lemmas, flat, with the two keels very narrowly winged. Anthers (FL, × 8) about 0·6 mm. long. Grain (CE, CH, × 5) enclosed by the lemma and palea, flat in front, rounded on the back, pale brown. *Ch. no.* 2n = 10.

A native of the Mediterranean Region, probably long ago introduced into the British Isles and now established as a weed on roadsides, in cultivated fields, and grassy places in S.W. England from Hampshire to the Scilly Isles; rather rare generally although sometimes locally abundant; also in S. Eire and in the Channel Islands. Elsewhere it occurs rarely on waste land or rubbish-tips, as an escape from cultivation, being grown as an ornamental grass in the same way as *B. maxima* on account of its decorative inflorescences. Flowering: June to September.

Briza minor may be distinguished from *B. media* by its annual duration, longer ligules, wider weaker leaf-blades, panicles usually with numerous spikelets, broader very deeply concave smaller lemmas, and by the smaller anthers.

The species of *Briza* may be separated from other British grasses by the following characteristics: spikelets broad, closely several- to many-flowered, borne in panicles; lemmas broad, blunt, firmly membranous, horizontally spreading, awnless, cordate at the base, rounded on the back, and 7–9-nerved.

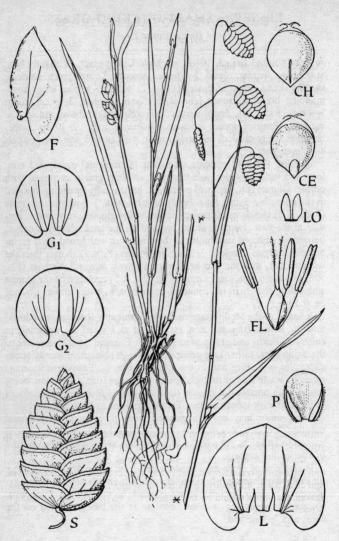

Briza maxima. Rare introduction.

BIG or LARGE QUAKING-GRASS
Briza maxima L.

Annual, 10–60 cm. high. Culms loosely tufted or solitary, erect, or bent below, slender, round, 2–4-noded, smooth. Leaves green, hairless; sheaths rounded, smooth; ligules oblong, blunt, 2–5-mm. long, membranous; blades finely pointed, mostly 5–20 cm. long, 3–8 mm. wide, flat, finely nerved, minutely rough only on the margins. Panicles loose, nodding, 3–10 cm. long, sparingly branched, bearing up to 12 spikelets, or only a single spikelet; branches slightly rough, bearing 1–3 spikelets on curved hair-like pedicels 6–20 mm. long.

Spikelets (S, × 2) nodding, ovate to oblong, plump, 14–25 mm. long, 8–15 mm. wide, 7–20-flowered, hairless, or usually minutely hairy, pale green, silvery, or often suffused with reddish-brown or purple. Glumes (G_1, G_2, × 3) persistent, horizontally spreading, broadly rounded, deeply concave, firmly membranous, 5–7 mm. long, 5–9-nerved. Lemmas (F, L, × 3) closely overlapping, rounded on the back, cordate at the base, very broad, 6–8 mm. long, hairless, or with minute gland-tipped hairs on the hardened centre of the back, and fine appressed hairs on the broad firmly membranous margins, 7–9-nerved. Paleas (P, × 3) broad, up to two-thirds as long as the lemmas, the two keels narrowly winged and minutely hairy. Anthers (FL, × 10), up to 2 mm. long. Grain (CE, CH, × 6) enclosed by the lemma and palea, flat in front, rounded on the back, 2·5 mm. long, pale brown. *Ch. no.* 2n = 14.

Native of the Mediterranean Region; naturalized on dry banks, rocky places and cultivated ground, in Jersey, Guernsey, and the Scilly Isles; occurs elsewhere in the British Isles as an escape from cultivation, occasionally persisting as a garden weed; now well established in most warm-temperate countries. Flowering: May to July.

On account of the ornamental value of its extremely beautiful spikelets it is frequently cultivated in gardens, either for use in the fresh state, or for drying as winter decoration, and for making bouquets. It is of easy cultivation, the seeds being sown outside from March to May, either in irregular patches for the adornment of flower borders, or in wide rows for drying. The inflorescences must be cut in dry weather when most spikelets are fully developed, but before the seeds mature, otherwise the spikelets break up on drying. After the removal of some of the lower leaves, the stems should be tied together in small bunches and hung in a cool airy dark room.

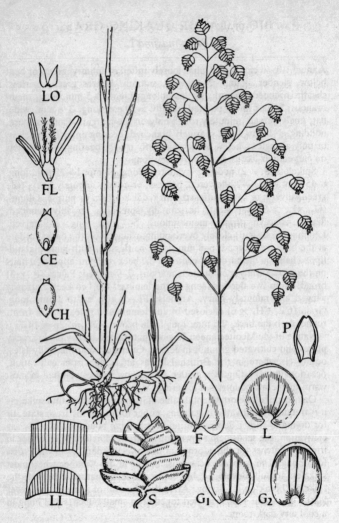

LO

FL

CE

CH

P

F

L

LI

S

G₁

G₂

Briza media. Frequent; grassland.

COMMON QUAKING-GRASS or TOTTER GRASS
Briza media L.

Perennial, forming loose tufts, 15–75 cm. high, with short rhizomes bearing leafy vegetative shoots. Culms mostly erect, slender, stiff, 2–3-noded, smooth. Leaves green, hairless; sheaths entire, soon splitting, smooth; ligules (LI, × 4) membranous, blunt, 0·5–1·5 mm. long; blades with a slender blunt tip, mostly 4–15 cm. long, flat, 2–4 mm. wide, minutely rough only on the margins. Panicles loose, more or less pyramidal, 4–18 cm. long and almost as wide; branches spreading, sparingly divided, with curved hair-like pedicels 5–20 mm. long.

Spikelets (S, × 4) drooping, loosely scattered, very broadly elliptic to broadly ovate, laterally compressed, 4–7 mm. long and wide, 4–12-flowered, shining, usually purplish. Glumes (G_1, G_2, × 5) horizontally spreading, persistent, deeply concave, hooded at the apex, 2·5–3·5 mm. long, 3–5-nerved, firmly membranous. Lemmas (F, L, × 5) similar to the glumes, about 4 mm. long, closely overlapping, cordate at the base, rounded on the back, 7–9-nerved, smooth, variegated with purple and green, and with whitish margins. Paleas (P, × 5) flat, slightly shorter than the lemmas, with the two keels narrowly winged. Anthers (FL, × 6) 2–2·5 mm. long. Grain (CE, CH, × 5) enclosed by the papery lemma and palea, rounded on the back, flattened in front, pale brown. *Ch. no.* 2n = 14, 28.

This very beautiful grass is widely distributed in the British Isles, being found in all counties except a few in the north of Scotland; it occurs also throughout Europe, N. and W. Asia. In Britain it is more frequent in the south, especially in hill grasslands on calcareous soils, but it is also prominent and sometimes abundant in old meadows and pastures on both heavy and light soils, and in dry and somewhat moist situations. Its altitudinal range varies from the low-lying water-meadows of the Thames Valley to 610 m. or more on the mountains of Scotland. Although grazed with other grasses, it produces little leafage and is of no importance as a herbage plant. Flowering: June to August.

The graceful panicles are often dried for winter decoration. In addition to the common form with purplish spikelets, two other variants may be found, one with greenish and the other with yellowish spikelets. It has a wealth of common names, the better known being Didder, Pearl, Rattle, Shivering, Trembling, Maiden Hair and Lady's Hair Grass, Cow Quakes, Doddering Dickies or Dillies, Quaker Grass, and Quakers.

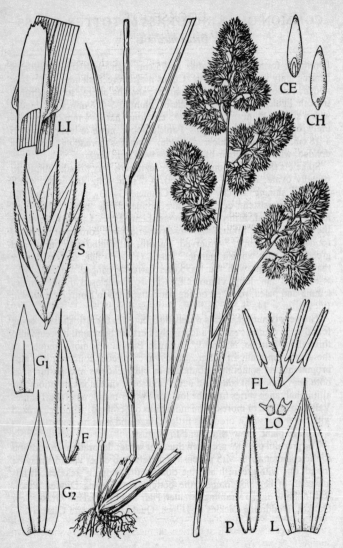

Dactylis glomerata. Very common; grassland.

COCKSFOOT
Dactylis glomerata L.

A densely tufted perennial, 15–140 cm. high, with compressed vegetative shoots. Culms erect or spreading, slender to stout, 3–5-noded, rough or smooth. Leaves green or greyish-green; sheaths keeled, at first entire, rough, hairless, or rarely short-hairy; ligules (LI, × 3) membranous, 2–12 mm. long; blades sharply pointed, 10–45 cm. long, at first folded, opening and 2–14 mm. wide, firm, rough. Panicles one-sided, erect, oblong to ovate, with the branches close together and spike-like, or usually with the lower distant, 2–30 cm. long, green, purplish, or yellowish; branches erect, spreading, or sometimes deflexed, stiff, angular, rough or hairy, rarely almost smooth, the longer bare at the base, up to 18 cm. long.

Spikelets (S, × 6) in dense one-sided masses at the ends of the branches, compressed, oblong or wedge-shaped, 5–9 mm. long, almost stalkless, 2–5-flowered, breaking up above the glumes. Glumes (G_1, G_2, × 6) persistent, lanceolate to ovate, finely pointed, membranous, 1–3-nerved, rough or hairy on the keel, 4–6·5 mm. long. Lemmas (F, L, × 6) closely overlapping, exceeding the glumes, 4–7 mm. long, lanceolate to oblong in side view, pointed or rather blunt, tipped with a rigid awn up to 1·5 mm. (rarely more) long, firm except for the membranous margins, 5-nerved, keels fringed with hairs or rough. Paleas (P, × 6) shorter than or as long as the lemmas, the two keels minutely hairy or rough. Anthers (FL, × 6) 3–4 mm. long. Grain (CE, CH, × 6) tightly enclosed by the hardened lemma and palea. *Ch. no.* 2n = 28.

A rather coarse grass of meadows, pastures, roadsides, and rough grasslands, widespread in the British Isles, formerly very abundant and much cultivated; occasional in open woodland. In most parts of Europe, N. Africa; temperate Asia; introduced into many temperate countries. Known in the United States as Orchard Grass. Flowering: June to September.

Formerly a very important pasture and hay grass, with numerous indigenous and introduced strains. Short plants with small dense flower-heads, growing in dry exposed places, have been named var. *collina* Schlechtd. The var. *variegata*, with the leaf-blades striped green and white, is sometimes cultivated in gardens. A closely related species, *D. polygama* Horvat. (*D. aschersoniana* Graebn.) of Central Europe, first noticed in 1951, is naturalized in Dorset and Buckinghamshire woodlands. It has looser panicles than *D. glomerata*, with fewer spikelets in the clusters; its lemmas are hairless on the keels, and have shorter awn-points (*Ch. no.* 2n = 14).

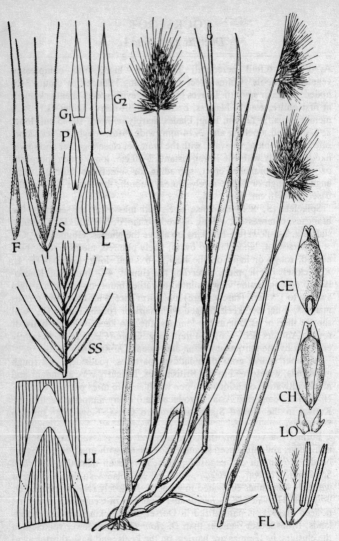

Cynosurus echinatus. Uncommon; arable and waste land.

ROUGH DOG'S-TAIL

Cynosurus echinatus L.

Annual, 10–100 cm. high. Culms tufted or solitary, erect or spreading, slender to somewhat stout, often branched, 2–6-noded, smooth. Leaves green, hairless; sheaths rounded on the back, smooth, the upper slightly inflated; ligules (LI, × 3) blunt, up to 10 mm. long, membranous; blades tapering to a fine point, 5–20 cm. long, 3–10 mm. wide, flat, rough above, smooth, beneath. Panicles spike-like, dense, ovate to oblong or almost globose, one-sided, bristly, 1–8 cm. long, 1–2 cm. wide, green or purplish, shining; axis smooth; branches short.

Spikelets densely clustered, of two kinds, fertile and sterile together, the latter more or less concealing the former. Fertile spikelets (S, × 3) wedge-shaped, 8–14 mm. long, 1–5-flowered, breaking up at maturity beneath each lemma. Glumes (G_1, G_2, × 3) persistent, nearly equal, narrowly lanceolate, very finely pointed, 7–12 mm. long, keeled, very thin, whitish, 1-nerved. Lemmas (F, L, × 3) rounded on the back, ovate when opened, 2-toothed or entire at the tip, 5–7 mm. long, becoming firm except for the membranous margins, rough upwards, 5-nerved, awned from near the tip, with the fine straight rough awn 6–16 mm. long. Paleas (P, × 3) about as long as the lemmas, 2-keeled. Anthers (FL, × 6) 2·5–4 mm. long. Grain (CE, CH, × 6) oblong, 3–4 mm. long, tightly enclosed by the hardened lemma and palea. Sterile spikelets (SS, × 3) persistent, broadly obovate, 7–13 mm. long, flattened, bearing up to 18 bracts, these narrowly lanceolate, tipped with a fine awn and including it 4–8 mm. long, firm to rigid, at first overlapping, finally separated and spreading. *Ch. no.* 2n = 14.

A native of the Mediterranean Region, now widespread as a weed in Europe, introduced into N. and S. America, Australia, etc. Of occasional occurrence in Great Britain, on rubbish tips, waste, and on cultivated land; more frequent in the south of England but mostly uncommon, sometimes persisting from year to year in the same locality; uncommon to rare in the north of England, rare in Scotland. Sometimes cultivated for ornament, its inflorescences being used fresh or dried for decorative purposes. Of no agricultural value. Flowering: June and July.

The genus *Cynosurus* may be distinguished from other British grasses by its two kinds of spikelets, fertile and sterile ones being mixed in dense clusters and borne on one side of the main axis of spike-like panicles, the inner spikelet of each pair being fertile and the outer composed of a number of sterile bracts and more or less concealing the former.

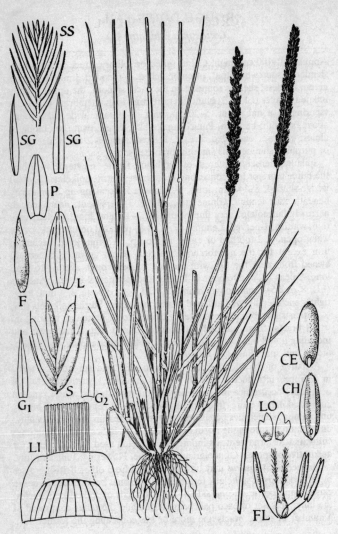

Cynosurus cristatus. Common; grassland.

CRESTED DOG'S-TAIL
Cynosurus cristatus L.

A compactly tufted perennial, 5–75 cm. high. Culms erect or slightly spreading, stiff, unbranched, 1–3-noded, smooth. Leaves green; sheaths rounded on the back, hairless, smooth; ligules (LI, × 6) very blunt, 0·5–1·5 mm. long, membranous; blades with a fine tip, up to 15 cm. long, 1–4 mm. wide, flat, roughish towards the tip, minutely hairy on the upper surface or hairless. Panicles spike-like, erect, or slightly curved, dense, one-sided, narrowly oblong, stiff, 1–14 cm. long, 4–10 mm. wide, green or tinged with purple; main axis rough or minutely hairy; branches very short.

Spikelets in dense clusters, of two kinds, fertile and sterile, mixed in the same cluster, the sterile almost concealing the fertile. Fertile spikelets (S, × 6) oblong or wedge-shaped, 3–6 mm. long, 2–5-flowered, breaking up at maturity beneath each lemma. Glumes (G$_1$, G$_2$, × 6) persistent, keeled, narrow, pointed, thin, 1-nerved, nearly equal, 3–5 mm. long. Lemmas (F, L, × 6) rounded on the back, their tips exceeding the glumes, oblong-ovate and blunt when opened out, 3–4 mm. long, usually tipped with an awn up to 1 mm. long, firm except for the membranous margins, rough upwards, finely 5-nerved. Paleas (P, × 6) slightly shorter than the lemmas, 2-keeled. Anthers (FL, × 6) about 2 mm. long. Grain (CE, CH, × 8) oblong, 2 mm. long, tightly enclosed by the hardened yellowish or brownish lemma and palea. Sterile spikelets (SS, × 6) persistent, ovate, becoming obovate, flattened, 4–6 mm. long, composed of up to 18 very narrow finely pointed 1-nerved bracts 3–5 mm. long (SG, × 6). *Ch. no.* 2n = 14.

Crested Dog's-tail grass is widely distributed in the British Isles, being recorded from every county, and from near sea-level up to about 610 m. It is usually common and sometimes abundant, particularly in old grasslands, both in the lowlands and on the hills, occurring on a wide range of soils from acid to basic and from light to very heavy, and in dry or damp situations. Also in most parts of Europe, S.W. Asia, and the Azores; introduced into N. America, Australia, and New Zealand. Flowering: June to August.

A low grass, leafy at the base, and thus suitable for grazing by sheep. Its yield is rather low and the proportion of wiry stem to leaf is high, but as it withstands drought and cold, and remains green during the winter, it is often included in seed-mixtures for permanent pastures on poor soils and in the uplands. Also sometimes used with other grasses in the formation of lawns and for sports grounds.

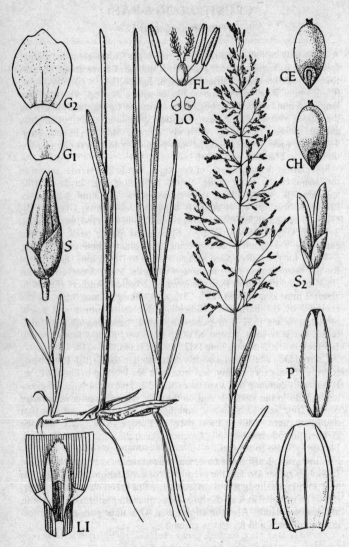

Catabrosa aquatica. Uncommon; wet places.

WATER WHORL-GRASS
Catabrosa aquatica (L.) Beauv.

A creeping perennial, 5–75 cm. high, spreading by stolons and rooting at the nodes. Culms erect or ascending from a bent base, slender to somewhat stout, succulent, unbranched, smooth. Leaves hairless, smooth; sheaths compressed, with free margins, the lower overlapping, the basal often purplish; ligules (LI, × 3) 2–8 mm. long, whitish, membranous; blades equally wide throughout, blunt, folded when young, afterwards flat, 4–14 cm. or more long, 2–10 mm. wide, rather thin, bright green. Panicles ovate to oblong, loose, 5–30 cm. long, 2·5–10 cm. wide, erect; branches clustered, spreading, very slender, minutely rough; pedicels short.

Spikelets (S, × 10, S₂, × 6) ovate to oblong, loosely 1–3-flowered, 3–5 mm. long, breaking up at maturity beneath each lemma, green, yellow, or brown, often variegated with purple. Glumes (G_1, G_2, × 10) persistent, thinly membranous, smooth, blunt, unequal, purple or white; lower ovate to elliptic, 1–1·5 mm. long; upper broader, 1·5–2·5 mm. long. Lemmas (L, × 10) elliptic-oblong to oblong, rounded on the back, truncate, 2·5–3·5 mm. long, firmly membranous except for the whitish tips, prominently 3-nerved, smooth, or with the nerves minutely hairy. Paleas (P, × 10) as long as the lemmas, 2-keeled, smooth, or minutely hairy on the keels. Anthers (FL, × 6) 1·5 mm. long. Grain (CE, CH, × 12) loosely enclosed between the lemma and palea. *Ch. no.* 2n = 20.

An aquatic grass, irregularly distributed in the British Isles, generally rather uncommon and of local occurrence, and in some districts rare; on the muddy margins of ponds, slow-running streams, in ditches and swampy places, sometimes floating in shallow water, preferring rich soils. Also throughout Europe, N.W. Africa, temperate Asia, and N. America. Flowering: May to July.

On account of its sweet stems and succulent foliage it is eagerly grazed by cattle; this factor, together with improved land-drainage systems, the clearing of ditches and ponds, are no doubt responsible for its disappearance from some localities.

Plants from the north and west coasts of Scotland, with larger lemmas than usual (up to 4 mm. long), have been named var. *grandiflora* Hack. Other plants from poor wet sandy soils near the sea at various places on our west and northern coasts have been referred to var. *uniflora* S. F. Gray (var. *littoralis* Parn.); they have shorter culms, leaves, and panicles, and 1-flowered spikelets. *Ch. no.* 2n = 20 (det. K. Jones, 1968 from Isle of Danna).

Catabrosa is a very distinct genus, recognized by its few-flowered spikelets, very blunt thin-tipped 3-nerved lemmas, and short broad-topped lodicules.

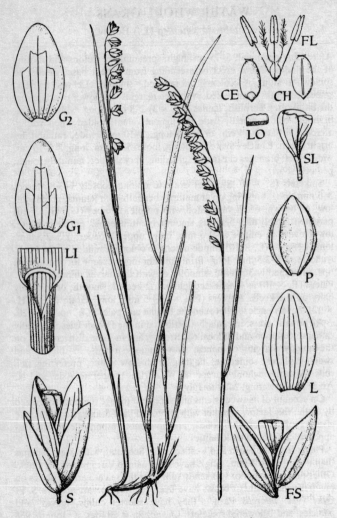

Melica nutans. Uncommon; woods, rocky places.

Labels on figure: G2, G1, LI, S, FL, CE, CH, LO, SL, P, L, FS

MOUNTAIN or NODDING MELICK
Melica nutans L.

Perennial, 20–60 cm. high, with slender rhizomes. Culms loosely clustered or solitary, erect or spreading, slender, angular, minutely rough near the raceme. Leaves rolled when young; sheaths tubular, 4-angled, minutely rough, the lower purplish; ligules (LI, × 3) very short, blunt, membranous; blades with a fine blunt tip, mostly 4–20 cm. long, 2–6 mm. wide, flat, bright green, short-haired above, minutely rough. Racemes loose, nodding, one-sided, sometimes branched, 3–15 cm. long; pedicels hair-like, curved, 3–15 mm. long, the tips minutely hairy.

Spikelets (S, × 4) solitary or paired, nodding, elliptic-oblong, or gaping, blunt, 6–8 mm. long, plump, purplish or reddish-purple, hairless, with 2–3 fertile florets (FS) and with the spikelet-axis terminating in a club-shaped mass of smaller sterile lemmas (SL), the florets falling together at maturity. Glumes (G_1, G_2, × 4) persistent, similar, slightly unequal, elliptic-ovate to elliptic, blunt, 4–6 mm. long, rounded on the back, papery-membranous, finely 5-nerved. Fertile lemmas (L, × 4) closely overlapping, with their tips slightly exceeding the glumes, elliptic or elliptic-oblong, blunt, 5–7 mm. long, rounded on the back, 7–9-nerved, becoming hardened, minutely rough. Paleas (P, × 4) as long as or shorter than the lemmas, elliptic, with the two keels thickened, narrowly winged and minutely hairy. Anthers (FL, × 4) 1·5–2 mm. long. Grain (CE, CH, × 4) tightly enclosed by the tough lemma and palea, elliptic, 3 mm. long, brown, *Ch. no.* 2n = 18.

An attractive grass of woods, wood margins, and shady banks; on calcareous rocks and soils, frequent on limestone; sometimes locally plentiful, but generally uncommon or rather rare; mainly in the western, central, and northern counties of England, northwards from Gloucestershire and Northamptonshire, and in Wales and in Scotland to the extreme north. Also in most parts of Europe, and in N. and S.W. Asia. Flowering: May to July.

Melica uniflora may be distinguished from *M. nutans* by the bristle-like outgrowth at the apex of the leaf-sheath, by its broader branched panicles, and especially by the structure of its spikelets, these having only one bisexual floret instead of two or three.

Melica altissima L. and its var. *atropurpurea* are cultivated in gardens for their beautiful spike-like panicles, those of the former being whitish, and of the latter, deep purple. *M. ciliata* L., with hairy whitish or purplish spikelets, is also occasionally cultivated for ornamental purposes.

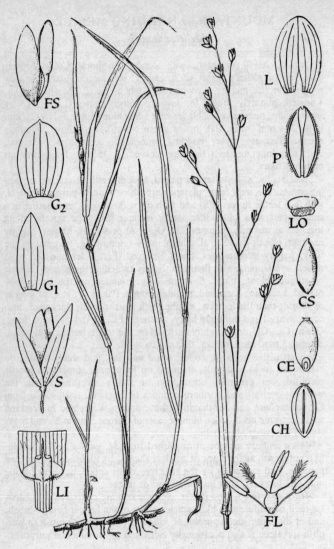

Melica uniflora. Common; woods, hedge-banks.

WOOD MELICK
Melica uniflora Retz.

Perennial, forming loose leafy patches, 20–60 cm. high, with slender creeping whitish rhizomes. Culms erect or spreading, slender, smooth. Leaf-sheaths tubular, tight, loosely hairy with short reflexed hairs, or hairless, produced at the apex into a slender bristle 1–4 mm. long on the side opposite the blade, the basal overlapping, usually purplish; ligules (LI, × 4) short, membranous; blades narrowed to a fine point 5–20 cm. long, flat, 3–7 mm. wide, rather thin, bright green, shortly hairy above, minutely rough beneath and on the margins. Panicles very loose, sparingly branched, erect or nodding, 6–22 cm. long, 1–12 cm. wide; branches spreading, naked below, bearing 1–6 spikelets towards the tips, fine, rough; pedicels 2–5 mm. long.

Spikelets (S, × 4) elliptic-oblong, or gaping, 4–7 mm. long, with 1 fertile floret and with 2–3 sterile lemmas in a club-shaped mass, the whole (FS) falling together at maturity. Glumes (G_1, G_2, × 4) persistent, rounded on the back, firmly membranous, smooth, purple or brownish, equal or slightly unequal, with the upper as long as the spikelet; lower narrowly elliptic, 3-nerved; upper elliptic, 5-nerved. Fertile lemma (L, × 4) broadly rounded on the back, boat-shaped, elliptic, blunt, 4–5·5 mm. long, green, eventually tough and rigid, 7-nerved, smooth. Palea (P, × 4) as long as the lemma, with the two keels tough, narrowly winged and minutely hairy. Sterile lemmas up to 3 mm. long. Anthers (FL, × 4) 1·5–2·3 mm. long. Grain (CE, CH, CS, × 4) about 3·5 mm. long, tightly enclosed between the hardened lemma and palea. *Ch. no.* 2n = 18.

Wood Melick is a common grass of woods and shady banks, on light as well as heavy soils; often very abundant and loosely carpeting the floor of open beech woods; scattered throughout Great Britain northwards from Cornwall but apparently absent from the north of Scotland; widespread in Ireland. Also in most parts of Europe, and in S.W. Asia. Flowering: May to July.

Var. *variegata*, with the leaf-blades longitudinally striped green and cream, is sometimes cultivated in gardens. Another attractive plant is an albino form with white spikelets which has been gathered in Kent, Sussex, Wiltshire, Somerset, and Monmouthshire.

The genus *Melica* may be recognized by its closed tubular leaf-sheaths, relatively large firmly membranous 3–5-nerved glumes, the club-shaped mass of sterile lemmas above the 1–3 fertile florets, the 7–9-nerved tough awnless lemmas, and the laterally fused lodicules.

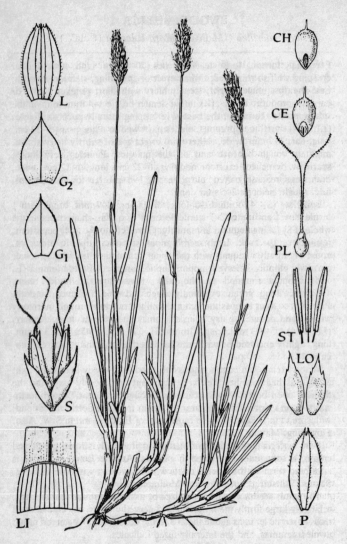

Sesleria caerulea subsp. *calcarea*. Uncommon; grassland, etc.

BLUE SESLERIA
Sesleria caerulea (L.) Ard. subsp. *calcarea* (Celak.) Hegi

A tufted perennial, 10–45 cm. high, with short slender rhizomes. Culms erect, slender, wiry, noded only near the base, smooth. Leaves mostly basal, hairless; sheaths persistent and coating base of plant, keeled upwards, smooth; ligules (LI, × 3) very short, membranous; blades equally wide to the abruptly pointed hooded tip, the basal up to 20 cm. (or more) long, the uppermost very short, folded or flat, 2–6 mm. wide, keeled beneath, firm, bluish-green above, rough on the margins and below on the middle nerve near the tip, otherwise smooth. Panicles spike-like, dense, ovate or oblong, cylindrical, 1–3 mm. long, 5–10 mm. wide, usually bluish-grey or purplish-grey, glistening, with short broad scales at the base; pedicels very short.

Spikelets (S, × 4) oblong, 4·5–7 mm. long, 2–3-flowered, breaking up at maturity beneath each lemma. Glumes (G$_1$, G$_2$, × 4) persistent, equal, or slightly unequal, 3–6 mm. long, ovate, mostly finely pointed, translucent, 1-nerved. Lemmas (L, × 4) with their tips equalling or projecting from the glumes, 4–5 mm. long, rounded on the back, keeled upwards, broadly oblong or elliptic, 3–5-nerved, with a broad 3–5-toothed tip, the nerves running into awn-points, the middle awn 0·5–1 mm. long, firm except for the membranous tips and margins, minutely rough or minutely hairy, especially on the nerves and margins. Paleas (P, × 4) as long as or slightly longer than the lemmas, densely short-hairy on the two keels. Anthers (ST, × 8) 2–2·5 mm. long. Grain (CE, CH, × 6) nearly 2 mm. long, hairy at the tip, loosely enclosed by the firm lemma and palea. *Ch. no.* 2n = 28.

This grass is of frequent occurrence on limestone in the north of England (Lancashire and Yorkshire northwards), and in W. Ireland; it is found also on micaceous schists in Scotland; in pastures, hill and mountain grassland, on cliffs and rock-ledges; from near sea-level to about 760 m. in the Lake District, and up to 910 m. in Perthshire. Also in similar situations in Central and S. Central Europe, and in Iceland. Known also as Blue Moor-grass. A form with whitish inflorescences has been called var. *luteo-alba* Opiz. Flowering: April to June.

Sesleria caerulea has been divided into two groups, these being variously treated as distinct species, subspecies, or varieties; the British plant, mainly of dry calcareous soils, being known as *S. calcarea* Opiz or *S. caerulea* subsp. or var. *calcarea*, whilst the name *S. caerulea* has been restricted to the Scandinavian and E. and Central European grass of wet habitats.

(*Sesleria albicans* Kit. ex Schultes.)

227

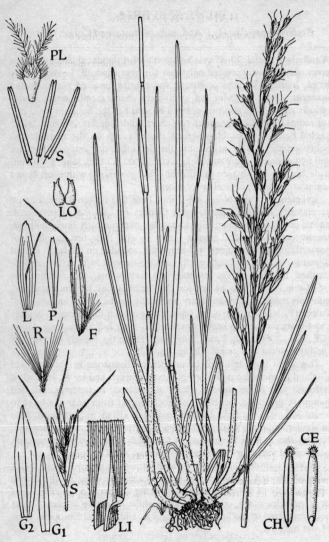

Helictotrichon pubescens. Common; grassland.

HAIRY OAT-GRASS
Helictotrichon pubescens (Huds.) Pilger

A loosely tufted perennial, 30–100 cm. high, with short rhizomes. Culms erect, or bent at the base, slender to somewhat stout, 2–3-noded, smooth. Leaves green, or with purple sheaths, these tubular at first, but soon splitting, the lower loosely hairy with spreading or deflexed hairs, the upper mostly smooth; ligules (LI, × 3) membranous, up to 8 mm. long; blades pointed or blunt, folded when young, afterwards flat, 2–6 mm. wide, softly hairy, or becoming hairless, the lower 4–30 cm. long. Panicles erect or nodding, loose, lanceolate to oblong, 6–20 cm. long, up to 6 cm. wide, green or purplish, glistening; branches clustered, fine, flexuous or straight, bearing 1–3 spikelets, slightly rough; pedicels 4–20 mm. long.

Spikelets (S, × $1\frac{1}{2}$) oblong, 11–17 mm. long, loosely 2–3-flowered, breaking up at maturity beneath each lemma; axis with hairs up to 7mm. long (R). Glumes (G_1, G_2, × 2) persistent, finely pointed, thin, 1–3-nerved; lower narrowly lanceolate, 7–13 mm. long; upper wider, 10–15 mm. long. Lemmas (F, L, × 2) narrowly oblong-lanceolate in side view, 9–14 mm. long, rounded on the back, toothed at the tip, tough except for the thin margins, 5-nerved, bearded at the base with hairs 2–5 mm. long, rough upwards, awned from the back about the middle, with the awn bent and twisted in the lower part and 12–20 mm. long. Paleas (P, × 2) nearly as long as the lemmas, with smooth keels. Anthers (ST, × 3) 5–7 mm. long. Grain (CE, CH, × 4) hairy at the top, enclosed by the hardened lemma and palea. *Ch. no.* 2n = 14.

Hairy Oat-grass is of frequent occurrence under suitable conditions in most parts of the British Isles; it is more common and occasionally locally abundant in lowland grassland and on the lower slopes of hills, especially on damp calcareous and gravelly soils, whereas the closely related *H. pratense* favours the higher and drier parts. Also throughout N., Central, and E. Europe and temperate Asia; introduced into N. America. Sometimes called Downy Oat-grass. Flowering: May to July.

Distinguished from *H. pratense* by its usually softly hairy and less stiff leaves, loose panicles, 2–3-flowered spikelets, and the longer hairs on the spikelet-axis. The genus *Trisetum* differs from *Helictotrichon* in having smaller spikelets (5–7 mm. long), and hairless ovaries and grains.

The two species of *Helictotrichon*, although grazed with other grasses are of little value as fodder plants, but their beautiful inflorescences are an attractive feature of natural grasslands.

(*Avenula pubescens* (Huds.) Dumort.)

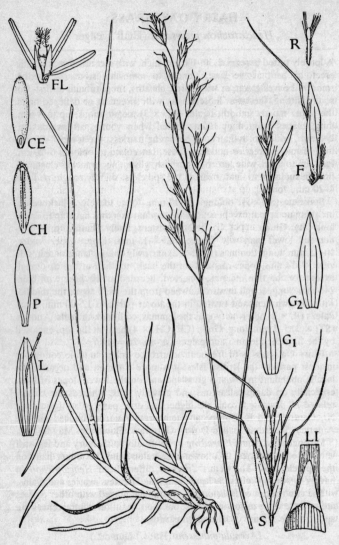

Helictotrichon pratense. Common; downs, grassland.

MEADOW OAT-GRASS
Helictotrichon pratense (L.) Pilger

A densely tufted perennial, 30–80 cm. high. Culms erect, slender, stiff, 1–2-noded in the lower part. Leaves hairless; sheaths rounded on the back, or keeled upwards, smooth or minutely rough; ligules (LI, × 3) membranous, the upper 2–5 mm. long, the lower shorter; blades with blunt tips, stiff to rigid, folded when young, opening out, 1–5 mm. wide, bluish-green above, minutely rough on the margins, smooth beneath, the basal 4–30 cm. long. Panicles erect, narrow, contracted, 4–18 cm. long, green or purplish, glistening; branches rough, paired or solitary, with 1–2 spikelets, the lower up to 3·5 cm. long, the upper shorter.

Spikelets (S, × 1½) narrowly oblong to oblong, 14–28 mm. long, 3–6-flowered, breaking up at maturity beneath each lemma; axis short-hairy (R). Glumes (G_1, G_2, × 2) persistent, lanceolate to oblong-lanceolate, finely pointed, firm except for the translucent margins, 3-nerved; lower 10–15 mm. long; upper 12–20 mm. long. Lemmas (F, L, tip of awn removed, × 2) narrowly oblong-lanceolate in side view, 10–17 mm. long, rounded on the back, toothed at the tip, tough except for the thin upper part and margins, 5-nerved, minutely rough upwards, bearded at the base with hairs 1–2 mm. long, awned from just above the middle, with the awn bent and twisted in the lower part, 12–22 mm. long. Paleas (P, × 2) with minutely hairy keels. Anthers (FL, × 3) 5–8 mm. long. Grain (CE, CH, × 4) hairy at the top, enclosed by the hardened lemma and palea. *Ch. no.* 2n = 42.

A stiff grass of short natural grasslands, mainly on chalk and limestone, widely distributed in Great Britain from S. Devon to the Orkneys; on chalk downs often locally very abundant, elsewhere less common; up to 1000 m. on Scottish mountains. In N. and Central Europe and temperate Asia. Known also as Perennial Oat-grass. Flowering: June and July.

The mountain plant of Scotland and N. England, in which the spikelets are larger than usual, has been treated as a distinct species, *H. alpinum* (Sm.) Henrard (*Avena alpina* Sm.), but as it appears to be connected with the southern type by a series of intermediates, it cannot be satisfactorily defined. *Ch. no.* 2n = 126.

Helictotrichon is often included in *Avena*, but the latter are annuals, with larger pendulous spikelets and 7–11-nerved glumes. *Arrhenatherum* resembles *Helictotrichon* but has mostly 2-flowered spikelets, with the lower flower male, and the florets falling together at maturity.

(*Avenula pratensis* (L.) Dumort.)

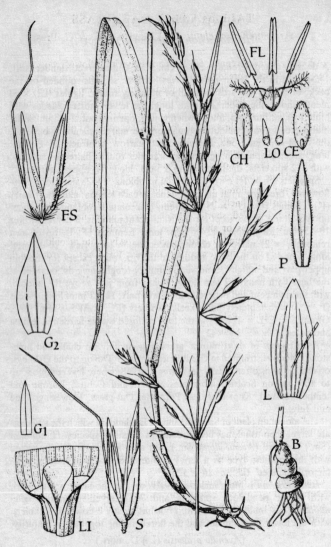

Arrhenatherum elatius. Very common; grassland.

232

TALL or FALSE OAT-GRASS
Arrhenatherum elatius (L.) Beauv. ex J. & C. Presl

A loosely tufted perennial, 50–150 cm. high, with yellowish roots. Culms erect or slightly spreading, stout, 3–5-noded, smooth, or hairy at the nodes. Leaves green; sheaths rounded on the back, smooth, rarely rough or loosely hairy; ligules (LI, × 3) 1–3 mm. long, membranous; blades finely pointed, 10–40 cm. long, 4–10 mm. wide, flat, loosely to sparsely hairy above, or hairless, rough. Panicles lanceolate to oblong, erect or nodding, loose or rather dense, 10–30 cm. long, green or purplish, shining; branches clustered, rough; pedicels 1–10 mm. long.

Spikelets (S, × 4) oblong or gaping, 7–11 mm. long, 2-(rarely 3–4-) flowered, the lower (or lowest) flower usually male, rarely bisexual like the uppper, the florets falling together at maturity. Glumes (G_1, G_2, × 4) persistent, finely pointed, membranous, minutely rough; lower lanceolate, 1-nerved, shorter than the upper; upper narrowly ovate, 3-nerved, as long as or shorter than the spikelet. Lemmas (FS, × 4) 8–10 mm. long, rounded on the back, narrowly ovate or oblong-ovate, pointed, 7-nerved, firm except for the thin tips, short-bearded at the base, the upper or both loosely hairy or hairless on the back, minutely rough upwards; lower (L. tip of awn removed, × 4) awned from the back in the lower third, the awn 10–17 mm. long; upper awnless, or with a fine short bristle from or near the tip, or with an awn from the back above the middle. Paleas (P, × 4) with minutely hairy keels. Anthers (FL, × 3) 4–5 mm. long. Grain (CE, CH, × 3) hairy, enveloped by the hardened lemma. *Ch. no.* 2n =28.

A coarse grass, very common in rough grasslands, hedgerows, road-sides, shingle and gravel banks, and waste ground; widespread in the British Isles. Distributed throughout Europe and W. Asia; introduced into N. America, Australia, New Zealand, etc. Flowering: June to September.

At one time included in seed-mixtures, it being very leafy, of rapid growth, deep rooted, drought-resistant, and on this account of con-siderable value for dry situations. It is of rather short duration, will not withstand heavy grazing, and is most suitable for hay. In the var. *bul-bosum* (Willd.) Spenner [*A. tuberosum* (Gilib.) F. W. Schultz] Onion Couch, the short basal internodes (B) of the culms are bulbous or pear-shaped and up to 1 cm. broad. This variety is sometimes a troublesome weed in arable land, being spread by the detached bulbous bases. A variegated form of this grass (var. *variegatum*), with the leaves striped green and white, is occasionally cultivated in gardens.

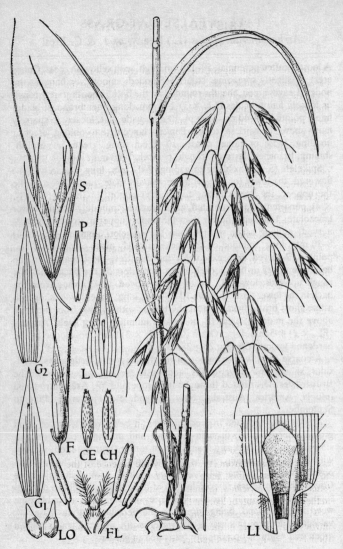

Avena strigosa. Local; arable land.

BRISTLE OR SMALL OAT

Avena strigosa Schreb.

Annual, 60–120 cm. high. Culms tufted or solitary, erect, or bent at the base, stout, 3–5-noded, smooth. Leaves green; sheaths rounded on the back, the lower loosely hairy, the upper smooth; ligules (LI, × 4) blunt, membranous, 2–5 mm. long; blades finely pointed, 8–25 cm. long, flat, 5–10 mm. wide, firm, rough. Panicles erect, narrowly ovate, nodding, 8–30 cm. long, up to 10 cm. wide, green; branches clustered, spreading, fine, loosely divided, rough; pedicels unequal.

Spikelets (S, × 1½) loosely scattered, pendulous, narrowly oblong or gaping, 17–26 mm. long, 2-flowered, not breaking up above the glumes or between the lemmas. Glumes (G₁, G₂, × 2) persistent, as long as the spikelet, equal or slightly unequal, lanceolate, finely pointed, rounded on the back, smooth, 7–9-nerved, becoming papery except for the narrow membranous margins. Lemmas (F, L, × 2) lanceolate or oblong-lanceolate in side view, 10–17 mm. long, finely 2-toothed at the tip with each tooth bearing a fine bristle 3–9 mm. long, becoming tough and rigid, stiffly hairy all over or only in the upper part, or hairless, rough upwards, 7-nerved, awned from about the middle of the back, with the stout awn 2–3·5 cm. long, rough, bent, dark brown and twisted in the lower part. Paleas (P, × 2) shorter than the lemmas, minutely hairy on the two keels. Anthers (FL, × 5) 2·5–4 mm. long. Grain (CE, CH, × 2) hairy, tightly enclosed by the hard lemma and palea. *Ch. no.* 2n = 14.

The Bristle Oat is cultivated in the mountainous districts of Wales, on the islands of W. and N. Scotland and in Ireland, usually in places where conditions are unfavourable for the Common Oat, *Avena sativa*. In these areas it is also widely spread as a weed in cornfields; elsewhere in the British Isles it occurs occasionally on waste ground. In addition it is cultivated here and there in W., Central, and E. Europe. Known also as Sand or Black Oat, and in Wales as Ceirch Llwyd and Blewgeirch. Flowering: July and August.

The other cultivated oat, *Avena sativa* L. (*Ch. no.* 2n = 42), may be easily distinguished from *A. strigosa* by the absence of the two bristles at the tip of the lemma. Both of these oats differ from the wild oats, *A. fatua* and *A. ludoviciana*, in their spikelets not shattering at maturity and in there being no tuft of hairs at the base of the lemmas. *A. barbata* Brot., a wild Mediterranean Region relative of *A. strigosa*, is sometimes introduced; it differs in the florets being readily deciduous at maturity, their bases being bearded and having a thickened basal scar.

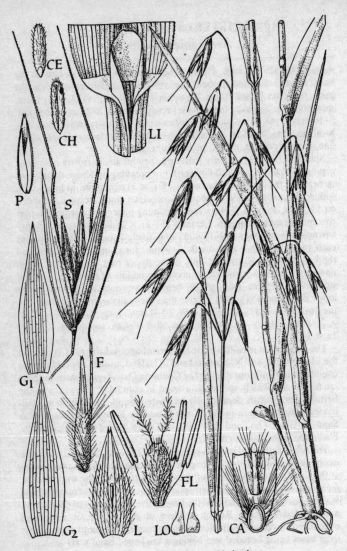

Avena fatua. Common; arable land.

SPRING or COMMON WILD OAT
Avena fatua L.

Annual, 30–150 cm. high. Culms tufted or solitary, erect, or bent at the base, stout, 3–5-noded smooth. Leaves green; sheaths rounded on the back, the basal usually loosely hairy, the rest smooth; ligules (LI, × 3) blunt, up to 6 mm. long, membranous; blades finely pointed, 10–45 cm. long, flat, 3–15 mm. wide, rough. Panicles nodding, narrowly to broadly pyramidal, loose, 10–40 cm. long, up to 20 cm. wide, green; branches widely spreading, mostly clustered, fine, loosely divided, rough; pedicels unequal.

Spikelets (S, × 2) loosely scattered, pendulous, narrowly oblong or gaping, 18–25 (rarely to 30) mm. long, 2–3-flowered, with all lemmas awned, breaking up at maturity beneath each lemma. Glumes (G$_1$, G$_2$, × 2) persistent, lanceolate, finely pointed, as long as the spikelet, equal or slightly unequal, smooth, 7–11-nerved, becoming papery except for the thinner margins. Lemmas (F, L, awn removed, × 2) narrowly oblong-lanceolate in side view, shortly 2–4-toothed at the apex, 14–20 mm. long, rounded on the back, becoming tough and rigid, stiffly hairy in the lower half, rough above, 7–9-nerved, finally brown, with a dense beard 1·5–4 mm. long around the horse-shoe-shaped basal scar (CA), awned from the middle of the back, with the stout awn 2·5–4 cm. long, bent, twisted, and dark brown in the lower part. Paleas (P, × 2) shorter than the lemmas, densely minutely hairy on the two keels. Anthers (FL, × 5) 3 mm. long. Grain (CE, CH, × 2) hairy, tightly enclosed by the hard lemma and palea. *Ch. no.* 2n = 42.

A common weed of arable land and waste places, often abundant among wheat, barley, and oats; introduced long ago, probably with seeds of cereals, now naturalized and widely distributed in the cultivated regions of the British Isles. Also throughout most of Europe, N. Africa, and Central Asia; introduced to N. America, etc. Flowering: June to September.

A very variable grass. In addition to the common variety, var. *fatua* (var. *pilosissima* S. F. Gray), described above, two others are of frequent occurrence. Var. *pilosa* Syme has very slightly hairy lemmas which become greyish at maturity, whilst in var. *glabrata* Peterm. the lemmas are hairless except for the short basal tuft and become yellowish when ripe. These three varieties are connected by a wide range of intermediates, probably the product of past hybridization. Hybrids between *A. fatua* and its derivative, the cultivated Oat. *A. sativa* L. (see p. 17), occur occasionally where the two grow together; they differ from the latter in having a hairy lower lemma.

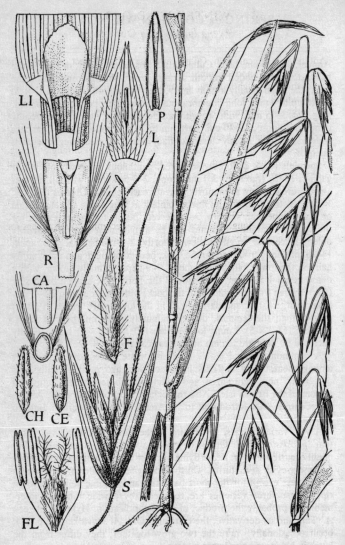

Avena ludoviciana. Locally common; arable land.

LI

P

L

R

CA

CH CE

F

FL

S

WINTER WILD OAT
Avena ludoviciana Durieu

Annual, 60–180 cm. high. Culms tufted or solitary, erect or bent at the base, stout, 2–4-noded, smooth. Leaves green; sheaths rounded on the back, the basal slightly hairy, the upper smooth; ligules (LI, × 3) blunt, membranous, up to 8 mm. long; blades finely pointed, up to 60 cm. long, 6–14 mm. wide, firm, rough, hairless. Panicles nodding, pyramidal, very loose, 15–45 cm. long, 8–25 cm. wide, green; branches clustered, spreading, rough; pedicels 5–35 mm. long.

Spikelets (S, × 2) scattered, pendulous, lanceolate, at length gaping, 23–32 mm. long, 2-awned, 2–3-flowered, breaking above the glumes but not between the florets, these falling together when ripe. Glumes persistent, lanceolate, finely pointed, rounded on the back, as long as the spikelet, 9–11-nerved, smooth, finally papery except for the thinner shining margins. Lemmas (F, L, awn removed, × 2) narrowly lanceolate, 15–22 mm. long, rounded on the back, becoming tough except for the 2-toothed membranous tip, mostly stiffly hairy except for the rough upper third, bearded at the base (CA) with hairs up to 5 mm. long, finally light to dark brown, 7-nerved, the lowest with a horse-shoe-shaped (CA) thickening at the base, awned from the middle of the back; awn stout, 3–5·5 cm. long, in the lower part bent, twisted, dark brown and minutely hairy. Paleas (P, × 2) with two minutely hairy keels. Anthers (FL, × 5) 2·5–3 mm. long. Grain (CE, CH, × 2) hairy, tightly enclosed by the hard lemma and palea. *Ch. no.* 2n = 42.

A weed of arable land, perhaps introduced with seed wheat from France during the 1914–18 war, now widespread in S. England, especially on heavy soils in the S. Midlands. Often very abundant and in the past a serious pest, particularly in fields of wheat, oats, barley, and beans; also on waste land. Distributed through S. and Central Europe, probably native in Central Asia; introduced into many parts of the world. Rather variable, perhaps on account of hybridization with other oats. The oldest name for this species is *A. persica* Steud. Flowering: July to August.

In the Spring Wild Oat, *Avena fatua*, the axis of the spikelet breaks naturally at maturity at the base of each lemma, the point of detachment being marked by a rounded scar. In *Avena ludoviciana*, however, the axis breaks at the base of the lowest lemma only and this is the only one with a scar (CA), the second lemma being continuous with the axis (R). *Avena sterilis* L., Animated Oats, is occasionally introduced and sometimes cultivated for ornament; it has larger spikelets than *A. ludoviciana*.

(*Avena sterilis* subsp. *ludoviciana* (Durieu) Nyman.)

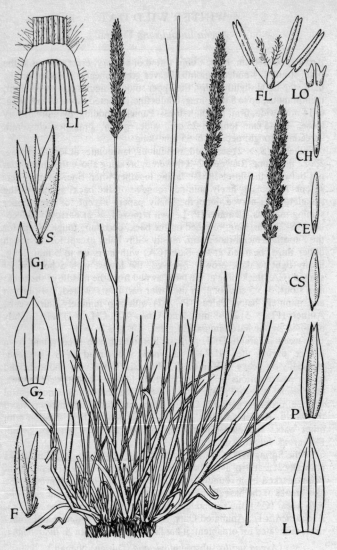

Koeleria cristata. Frequent; grassland.

CRESTED HAIR-GRASS
Koeleria cristata (L.) Pers.

A compactly tufted perennial, 10–60 cm. high, sometimes with slender wiry rhizomes. Culms erect, or slightly curved at the base, slender, stiff, 1–3-noded, downy especially towards the panicle, or hairless. Leaves green or grey-green; sheaths rounded on the back, at first entire, densely to loosely hairy especially the lower, or the upper hairless; ligules (LI, × 6) up to 1 mm. long, membranous; blades with a fine blunt tip, up to 20 cm. long, rolled and bristle-like, or opening out and 1–2·5 mm. wide, finely hairy, or hairless and smooth. Panicles spike-like, erect, very dense, often lobed or interrupted in the lower part, narrowly oblong, or tapering upwards, 1–10 cm. long, 5–20 mm. wide, silvery-green or purplish, glistening; branches very short, hairy.

Spikelets (S, × 6) densely clustered, on very short pedicels, oblong or wedge-shaped, compressed, 4–6 mm. long, 2–3-flowered, breaking up at maturity beneath the lemmas, hairless or downy-hairy. Glumes (G$_1$, G$_2$, × 6) persistent, pointed, with thin membranous margins; lower three-fourths the length of the upper, narrowly oblong, 1-nerved; upper oblong or elliptic-oblong, 4–5·5 mm. long, 3-nerved. Lemmas (F, L, × 6) as long as the upper glume or with their tips exserted, pointed, keeled upwards, oblong, 3·5–5·5 mm. long, firm except for the thin margins, 3-nerved. Paleas (P, × 6) about as long as the lemmas, thin, 2-keeled. Anthers (FL, × 6) 2 mm. long. Grain (CE, CH, CS, × 6) 2·5–3 mm. long, enclosed by the hardened lemma. *Ch. no.* 2n = 28.

A common plant of dry grasslands, especially those on calcareous soils; widely distributed in the British Isles from near sea level to about 610 m. frequent in hill and downs grasslands, but also in dry lowland meadows and pastures, as well as in sandy places. Widespread in Europe, temperate Asia, and N. America. Sometimes called *Koeleria gracilis* Pers. Flowering: June and July.

This grass varies somewhat in size, hairiness, rigidity of the leaf-blades, colour, and density of the panicles. Such ranges in structure are frequent among grasses. A coastal sand-dune variant has been named *Koeleria albescens* DC., but the British plant referred to it is scarcely distinguishable from inland *K. cristata*, except perhaps by its whitish panicles. *K. britannica* (Domin) Druce is a dwarf variant with short dense panicles.

The genus *Koeleria* may be recognized by its dense spike-like panicles, 2–4-flowered flattened spikelets, and the thin shinning margins of the glumes and lemmas.

(*Koeleria macrantha* (Ledeb.) Schultes.)

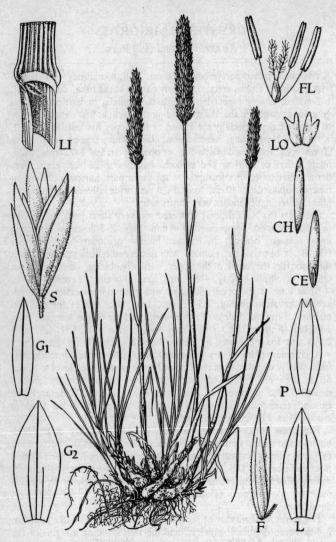

Koeleria vallesiana. Rare; Somerset limestone hills.

SOMERSET GRASS
Koeleria vallesiana (Honck.) Bertol.

A densely tufted perennial, 10–40 cm. high, thickened at the base. Culms erect, slender, stiff, 1–3-noded below the middle, downy with very fine short hairs especially towards the panicle. Leaves greyish-green; sheaths smooth, rounded on the back, the basal splitting into fibres, these persisting and forming a dense thickened fibrous network at the base of the plant; ligules (LI, × 6) membranous, up to 0·5 mm. long; blades very narrow, straight or curved, blunt, 3–12 cm. long, rolled and bristle-like, or opening out and up to 3 mm. wide, stiff, closely ribbed above, smooth except for the rough margins. Panicles spike-like, dense, oblong to ovate-oblong, blunt, 1·5–7 cm. long, 6–12 mm. wide, silvery-green or tinged with purple; pedicels extremely short.

Spikelets (S, × 6) oblong or wedge-shaped, flattened, densely overlapping, 4–6 mm. long, 2–3-flowered, breaking up at maturity beneath the lemmas. Glumes (G_1, G_2, × 6) persistent, pointed, equal or slightly unequal, rough or minutely hairy on the keels above the middle, firm and green about the nerves, the rest very thin and whitish; lower narrow, 3·5–4·5 mm. long, 1-nerved; upper elliptic or obovate, 4–5·5 mm. long, 3-nerved. Lemmas (F, L, × 6) overlapping, their tips shortly exceeding those of the glumes, 4–5 mm. long, keeled upwards elliptic, pointed, sometimes with a very short awn from the tip, similar in texture to the glumes, 3-nerved, minutely rough, or short-haired. Paleas (P, × 6) slightly shorter than the lemmas, 2-keeled, thin. Anthers (FL, × 6) 2–2·5 mm. long. Grain (CE, CH, × 6) enclosed by the slightly hardened lemma and palea. *Ch. no.* 2n = 42.

A rare grass restricted to a few limestone hills near Weston-super-Mare in N. Somerset, namely Brean Down, Uphill, Crook Peak, Worle Hill, and Purn Hill; on rock ledges or in the short grassy turf. Also in France, Spain, Switzerland, N. Italy, and N.W. Africa. Flowering: June to August.

This very distinct species may be easily separated from the common *Koeleria cristata* by the dense network of fibrous remains of old leaf-sheaths thickly clothing the base of the plant. It was first discovered in England on Brean Down and Uphill in 1726 by Dillenius, Professor of Botany at Oxford, during a tour of the west of England and Wales in search of plants. Although many other botanists visited these hills. it remained unknown until the late Dr G. C. Druce rediscovered it in 1904, as a result of his studies of Dillenius's specimens.

The annual, *K. phleoides* Pers., of the Mediterranean Region, is occasionally introduced.

Hybrids between *K. vallesiana* (2n = 42) and *K. cristata* (2n = 28) recorded by R. S. Callar (Linnean Society Symposium 1974). Pentaploid (2n = 35) and heptaploid hybrids.

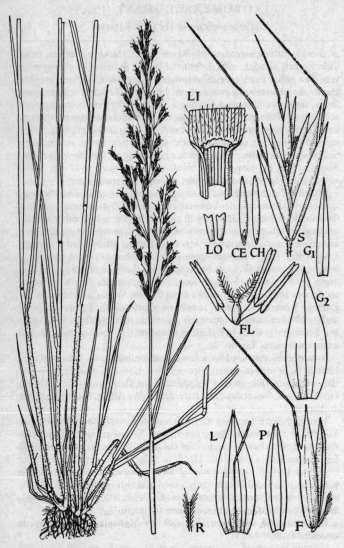

LI

LO CE CH S G₁

G₂

FL

L P F

R

Trisetum flavescens. Common; grassland.

YELLOW or GOLDEN OAT-GRASS
Trisetum flavescens (L.) Beauv.

A loosely tufted perennial, 20–80 cm. high. Culms erect or spreading, slender, stiff to weak, unbranched, 2–5-noded, hairy near the nodes, or quite smooth. Leaves green, softly hairy or hairless; sheaths rounded on the back, the lower often hairy; ligules (LI, × 4) 0·5–2 mm. long, membranous; blades narrowed to a fine point, up to 15 cm. long, 2–4 mm. wide, flat, firm, often hairy above, mostly smooth beneath. Panicles erect or nodding, loose to rather dense, 5–17 cm. long, 1·5–7 cm. wide, usually yellowish, less often greenish, purplish, or variegated with yellow and purple, glistening; branches clustered, fine, loosely divided, rough; pedicels 1–4 mm. long.

Spikelets (S, × 6) oblong or finally wedge-shaped and gaping, compressed, 5–7 mm. long, 2–4-flowered, breaking up at maturity beneath each lemma, the spikelet-axis (R) short-hairy. Glumes (G_1, G_2, × 6) persistent, keeled, finely pointed, membranous, rough on the keels, shining, unequal; lower narrowly lanceolate, 3–4 mm. long, 1-nerved; upper elliptic, 4–6 mm. long, 3-nerved. Lemmas (F, L, × 6) loose, narrowly lanceolate or narrowly oblong in side view, 4–5·5 mm. long, narrowed upwards and tipped with 2 fine short teeth or bristle-points, firm except for the thinly membranous tips and margins, finely 5-nerved, minutely rough upwards, awned from or near the middle of the back, the awn 5–9 mm. long, bent at and twisted below the middle when dry. Paleas (P, × 6) nearly as long as the lemmas, whitish and very thin. Anthers (FL, × 6) 2–3 mm. long. Grain (CE, CH, × 6) about 3 mm. long, enclosed by the firm back of the lemma. *Ch. no.* 2n = 28.

Yellow Oat-grass is widely distributed in Europe and temperate Asia, and has been introduced into N. America. In England and Ireland it is common on road-verges, in old pastures, and hill grasslands, especially those on calcareous soils; less frequent in Wales and rare in or absent from S.W., Central, and N. Scotland. Flowering: June and July.

Although this grass is not included nowadays in seed-mixtures for pastures or hay, it has some desirable qualities. It is fairly drought-resistant, tolerates a wide range of soils, and above all is highly palatable to sheep and cattle.

Trisetum is most closely allied to *Helictotrichon*, which may be separated by its considerably larger green or purplish spikelets, firmer 5–11-nerved lemmas, and the hairy-topped ovary. *Gaudinia fragilis* (L.) Beauv., of the Mediterranean Region, is occasionally introduced; it is a slender annual, with a narrow spike of awned spikelets borne in two opposite rows.

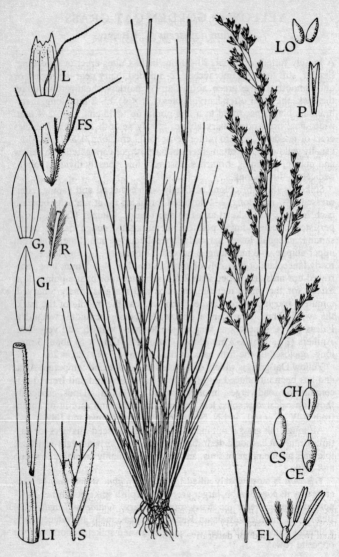

Deschampsia setacea. Uncommon; wet places.

BOG HAIR-GRASS
Deschampsia setacea (Huds.) Hack.

A densely tufted perennial, 20–60 cm. high, with numerous closely packed vegetative shoots. Culms erect, slender, stiff, 2–3-noded, smooth. Leaves green, hairless; sheaths tight, smooth; ligules (LI, × 8) narrowly lanceolate, finely pointed, 2–8 mm. long, membranous; blades bristle-like, very fine, sharply pointed, 5–20 cm. long, inrolled, 0·2–0·4 mm. in diameter, or opening out and up to 1 mm. wide, rough. Panicles loose, lanceolate to ovate, 6–15 cm. long, up to 7 cm. wide; main-axis rough; branches hair-like, rough, divided towards the tips; pedicels 1–4 mm. long.

Spikelets (S, × 6) in clusters towards and at the tips of the branches, narrowly oblong, becoming wedge-shaped, 4–5 mm. long, 2-flowered (FS), breaking up at maturity above the glumes, variegated with purple and pale yellow, with the axis hairy (R). Glumes (G_1, G_2, × 6) persistent, blunt or pointed, membranous, shining; lower slightly shorter than the upper, narrowly oblong, 1-nerved; upper as long as the spikelet, elliptic-oblong, 3-nerved. Lemmas (FS, L, × 6) rounded on the back, oblong, unequally 4-toothed with the outer teeth longest, 2·5–3 mm. long, short-bearded at the base, membranous, finely 4-nerved, minutely rough upwards, awned from near the base, with the bent awn brown and twisted in the lower half, up to 6 mm. long. Paleas (P, × 6) nearly as long as the lemmas, 2-keeled; keels minutely hairy upwards. Anthers (FL, × 6) 1·5–2 mm. long. Grain (CE, CH, CS, × 6) brown, 1·5 mm. long, enclosed between the slightly hardened lemma and palea. *Ch. no.* 2n = 14.

A rather rare grass of peaty margins of pools and boggy places on heaths, occurring in isolated localities scattered throughout the British Isles, and in W. Ireland; also in W. Europe from S. Scandinavia to Spain, and in S. Chile. Flowering: July and August.

Distinguished from *D. flexuosa* by its narrow pointed ligules, smooth leaf-sheaths, spaced florets, and by the unequally 4-toothed broader tips of the lemmas, and from *D. caespitosa* and *D. alpina* by its very narrow bristle-like leaf-blades.

The species of *Deschampsia* have been included in *Aira* in some British Floras. They may be separated from that genus (pp. 257–259), by their perennial duration, 3-nerved upper glume, and 2-lobed, truncate or toothed lemmas. They have no value as pasture or hay plants. However, most species possess very attractive glistening panicles which may be used fresh or dried for decorative purposes.

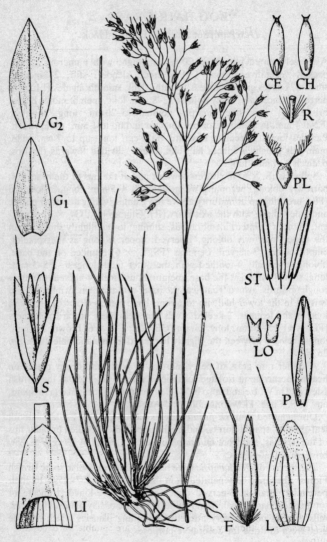

Deschampsia flexuosa. Common; moors, heaths.

WAVY HAIR-GRASS
Deschampsia flexuosa (L.) Trin.

A loosely to densely tufted perennial, 20–100 cm. high, sometimes with slender rhizomes. Culms erect or bent at the base, slender, wiry, 1–3-noded, smooth. Leaves green, hairless; sheaths rounded on the back, often slightly rough upwards; ligules (LI, × 8) blunt, 0·5–3 mm. long, membranous; blades bristle-like, pointed or blunt-tipped, up to 20 cm. (or more) long, tightly inrolled, 0·3–0·8 mm. wide, rather stiff, rough towards the tip. Panicles open and very loose, 4–15 cm. long, up to 8 cm. wide; main axis rough upwards; branches hair-like, rough, flexuous, divided in the upper part, spreading; pedicels 3–10 mm. long.

Spikelets (S, × 6) oblong or slightly wedge-shaped, loosely scattered, 4–6 mm. long, usually 2-flowered, breaking up at maturity above the glumes, purplish, brownish, or silvery. Glumes (G_1, G_2, × 6) persistent, keeled upwards, very thin, pointed, minutely rough, or smooth; lower slightly shorter than the upper, ovate, 1-nerved; upper elliptic-ovate, as long as the spikelet, 1–3-nerved. Lemmas (F, L, × 6) rounded on the back, 3·5–5·5 mm. long, elliptic-oblong, blunt and minutely toothed at the tip, membranous, minutely rough, short-bearded at the base, finely 4-nerved, awned from near the base, with the awn brown and twisted in the lower half, 4–7 mm. long. Paleas (P, × 6) about as long as the lemmas, 2-keeled, rough on the keels. Anthers (ST, × 10) 2–3 mm. long. Grain (CE, CH, × 6) 2–2·5 mm. long, enclosed by the slightly hardened lemma and palea. *Ch. no.* 2n = 28.

A very beautiful grass, widespread in Great Britain from Cornwall to the Shetlands and throughout Ireland; on sandy and peaty soils; usually in dry places, but occasionally in damp or wet habitats; often abundant on moors and heaths, also in open woodlands; from low altitudes to nearly 1220 m. on Scottish mountains. The alpine plant (var. *montana* (L.) Huds.) has smaller contracted panicles, with fewer spikelets 6–7 mm. long. Distributed through Europe, N. Asia, N.E. America, and temperate S. America. Flowering: June and July.

In the genus *Deschampsia* the spikelets are mostly 2–3-flowered and borne in open or contracted panicles, with rather delicate shining glumes and lemmas, the latter more or less enclosed by the glumes, blunt or toothed at the tip, and bearing a bent and twisted awn on the rounded back.

Wavy Hair-grass may be used as a lawn-grass on very acid soils, and also for planting in open woodlands on similar soils. Like other species of *Deschampsia*, the very attractive panicles are suitable for decorative purposes.

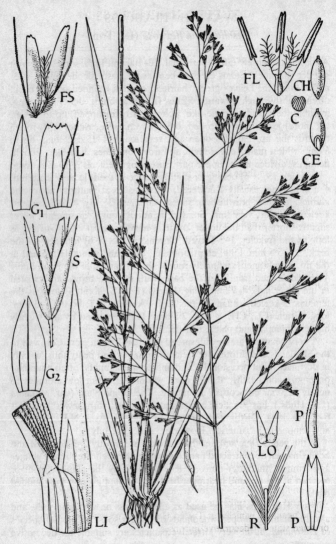

Deschampsia caespitosa. Very common; wet grassland, etc.

TUFTED HAIR-GRASS
Deschampsia caespitosa (L.) Beauv.

A densely tufted perennial, 20–200 cm. high, forming large tussocks. Culms erect, or slightly bent at the base, moderately slender to stout, stiff, 1–3-noded, smooth. Leaves hairless, green; sheaths rounded on the back, or somewhat keeled, smooth, or rough upwards; ligules (LI, × 4) narrow, up to 15 mm. long; blades sharply pointed or somewhat blunt, 10–60 cm. long (rarely less), flat or rolled, 2–5 mm. wide, coarse, ribbed above, with the ribs and margins very rough, smooth beneath. Panicles open, loose, rarely contracted, erect or nodding, ovate to oblong, 10–50 cm. long, up to 20 cm. wide, green, silvery, golden, purple, or variegated with these colours; branches very slender, spreading, rough, bare below; pedicels 1–6 mm. long.

Spikelets (S, × 6) loosely scattered or clustered, lanceolate to narrowly oblong, 4–6 mm. long, 2-flowered (FS), breaking up at maturity beneath each lemma; axis hairy (R). Glumes (G_1, G_2, × 6) persistent, as long as the spikelet or slightly shorter, keeled, membranous, shining, equal or nearly so, pointed; lower narrowly lanceolate, 1-nerved; upper wider, 3-nerved. Lemmas (FS, L, × 6) enclosed in the glumes or with their tips protruding, rounded on the back, 3–4 mm. long, oblong, with a broad toothed tip, membranous, finely 5-nerved, bearded at the base, with a fine straight awn up to 4 mm. long from near the base. Paleas (P, × 6) slightly shorter than the lemmas. Anthers (FL, × 6) 1·5–2 mm. long. Grains (C, CE, CH, × 6) enclosed by the thin firm lemma and palea. *Ch. no.* 2n = 26(28).

A coarse worthless grass of wet and badly drained soils, common throughout the British Isles, often very abundant in marshy fields, rough grassland, and moorland; from low altitudes up to about 1220 m. on Scottish mountains. Widely distributed in temperate and arctic regions, occurring on mountains in tropical Africa and Asia. Sometimes called Tussock-grass or Hassocks. Also spelt *D. cespitosa*. Flowering: June to August.

A rather variable grass, especially in size, length of leaves and in the colour of the spikelets. One variant, var. *parviflora* (Thuill.) Coss. & Germ., of damp shady places, is frequent on heavy soils in the oak woods of S. England, and extends to Central Scotland. It differs from typical. *D. caespitosa* in having narrower, less rough leaf-blades (up to 2·5 mm. wide) and smaller spikelets (2·5–3·5 mm. long).

The beautiful panicles of Tufted Hair-grass may be used in the fresh or dried state for decorative purposes.

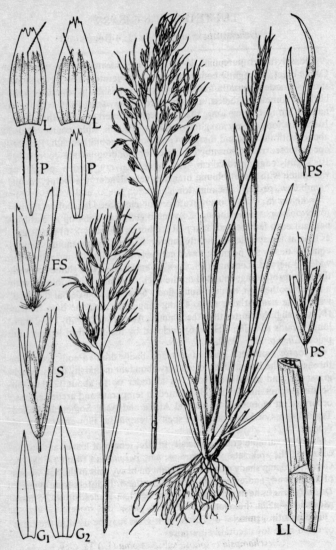

Deschampsia alpina. Rare; mountains.

ALPINE HAIR-GRASS
Deschampsia alpina (L.) Roem. & Schult.

A densely tufted perennial, 10–40 cm. high. Culms erect, or bent near
the base, slender, 1–2-noded, smooth. Leaves green, hairless; sheaths
rounded on the back, smooth; ligules (LI, × 4) 3–10 mm. long, membranous; blades with blunt or abruptly pointed tips, mostly 2–15 (rarely
up to 25 or more) cm. long, flat or inrolled, 2–4 mm. wide, stiff, prominently ribbed above, rough upwards on the ribs and margins, smooth
beneath. Panicles erect, loose, or rather dense, 5–16 cm. long, purplish
or green, sexual, or usually proliferous; branches fine, divided, smooth
or slightly rough; pedicels 1–4 mm. long.

Spikelets (S, × 6) oblong or gaping, 2–3-flowered (FS), 4–5·5 mm.
long, breaking up beneath each lemma, or longer and with the upper
flower replaced by a plantlet (PS). Glumes (G_1, G_2, × 6) persistent,
keeled, pointed, membranous, minutely rough on the keels towards the
tips, shining, variegated with purple and yellow, green or white, equal
or slightly unequal, 4–7 mm. long; lower lanceolate, 1-nerved; upper
lanceolate to elliptic, 3-nerved. Lemmas (FS, L, × 6) 3·5–5 mm. long,
or the lower 5–8 mm. long in proliferating spikelets, rounded on the
back, ovate or oblong, toothed or lobed at the apex, membranous, 5-
nerved, short-bearded at the base, awned on the back from the middle
upwards or from the tip, with the awn 0·5–4 mm. long. Paleas (P, × 6)
with rough keels. Anthers about 2 mm. long. Apomictic. *Ch. no.*
2n = 39, 41, 48, 49, 52, 56.

A rare grass of moist stony ground, wet rocks, and grassy slopes of
the higher mountains of Central and N. Scotland, Wales (Caernarvon)
and Eire (Kerry and Mayo), at altitudes from 910 to 1250 m. Also in
Scandinavia, Iceland, Arctic Russia, Siberia, and Arctic America.
Flowering: July and August.

Usually proliferous, as illustrated; that is, with the upper part of the
spikelet replaced by a miniature plant. In such spikelets the lemmas are
usually longer than in sexual spikelets, and all degrees of transition
between a normal lemma and a small leaf may be found (PS). The lower
lemmas of proliferating spikelets frequently bear sexual organs in their
axils. *D. caespitosa* and *D. alpina* appear to be very closely related. The
former is very rarely proliferous (var. *vivipara* S. F. Gray), and then
usually taller and with larger panicles than in *D. alpina*, whilst in its
sexual spikelets the awn arises near the base, not from or above the
middle of the lemma.

(*Deschampsia cespitosa* subsp. *alpina* (L.) Tzvelev.)

253

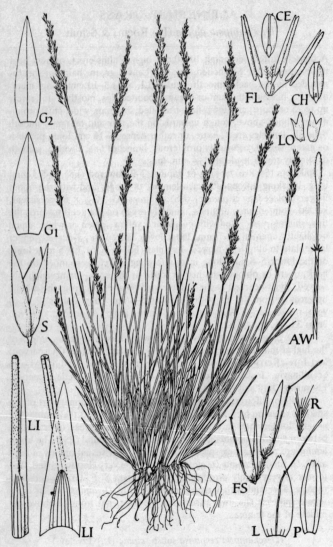

Corynephorus canescens. Rare; coastal dunes.

GREY HAIR-GRASS

Corynephorus canescens (L.) Beauv.

A densely tufted perennial, 10–35 cm. high. Culms erect or spreading, very slender, 2–7-noded below the middle, smooth or slightly rough. Leaves hairless; sheaths usually purplish, minutely rough; ligules (LI, × 6) pointed, 2–4 mm. long, membranous; blades numerous, bristle-like, stiff, sharply pointed, up to 6 cm. long, tightly inrolled, 0·3–0·5 mm. wide, greyish, minutely and densely rough. Panicles narrow, lanceolate to narrowly oblong, loose when in flower, afterwards rather dense, 1·5–8 cm. long, 0·5–1·5 cm. wide, purple, or variegated with pale green; branches short; pedicels 1–3 mm. long.

Spikelets (S, × 7) lanceolate to narrowly oblong, compressed, 3–4 mm. long, breaking up at maturity below each lemma, 2-flowered (FS). Glumes (G_1, G_2, × 8) persistent, narrowly lanceolate and pointed in side view, equal or nearly so, shining, membranous with thinner white tips and margins, 1-nerved. Lemmas (FS, L, × 10) enclosed by the glumes 1·5–2 mm. long, ovate, blunt, thin, obscurely nerved, with a tuft of minute hairs at the base, awned from the base, the awn (AW) with its lower half orange or brown and twisted when dry, bearing a ring of minute hairs at the middle, and with the terminal part club-shaped, and enclosed by the glumes. Paleas (P, × 10) nearly as long as the lemmas. Anthers (FL, × 12) 1–1·5 mm. long. Grain (CE, CH, × 10) enclosed by the lemma and palea. *Ch. no.* 2n = 14.

A rather rare grass of coastal sand-dunes, native in Norfolk, Suffolk, and the Channel Islands, also occurring in similar situations in Moray and Inverness, where, although now well established, it appears to have been introduced. In some places it is locally very abundant on the older (consolidated) parts of the sand-dunes, growing on the looser sand among the scattered shoots of Marram Grass and the Sand Fescue, or forming pure masses on the firmer sand or sandy shingle. Its area of distribution extends from Scandinavia to Portugal, Spain, and Italy, and inland to Russia. Flowering: June to July.

The name *Corynephorus* is derived from two Greek words meaning bearing a club, alluding to the terminal club-like portion of the very remarkable awn. The awn provides the best means of distinguishing this genus from all other British grasses, but it may also be separated from *Aira*, in which it was at one time included, by its perennial habit, stiffer culms, and the dense tufts of very rough bristle-like greyish leaf-blades.

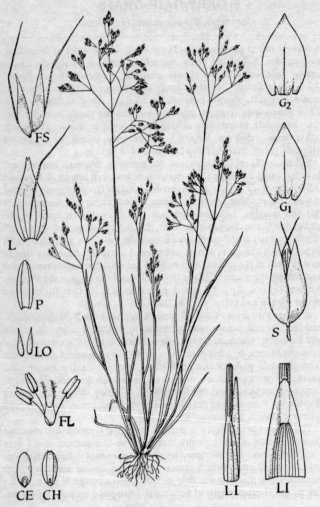

Aira caryophyllea. Common; sandy soils.

SILVERY HAIR-GRASS
Aira caryophyllea L.

Annual, 3–40 cm. high. Culms few to many in tufts, or solitary, erect or spreading, very slender, 2–3-noded below the middle, smooth. Leaves hairless, greyish-green; sheaths minutely rough upwards; ligules (LI, × 4) toothed, up to 5 mm. long, membranous; blades thread-like, blunt, 0·5–5 cm. long, inrolled, about 0·3 mm. wide, minutely rough on the nerves. Panicles very loose, with widely spreading branches, 1–12 cm. long and wide; main-axis often wavy; branches bare at the base, usually loosely divided into threes at intervals, hair-like; pedicels 1–10 mm. long.

Spikelets (S, × 8) in small loose clusters at the tips of the branches, ovate to oblong, 2-flowered (FS), silvery or tinged with purple, 2·5–3·5 mm. long. Glumes (G_1, G_2, × 8) persistent, similar, obliquely lanceolate and pointed in side view, minutely rough on the keel, shining, thinly membranous, 1–3-nerved. Lemmas (FS, L, × 9) slightly shorter than and enclosed by the glumes, narrowly ovate, finely 2-toothed, minutely rough above, with a tuft of short hairs at the base, firm, awned from the back one-third above the base, the awns twisted and bent below the middle, projecting from the tips of the glumes. Paleas (P, × 9) shorter than the lemmas. Anthers (FL, × 10) 0·3–0·6 mm. long. Grain (CE, CH, × 9) tightly enclosed by the firm brown lemma and palea. *Ch. no.* 2n = 14.

This graceful grass is recorded from all counties in the British Isles; it is of frequent occurrence on dry gravelly and sandy soils, in short grassland, on heaths and commons, and in open woodland, from low altitudes up to 610 m. in Scotland. Widespread in Europe; N. Africa, W. Asia; on mountains of tropical Africa; introduced into N. and S. America, etc. Flowering: May to July.

The closely related *A. multiculmis* Dum., of S.W. Europe and N.W. Africa, is of rare occurrence in S. England. It has 28 chromosomes (2n), but is difficult to separate from *A. caryophyllea* L.; it forms denser and larger tufts of usually numerous taller and less slender stems, with the slightly smaller spikelets on shorter pedicels.

Aira elegans Willd. (*A. capillaris* Host) of the Mediterranean Region, is sometimes cultivated in gardens on account of its delicate loose panicles which are dried for decorating small vases, etc. It has smaller (1–2 awned) spikelets than *Aira caryophyllea*. Both it and *A. cupaniana* Guss. are occasionally found on port tips. None of the species of *Aira* is of any agricultural value.

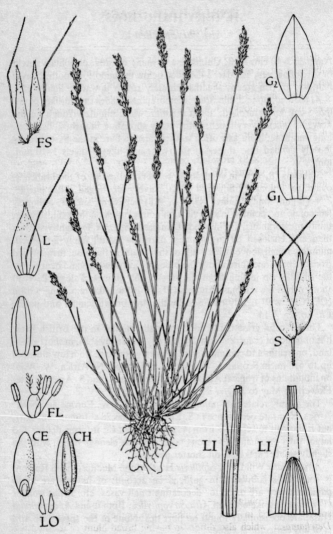

Aira praecox. Common; sandy soils.

EARLY HAIR-GRASS
Aira praecox L.

A delicate annual, 2–20 cm. high. Culms few to many in small tufts, or solitary, erect, spreading or prostrate, very fine, 2–3-noded, smooth or very minutely hairy. Leaves hairless, green; sheaths smooth; ligules (LI, × 5) blunt, up to 3 mm. long, membranous; blades blunt, up to 5 cm. long, involute, about 0·3–0·5 mm. wide, smooth, or minutely rough. Panicles spike-like, narrowly oblong, 0·5–5 cm. long, 2–8 mm. wide, silvery, purplish or pale green; branches erect, very short; pedicels 1–3 mm. long.

Spikelets (S, × 8) crowded, ovate or oblong, 2·5–3·5 mm. long, 2-flowered (FS). Glumes (G_1, G_2, × 8) persistent, as long as the spikelet, similar, obliquely lanceolate in side view, pointed, keeled upwards, minutely rough on the keels, shining, with thin membranous tips and margins, 1–3-nerved. Lemmas (FS, L, × 8) similar, slightly shorter than and enclosed by the glumes, narrowly lanceolate, rounded on the back, finely 2-toothed at the narrowed tip, minutely rough upwards, with a tuft of very short hairs at the base, finely 5-nerved, firm, bearing an awn on the back one-third above the base, the awn yellowish-brown, twisted and bent below the middle, projecting from the tips of the glumes. Paleas (P, × 8) shorter than the lemmas. Anthers (FL, × 15) 0·3 mm. long. Grain (CE, CH, × 10) tightly enclosed by the firm brown lemma and palea. *Ch. no.* 2n = 14.

Early Hair-grass is widespread in the British Isles, being found in every county from Cornwall to the Shetland Islands, and throughout Ireland. It prefers acid sandy soils, and is frequent on heaths, commons, dry fields, and open places in woods; it occurs also on dry rocky slopes, stone-walls, sand-dunes, from near sea-level up to 680 m. Generally distributed in N., Central, and W. Europe, extending to the Azores; naturalized in N. and S. America, and Australia. Flowering: April to early June.

Aira caryophyllea differs from *A. praecox* by its very loose panicles, with the spikelets in loose clusters at the tips of the branches, and by the rough leaf-sheaths.

The genus *Aira* is now restricted to annual grasses, with small 2-flowered spikelets in panicles, persistent equal membranous glumes as long as the spikelet, and with firm minutely 2-toothed finely 5-nerved lemmas, each rounded on and awned from the back. The perennial species included in *Aira* by Linnaeus and others are now placed in *Deschampsia*, which also differs in having broad blunt or toothed tips to the lemmas.

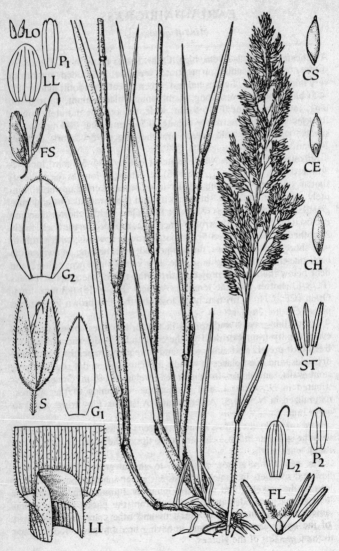

Holcus lanatus. Very common; grassland.

YORKSHIRE FOG

Holcus lanatus L.

A loosely to compactly tufted softly hairy perennial, 20–100 cm. high. Culms erect or ascending from a bent base, slender to somewhat stout, 2–5-noded, downy like the nodes, rarely almost hairless. Leaves greyish-green or green, softly hairy, rarely almost hairless; sheaths usually with reflexed hairs, rounded on the back; ligules (LI, × 4) 1–4 mm. long, membranous; blades narrowed to a fine point, 4–20 cm. long, flat, 3–10 mm. wide. Panicles lanceolate to oblong or ovate, very dense to rather loose, erect or nodding, whitish, pale green, pinkish, or purple 3–20 cm. long, 1–8 cm. wide; branches hairy, closely divided; pedicels 1–4 mm. long.

Spikelets (S, × 6) oblong to elliptic, or gaping, compressed, 4–6 mm. long, falling entire at maturity, 2-flowered (FS), with the lower flower bisexual (FL) and the upper usually male (ST), rarely bisexual. Glumes (G_1, G_2, × 6) equal, or with the upper longer and broader, as long as the spikelet, stiffly hairy on the keels and nerves, minutely rough or hairy on the sides, thinly papery; lower narrowly lanceolate or oblong, 1-nerved; upper ovate to elliptic, usually tipped with an awn up to 1 mm. long, 3-nerved. Lemmas (FS) 2–2·5 mm. long, enclosed by the glumes, keeled upwards, obscurely 3–5-nerved, firm, shining; lower (LL, × 6) boat-shaped, blunt, awnless, with an equally long palea (P_1, × 6); upper (L_2, × 6) narrower, awned on the back near the tip, with the awn up to 2 mm. long, becoming recurved like a fish-hook when dry, the palea (P_2, × 6) shorter than the lemma. Anthers (FL, ST, × 6) 2–2·5 mm. long. Grain (CE, CH, CS, × 6) enclosed by the hardened lemma and palea. *Ch. no.* 2n = 14.

A very common grass, found in a great variety of situations; frequent as a weed in meadows and pastures, often abundant in rough grassland, on waste land, and in open woodland, etc., growing on a wide range of soils, from heavy loams to sands, and under dry and wet conditions; distributed through all parts of the British Isles; also throughout Europe, temperate Asia, and N.W. Africa; introduced to N. America and other temperate parts of the world. Known also as Tufted or Meadow Soft-grass, and in N. America as Velvet Grass. Flowering: May to August.

Yorkshire Fog is generally regarded as a weed, but when young it has some value for grazing, especially on poor soils unsuitable for more desirable grasses. It may be distinguished from *Holcus mollis* by the absence of rhizomes, the beardless nodes of the culm and by the awn of the upper lemma becoming hooked when dry and not projecting beyond the tips of the glumes.

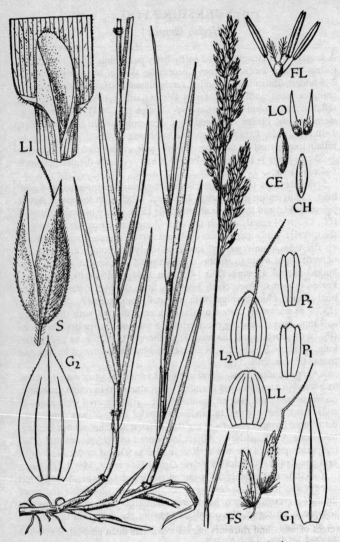

Holcus mollis. Common; shaded places and arable land.

CREEPING SOFT-GRASS
Holcus mollis L.

Perennial, 20–100 cm. high, with tough creeping rhizomes, forming compact tufts or loose mats. Culms erect or more often spreading, slender, 4–7-noded, loosely to densely bearded at the nodes, otherwise smooth. Leaves greyish-green; sheaths rounded on the back, hairless or softly hairy; ligules (LI, × 5) blunt, 1–5 mm. long, membranous; blades pointed, 4–20 cm. long, flat, 3–12 mm. wide, short-haired or hairless, rough or nearly smooth. Panicles narrowly oblong to ovate, compact to somewhat loose, 4–12 cm. long, whitish, pale grey or purplish; branches hairy; pedicels 1–4 mm. long.

Spikelets (S, × 6) elliptic or oblong, flattened, 4–6 (rarely 7) mm. long, falling entire at maturity, 2- rarely 3-flowered (FS,), with the lower flower bisexual and the upper functionally male or bisexual. Glumes (G_1, G_2, × 6) slightly unequal, the upper as long as the spikelet, pointed, thinly papery, with short stiff hairs on the keels and nerves, minutely rough on the sides; lower narrowly lanceolate, 1-nerved; upper elliptic or ovate, 3-nerved. Lemmas (FS) obliquely lanceolate in side view, 2·5–3 mm. long, enclosed by the glumes, obscurely 5-nerved, bearded at the base, smooth or minutely hairy above, firm, shining; lower (LL, × 6) awnless; upper (L_2, × 6) awned on the back just below the apex, with the awn 3·5–5 mm. long, slightly bent and protruding beyond the glumes. Paleas (P_1, P_2, × 6) about as long as the lemmas, minutely hairy on the nerves. Anthers (FL, × 6) 2 mm. long. Grain (CE, CH, × 6) enclosed between the lemma and palea. *Ch. no.* 2n = 28, 35, 42, 49.

A polymorphic species, widely distributed throughout the British Isles; frequent in open woodland, often carpeting the ground, also in shady situations such as shrubby heaths and hedgerows; occasionally in poor grassland; also a common weed of sandy arable land; on various soils from sands to heavy loams. Scattered through Europe; introduced into N. America. A male-sterile hybrid with *H. lanatus*, having 2n = 21 chromosomes, has been reported. Var. *variegatus*, with the leaves striped green and white, is sometimes cultivated. Flowering: June to August.

By means of its extensively creeping rhizomes, this grass has become a troublesome weed in sandy fields. It is most difficult to eradicate, as each small piece is capable of developing into a fresh plant. Investigations have shown that within 6–8 in. of the surface, a square foot of infested sandy soil may contain up to 110 ft of its rhizomes, whilst the weight of roots and rhizomes in such cases has been estimated at over 7½ tons per acre.

Holcus mollis var. *parviflorus* Parin. Breckland woodland on sandy and gravelly soils. Lemmas 2 mm., anthers 1·2 mm. (ex Libby and Swann).

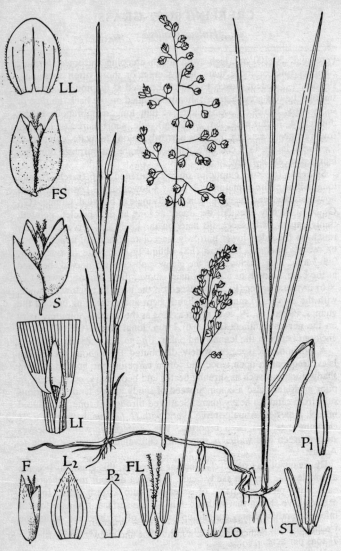

Hierochloë odorata. Very rare; wet places.

HOLY GRASS
Hierochloë odorata (L.) Beauv.

An aromatic perennial, 20–50 cm. high, with slender creeping rhizomes, forming compact tufts or patches. Culms erect, slender, few-noded, slightly rough near the panicle, or smooth. Leaf-sheaths rounded on the back, minutely rough; ligules (LI, × 3) blunt, 2–4 mm. long, membranous; lower blades up to 30 cm. long and 10 mm. wide, finely pointed, flat, sparsely and minutely hairy above, or hairless, glossy green beneath, rough on the margins, upper blades very short. Panicles ovate, loose, 4–10 cm. long, up to 8 cm. wide; branches spreading, naked below, smooth; pedicels up to 4 mm. long, smooth.

Spikelets (S, × 5) broadly elliptic, 3·5–5 mm. long, rather plump, green or purplish at the base, golden-brown upwards, 3-flowered, the lower two flowers male, the uppermost (F) bisexual, breaking up above the glumes at maturity, the florets (FS) falling together. Glumes persistent, broad, blunt, slightly shorter than or as long as the florets, keeled, membranous, shining, 1–3-nerved. Lower two lemmas (LL, × 5) broadly elliptic, very blunt, 3·5–4·5 mm. long, rough with minute hairs, short-haired on the margins, firm except for the thin tip, 5-nerved; paleas (P$_1$, × 5) with two minutely rough keels; anthers (ST, × 6) 3, up to 3 mm. long. Terminal lemma (L$_2$, × 5) slightly shorter than the others, ovate, becoming hardened, short-haired at the tip, 3–5-nerved; palea (P$_2$, × 5) 1-nerved; anthers (FL, × 6) 2, 2·5 mm. long. Apomictic. *Ch. no.* 2n = 28, 42, 56.

A very rare grass of wet grassy places and river-margins, in Angus, Caithness, Kirkcudbright, Outer Hebrides, Renfrew and Roxburghshire in Scotland, and on the banks of Lough Neagh in Ireland. First discovered by George Don in 1812 in Angus. Widespread in northern America, Asia, and Europe. Known in N. America as Sweet Grass or Vanilla Grass. Flowering: end of March to May.

When cultivated in the south of England, it is the first perennial grass to come into flower, a few panicles emerging towards the end of March, the rudiments of which develop the previous October. It spreads rapidly by means of its whitish rhizomes, its luxuriant growth being strongly scented with coumarin. In this respect it resembles its relative *Anthoxanthum odoratum*, which, however, possesses dense spike-like panicles, unequal glumes, barren awned lower lemmas, and green or purplish spikelets.

It was named *Hierochloë* or Holy Grass because in some parts of Prussia it was dedicated to the Virgin Mary and strewn before the doors of churches on festival days.

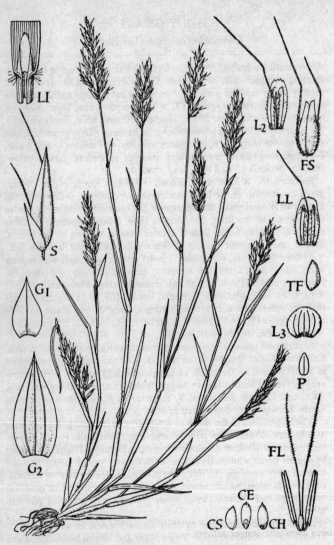

Anthoxanthum puelii. Rare; arable and waste land.

ANNUAL VERNAL-GRASS
Anthoxanthum puelii Lecoq & Lamotte

Annual, 10–40 cm. high. Culms loosely tufted, or solitary, erect or spreading, slender, 4–5-noded, branched, especially in the lower part, smooth. Leaves green; sheaths rounded on the back, with a few spreading hairs near the ligule, smooth; ligules (LI, × 5) up to 2 mm. long, membranous; blades finely pointed, 0·8–6 cm. long, flat, 1–5 mm. wide, thin, hairless, or sparsely hairy above. Panicles spike-like, moderately dense to loose, lanceolate to ovate or oblong, 1–4 cm. long, up to 12 mm. wide, pale green; branches short; pedicels up to 0·3 mm. long.

Spikelets (S, × 4) lanceolate to oblong, compressed, 5–7·5 mm. long, with three florets, the lower two barren, the uppermost (TF) bisexual, the florets (FS) falling together at maturity. Glumes (G_1, G_2, × 4) persistent, hairless, finely pointed, sometimes tipped with a short awn-point, rough on the keel, thinly membranous; lower ovate, about half the length of the upper, 1-nerved; upper as long as the spikelet, and enclosing the florets, ovate or elliptic, 3-nerved. Sterile lemmas (LL, L_2, × 4) narrowly oblong, 2-lobed or entire and toothed at the tip, keeled, 3–4 mm. long, brown, firm and hairy except for the whitish membranous tips, finely 4–5-nerved, the lower with a fine awn 4–5 mm. long from just above the middle, the upper with stouter awn 7–10 mm. long from near the base, the awns bent and the upper tightly twisted and dark brown below the middle; paleas absent. Fertile lemma (L_3, TF, × 4) orbicular, 2 mm. long, firm, smooth, and shiny; palea (P, × 4) 1-nerved. Anthers (FL, × 4) 2, 2·5–3·5 mm. long. Grain (CE, CH, CS, × 4) tightly enclosed by the hardened lemma and palea. *Ch. no.* 2n = 10.

A slender branched annual weed of cultivated and waste land, very probably introduced from France in the latter half of the 19th century with seeds of fodder plants; for some time widely scattered in England, now comparatively rare, but seeding and persisting in some sandy fields; very rare in Wales and Scotland. Native of S.W. Europe. Often considered synonymous with *A. aristatum* Boiss. Flowering: June to August.

The species of *Anthoxanthum* are scented with coumarin, like those of their close relative Hierochloë. The latter may be distinguished by its loose panicles, golden-brown spikelets, equal glumes and male lower florets. *Anthoxanthum odoratum* differs from *A. puelii* in being a perennial, with unbranched mostly stouter culms, hairy glumes, less conspicuous awns, and longer anthers.

(*Anthoxanthum aristatum* Boiss.)

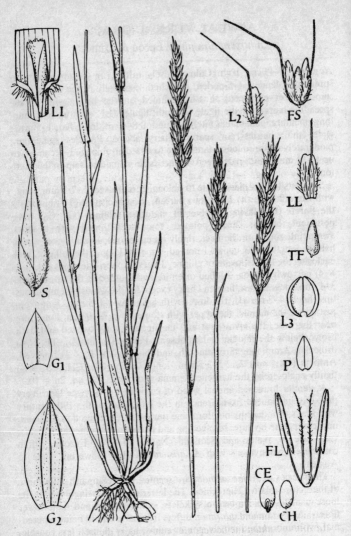

Anthoxanthum odoratum. Very common; grassland.

SWEET VERNAL-GRASS
Anthoxanthum odoratum L.

A tufted perennial, 10–100 cm. high. Culms erect or spreading, slender to relatively stout, unbranched, 1–3-noded, rather stiff, smooth. Leaves green; sheaths rounded on the back, loosely to densely bearded at the apex, otherwise smooth or loosely hairy; ligules (LI, × 4) 1–5 mm. long, blunt, membranous; blades finely pointed, variable in size, mostly 1–12 cm. long and 1·5–5 mm. wide, or up to 30 cm. long and 9 mm. wide on plants from wet places, flat, loosely hairy or hairless, rough or smooth. Panicles spike-like, very dense to somewhat loose, ovate to narrowly oblong, 1–12 cm. long, 6–15 mm. wide, green or purplish; branches short; pedicels up to 1 mm. long, hairy.

Spikelets (S, × 4) lanceolate, compressed, 6–10 mm. long, with 3 florets (FS), the lower two barren, the third bisexual (TF), the three falling together at maturity. Glumes (G_1, G_2, × 4) persistent, keeled, finely pointed, loosely to sparingly hairy, thinly membranous; lower ovate, about half the length of the upper, 1-nerved; upper as long as the spikelet, enclosing the florets, ovate to elliptic, 3-nerved. Sterile lemmas (LL, L_2, × 4) 3–3·5 mm. long, narrowly oblong, bluntly 2-lobed at the tip, firm, brown and hairy except for the white membranous tip, 4–5-nerved, the lower (LL) awned from above the middle, with the awn straight and 2–4 mm. long, the upper (L_2) with a stouter bent awn from the base, the awn dark brown and strongly twisted below, 6–9 mm. long. Fertile lemma (TF, L_3, × 4) 2 mm. long, rotund, smooth, shining, brown; palea (P, × 4) as long as the lemma, 1-nerved. Anthers (FL, × 4) 2, 3–4·5 mm. long. Grain (CE, CH, × 4) 2 mm. long, enclosed between the lemma and palea. *Ch. no.* 2n = 20.

An early flowering grass, strongly scented with coumarin, distributed throughout the British Isles in a great variety of habitats, often very abundant; on heaths and moors, in hill grassland, old pastures, meadows, and open woodlands; on a wide range of soils from sands to clays; in dry and damp places. Widespread in Europe and temperate Asia, introduced into N. America, etc. Flowering: late April to July.

A very polymorphic grass, varying considerably in size, leafiness, and hairiness. At one time included in seed-mixtures for pasturage or hay on account of its fragrant smell, but as it is not very palatable to stock, and moreover has a high proportion of stem to leaf, its inclusion is not generally recommended.

In *Anthoxanthum* the flowers are protogynous, the stigmas appearing before the anthers, as in other grasses lacking lodicules.

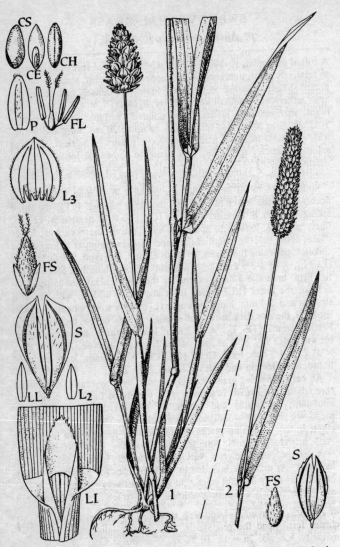

Phalaris canariensis (1) and *P. minor* (2). Uncommon; arable and waste land.

CANARY GRASS

Phalaris canariensis L. (Figure 1)

Phalaris minor Retz. (Figure 2)

A tufted annual, 20–120 cm. high. Culms erect, or bent at the base, slender to rather stout, stiff, smooth. Leaves green, hairless; sheaths smooth, or roughish, rounded on the back, the upper somewhat inflated; ligules (LI, × 3) membranous, 3–8 mm. long; blades narrowed to a fine point, 5–25 cm. long, 4–12 mm. wide, flat, rough. Panicles ovate to ovate-oblong, erect, very dense, spike-like, 1·5–6 cm. long, 12–22 mm. wide, stiff, whitish except for the green nerves; branches very short.

Spikelets (S, × 3) much flattened, closely packed, obovate, 6–10 mm. long, up to 6 mm. wide, 1-flowered, breaking up above the glumes at maturity. Glumes persistent, as long as the spikelet, equal, similar, oblanceolate, abruptly pointed, keeled, with the green keel broadly winged above the middle, minutely rough, firm, 3–5-nerved, slightly hairy. Florets 3 (FS, × 3). Sterile lemmas (LL, L_2, × 3) 2, 3–4·5 mm. long. Fertile lemma (L_3, × 3) broadly elliptic opened out, keeled, 5–6 mm. long, tough, hairy, 5-nerved, becoming smooth and glossy. Palea (P, × 3) 2-nerved. Anthers (FL, × 3) 3–4 mm. long. Grain (CE, CH, CS, × 3) tightly enclosed by the hardened lemma and palea. *Ch. no.* 2n = 12.

Canary Grass, a native of the western Mediterranean Region, is now widely cultivated in warm-temperate countries for its small yellowish fruits, which are used as food for cage-birds. In the British Isles, especially in the south, wasted seeds germinate and come to maturity on cultivated and waste land; in some places persisting for a few years. Flowering: end of June to September.

Phalaris minor Retz., Lesser Canary Grass (figure 2), of the Mediterranean Region, occurs as a casual, especially in the south. It is a tufted annual, 10–100 cm. high, with ovate or oblong soft dense panicles 1–5·5 cm. long and 8–16 mm. wide; spikelets (S, × 3) 4·5–5·5 mm. long, 2·5–3 mm. wide; glumes narrowly oblong, winged on the keels in the upper part, usually with the wings slightly toothed; sterile lemmas 2, one about 1 mm. long, the other minute; fertile lemma (FS, × 3) 3 mm. long. *Ch. no.* 2n = 28.

Phalaris paradoxa L., of the Mediterranean Region, is occasionally introduced into cultivated and waste places. It differs from other species of *Phalaris* in having 6–7 spikelets in a cluster, the central one of the cluster fertile and the rest sterile, each cluster falling as a whole at maturity. *Ch. no.* 2n = 14. In its var. *praemorsa* Coss. & Dur. [var. *appendiculata* (R. & S.) Chiov.], found on tips, etc., the glumes of the sterile spikelets are all deformed and club-shaped. *P. angusta* Nees of S. America, also occasionally introduced, has spikelets 2–3·5 mm. long.

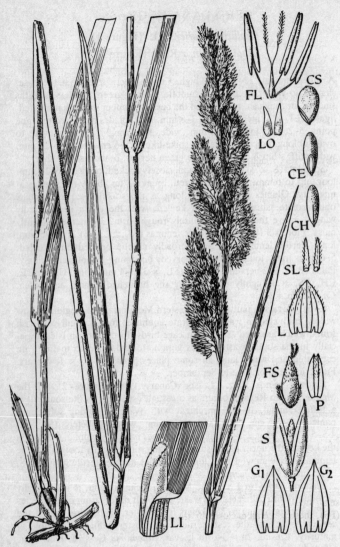

FL

CS

LO

CE

CH

SL

L

FS

P

S

G₁ G₂

Phalaris arundinacea. Frequent; wet places.

REED CANARY-GRASS

Phalaris arundinacea L.

A robust perennial, 60–200 cm. high, spreading extensively by creeping rhizomes. Culms stout, erect, or bent at the base, 4–6-noded, smooth. Leaves hairless, green or whitish-green, with cross-nerves between the nerves; sheaths smooth, rounded on the back; ligules (LI, × 2) blunt, becoming torn, 2·5–16 mm. long, membranous; blades finely pointed, 10–35 cm. long, 6–18 mm. wide, flat, firm, rough in the upper part. Panicles lanceolate to oblong, dense or somewhat loose below, lobed, 5–25 cm. long, 1–4 cm. wide; branches spreading when in flower, closely divided, very rough; pedicels very short.

Spikelets (S, × 4) densely crowded, oblong, or gaping, 5–6·5 mm. long, flattened, 1-flowered, breaking up at maturity above the glumes, greenish, purplish, or whitish-green. Glumes (G_1, G_2, × 4) equal, or the upper slightly longer, as long as the spikelet, narrowly lanceolate in side view, pointed, firm, minutely rough, 3-nerved. Sterile lemmas (SL, × 6) narrow, 1–2 mm. long, one on each side of fertile lemma (FS), short-haired. Fertile lemma (L, × 4) enclosed by the glumes, broadly lanceolate in side view, pointed, 3–4 mm. long, keeled, firm, 5-nerved, with appressed hairs, becoming smooth and glossy below. Palea (P, × 4) as long as the lemma, 2-nerved. Anthers (FL, × 6) 2·5–3 mm. long. Grain (CE, CH, CS, × 6) tightly enclosed by the hardened lemma and palea. *Ch. no.* 2n = 28, 42.

A leafy deep-rooting grass of wet places, widely distributed in the British Isles, of frequent occurrence on the margins of rivers, streams, lakes, and pools, and in marshes, often forming large masses. Also throughout Europe, temperate Asia and N. America, and in S. Africa. Also known as Reed-grass. Flowering: June to August.

A useful grazing or hay grass when young, especially on land subject to flooding, such as in river valleys. It yields a large amount of palatable succulent herbage over a long period, and on this account has been cultivated in the United States and on the Continent. When fringing rivers it protects the banks from erosion. Var. *picta* L., known as Ribbon Grass or Gardener's Garters, with the leaf-blades striped green and cream, is occasionally cultivated in gardens for ornament.

The species of *Phalaris* may be recognized by their contracted or dense panicles, flattened spikelets, similar 3-nerved keeled glumes, and by two small sterile lemmas at the base of the single awnless firm fertile lemma (FS), these three all enclosed by the glumes.

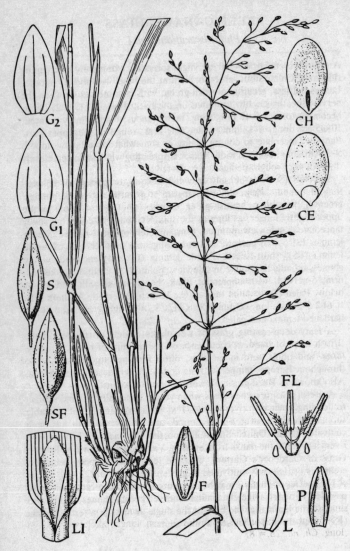

Milium effusum. Frequent; woods.

274

WOOD MILLET
Milium effusum L.

A loosely tufted perennial, 45–180 cm. high. Culms erect, or bent at the base, slender to stout, 3–5-noded below the middle, smooth. Leaves dull green, hairless; sheaths rounded on the back, smooth; ligules (LI, × 2) 3–10 mm. long, membranous; blades pointed, 10–30 cm. long, 5–15 mm. wide, flat, rough on the margins, smooth or only slightly rough on the nerves. Panicles lanceolate to ovate or oblong, very loose, nodding, 10–40 cm. long, up to 20 cm. wide; main-axis smooth; branches in clusters, fine, flexuous, spreading or deflexed, rough in the upper part; pedicels 1–3 mm. or more long.

Spikelets (S, SF, × 6) narrowly elliptic to ovate, pointed or at length blunt, 3–4 mm. long, slightly compressed from the back, 1-flowered, breaking up above the glumes at maturity, pale green, rarely purple. Glumes (G_1, G_2, × 6) persistent, ovate to elliptic-ovate, as long as the spikelet, greenish, membranous except for the whitish margins, minutely rough, 3-nerved, equal; the upper narrower than the lower. Lemma (L, × 6) lanceolate to elliptic in back view, pointed, as long as the glumes or usually slightly shorter, rounded on the back, becoming hard and tough, very smooth and shining, finely 5-nerved. Palea (P, × 6) as long as the lemma and similar in texture. Anthers (FL, × 6) 2–3 mm. long. Grain (CE, CH, × 10) tightly enclosed by the hard brown lemma and palea. *Ch. no.* 2n = 28.

A handsome grass, occurring throughout the British Isles; more frequent in England, becoming sparsely distributed or rare in Ireland and Wales, and northwards in Scotland; locally abundant in oak and beech woods, especially on damp heavy and calcareous soils with humus. At one time sown in woodlands for ornamental purposes, its seeds providing food for game birds. A variety (var. *aureum*) with yellow leaves and panicles is sometimes cultivated in gardens. Known also as Spreading Millet. In most parts of Europe, temperate Asia, and in N. America. Flowering: May to July.

Milium scabrum Rich., Early Millet, first collected in Guernsey in April 1899, was not re-found until fifty years later. It grows abundantly in the almost closed short turf of fixed dunes. Also on the coast of W. Europe from Holland to Spain, Flowering: April and May. A slender annual, 5–45 cm. high, with erect or spreading culms; leaf-sheaths minutely rough; ligules 2–3 mm. long; blades up to 5 cm. long, 1·5–3 mm. wide; panicles narrow, 1·5–5 cm. long; spikelets 2·5–3 mm. long. *Ch. no.* 2n = 8.

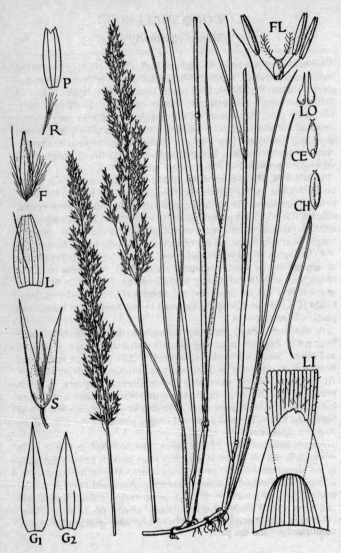

Calamagrostis scotica. Very rare; N. Scotland.

276

SCOTTISH SMALL-REED
Calamagrostis scotica (Druce) Druce

Perennial, forming compact tufts, up to 90 cm. high, with slender creeping rhizomes. Culms erect or slightly spreading, slender, 2–3-noded, smooth. Leaves green; sheaths smooth; ligules (LI, × 6) membranous, blunt, up to 3 mm. long; blades finely pointed, up to 30–56 cm. or more long, inrolled, or flat and 2–5 mm. wide, shortly hairy and prominently nerved above, smooth beneath. Panicles lanceolate to narrowly oblong, erect, rather dense, 7–16 cm. long, 1–3 cm. wide, brownish or tinged with purple; main-axis rough in the upper part; branches erect after flowering, closely divided, very rough, the lower up to 6 cm. long; pedicels 1–3 mm. long.

Spikelets (S, × 6) densely clustered, lanceolate, or gaping, 4·5–6 mm. long, 1-flowered. Glumes (G_1, G_2, × 6) persistent, narrowly lanceolate in side view, finely pointed, similar, equal or nearly so, firmly membranous, rough on the keels and minutely so on the sides, 3-nerved, or the lower 1-nerved. Lemma (F, L, × 6) three-fourths to four-fifths the length of the glumes, ovate, with a blunt minutely toothed tip, membranous, 5-nerved, minutely rough, ringed at the base with white hairs up to three-fourths as long as the lemma, bearing a fine straight awn on the back one-third above the base, the awn reaching or slightly exceeding the tip of the lemma. Palea (P, × 6) about two-thirds the length of the lemma, membranous. Anthers (FL, × 6) 2–2·5 mm. long. Grain (CE, CH, × 6) enclosed by the papery lemma and palea, about 1·6–2 mm. long.

An exceedingly rare grass, only known to occur in bogs in the northern part of Caithness and nowhere else in Europe. At one time it was considered identical with the Scandinavian *C.* × *strigosa* (Wahl.) Hartm, now thought to be the product of hybridization between *C. epigejos* and *C. stricta*. The Scottish plant is, however, quite distinct, and moreover fertile Flowering: July and August.

Calamagrostis stricta is very similar to *C. scotica*, but may be distinguished by its smaller spikelets, with less finely pointed or somewhat blunt glumes, these being 3–4 mm. long. These two species have minutely rough firm lemmas, and the spikelet-axis is produced as a minute hairy bristle (R) beyond the palea. On account of these features, they are often placed in the genus *Deyeuxia*. In typical species of *Calamagrostis*, such as *C. epigejos* and *C. canescens*, the lemmas are delicately membranous and smooth, and the spikelet-axis is not usually continued beyond the palea.

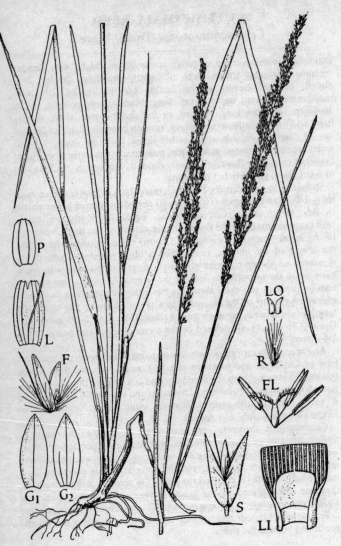

Calamagrostis stricta. Rare; wet places.

NARROW SMALL-REED
Calamagrostis stricta (Timm) Koel.

Perennial, forming compact tufts, 30–100 cm. high, with slender creeping rhizomes. Culms erect or slightly spreading, slender, 2–3-noded, rough near the panicle, or smooth. Leaves green; sheaths smooth; ligules (LI, × 6) membranous, 1–3 mm. long; blades finely pointed, up to 60 cm. long, inrolled, or flat and 1–5 mm. wide, shortly hairy and closely nerved above, smooth beneath, rough on the margins. Panicles erect, lanceolate to narrowly oblong, dense to somewhat loose, yellowish-brown, purple or greenish 5·5–20 cm. long 0·5–3 cm. wide; main-axis rough; branches erect or nearly so, rough, the lower up to 6 cm. long; pedicels 0·5–2 mm. long.

Spikelets (S, × 6) densely clustered, lanceolate, or gaping, 3–4 mm. long. Glumes (G_1, G_2, × 6) persistent, lanceolate and more or less pointed in side view, equal or nearly so, firmly membranous, rough on the keel and minutely so on the sides, 1-nerved, or the upper 3-nerved. Lemma (F, L, × 6) three-fourths to four-fifths the length of the glumes, ovate-oblong, with a broad-toothed tip, membranous, minutely rough, 5-nerved, with a ring of white hairs at the base up to three-fourths as long as the lemma, bearing a fine straight awn on the back one-third to half-way above the base, the awn reaching or slightly exceeding the tip of the lemma. Palea (P, × 6) about two-thirds the length of the lemma, 2-keeled. Anthers (FL, × 6) 2–2·5 mm. long. *Ch. no.* 2n = 28, 42, 56.

A rare grass of bogs and marshes, occurring in a few widely scattered localities in the British Isles. In Scotland, it has been recorded from the counties of Caithness, Perth, Angus, Roxburghshire, Selkirkshire and Ayrshire; in England from Yorkshire, Cheshire, W. Norfolk and W. Suffolk; and in N. Ireland from the shores and islands of Lough Neagh; also through-out northern Europe, temperate Asia, and N. America, S. Chile and S. Argentina. Flowering: June to August.

Calamagrostis stricta is a rather variable grass, plants from the more distant areas being slightly different and on this account sometimes classified as distinct varieties. These differences may be due to long isolation, or in some cases to past hybridization with other species. For example, where *C. stricta* and *C. canescens* grow together plants intermediate in structure have been observed. *C. canescens* differs from *C. stricta* by its looser panicles, larger spikelets, narrower and more finely pointed glumes, and the longer hairs surrounding the lemma and palea.

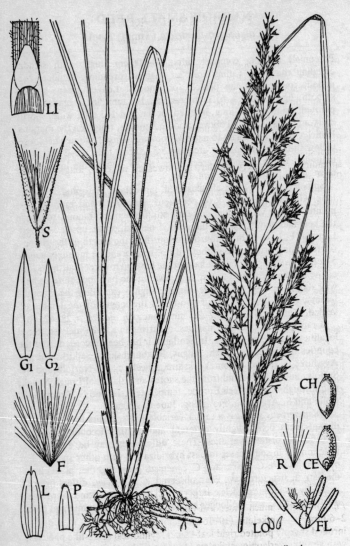

Calamagrostis canescens. Uncommon; fens and damp woodland.

PURPLE SMALL-REED
Calamagrostis canescens (Weber) Roth

Perennial, forming loose tufts, or patches, 60–120 cm. high, with slender rhizomes. Culms erect or slightly spreading, moderately slender, 3–5-noded, smooth. Leaves green; sheaths smooth; ligules (LI, × 2) 2–5 mm. long, membranous; blades finely pointed, up to 40 cm. or more long, flat, 3–6 mm. wide, short-haired above, rough on both sides, closely nerved. Panicles lanceolate to oblong, moderately loose, becoming flexuous or finally nodding, 10–25 cm. long, 2·5–6 cm. wide, purplish or greenish, rarely yellowish; main-axis rough; branches slightly spreading, rough, very slender, the lower up to 8 cm. long; pedicels 0:5–3 mm. long.

Spikelets (S, × 6) clustered, lanceolate, or finally gaping, 4·5–6 (rarely 7) mm. long. Glumes (G_1, G_2, × 6) persistent, narrowly lanceolate in side view, finely pointed, slightly unequal, membranous, 1-nerved, minutely rough. Lemma (F, L, × 6) half to nearly two-thirds the length of the glumes, ovate, thinly membranous, smooth, finely 3–5-nerved, with a very short fine awn from the narrowly two-toothed tip, surrounded and shortly exceeded by long fine white hairs from the base (F). Palea (P × 6) about two-thirds the length of the lemma, finely 2-nerved. Anthers (FL, × 6) about 1·5 mm. long. Grain (CE, CH, × 12) enclosed by the delicate lemma and palea. *Ch. no.* 2n = 28, 42, 56.

The Purple Small-reed occurs in marshes, fens, and wet open woodland, here and there in the lowlands from S., E., and Central England to the Border and in a few places in Wales and E. Scotland. It is generally infrequent or rather rare, but in favourable habitats it may be locally abundant. Also in W., N., and Central Europe. Flowering: June and July.

Calamagrostis epigejos differs from *C. canescens* in having the leaf-blades hairless on the upper surface, in its denser panicles, narrower more finely pointed glumes, and comparatively longer hairs round the lemmas. *C. stricta* has denser panicles and smaller spikelets (3–4 mm. long). A hybrid *C.* × *gracilescens* between *C. canescens* and *C. stricta* has been recorded from S.E. Yorkshire. *Ch. no.* 2n = 56 (ex Crackles, 1972).

Phragmites communis and *Ammophila arenaria* agree with *Calamagrostis* in the lemmas being surrounded by long silky hairs from the base. *Phragmites* has much wider leaf-blades (10–30 mm. wide), and larger 2–6-flowered spikelets (10–16 mm. long). *Ammophila* has tightly inrolled sharply pointed rigid leaf-blades, cylindrical spike-like panicles, with closely overlapping spikelets (10–16 mm. long).

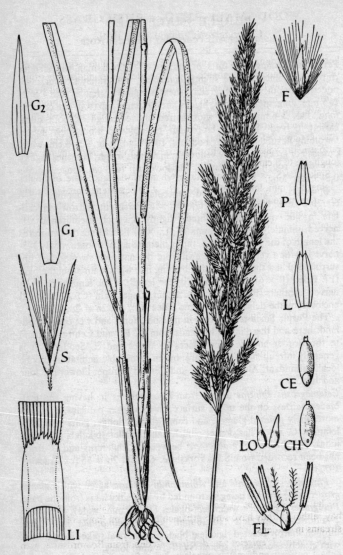

Calamagrostis epigejos. Frequent; damp open woods, fens.

WOOD SMALL-REED or BUSH GRASS
Calamagrostis epigejos (L.) Roth

Perennial, forming tufts or tussocks, 60–200 cm. high, with creeping rhizomes. Culms erect or slightly spreading, slender to moderately stout, 2–3-noded, rough near the panicle, otherwise smooth. Leaves dull green, hairless; sheaths smooth; ligules (LI, × 2) 4–12 mm. long, membranous, becoming torn; blades finely pointed, up to 70 cm. long, flat, 4–10 mm. wide, rather coarse, rough, closely nerved. Panicles erect, lanceolate to oblong, dense before and after flowering, 15–30 cm. long, 3–6 cm. wide, purplish, brownish, or green; main-axis rough upwards; branches very rough, up to 8 cm. long; pedicels 0·3–1 mm. long.

Spikelets (S, × 6) densely clustered, narrowly lanceolate or finally gaping, 5–7 mm. long. Glumes (G_1, G_2, × 6) persistent, equal or nearly so, very narrowly lanceolate and finely pointed in side view, firmly membranous, 1-nerved or the upper 3-nerved, rough on the keels. Lemma (F, L, × 6) about half the length of the glumes, lanceolate-oblong, thinly membranous smooth, finely 3-nerved, with a fine short awn from the toothed tip or from the back, surrounded by fine white hairs from the base (F), these much exceeding the lemma. Palea (P, × 6) up to two-thirds the length of the lemma, 2-nerved. Anthers (FL, × 6) about 2 mm. long. Grain (CE, CH, × 12) enclosed by the thin lemma and palea. *Ch. no.* 2n = 28 from Britain, 42, 56.

Calamagrostis epigejos is a coarse grass of open places in damp woods, in thickets, ditches, and fens, usually on heavy soils. It is widely distributed in England, being found in many counties from Cornwall northwards to the Border, and, although sometimes local, it is occasionally very abundant. In Scotland and Wales it is sparsely distributed, and in Ireland very rare. Outside the British Isles, it extends through Europe to E. Asia, whilst a variety occurs on the mountains of E. Africa and in S. Africa. Flowering: June to August.

The genus *Calamagrostis* may be recognized by the following combination of characters: spikelets narrow, one-flowered, borne on short pedicels in dense to somewhat loose panicles, breaking up at maturity, the glumes persisting, and the grain falling enclosed between the lemma and palea; lemma shorter than the glumes, membranous, 3–5-nerved, surrounded by long hairs from the base (F), with an awn arising on the back or from the tip.

The British species of *Calamagrostis* are of no value for grazing or hay, although they have some ornamental value on banks of lakes and streams in gardens.

Calamagrostis epigejos var. *densiflora* Ledeb. from Bedfordshire, with denser panicles and smaller spikelets (3·5–4·5 mm.).

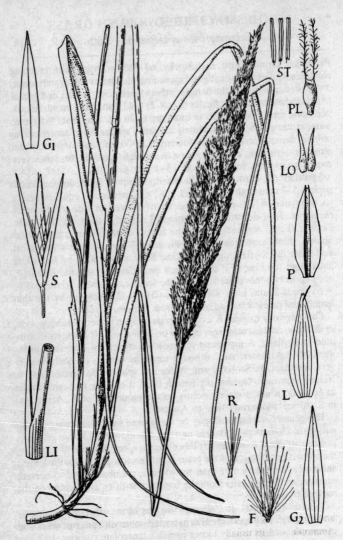

ST

PL

LO

P

R

L

F

G₁

S

LI

G₂

× *Ammocalamagrostis baltica*. Rare; coastal dunes.

HYBRID MARRAM
× *Ammocalamagrostis baltica* (Fluegge ex Schrad.) P. Fourn.

Perennial, up to 150 cm. high, spreading extensively by stout rhizomes. Culms erect or spreading, stout, few-noded, rough near the panicle or smooth. Leaf-sheaths rigid, rounded on the back, smooth; ligules (LI, × 1) lanceolate, 1–2·5 cm. long; blades finely pointed, up to 100 cm. long and 7 mm. wide, flat and spreading on the sand with the lower surface uppermost, or becoming inrolled, tough, prominently ribbed above, with the ribs rough or minutely and stiffly hairy, smooth and green or purplish below. Panicles linear-lanceolate to lanceolate, tapering upwards, very dense, 13–25 cm. long, 1·7–3 cm. wide, purplish or pale green; branches rough, the lower up to 7 cm. long; pedicels 1–4 mm. long, rough.

Spikelets (S, × 3) narrow, closely overlapping, compressed, 9–12 mm. long, 1-flowered. Glumes (G_1, G_2, × 3) narrowly lanceolate, finely pointed, equal or slightly unequal, as long as the spikelet, firm, keeled upwards, rough on the keels; lower 1–3-nerved; upper 3-nerved. Lemma (F, L, × 3) lanceolate and pointed in side view, 7–9 mm. long, firm, minutely rough, 3–7-nerved, with a straight awn 1–2 mm. long from just below the minutely 2-toothed tip, densely bearded at the base with fine silky hairs 5–7 mm. long. Palea (P, × 3) slightly shorter than the lemma, 2–4-nerved. Anthers (ST, × 3) 4–4·5 mm. long. *Ch. no.* 2n = 28, 42.

A sterile intergeneric hybrid, the product of the crossing of *Ammophila arenaria* and *Calamagrostis epigejos*, known in the British Isles only from a few isolated coastal areas; on the sand-dunes of E. Norfolk from Caister to Horsey; on Ross Links, Northumberland; on cliffs, Handa Island, Sutherland. Following the 1953 sea-flood it was planted on sand-dunes in Norfolk, Suffolk and Dorset, and has proved to be a valuable sand-binder. Also on the sandy coasts of W. Europe from southern Scandinavia to N.E. France. Known also as Purple Marram. Flowering: end of June to August.

The British hybrids are slightly different from one another, but are nearer to the *Ammophila* parent in spikelet-size, whereas on the Baltic coast another hybrid occurs with more *Calamagrostis* characteristics. In the Norfolk plant the lemma is 5–7-nerved and the palea 2-nerved, but in the Northumberland and Handa plants they are respectively 3–5-nerved and 4-nerved. In both hybrid groups the anthers remain closed and the pollen is imperfect. This hybrid grass may be distinguished from *Ammophila* by its usually looser purplish lanceolate panicles, less rigid and often flat leaf-blades, lanceolate glumes, longer hairs from the base of the lemma, and by the smaller anthers.

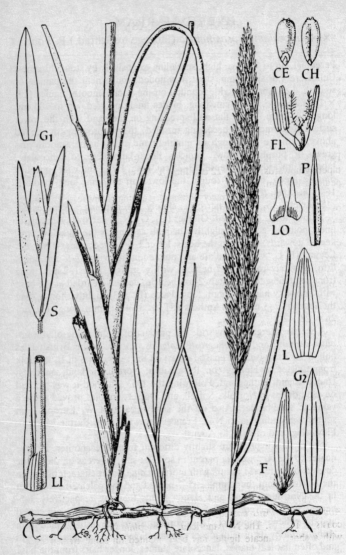

Ammophila arenaria. Common; coastal dunes.

MARRAM GRASS
Ammophila arenaria (L.) Link

Perennial, 50–120 cm. high, spreading extensively by stout branched, horizontally-spreading or vertical rhizomes, forming compact tufts. Culms erect or spreading, moderately stout, rigid, few-noded, smooth. Leaves greyish-green; sheaths overlapping, smooth; ligules (LI, × 1) narrow, 1–3 cm. long, firm; blades sharp-pointed, up to 90 cm. long, tightly inrolled, up to 6 mm. wide when opened out, rigid, closely ribbed above, with the ribs minutely and densely hairy, smooth beneath. Panicles spike-like, narrowly oblong to lanceolate-oblong, cylindrical, tapering upwards, pale, 7–22 cm. long, 1–2·5 cm. wide; branches erect; pedicels 1–4 mm. long.

Spikelets (S, × 4) narrowly oblong, or gaping, compressed, closely overlapping, 10–16 mm. long, 1-flowered, breaking up at maturity above the glumes. Glumes (G_1, G_2, × 3) persistent, narrow, pointed or blunt, equal or slightly unequal, minutely rough on the sides and on the keels, firm; lower mostly 1-nerved; upper 3-nerved. Lemma (F, L, × 3) lanceolate, blunt, keeled, 8–12 mm. long, firm, 5–7-nerved, minutely rough, bearing a projecting point 0·2–0·8 mm. long near the apex, surrounded at the base with fine white hairs 3–5 mm. long. Palea (P, × 3) nearly as long as the lemma, 2–4-nerved. Anthers (FL, × 3) 4–7 mm. long. Grain (CE, CH, × 3) enclosed by the hardened lemma and palea. *Ch. no.* 2n = 28.

A common grass of sand-dunes round the coasts of the British Isles, often very abundant and usually the dominant plant; sometimes growing in association with Lyme Grass, Sand Fescue, and Sand Couch. Widespread along the coasts of W. Europe; introduced into N. America and Australia. Also known as Sea Mat-grass, and in the United States as European Beach-grass. Flowering: end of June to August.

Marram Grass is most valuable as a binder and consolidator of drifting sand. It has been extensively and very effectively planted for this purpose, both in the British Isles and overseas. Its rhizomes spread rapidly through loose sand, rooting and branching at the nodes, and giving rise to erect shoots. These are capable of growing up through increasing layers of sand, their leaves and culms breaking the force of the wind and causing the blown sand to be deposited.

It hybridizes with *Calamagrostis epigejos*, the sterile hybrid (× *Ammocalamagrostis baltica*, p. 285) occurring at a few points on the coasts of Britain. The N. American, *Ammophila breviligulata* Fernald, with a short truncate ligule, has been planted on some British sand-dunes.

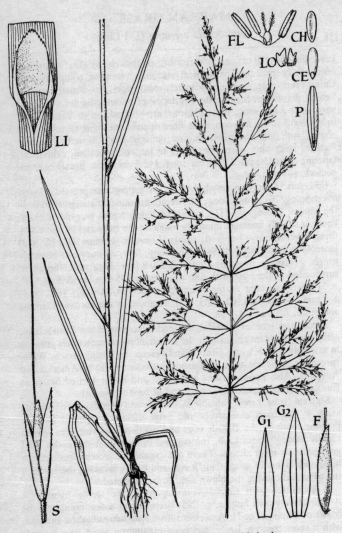

LI

FL CH

LO CE

P

G₁ G₂ F

S

Apera spica-venti. Locally common; arable land.

LOOSE SILKY-BENT
Apera spica-venti (L.) Beauv.

Annual, 20–100 cm. high. Culms tufted or solitary, erect, or kneed at
the base, slender to relatively stout, 3–5-noded below the middle,
smooth. Leaves hairless; sheaths smooth, or rough near the apex, green
or purple; ligules (LI, × 3) oblong, 3–10 mm. long, membranous; blades
pointed, flat, 7–25 cm. long, 3–10 mm. wide, rough all over, or smooth
beneath, green. Panicles ovate to oblong, usually open and very diffuse,
or sometimes appearing congested, much-branched, 10–25 cm. long,
3–15 cm. wide, green or purplish; branches usually numerous,
spreading, very fine, rough; pedicels 1–3 mm. long.

Spikelets (S, × 10) scattered, narrowly oblong, mostly 2·5–3 mm.
long, 1-flowered, breaking up at maturity, Glumes (G_1, G_2, × 10)
slightly to markedly unequal, finely pointed, rough on the keels above
the middle, membranous; lower three-fourths or more the length of the
upper, narrowly lanceolate, 1-nerved; upper oblong-lanceolate, 3-
nerved. Lemma (F, part of awn removed, × 10) as long as the upper
glume or slightly shorter, rounded on the back, lanceolate-oblong, and
pointed in side view, minutely rough above the middle, minutely
bearded at the base, firmly membranous, finely 5-nerved, awned from
near the tip, with the fine straight or flexuous awn 5–10 mm. long. Palea
(P, × 10) as long as the lemma or slightly shorter, 2-nerved. Anthers
(FL, × 6) 1–2 mm. long. Grain (CE, CH, × 6) tightly enclosed between
the hardened lemma and palea. *Ch. no.* 2n = 14.

A doubtful native, probably introduced long ago with seeds of cereals,
now well established and widely distributed in England, especially on
sandy or light loam soils in the eastern, south-eastern, and southern
counties, where it is often frequent as a weed on arable land; elsewhere
less common and mostly on waste ground; uncommon to rare in Wales
and Scotland. Also throughout Europe and northern Asia; introduced
into N. America. Also known as Wind Grass. Flowering: June to early
August.

In fields of cereals this grass is occasionally very abundant, so much
so that it may become a serious pest, depriving the crops of moisture
and nutriment. The seeds are very small and light, being produced in
large numbers from each panicle and shed before the corn matures. For
these reasons it spreads rapidly on suitable soils, especially when several
cereal crops are taken in succession, so that weeding is not possible. As
it has such elegant panicles it is sometimes cultivated in gardens the
panicles being dried for winter decoration or for bouquets.

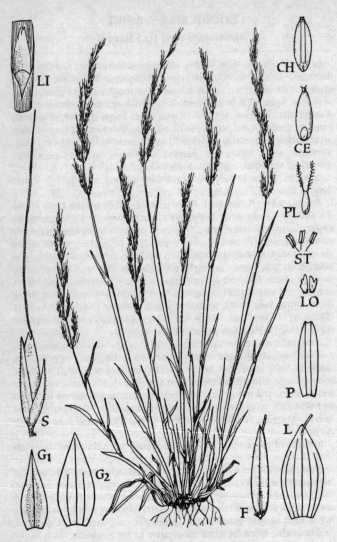

Apera interrupta. Rare; local; East Anglia, etc.

DENSE SILKY-BENT
Apera interrupta (L.) Beauv.

Annual, 10–70 cm. high. Culms tufted or solitary, erect, or bent at the base, slender, 2–4-noded below the middle, smooth. Leaves green, or with purple sheaths, the latter smooth; ligules (LI, × 3) oblong, 2–5 mm. long, membranous; blades pointed, up to 12 cm. long, but usually much shorter, 1–4 mm. wide, flat, or rolled when dry, minutely hairy or rough on the nerves above, smooth beneath except towards the tip. Panicles erect, contracted, more or less interrupted below, continuous and moderately dense above, 3–20 cm. long, 4–15 mm. (rarely more) wide, green, or purplish; branches erect or slightly spreading, bearing spikelets close to the base, rough; pedicels 0·5–2 mm. long.

Spikelets (S, × 10) narrowly oblong, 2–2·5 mm. long, 1-flowered, breaking up at maturity. Glumes (G_1, G_2, × 10) persistent, unequal, pointed, membranous, rough on the keel above the middle; lower lanceolate, 1·5–2 mm. long, 1-nerved; upper broader, 3-nerved, about as long as the spikelet. Lemma (F, L, part of awn removed, × 10) from slightly shorter to slightly longer than the upper glume, rounded on the back, lanceolate-oblong and pointed in side view, firmly membranous, finely 5-nerved, minutely rough above the middle, minutely hairy at the base, awned from near the tip; the very fine straight awn 4–10 mm. long. Palea (P, × 10) about three-fourths the length of the lemma. Anthers (ST, × 10) 0·3–0·4 mm. long. Grain (CE, CH, × 10) enclosed by the lemma and palea. *Ch. no.* 2n = 14.

A slender grass of dry sandy soils, locally frequent in parts of W. Norfolk and W. Suffolk. In this area of East Anglia, mainly Breckland, it may be native although there is a possibility that it was introduced in early times with seeds of cereals from Central Europe. It grows in disturbed soil on heaths, in poor thin grassland, in sandpits, and on roadsides; of rare occurrence in a few widely scattered localities from Yorkshire and Lancashire southwards to Berkshire. Also W., S., and Central Europe; Asiatic Russia; introduced to N. America. Flowering: June, July.

Distinguished from *A. spica-venti* by its contracted, usually dense, or interrupted panicles, and very small anthers. *A. intermedia* Hack., a native of S.W. Asia, has been found in a few places in England and Scotland; it differs from *A. interrupta* in the glumes being very short-awned and in its larger (1·5 mm.) anthers.

The genus *Apera* has been included in *Agrostis*, from which it differs by the firmer long-awned lemma, which is about as long as the glumes, with the awn arising from near the tip.

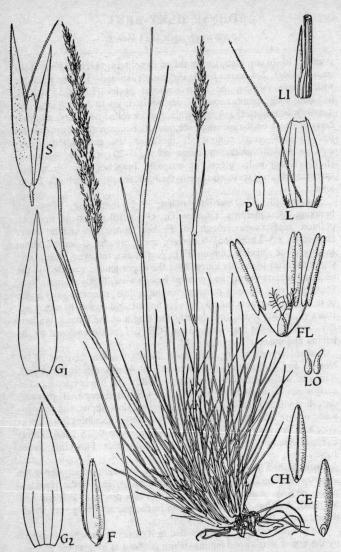

Labels on figure: S, LI, L, P, G₁, FL, LO, G₂, F, CH, CE

Agrostis setacea. Locally common, S.W. England; heaths, moors.

BRISTLE-LEAVED BENT
Agrostis setacea Curt.

A densely tufted perennial, 10–60 cm. high, with numerous slender vegetative shoots, growing in isolated tufts, or forming a close turf. Culms erect, or sometimes bent below, very slender, 2–3-noded, rough towards the nodes and panicles. Leaves hairless; sheaths rounded on the back, slightly rough, the basal straw-coloured; ligules (LI, × 5) narrow, 2–4 mm. long, membranous; blades very fine, bristle-like, finely pointed, the basal up to 20 cm. long, usually much shorter, erect or flexuous, grooved above, 0·2–0·3 mm. wide, green or greyish-green, minutely rough. Panicles erect, narrowly oblong or lanceolate, 3–10 cm. long, 5–15 mm. wide, dense and spike-like before and after flowering, purple or green; branches clustered, divided, minutely rough; pedicels 1–4 mm. long.

Spikelets (S, × 12) lanceolate or narrowly oblong, 3–4 mm. long, 1-flowered, breaking up at maturity above the glumes. Glumes (G_1, G_2, × 12) persistent, lanceolate, finely pointed, rounded on the back below, keeled above, firmly membranous, minutely rough, unequal, the upper three-fourths of the length to nearly as long as the lower, 1-nerved, or the upper 3-nerved. Lemma (L, F, × 12) about two-thirds the length of the glumes, ovate-oblong, very blunt, thin, minutely bearded at the base, finely 5-nerved, with the outer nerves produced at the tip into minute points, awned from near the base, with the very fine awn up to 5 mm. long, projecting from the glumes. Palea (P, × 12) very small. Anthers (FL, × 12) 1·5–2 mm. long. Grain (CE, CH, × 12) 1·5 mm. long, covered by the thin lemma. *Ch. no.* 2n = 14.

This fine-leaved bent-grass is restricted to the southern and south-western counties of England, from Berkshire, Surrey, and Sussex westwards to Cornwall, and to Glamorgan in South Wales; on dry sandy and peaty heaths and moors; locally often very abundant and sometimes becoming the dominant grass; ascending to 425 m. on Exmoor and to 610 m. on Dartmoor. Also in S.W. Europe (France, Spain, and Portugal). Flowering: June and July.

The species of *Agrostis* may be recognized by the following characters: spikelets small, 1-flowered, borne in panicles; glumes narrow, as long as the spikelet, equal or slightly unequal, with the upper shorter, 1–3-nerved; lemmas shorter and thinner than the glumes, 3–5-nerved, awned or awnless, minutely hairy at the base or hairless.

(*Agrostis curtsii*, Kerguélen)

293

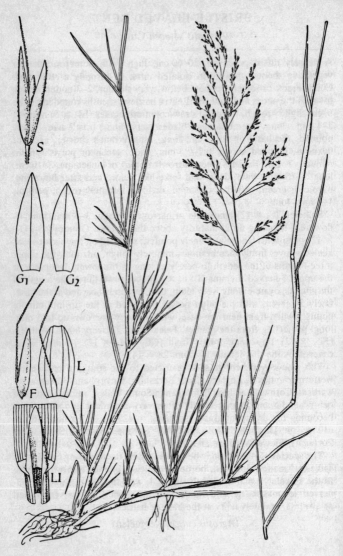

Agrostis canina subsp. *canina*. Common; damp grassland.

VELVET BENT

Agrostis canina L. subsp. *canina*

A tufted perennial, 15–75 cm. high, with slender creeping stolons, rooting at the nodes and producing there tufts of fine leafy shoots, and eventually forming a rather close turf. Culms erect, or more often ascending from a bent or prostrate base, sometimes branching and rooting in the lower part, slender, 2–4-noded, smooth. Leaves bright green or grey-green, hairless; sheaths rounded on the back, rough upwards, or usually smooth; ligules (LI, × 6) often pointed, 2–4 mm. long, membranous; blades finely pointed, 2–15 cm. long, flat or rolled, 1–3 mm. wide, soft, finely ribbed above, rough. Panicles lanceolate to broadly ovate, usually rather loose and open, or becoming somewhat dense, erect or nodding, 3–16 cm. long, up to 7 cm. wide, purplish, reddish, or green; branches clustered, hair-like, bare in the lower part, divided above, minutely rough, spreading when in flower; pedicels 1–3 mm. long.

Spikelets (S, × 12) lanceolate or narrowly oblong, 1·7–3 mm. long, 1-flowered, breaking up above the glumes at maturity. Glumes (G₁, G₂, × 12) persistent, lanceolate, pointed, 1-nerved, membranous, the lower as long as the spikelet, minutely rough on the keel, the upper slightly shorter, rough only near the tip. Lemma (F, L, × 12) two-thirds the length of the glumes, ovate-oblong, blunt, very thin, 4–5-nerved, minutely hairy at the base, awned from near the base, with the bent awn projecting from the glumes or often awnless. Palea minute. Anthers 1–1·5 mm. long. Grain enclosed by the thin lemma. *Ch. no.* 2n = 14.

A fine-leaved grass of damp or wet places, widely distributed in the British Isles; in low-lying meadows, ditches, hollows, pond-margins, swamps, and marshy ground; often growing with rushes; occasional in open woodland on heavy soils; locally abundant. Also throughout Europe, in temperate Asia and N.E. America. Flowering: end of June to August.

On account of its short, soft, green growth, Velvet Bent has been used as a lawn grass. It may be separated from Brown Bent (*A. canina* subsp. *montana*) by its creeping leafy stolons which form a close carpet, whereas plants of the latter subspecies form dense tufts, have stiffer leaves, and spread by underground scaly rhizomes. *Agrostis tenuis* differs in its shorter blunt ligule, very loose open panicle, usually awnless spikelets, and the larger palea. *A. stolonifera* has a blunt ligule, much denser panicles, awnless spikelets, and a longer palea.

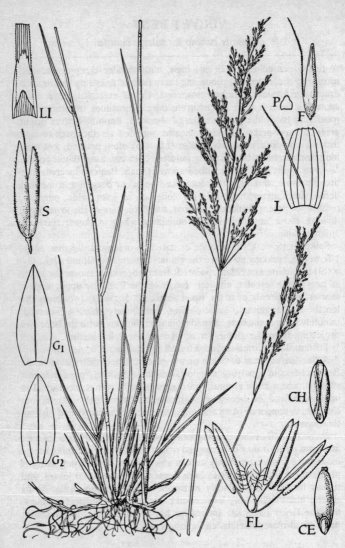

Agrostis canina subsp. montana. Common; dry grassland.

BROWN BENT

Agrostis canina L. subsp. *montana* (Hartm.) Hartm.

A densely tufted perennial, 10–60 cm. high, with slender creeping scaly rhizomes. Culms erect or bent at the base, slender, 1–2-noded, smooth. Leaves green or greyish-green, hairless; sheaths rounded on the back, smooth; ligules (LI, × 3) membranous, 1–5 mm. long, the uppermost pointed; blades finely pointed, 2–15 cm. long, flat or rolled, 1–3 mm. wide, firm, sometimes bristle-like, closely nerved above, rough on both sides, or smooth beneath. Panicles usually contracted and somewhat dense before and after flowering, lanceolate to oblong or narrowly ovate, 2–20 cm. long, green, purplish, or brownish; branches clustered, hair-like, mostly erect, rough, divided above the naked base; pedicels 0·5–2 mm. long.

Spikelets (S, × 12) rather closely clustered, lanceolate to narrowly oblong, 2–3·3 mm. long, 1-flowered, breaking up at maturity above the glumes. Glumes (G_1, G_2, × 12) persistent, as long as the spikelet, equal or slightly unequal with the upper shorter, membranous, 1-nerved, or the upper 3-nerved, the lower rough on the keel, the upper smooth or nearly so. Lemma (F, L, × 12) about three-fourths the length of the glumes, ovate or ovate-oblong, very blunt, thin, minutely rough, 4–5-nerved, minutely hairy at the base, with a fine bent awn 2–4·5 mm. long on the back near the base or in the lower third, or awnless. Palea (P, × 12) minute. Anthers (FL, × 12) 1–1·8 mm. long. Grain (CE, CH, × 12) enclosed by the thin lemma. *Ch. no.* 2n = 28.

Brown Bent is widespread in the British Isles, being abundant on heaths, hill, and mountain grassland; on sandy or peaty soils; frequently associated with *Agrostis tenuis* but usually less common. Distributed through Europe and temperate Asia. Usually known as *A. canina* var. *arida* Schlechtd. Flowering: June to August.

A drought-resistant lawn grass, spreading by its rhizomes to form a fine compact turf. Like other widely distributed grasses it is rather variable; the awn of the lemma is occasionally absent, whilst the spikelets are larger (3–4 mm.) in plants from high elevations. The spikelets are sometimes diseased, the ovaries being infected by a nematode (*Anguillina agrostis*) which causes elongation of the lemmas, or by a smut (*Tilletia decipiens*) when the plants are stunted. Male-sterile hybrids between *A. canina* subsp. *montana* and *A. tenuis* and *A. stolonifera* may be found where they grow together; the hybrids are more or less inter-mediate in structure between their parents.

(*Agrostis vinealis* Schreber)

297

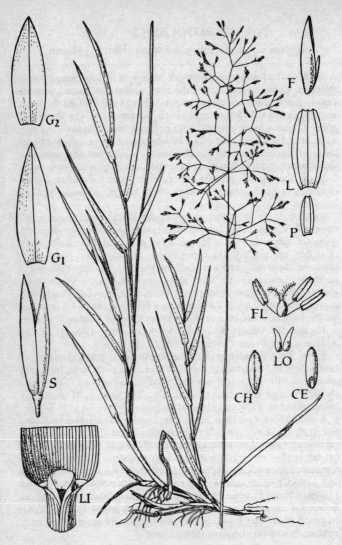

Agrostis tenuis. Very common; grassland.

298

COMMON BENT OR BROWN TOP
Agrostis tenuis Sibth.

A tufted perennial, 10–70 cm. high, spreading by short rhizomes and sometimes by stolons, forming a loose or dense turf. Culms erect or spreading, slender, 2–5-noded, usually smooth. Leaves green, hairless; sheaths rounded on the back, smooth; ligules (LI, × 6) 0·5–2 mm. long, mostly shorter than broad, membranous; blades finely pointed, 1–15 cm. (or more) long, flat, or inrolled, 1–5 mm. wide, soft to stiff, rough or nearly smooth. Panicles oblong to ovate or pyramidal, open and very loose, rarely somewhat dense, erect or slightly nodding, 1–20 cm. long, 1–12 cm. wide, green or purplish; main-axis smooth, or rough above; branches clustered, spreading, hair-like, bare in the lower part, divided above, smooth or rough; pedicels 1–3 mm. long.

Spikelets (S, × 12) lanceolate to narrowly oblong, 2–3·5 mm. long, 1-flowered, breaking up at maturity above the glumes. Glumes (G_1, G_2, × 12) persistent, equal or slightly unequal (the upper shorter), as long as the spikelet, lanceolate, finely pointed, membranous except for the thinner margins, 1-nerved, the lower slightly rough on the keel above the middle. Lemma (F, L, × 12) two-thirds to three-fourths the length of the spikelet, ovate or elliptic, blunt, 3–5-nerved, very thin, minutely hairy at the base, awnless, or rarely with a short awn on the back. Palea (P, ×12) half to two-thirds the length of the lemma. Anthers (FL, × 6) 1–1·5 mm. long. Grain (CE, CH, × 12) enclosed by the thin lemma and palea. *Ch. no.* 2n = 28.

Common Bent is abundant and widely distributed in the British Isles; on heaths, moorlands, pastures, waste ground, etc., from sea-level to about 1220 m.; on a wide range of soils from sands to clays, but especially prevalent on poor dry acid types. Throughout Europe and temperate Asia; introduced and established in N. and S. America, Australia, and New Zealand. Male-sterile hybrids between this species and *A. canina*, *A. gigantea*, and *A. stolonifera* have been recorded. Known also as Fine, New Zealand, or Colonial Bent. Flowering: end of June to August.

Large areas of permanent grassland, particularly on poorer soils, on hills and mountains, are dominated by this grass. It is of relatively low agricultural value except in the aforementioned situations where high-class grazing grasses do not flourish. For fine lawns, putting and bowling greens, Common Bent forms a short even turf used alone, or with Chewings Fescue or other lawn grasses. It is extensively sown for this purpose in the British Isles, our main source of seed now being the United States and Europe.

A recent introduction in amenity grass seed-mixtures is *Agrostis castellana*, described on p. 372.

(described on p. 372.)

(*Agrostis capillaris* L.)

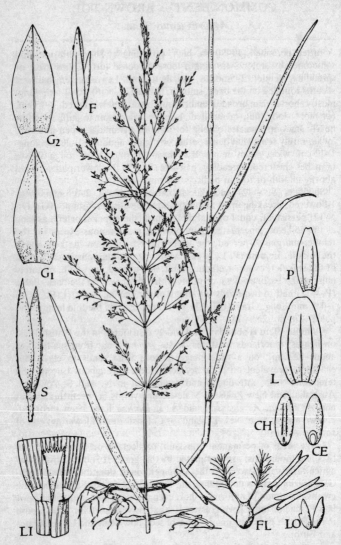

Agrostis gigantea. Common; arable and waste land, etc.

BLACK BENT or RED TOP
Agrostis gigantea Roth

A loosely tufted perennial, 40–120 cm. high, with tough creeping rhizomes. Culms erect, or ascending from a curved or procumbent base, rooting and branching from the lower nodes, slender to stout, 3–6-noded, smooth. Leaves dull green, hairless; sheaths rounded on the back, smooth or roughish; ligules (LI, × 3) very blunt, 1·5–6 mm. long, toothed, membranous; blades finely pointed, 5–20 cm. long, 2–8 mm. wide, rolled when young, afterwards flat, firm, rough. Panicles erect, oblong to ovate, usually open and very loose, 8–25 cm. long, 3–15 cm. wide, much-branched, green or purplish; branches clustered, spreading, divided above the naked base, rough; pedicels 0·5–3 mm. long.

Spikelets (S, × 12) very numerous, lanceolate to oblong, 2–3 mm. long, 1-flowered, breaking up above the glumes at maturity. Glumes (G$_1$, G$_2$, × 12) persistent, lanceolate in side view, finely pointed, as long as the spikelet, equal or slightly unequal with the upper shorter, membranous, 1-nerved, rough on the keels. Lemma (F, L, × 12) two-thirds to three-fourths the length of the glumes, ovate-oblong or oblong, very blunt, 3–5-nerved, minutely hairy at the base, thin, awnless, rarely with a short awn from or near the tip. Palea (P, × 12) half to two-thirds the length of the lemma. Anthers (FL, × 12) 1–1·5 mm. long. Grain (CE, CH, × 12) enclosed by the delicate lemma and palea. *Ch. no.* 2n = 42.

Widely distributed in the lowland districts of the British Isles. Owing to confusion with other species of *Agrostis* its complete range is not known, but it is of frequent occurrence in England, less common to rare in Wales, Scotland, and Ireland; in open woodlands, rough grassland, hedgerows, roadsides, waste ground, and as a bad weed on arable land, particularly on light sandy or gravelly soils. Also in most parts of Europe, temperate Asia; introduced into N. America, etc. Flowering: late June to August.

Agrostis gigantea and *A. stolonifera* are sometimes called incorrectly *A. alba* L. Both species are similar to *A. tenuis* in being of rather low agricultural value. *A. gigantea* is cultivated for hay and as a soil-binder in the United States, and has been sown on sports-grounds and on road-sides in the British Isles, but its cultivation here is not recommended on account of it becoming a pest on arable land. It differs from *A. tenuis* in its longer ligules and larger leaf-blades, and from *A. stolonifera* by its rhizomes and very loose panicles. Male-sterile hybrids with *A. tenuis* (*Ch. no.* 2n = 35) and *A. stolonifera* have been recorded.

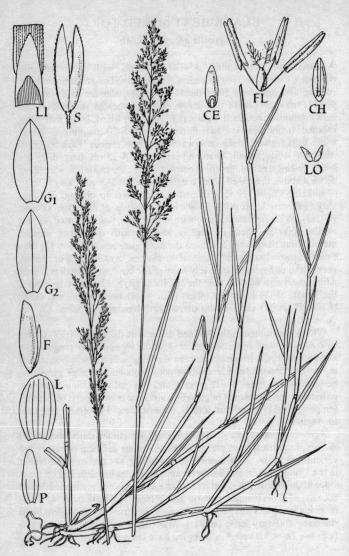

Agrostis stolonifera. ∇ery common; grassland, etc.

CREEPING BENT
Agrostis stolonifera L.

A tufted perennial, 8–40 cm. high, spreading by leafy stolons and forming a close turf. Culms erect or ascending from a bent or prostrate base, rooting from the lower nodes, slender, 2–5-noded, smooth. Leaves green, greyish-, or bluish-green, hairless; sheaths rounded on the back, mostly smooth; ligules (LI, × 3) blunt, 1–6 mm. long, membranous; blades finely pointed, 1–10 cm. long, rolled when young, afterwards flat, 0·5–5 mm. wide, closely nerved, minutely rough. Panicles linear to lanceolate, or oblong, 1–13 cm. long, 0·4–2·5 cm. wide, open in flower, afterwards contracted and often dense, or only loose below, frequently lobed, green, whitish, or purplish; branches clustered, closely divided, rough pedicels 0·5–2 mm. long.

Spikelets (S, × 12) densely clustered, lanceolate to narrowly oblong, 2–3 mm. long, 1-flowered, breaking up above the glumes at maturity. Glumes (G$_1$, G$_2$, × 12) persistent, as long as the spikelet, equal or slightly unequal, narrowly lanceolate to oblong-lanceolate in side view, pointed, membranous, 1-nerved, rough upwards on the keels. Lemma (F, L, × 12) up to three-fourths the length of the glumes, ovate or oblong, very blunt, finely 5-nerved, thin, usually awnless, rarely with a short awn from near the tip. Palea (P, × 12) up to two-thirds the length of the lemma. Anthers (FL, × 12) 1–1·5 mm. long. Grain (CE, CH, × 12) enclosed by the delicate lemma and palea. *Ch. no.* 2n = 28, 42.

An extremely variable grass, frequent to very common in the British Isles in a wide range of situations; in lowland and hill grassland, salt-marshes, on chalk-downs, roadsides, inland and coastal sands, on cliffs, in open woodland, and as a weed on cultivated land; on light or heavy soils; from sea-level to 760 m. Also called Fiorin or White Bent. Throughout Europe, temperate Asia, N. America; introduced into Australia, New Zealand, S. America etc. Hybrids with *A. canina, A. gigantea,* and *A. tenuis* have been recorded. Flowering: July and August.

Dwarf varieties, such as those found in sea-marsh turf, are used in the formation of lawns. Marsh Bent, *A. stolonifera* var. *palustris* (Huds.) Farw. (*A. palustris* Huds.), is widespread in wet places in the lowlands. It has extensively creeping stolons which mat loosely together and do not form a turf as in typical *A. stolonifera* (i.e. var. *stolonifera*). Its culms are 20–60 cm. high; leaf-blades 6–20 cm. long, 3–7 mm. wide; ligules up to 8 mm. long; panicles lanceolate to narrowly ovate, 8–30 cm. long, up to 10 cm. wide; spikelets 2·5–3·5 mm. long.

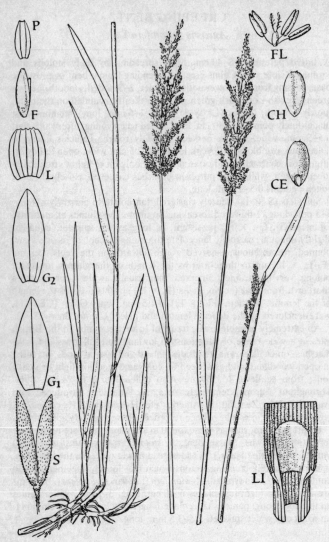

Agrostis semiverticillata. Rare; introduced.

WATER BENT

Agrostis semiverticillata (Forsk.) C. Christ.

Perennial or annual, loosely tufted, 10–60 cm. high, with long trailing stolons, rooting from the nodes. Culms ascending from a bent or prostrate base, slender, often branching in the lower part, smooth. Leaves greyish-green or green, hairless; sheaths rounded on the back, rather loose, smooth; ligules (LI, × 4) blunt, 1·5–6 mm. long, membranous; blades pointed, 3–18 cm. long, 2–10 mm. wide, flat, closely nerved, rough. Panicles erect, ovate to oblong, dense, lobed, sometimes interrupted below, 2–15 cm. long, 0·6–4 cm. wide, pale green or purplish; branches clustered, closely divided, crowded with spikelets mostly right to the base, rough; pedicels very short, jointed on the branches.

Spikelets (S, × 12) very numerous, oblong, awnless, 1·7–2·2 mm. long, 1-flowered, falling at maturity with the pedicel attached. Glumes (G_1, G_2, × 12) equal, as long as the spikelet, oblong or elliptic and blunt when opened out, rounded on the back below, keeled above the middle, minutely rough, 1-nerved, or the upper 3-nerved, firmly membranous. Lemmas (F, L, × 12) about half the length of the glumes, rounded on the back, broadly elliptic, with a very blunt minutely toothed broad tip, smooth, finely 5-nerved, thin. Palea (P, × 12) nearly as long as the lemma and similar in texture, 2-nerved. Anthers (FL, × 12) 0·5–0·7 mm. long. Grain (CE, CH, × 12) pale brown, 1 mm. long, enclosed by the thin lemma and palea. *Ch. no.* 2n = 28.

A native of wet places in the Mediterranean Region and N.E. Africa; naturalized in the Channel Islands; occasionally introduced into England, and found on rubbish tips, waste and cultivated ground. Introduced into N. and S. America, Australia, and S. Africa. Flowering: June to August.

A male-sterile hybrid, intermediate in structure between its parents, *Agrostis stolonifera* and *A. semiverticillata*, has been found on the coastal sands of Guernsey.

The other British species of *Agrostis* differ from Water Bent in their pedicels and glumes persisting on the branches at maturity, in the markedly unequal lemma and palea, and in the larger anthers. Water Bent resembles *Polypogon* in its pedicels being articulated and falling attached to the mature spikelet and in its epidermal structure, but this genus may be readily distinguished by the 2-notched or 2-lobed and awned tips of the glumes.

A. avenacea J. F. Gmel. of Australia and New Zealand is occasionally introduced with 'shoddy' from wool; it differs from our native species by its very loose panicles and hairy lemmas.

(*Polypogon viridis* (Gouan) Breistr.)

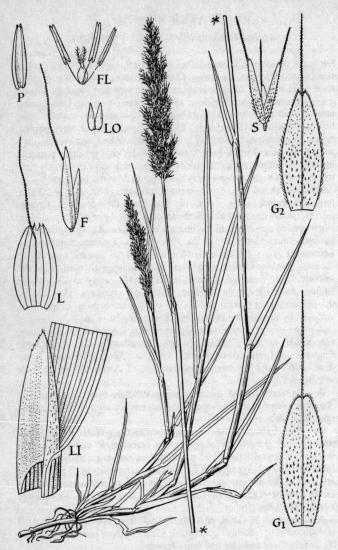

P

FL

LO

S

F

G₂

L

LI

G₁

× *Agropogon littoralis.* Rare; salt-marshes.

PERENNIAL BEARD-GRASS

× *Agropogon littoralis* (Sm.) C. E. Hubbard

Perennial, loosely tufted or creeping, 8–60 cm. high. Culms kneed at the base and then erect, or ascending from a prostrate many-noded base, usually branched in the lower part, slender, smooth. Leaves hairless, greyish-green; sheaths smooth; ligules (LI, × 5) blunt, becoming toothed, 3–7 mm. long, membranous; blades finely pointed, flat, 3–20 cm. long, 2–11 mm. wide, rough towards the tips, or all over. Panicles erect, moderately to very dense, lanceolate to narrowly ovate, or oblong, more or less lobed, 2–18 cm. long, 0·6–7 cm. wide, green or purplish; branches closely divided, rough; pedicels very short.

Spikelets (S, × 6) persistent, narrowly oblong, or gaping, 2–3 mm. long, laterally compressed, 1-flowered. Glumes (G_1, G_2, × 12) similar, narrowly oblong or elliptic, narrowed upwards, minutely notched at the tip, rounded on the back below, keeled above, membranous, 1-nerved, rough-pointed, especially in the lower half, awned from the tip, with the fine straight awn up to about 2 mm. long. Lemma (F, L, × 12) between half and two-thirds the length of the glumes, elliptic-oblong, with a very blunt minutely toothed tip, smooth, very thin, obscurely 5-nerved, awned from the back just below the tip, with the awn up to 3 mm. long. Palea (P, × 12) about three-fourths the length of the lemma, finely 2-nerved. Anthers (FL, × 12) about 1 mm. long. *Ch. no.* 2n = 28.

A rare intergeneric hybrid sometimes known as *Polypogon × littoralis* Sm., resulting from the crossing of *Polypogon monspeliensis* with *Agrostis stolonifera*. Found on a few muddy salt-marshes of S. England, from Dorset to Norfolk, in Gloucestershire and Glamorgan; also in France. Flowering: end of June to September.

A rather variable grass, usually decidedly perennial, like the *Agrostis* parent, but occasionally with few vegetative shoots and resembling an annual. It varies considerably in vigour, perhaps owing to the *Polypogon* hybridizing with different varieties of the *Agrostis*, or alternatively it may be as a result of growth under poor or good habitat conditions. The hybrid differs from both parents in being male-sterile, its anthers remaining closed and being devoid of good pollen. From the *Polypogon* it may be distinguished by its habit, persistent spikelets, less blunt short-awned glumes, and the awn from the back of the lemma. It may be separated from the *Agrostis* by its awned and minutely notched rough-pointed glumes, and by the awned lemma. Sometimes known incorrectly as *Polypogon lutosus* (Poir.) Hitchc.

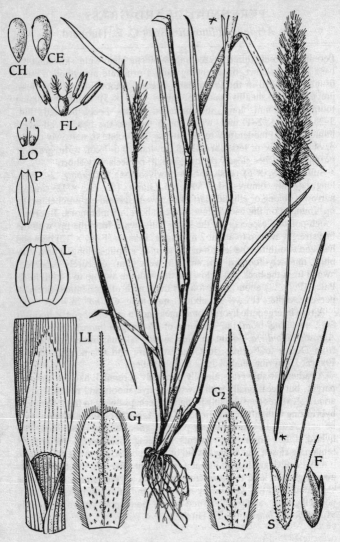

CH CE

FL

LO

P

L

LI

G₁

G₂

S

F

Polypogon monspeliensis. Uncommon; salt-marshes.

ANNUAL BEARD-GRASS
Polypogon monspeliensis (L.) Desf.

Annual, 6–80 cm. high. Culms in small tufts, or solitary, erect, or kneed towards the base, slender to somewhat stout, 3–6-noded, usually branched near the base, rough beneath the panicle, or smooth. Leaves hairless, green; sheaths smooth, or rough upwards, the upper somewhat inflated; ligules (LI, × 4) oblong, toothed, 3–15 mm. long, membranous; blades pointed, flat, mostly 5–15 cm. long, and 2–8 mm. wide, but longer on big plants, rough on the nerves. Panicles very dense, covered with fine bristles, narrowly ovate to narrowly oblong, cylindrical or sometimes lobed, 1·5–16 cm. long, 1–3·5 cm. wide, pale, green, or yellowish; branches closely divided; pedicels very short, jointed.

Spikelets (S, × 6) narrowly oblong, 2–3 mm. long, 1-flowered, falling entire at maturity with a minute piece of the pedicel. Glumes (G_1, G_2, × 12) similar, rounded on the back below, keeled above, narrowly oblong when opened out, blunt and slightly notched at the apex, rough with minute points especially in the lower part, minutely hairy on the margins, 1-nerved, awned from the tip, with the fine straight awn 4–7 mm. long. Lemma (F, L, × 12) about half the length of the glumes, very smooth and shining, broadly elliptic, with a broad blunt minutely toothed tip, very thin, obscurely 5-nerved, awnless, or with an awn up to 2 mm. long from the tip. Palea (P, × 12) slightly shorter than the lemma. Anthers (FL, × 12) 0·4–0·7 mm. long. Grain (CE, CH, × 12) enclosed by the lemma and palea. *Ch. no.* 2n = 28.

Growing naturally in damp brackish pastures and salt-marshes here and there along the coasts of southern and southern-eastern England and the Channel Islands, and a chance introduction on waste land and rubbish tips near ports; occasionally escaping from garden cultivation. Rather uncommon generally, though sometimes locally abundant, especially on the bare edges of pools, gullies, and ditches in maritime grasslands. Widespread in Europe, N. Africa, and Asia, extending to N.E. tropical and S. Africa; introduced into and now naturalized in most warm-temperate countries. Known in N. America as Rabbitfoot Grass. Flowering: June to August.

This species of Beard-grass is occasionally cultivated in gardens on account of its attractive silky panicles. It crosses with *Agrostis stolonifera* in its native habitats, producing the sterile hybrid known as × *Agropogon littoralis* (p. 307), which may be distinguished by its persistent spikelets, short-awned glumes, and barren stamens. *Polypogon maritimus* Willd., of the Mediterranean Region, with prominently 2-lobed glumes, is occasionally introduced.

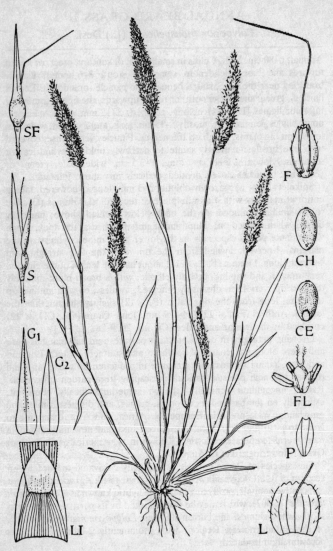

Gastridium ventricosum. Uncommon; grassland, arable land.

NIT GRASS

Gastridium ventricosum (Gouan) Schinz & Thell.

Annual, 10–60 cm. high. Culms loosely tufted or solitary, slender, erect, or bent at the base, 2–4-noded, smooth. Leaves green, hairless; sheaths rounded on the back, minutely rough upwards or smooth; ligules (LI, × 4) 1–3 mm. long, membranous; blades finely pointed, 2–10 cm. long, 2–4 mm. wide, flat, rough, or smooth except on margins. Panicles narrowly lanceolate to narrowly oblong, cylindrical, or tapering upwards, 2–10 cm. long, 5–12 mm. wide, open in flower, afterwards rather dense, pale green, shining; branches closely divided, rough; pedicels 0·5–2 mm. long.

Spikelets (S, SF, × 6) densely overlapping, narrowly oblong, 3–5 (mostly 4) mm. long, 1-flowered, breaking up above the glumes at maturity. Glumes (G_1, G_2, × 6) persistent, narrowly lanceolate, rounded on the back, hardened, shining, and swollen near the base, then slightly constricted, keeled, narrowed above and pointed, rough on the keels, 1-nerved, unequal, the lower as long as the spikelet, the upper three-fourths or more the length of the lower. Lemma (F, L, tip of awn removed, × 12) rounded on the back, broadly elliptic, with a blunt minutely toothed tip, about 1 mm. long, thin, finely 5-nerved, minutely hairy at the base, sparingly short-hairy on the sides, or hairless, awned from the back near the apex, or awnless, the awn very slender, bent at and twisted below the middle, 3–4 mm. long. Palea (P, × 12) as long as the lemma, 2-nerved. Anthers (FL, × 12) 0·6–0·8 mm. long. Grain (CE, CH, × 12) tightly enclosed between the lemma and palea. *Ch. no.* 2n = 14.

Formerly, locally abundant in cornfields on light or heavy soils and as a weed of waste land in S. England and Wales, from Cornwall, Glamorgan, and Gloucestershire eastwards to Kent, Essex, Suffolk and Norfolk. Possibly native in short grassland on limestone and chalk, but now comparatively rare and confined to sites in Dorset and Hampshire. Also in S. Europe, from France and the Iberian Peninsula eastwards to the Balkan Peninsula, N.W. Africa, and Azores. Introduced to the Pacific and East coasts of the U.S.A. and to New Zealand. Flowering: June to August.

The spikelets may be awned or awnless, the two kinds occurring mixed in the same panicles. The lemmas with awns are hairy, whilst those without awns are usually quite hairless.

Gastridium phleoides (Nees & Meyen) C. E. Hubbard, of the Mediterranean Region and N.E. Africa, has been found on rubbish tips, in wool shoddy or as a weed. It has larger panicles (up to 18 cm. long) and spikelets (5–7·5 mm. long), whilst the awned lemmas are loosely to densely hairy and have awns up to 7 mm. long.

These grasses have no economic value.

311

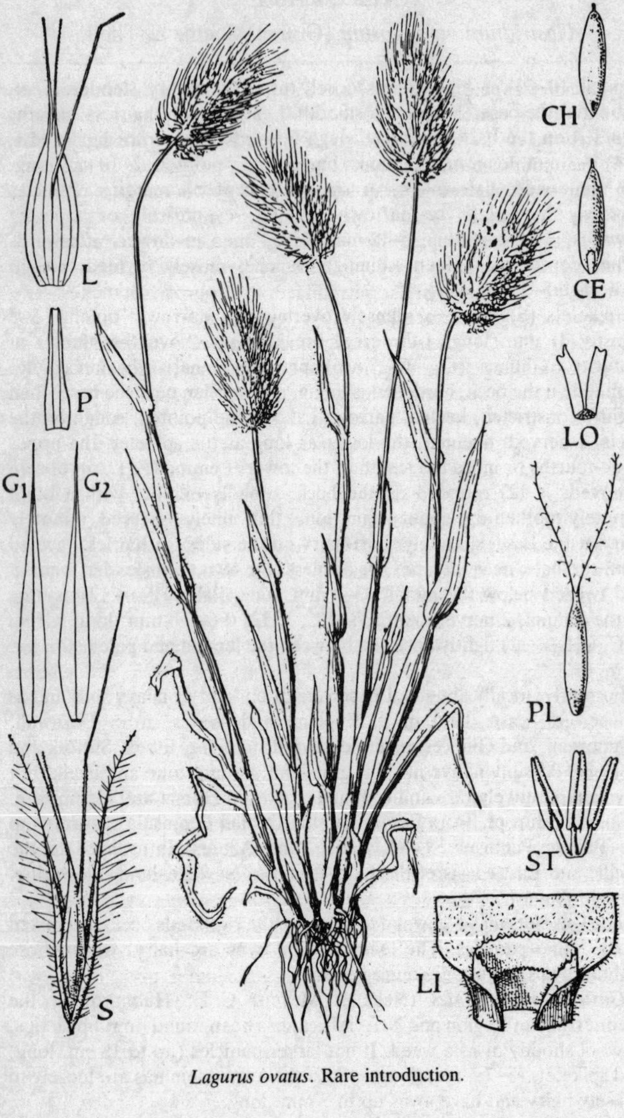
L
P
G1
G2
S
CH
CE
LO
PL
ST
LI

Lagurus ovatus. Rare introduction.

HARE'S-TAIL
Lagurus ovatus L.

A softly hairy annual, 5–60 cm. high. Culms solitary or tufted, erect, or ascending from a bent base, slender, few-noded, like the leaves loosely to densely hairy. Leaves greyish-green; sheaths loose, rounded on the back, the upper somewhat inflated; ligules (LI, × 3), blunt, up to 3 mm. long, membranous, hairy; blades linear to narrowly lanceolate, pointed, 1–20 cm. long and 2–14 mm. wide depending on the size of the plant, flat, velvety. Panicles spike-like, dense, globose to ovoid or oblong-cylindrical, 1–7 cm. long, 0·6–2 cm. wide, very softly hairy, bristly, erect or at length nodding, pale, rarely tinged with purple; branches very short; pedicels 0·5–2 mm. long.

Spikelets (S, × 4) densely overlapping, narrow, 8–10 mm. long, 1-flowered, breaking up at maturity above the glumes. Glumes (G_1, G_2, × 4) persistent, equal, narrowly lanceolate, each tapering into a fine bristle, as long as the spikelet, thinly membranous, 1-nerved, closely hairy with fine spreading hairs. Lemma (L, × 4) rounded on the back, elliptic, 4–5 mm. long, narrowed into two teeth, with each tooth terminated by a fine straight bristle 3–5 mm. long, membranous, 5-nerved, hairy near the base, awned from the back in the upper third, the awn bent and twisted below the middle, 8–18 mm. long. Palea (P, × 4) narrow, shorter than the lemma, 2-keeled. Anthers (ST, × 5) 1·5–2 mm. long. Grain (CE, CH, × 6) 2·5–3 mm. long, enclosed by the hardened lemma and palea. *Ch. no.* 2n = 14.

A native of the Mediterranean Region, probably introduced into the Channel Islands, but now well established there in sandy places; occasional in the British Isles and mainly in S. England; on rubbish dumps, waste and cultivated land, in some localities becoming naturalized; sometimes escaping from cultivation. Introduced into N. and S. America, Australia, S. Africa, etc. Flowering: June to August.

A beautiful grass, frequently cultivated in gardens for ornamental purposes, the panicles also being dried and sometimes dyed with bright colours and used for winter decorations, bouquets, and for adorning confectionery. The seed, which is sold by florists and seedsmen, may be sown in pots in August and September and planted out in the spring, or sown thinly in the spring in patches in the open border, or in rows for drying. The flowering stems should be cut in dry weather, tied in small bunches and hung in a dark airy room until the stems are rigid.

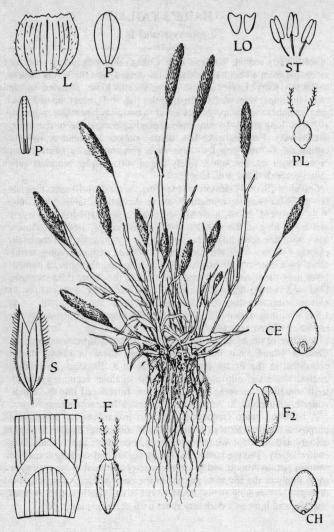

Phleum arenarium. Common; coastal dunes.

SAND CAT'S-TAIL
Phleum arenarium L.

Annual, 1–15 (or up to 30) cm. high. Culms tufted or solitary, erect, or bent at the base, very slender, stiff, 1–4-noded below the middle, smooth. Leaves hairless, whitish-green or pale green; sheaths rounded on the back, smooth, the uppermost somewhat inflated; ligules (LI, × 4) membranous, up to 7 mm. long; blades narrowed to a fine tip, 0·5–6 cm. long, up to 4 mm. wide, flat, closely nerved above, minutely rough on the margins. Panicles spike-like, very dense, narrowly cylindrical or abovoid, usually narrowed at the base, rounded at the tip, 0·5–5 cm. long, 3–7 mm. wide, pale green or whitish-green, sometimes tinged with purple; pedicels extremely short.

Spikelets (S, × 6) lanceolate to oblong, densely overlapping, 3–4 mm. long, flattened, 1-flowered, breaking up at maturity above the glumes. Glumes persistent, equal, as long as the spikelet, gradually narrowed into a sharply pointed rough tip, keeled, firmly membranous, 2–3-nerved, with short stiff spreading hairs on the keel above the middle. Lemma (L, × 12) about one-third the length of the glumes, rounded on the back, broad, very blunt, finely 5–7-nerved, membranous, minutely hairy. Palea (P, × 12) narrow, as long as the lemma. Anthers (ST, × 8) 0·3–1 mm. long. Grain (CE, CH, × 12) enclosed between the thin lemma and palea (F_2, × 12) *Ch. no.* 2n = 14.

A small stiff grass of sand-dunes and sandy shingles, widely distributed round the coasts of the British Isles, most frequent in England and sometimes locally very common, especially on the east coast; of rare occurrence on inland sandy soils. Generally distributed along or near the coasts of W. Europe from Sweden southwards, and in the Mediterranean. Known also as Sand Timothy. Flowering: May to July.

Three slender annual species of the Mediterranean Region, *Phleum paniculatum* Huds. (*P. asperum* Jacq.), *P. subulatum* (Savi) Aschers. & Graebn. (*P. tenue* Schrad.), and *P. exaratum* Griseb. (*P. graecum* Boiss. & Heldr.) occur occasionally on rubbish tips and port dumps in Britain. In the first the glumes are about 2 mm. long, hairless, widened, and swollen upwards and abruptly tipped with a minute point. In the second the glumes are about 3 mm. long, usually hairless, and narrowed to a pointed tip. The third resembles *P. arenarium*, but the cylindrical panicles are not narrowed at the base, the glumes are more finely pointed, and the anthers larger (about 2 mm. long).

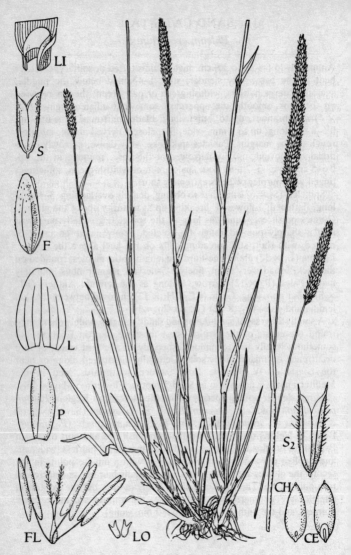

Phleum phleoides. Local; grasslands, S.E. England.

PURPLE-STEM CAT'S-TAIL
Phleum phleoides (L.) Karst.

A densely tufted perennial, 10–70 cm. high. Culms erect, or nearly so, slender, 2–3-noded below the middle, smooth, often purplish. Leaves hairless, greyish-green; sheaths smooth, rounded on the back; ligules (LI, × 4) very blunt, membranous, up to 2 mm. long; blades narrowed to a fine blunt tip, flat or rolled, 1–3·5 mm. wide, rough especially on the margins, the lower up to 12 cm. long, the upper much shorter. Panicles erect, very dense, spike-like, narrowly cylindrical, 1·5–10 cm. long, 4–6 mm. wide, green or purplish; pedicels extremely short.

Spikelets (S, S_2, × 6) oblong, densely overlapping, compressed, 2·5–3 mm. long, 1-flowered, breaking up above the glumes at maturity. Glumes persistent, similar, equal, as long as the spikelet, narrowly oblong, abruptly narrowed into a rough point up to 0·5 mm. long, keeled, rigid about the keels, the margins membranous, 3-nerved, rough (S), or with short stiff hairs on the keels (S_2). Lemma (F, L, × 12) two-thirds to three-fourths the length of the glumes, rounded on the back, ovate, blunt, firm, finely 5-nerved, minutely hairy or smooth. Palea (P, × 12) about as long as the lemma, oblong, 2-nerved. Anthers (FL, × 12) 1·5 mm. long. Grain (CE, CH, × 12) about 1·3 mm. long, enclosed in the hardened lemma and palea. *Ch. no.* 2n = 14, 28.

A native of dry sandy and chalky soils in S.E. England, confined to W. Norfolk, W. Suffolk, Cambridge, Bedford, Hertford, and Essex; locally abundant in some hill and downs grasslands, but generally rather uncommon. Widespread in Europe; extending to N. Asia and N.W. Africa. Known also as Boehmer's Cat's-tail and Pointed Cat's-tail. Flowering: June to August.

Phleum phleoides resembles *P. bertolonii* DC., but the latter may be distinguished by the usually swollen bases of its culms, longer ligules, wider leaf-blades, and the very blunt tips of the glumes.

The species of *Phleum* may be recognized by the following combination of characters: spikelets 1-flowered, compressed laterally, breaking up at maturity above the persistent glumes, borne on very short pedicels in dense spike-like panicles; glumes keeled, often with short-pointed or awned tips; lemma shorter than the glumes, awnless, membranous. In the genus *Alopecurus*, which possesses similar cylindrical but softer panicles, the spikelets fall entire at maturity, the glumes are often united by their margins in the lower part, and the lemma is usually awned on the back.

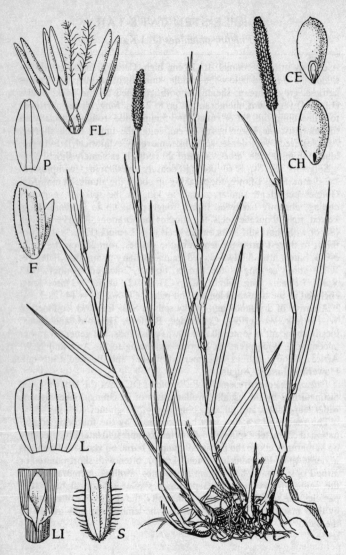

Phleum bertolonii. Common; grassland.

SMALL-LEAVED TIMOTHY-GRASS
Phleum bertolonii DC.

A loosely to compactly tufted perennial, 10–50 cm. high, sometimes with leafy stolons. Culms erect, or ascending from a bent or prostrate base, slender, stiff, smooth, 2–6-noded, the basal (1–2) internodes short, usually swollen or bulbous. Leaves green to greyish-green, hairless; sheaths rounded on the back, smooth, the basal becoming dark brown, the upper slightly inflated; ligules (LI, × 3) 1–4 mm. long, membranous; blades finely pointed, 3–12 cm. long, flat, 2–5 mm. wide, firm, minutely rough on the nerves and margins, or only on the latter. Panicles dense, spike-like, narrowly cylindrical, mostly 1–6 (rarely 8) cm. long and 3–5 mm. wide, pale- or whitish-green, or tinged with purple; pedicels extremely short.

Spikelets (S, × 6) oblong, tightly packed, flattened, 2–3 mm. long, 1-flowered, breaking up at maturity above the glumes. Glumes persistent, narrowly oblong, truncate, keeled, with a rough awn-point 0·4–1 mm. long, minutely rough or minutely hairy on the membranous sides, 3-nerved, the keels fringed with stiff white spreading hairs, and the margins of the lower glume softly hairy. Lemma (F, L, × 12) two-thirds to three-fourths the length of the glumes, very broad and blunt, membranous, 5–7-nerved, minutely hairy on the nerves. Palea (P, × 12) nearly as long as the lemma. Anthers (FL, × 12) 1–2 mm. long. Grain (CE, CH, × 12) enclosed by the thin lemma and palea.. *Ch. no.* 2n = 14.

An important constituent of old pastures, and of short-grass hill and downs grassland, on a wide range of soils from heavy clays to those of a calcareous or sandy nature. Found throughout the British Isles; generally common, particularly in England. Also in most parts of Europe from Scandinavia to Portugal and the Balkans. Known in the past as *P. nodosum* L., the type of which is a weak state of *P. pratense*. Flowering: June to August.

This native Timothy-Grass or Smaller Cat's-tail has usually been regarded as a variety of *Phleum pratense*, the common Timothy-grass, but whereas that is a robust plant with 42 chromosomes (2n), *P. bertolonii* is more slender and smaller in all its parts, and has only 14 chromosomes (2n). It comprises a large number of strains, differing mainly in their form of growth, from those that are almost prostrate and spread by creeping stolons to others stiffly erect. The British strains selected from our old grasslands on account of their leafy growth, high yield, great palatability to stock, and persistence, are very suitable for permanent pasture. They form a compact turf in association with other herbage plants.

(*Phleum pratense* subsp. *bertolonii* (DC.) Bornm.)

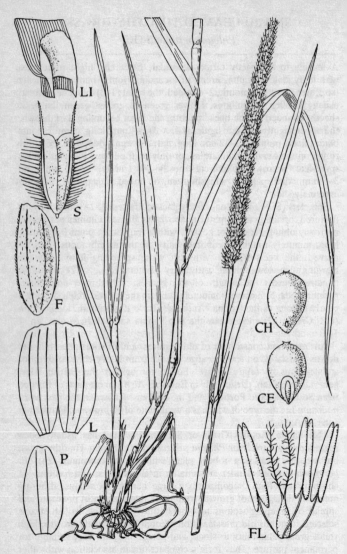

Phleum pratense. Common; grassland.

LARGE-LEAVED TIMOTHY-GRASS
Phleum pratense L.

A loosely to densely tufted perennial, 40–150 cm. high. Culms erect, or ascending from a bent base, mostly stout, 3–6-noded, smooth or nearly so, the basal 1–3 internodes very short and usually swollen or bulbous. Leaves hairless, green or greyish-green; sheaths smooth, rounded on the back, the basal becoming dark brown; ligules (LI, × 3) blunt, up to 6 mm. long, membranous; blades narrowed to a fine tip, flat, 3–9 mm. wide, firm, rough all over, or only on the upper part and margins, the lower up to 45 cm. long, the upper shorter. Panicles dense, spike-like, cylindrical, most 6–15 (rarely up to 30 cm. or less to 2) cm. long, 6–10 mm. wide, green, greyish-green, or purplish; pedicels extremely short.

Spikelets (S, × 6) oblong, flattened, tightly packed, 3–3·8 mm. long, 1-flowered, breaking up at maturity above the glumes. Glumes persistent, narrowly oblong, truncate, keeled, minutely rough on the membranous sides, 3-nerved, the keels fringed with stiff spreading white hairs, and produced at the tip into a rigid rough awn 1–2 mm. long, the lower glume softly hairy on the margins. Lemma (F, L, × 12) two-thirds to three-fourths the length of the glumes, broad and very blunt, 5–7-nerved, membranous, minutely hairy. Palea (P, × 12) about as long as the lemma. Anthers (FL, × 12) 2 mm. long. Grain (CE, CH, × 8) enclosed between the thin lemma and palea. *Ch. no.* 2n = 42.

Timothy-grass or Cat's-tail is now widespread in the British Isles, being grown extensively for grazing and hay . It is also common on field margins, roadsides, and waste places, but is probably native only on the moist soils of water-meadows and other low-lying grasslands. Also throughout N., W., and Central Europe; introduced into most temperate countries. Called also Meadow Cat's-tail. Flowering: June to August.

There are numerous strains of this important fodder plant which vary considerably in growth and in value to the farmer. Some of the older varieties are short-lived and very stemmy, the seeds being taken from plants bearing relatively few vegetative shoots. More persistent strains with a greater amount of very palatable leafy growth are now available for both hay and grazing. Timothy-grass is shallow-rooting, succeeding best on moist heavy soils, and, being very hardy, is widely grown in cold countries. The name Timothy is derived from Timothy Hanson, who about 1720 introduced this grass to the United States. It may be distinguished from *P. bertolonii* by its larger size, longer and wider leaf-blades and panicles, and longer awns.

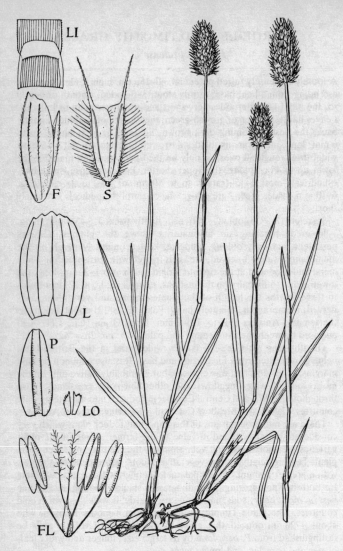

Phleum alpinum. Rare; mountains.

ALPINE CAT'S-TAIL
Phleum alpinum L.

A loosely tufted perennial, 10–50 cm. high, with short creeping rhizomes. Culms erect, or ascending from a bent or curved base, slender, 2–4-noded, smooth. Leaves green, hairless; sheaths rounded on the back, smooth, the basal becoming dark brown, the upper somewhat inflated; ligules (LI, × 3) very blunt, up to 2 mm. long, membranous; blades narrowed to a fine blunt tip, flat, up to 6 mm. wide, minutely rough on the margins, otherwise smooth, the lower up to 12 cm. long, the upper shorter. Panicles spike-like, very dense, erect, short-bristled, oblong, broadly cylindrical, 1–5 cm. long, 6–12 mm. wide, usually purplish; pedicels extremely short.

Spikelets (S, × 6) oblong, densely packed, compressed, 3–3·8 mm. long, 1-flowered, breaking up at maturity above the glumes. Glumes narrowly oblong, truncate, keeled, tough about the keels, with broad minutely rough membranous sides, 3-nerved, the keels fringed with stiff white spreading hairs, produced at the tip into a rough rigid straight or slightly curved awn 2–3 mm. long; lower glume with softly hairy margins. Lemma (F, L, × 12) about two-thirds the length of the glumes, broadly elliptic-oblong, very blunt, membranous, finely 3–5-nerved, minutely hairy on the nerves. Palea (P, × 12) slightly shorter than the lemma, membranous. Anthers (FL, × 12) 1–1·5 mm. long. *Ch. no.* 2n = 28.

A rare alpine grass of wet slopes and rock-ledges, restricted to the higher mountains of north and central Scotland and north-west England, from about 610 to 1220 m.; recorded from Ross, Inverness, Banff, Aberdeen, Angus, Perth, Cumberland, and Westmorland. It is the most widespread of all the species of *Phleum*, occurring from Arctic Regions southwards on mountains to those of Central and S. Europe, W. and Central Asia, the Himalaya, China, United States, and Mexico; also on the Andes of Chile and Argentina, and on S. Georgia. Known also as Alpine Timothy. Flowering: July and August.

In recent years this species has been incorrectly named *P. commutatum* Gaud., to distinguish it from the alpine plant of Central and S. European mountains which has only 14 (2n) chromosomes, and may be recognized by its hairy awns. *P. alpinum* may be separated from *P. bertolonii* and *P. pratense* by its short relatively broad panicles and the longer awns of its glumes.

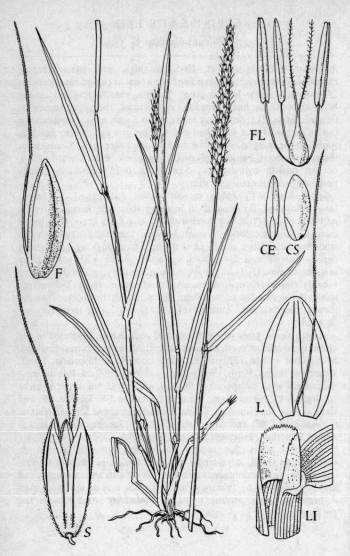

Alopecurus myosuroides. Common; arable and waste land.

SLENDER FOX-TAIL or BLACK GRASS

Alopecurus myosuroides Huds.

Annual, 20–80 cm. high. Culms loosely to compactly tufted, or sometimes solitary, erect, or kneed at the base, slender, few-noded, smooth. Leaves hairless; sheaths smooth, green, or purplish, the uppermost somewhat inflated; ligules (LI, × 4) blunt, membranous, 2–5 mm. long; blades pointed, 3–16 cm. long, 2–8 mm. wide, flat, rough on both sides, or smooth beneath, green. Panicles spike-like, dense, 2–12 cm. long, 3–6 mm. wide, narrowly cylindrical, tapering upwards, yellowish-green, pale green, or purplish; pedicels very short.

Spikelets (S, × 6) narrowly oblong or lanceolate-oblong, 4·5–7 mm. long, flattened, 1-flowered, falling entire at maturity. Glumes united by their margins for one-third to half their length, narrowly oblong to lanceolate, pointed, 3-nerved, firm, narrowly winged on the keels, minutely hairy there and on the nerves near the base. Lemma (F, L, × 6) as long as or slightly longer than the glumes, ovate, blunt, keeled, with the margins united for one-third above the base, membranous, 4-nerved, smooth, awned on the back from near the base, with the awn exceeding the tip of the lemma by 4–8 mm. Palea absent. Anthers (FL, × 6) 3–4 mm. long. Grains (CS, CE, × 6) tightly enclosed in the lemma between the hardened glumes. *Ch. no.* 2n = 14.

Black Grass or Black Twitch is a common weed of arable land and waste places, on both heavy and light soils, frequently becoming a serious pest in fields of cereals. It is scattered throughout the British Isles, but most abundant in the areas of cultivated land in S.E. England, infrequent in the north of England, rare in Scotland and Ireland. Widespread in Europe and temperate Asia; introduced to N. America and other temperate regions. Often known in the past as *A. agrestis* L. Flowering: May to August.

It is not easy to eradicate this grass from arable land when several cereal crops are grown in succession. Seed is produced in great abundance, and, being shed before the corn is cut, leads to greater quantities of the weed in the next season's crop. As the seeds have a very short period of dormancy and viability, experiments have shown that this grass may be considerably reduced by surface cultivation after harvest, or by growing a crop which permits of hoeing. It may be almost entirely eliminated by two years' fallow, but the few viable seeds which remain in the soil are sufficient to provide fresh stock for a new infestation where cultural conditions are favourable and weeding is not possible.

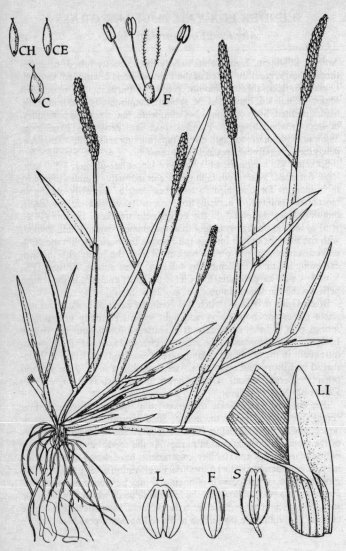

Alopecurus aequalis. Uncommon; wet places, ponds.

Labels on figure: CH, CE, C, F, LI, L, F, S

ORANGE OR SHORT-AWN FOX-TAIL

Alopecurus aequalis Sobol.

Annual, biennial, or short-lived perennial, 10–35 cm. high. Culms usually ascending from a kneed or prostrate base, sometimes rooting at the nodes, slender, few- to many-noded, smooth, whitish-green towards the panicle. Leaves hairless; sheaths smooth, the upper whitish-green, somewhat inflated; ligules (LI, × 6) blunt, up to 5 mm. long, membranous; blades pointed, 2–10 cm. long, 2–5 mm. wide, flat, finely nerved, with the nerves rough, green. Panicles very dense, spike-like, narrowly cylindrical, 1–5 cm. long, 3–6 mm. wide, pale- or greyish-green sometimes tinged with blue; pedicels very short.

Spikelets (S, × 6) elliptic or oblong, very blunt, 2–2·5 mm. long, flattened, 1-flowered, falling entire at maturity. Glumes similar, keeled, with margins free nearly to the base, narrowly oblong, blunt, thinly membranous, 3-nerved, with a fringe of silky hairs on the keels and shorter ones on the sides. Lemma (F, L, × 6) as long as or very slightly longer than the glumes, keeled, broadly elliptic, very blunt, thinly membranous, 4-nerved, smooth, with the margins united for up to half their length, awned on the back just below the middle, with the awn included in the glumes or very slightly protruding from them. Palea absent. Anthers (FL, × 4) 1–1·3 mm. long. Grain (C, CE, CH, × 7) enclosed in the lemma between the thin glumes. *Ch. no.* 2n = 14.

Although *Alopecurus aequalis* is widely distributed in England, from the Isle of Wight and Wiltshire to Kent, northwards to Lancashire and Yorkshire, it is of rather local occurrence; rare in E. Wales and Scotland (Inverness); also throughout Europe, temperate Asia, and N. America. It grows on the margins of pools, reservoirs, and in ditches, in shallow water, and especially on drying mud, where it may sometimes form dense carpets. Flowering: June to September.

Orange Fox-tail is named on account of the colour of its anthers, these being bright orange or golden-yellow at maturity. They provide a reliable distinction between it and the more common *Alopecurus geniculatus*, which is a perennial grass, with longer and more conspicuous awns.

The species of *Alopecurus* may be recognized by the following characters: spikelets 1-flowered, protogynous, strongly laterally compressed, borne on very short stalks in cylindrical spike-like panicles, falling entire from their stalks at maturity; glumes similar, keeled, 3-nerved, often with their margins united below; lemmas membranous, 4–5-nerved, usually bearing an awn on the back; palea and lodicules absent.

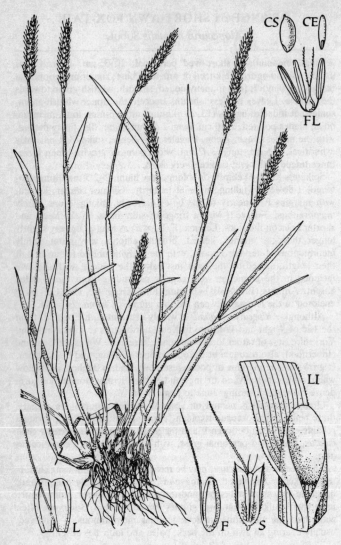

CS CE

FL

LI

L F S

Alopecurus bulbosus. Uncommon; salt-marshes.

TUBEROUS or BULBOUS FOX-TAIL

Alopecurus bulbosus Gouan

Perennial, forming small compact or spreading tufts, 15–20 cm. high. Culms erect, or ascending from a bent base, slender, unbranched, few-noded, smooth, the basal one or two joints swollen or bulbous. Leaves greyish-green or green, hairless; sheaths smooth, the uppermost some-what inflated; ligules (LI, × 6) blunt, 2–6 mm. long, membranous; blades narrow, pointed, 1·5–12 cm. long, 1–3·5 mm. wide, flat or rolled, closely nerved, smooth except for the rough margins. Panicles spike-like, very dense, narrowly cylindrical, 1·5–7 cm. long, 3–5 mm. wide, green, tinged with bluish-grey or purple; pedicels extremely short.

Spikelets (S, × 6) oblong, 3–4 mm. long, flattened, 1-flowered, falling entire at maturity. Glumes similar, free to the base, as long as the spikelet, keeled, narrowly oblong, sharply pointed, 3-nerved, firmly membranous, short-hairy on the keels and on the sides below the middle. Lemma (F, L, × 6) up to four-fifths the length of the glumes, keeled, broadly oblong, very blunt, with the margins free to the base, membra-nous, 4-nerved, minutely hairy at the tip, otherwise hairless, awned on the back from near the base, the awn protruding beyond the glumes for 3–4 mm. Palea and lodicules absent. Anthers (FL, × 6) 2 mm. long. Grain (CS, CE, × 6) compressed, elliptic-oblong in side view, about 1·6 mm. long, enclosed in the lemma between the glumes and falling with them at maturity. *Ch. no.* 2n = 14.

This small slender Fox-tail of tidal salt-marshes and brackish seaside meadows is generally uncommon, although in some localities it may be very abundant among other maritime grasses. It is to be found round the coasts of England and S. Wales from Sussex to Cornwall and north-wards to S. Yorkshire and S. Lancashire; in Scotland it is very rare or absent. On the Continent its distribution extends along the coast from Holland to the Iberian Peninsula, and in the Mediterranean to France, Italy, and Greece. Flowering: May to August.

Tuberous Fox-tail is not likely to be confused with other British species of the genus, for they normally lack the bulbous base, this being formed of one or two globose or pear-shaped internodes of the culm containing food-reserves, and clothed with the remains of the leaf-sheaths. It is most closely related to *Alopecurus geniculatus*, of which it has been treated by some as a subspecies or variety, but from which it may also be distinguished by the sharp-pointed tips to its glumes, and its more erect tufted form of growth.

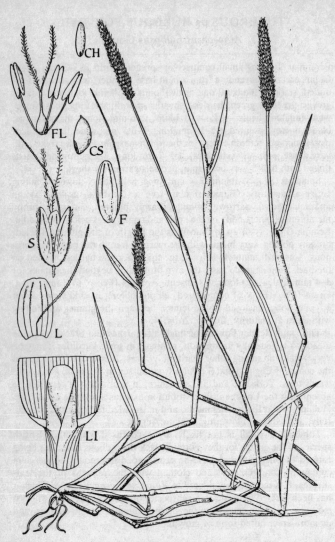

Alopecurus geniculatus. Common; wet places.

MARSH or FLOATING FOX-TAIL

Alopecurus geniculatus L.

Perennial, 15–45 cm. high. Culms spreading, usually ascending from a kneed or prostrate base and rooting at the nodes, sometimes extensively creeping, occasionally floating in water, slender, few- to many-noded, smooth, whitish-green in the upper part, rarely slightly tuberous at the base. Leaves hairless; sheaths smooth, whitish-green, the upper somewhat inflated; ligules (LI, × 6) blunt, 2–5 mm. long, membranous; blades pointed, 2–12 cm. long, 2–7 mm. wide, flat, spreading, green or greyish-green, rough on the nerves, or smooth beneath. Panicles very dense, spike-like, narrowly cylindrical, blunt, 1·5–7 cm. long, 3–7 mm. wide, green, or tinged with blue, or purplish; pedicels very short.

Spikelets (S, × 6) oblong, 2·5–3·3 mm. long, 1-flowered, flattened, falling entire at maturity. Glumes narrowly oblong, blunt, keeled, with the margins free nearly to the base, thinly membranous, 3-nerved, fringed with silky hairs on the keel and with appressed hairs on the sides. Lemma (F, L, × 6) slightly shorter than or as long as the glumes, broadly oblong or ovate, very blunt, keeled, with the margins united near the base, thinly membranous, smooth, 4-nerved, awned just above the base, with the awn exceeding the glumes by 2–3 mm. Palea absent. Anthers (FL, × 6) 1·5–2 mm. long, yellow or purple. Grain (CS, CH, × 6) enclosed in the lemma between the thin glumes. *Ch. no.* 2n = 28.

A low grass of wet or moist places such as the muddy margins and shallow water of pools, rivers, streams, and ditches, and of damp depressions in meadows. It is widespread and of frequent occurrence in the British Isles, having been recorded from every county. Also throughout Europe, N. Asia, and N. America. Flowering: June to August.

As the stigmas mature before the stamens, cross-pollination can often take place when two or more species of *Alopecurus* grow together. The progeny of two hybrids produced in this way have been discovered in the British Isles. Both are male-sterile, their anthers being devoid of good pollen and remaining closed. One hybrid between *A. geniculatus* and *A. pratensis* (= *A.* × *hybridus* Wimm.) is fairly widespread in S. England, occurring in marshy fields in at least ten counties. It is intermediate in structure between its parents, the culms spreading and geniculate, the uppermost ligule up to 5 mm. long, the spikelets 3·5–4·5 mm. long, with slightly pointed or somewhat blunt glumes, and anthers 2 mm. long. The other hybrid, between *A. geniculatus* and *A. aequalis* (= *A.* × *haussknechtianus* A. & G.), has been found in W. Norfolk.

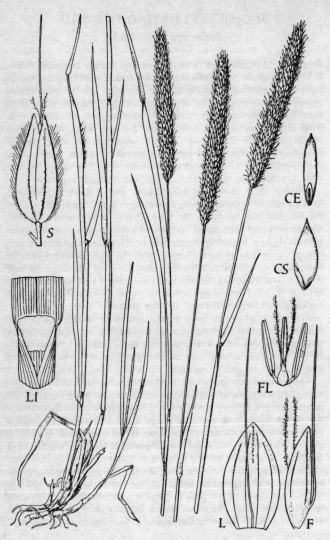

Alopecurus pratensis. Very common; meadows.

MEADOW or COMMON FOX-TAIL
Alopecurus pratensis L.

A loosely or compactly tufted perennial, 30–120 cm. high. Culms erect, or kneed at the base, slender to moderately stout, few-noded, smooth, green, or whitish-green in the upper part. Leaves hairless; sheaths smooth, cylindrical, split, the basal turning dark brown, the upper green or whitish-green, somewhat inflated; ligules (LI, × 4) 1–2·5 mm. long, membranous; blades finely pointed, finally flat, green, rough or nearly smooth, the lower 6–40 cm. long, 3–10 mm. wide, the upper shorter. Panicles very dense, spike-like, cylindrical, blunt, soft, 2–13 cm. long, 5–10 mm. wide, green or purplish; branches short, erect; pedicels very short.

Spikelets (S, × 6) lanceolate-oblong or elliptic, 4–6 mm. long, flattened, 1-flowered, falling entirely at maturity. Glumes narrowly lanceolate and pointed in side view, with their margins united towards the base, 3-nerved, firm, fringed with fine hairs on the keels, hairy on the sides. Lemma (F, L, × 6) as long as or slightly longer than the glumes, ovate or elliptic, rather blunt, keeled, with the margins united below the middle, 4-nerved, membranous, smooth, awned from the lower third on the back, with the awn exceeding the glumes by 3–5 mm. Palea absent. Anthers (FL, × 6) 2–3·5 mm. long, yellow or purple. Grain (CS, CE, × 6) enclosed in the lemma between the glumes. *Ch. no.* 2n = 28.

Meadow Fox-tail occurs throughout the British Isles, being most abundant in low-lying areas and river valleys, especially in water-meadows or old grasslands on rich moist soils. It is widespread in Europe and N. Asia; introduced into N. America and elsewhere. Flowering: April to June or July.

In addition to our indigenous strains, numerous varieties from overseas have been sown here, so that we now possess a wide range of forms. Some yield leafy succulent herbage, particularly those from old native grasslands, others are rather stemmy and of little value to the farmer. The former are very nutritious and palatable to stock, withstand cold, and remain green throughout the winter. They commence growth early in the year, are among the first grasses to flower, and are highly productive, providing valuable grazing and hay crops. The larvae of certain gall-midges do serious damage to the ovaries and so lower the percentage of viable seed. *Alopecurus pratensis* var. *aureo-variegatus* and var. *aureus*, with the leaves striped green and yellow or wholly yellow respectively, are occasionally cultivated in gardens.

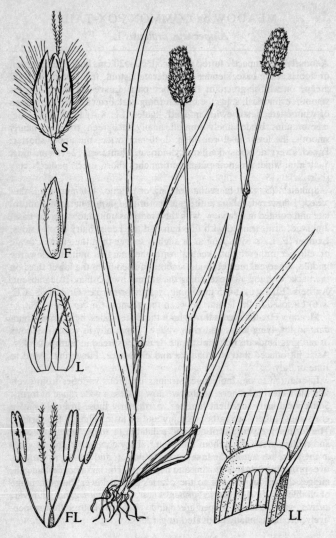

Alopecurus alpinus. Very rare; mountains.

ALPINE FOX-TAIL

Alopecurus alpinus Sm.

Perennial, forming loose tufts, 10–45 cm. high, with slender creeping rhizomes. Culms erect, or bent at the base, slender, 2–3-noded, smooth. Leaves green, hairless; sheaths smooth, the upper somewhat inflated; ligules (LI, × 6) 1–2 mm. long, membranous; blades narrowly lanceolate, pointed, flat, 2·5–6 mm. wide, closely nerved and slightly rough above, smooth beneath, the basal up to 22 cm. long, the upper much shorter. Panicles spike-like, very dense, erect, broadly cylindrical or ovoid, 1–3 cm. long, 7–12 mm. wide, greyish-green or tinged with purple, silkily hairy; pedicels extremely short.

Spikelets (S, × 6) elliptic or ovate, blunt, 3–4·5 mm. long, 1-flowered, flattened, falling entire at maturity. Glumes with their margins united near the base, semi-elliptic and pointed in side view, 3-nerved, with the nerves green, membranous, clothed with fine spreading hairs, especially on the keels. Lemma (F, L, × 6) as long as the glumes or slightly longer, keeled, broadly ovate, very blunt, with the margins united towards the base, 4-nerved, membranous, slightly hairy near the margins or hairless, awnless or awned on the back from one-third above the base, with the awn sometimes projecting beyond the tip of the spikelet. Palea and lodicules absent. Anthers (FL, × 6) 2–2·5 mm. long. *Ch. no.* 2n = 100–130.

A very rare alpine grass of wet grassy slopes, moist rocks, and stream margins on Scottish mountains in Dumfriesshire, Perth, Angus, Aberdeen, Banff, Inverness, and East Ross, at elevations from 760 to 1220 m.; also in Cumberland, Westmorland, and Durham. It occurs all over the Arctic; in Spitsbergen, Novaya Zemlya, N. Russia and N. America, extending to N. Greenland, but has not been found in Scandinavia or Iceland. Flowering: mid-June to August.

The Scottish plants are somewhat variable in structure. Their spikelets may be without awns, as in the plants first found on Lochnagar in Aberdeenshire by Robert Brown in August 1794; or they may have awns extending for one-third their length beyond the tips of the glumes. Such plants have been named var. *watsonii* Syme. The flowers of *Alopecurus* are termed protogynous, because the stigmas mature and become exserted from the spikelet a day or more before the anthers, a circumstance which favours hybridization when two or more species of the genus grow together. It is interesting to note that all our protogynous grasses lack lodicules; besides *Alopecurus*, these include *Anthoxanthum*, *Nardus*, and *Spartina*.

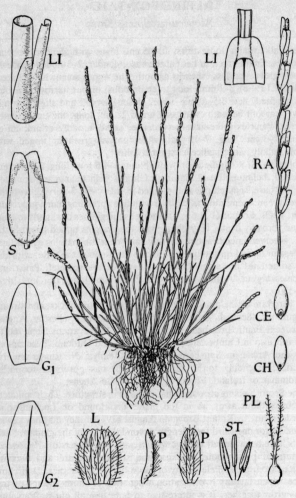

Mibora minima. Very rare; coastal sands, Anglesey, etc.

EARLY SAND-GRASS or SAND BENT
Mibora minima (L.) Desv.

A compactly tufted annual, 2–15 cm. high. Culms erect or spreading, numerous, very slender, hair-like, unbranched, smooth, closely sheathed at the base, the upper part exserted and green or purplish. Leaves mostly at the base of the plant, smooth and hairless; sheaths round, overlapping, delicate; ligules (LI, × 7) very blunt, up to 1 mm. long, thinly membranous; blades very narrow, blunt, up to 2 cm. (rarely more) long, flat or with inrolled margins, about 0·5 mm. wide, green. Racemes (RA, × 3) spike-like, very slender, one-sided, erect, 0·5–2 cm. long, up to 1 mm. wide, reddish, purple or green; main axis very slender, smooth.

Spikelets (S, × 12) almost stalkless, appressed to and loosely to closely overlapping in two rows on one side of the axis, oblong, blunt, 1·8–3 mm. long, one-flowered, breaking up at maturity above the glumes. Glumes (G_1, G_2, × 12) persistent, as long as the spikelet, equal or nearly so, oblong or elliptic-oblong, very blunt, rounded on the back, thinly membranous, 1-nerved, smooth. Lemma (L, × 12) about two-thirds the length of the glumes, very broad, truncate or minutely toothed at the apex, shortly and densely hairy, thinner than the glumes, finely 5-nerved. Palea (P, × 12) as long as the lemma, 2-nerved, shortly hairy. Anthers (ST, × 15) 1–1·7 mm. long. Grain (CE, CH, × 10) loosely enclosed between the delicate lemma and palea. *Ch. no.* 2n = 14.

This delicate little plant, one of the smallest of our grasses, grows in moist sandy places near the sea on the islands of Anglesey, Jersey, and Guernsey, and on sand-dunes in East Lothian. It was apparently accidentally introduced long ago, perhaps by seed on the roots of plants from the Channel Islands, into a nursery at Ferndown in Dorset; here on the light sandy soil it is well established, and has spread to a few other places in Hampshire and Dorset. It has also been found under similar conditions in Suffolk. A native of S.W. and S. Europe, and N.W. Africa; introduced into Australia and the United States. Flowering: February to May, according to the mildness or otherwise of the winter, sometimes flowering again in the late summer and even as late as December.

The genus *Mibora* may be easily recognized among British grasses with one-flowered spikelets by the arrangement of its spikelets along one side of the fine axis of the slender racemes. *Mibora* may be cultivated in sandy soil in a pot or pan, the seed being sown thinly in the late summer or autumn, otherwise it will not flower in the spring. Grown in this way it forms an unusual dwarf decorative plant.

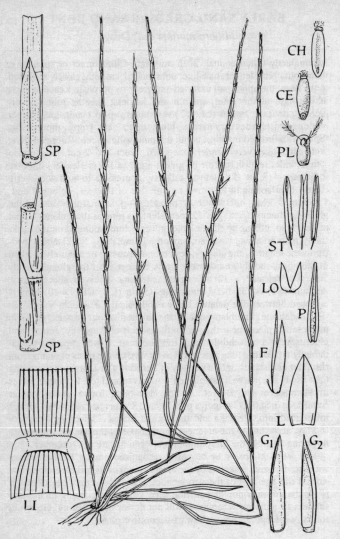

Parapholis strigosa. Common; salt-marshes.

SEA HARD-GRASS

Parapholis strigosa (Dum.) C. E. Hubbard

Annual, up to 40 cm. high. Culms loosely tufted or solitary, erect, or bent or curved and spreading, very slender, usually loosely branched, few- to many-noded, smooth. Leaves greyish-green or green, hairless; sheaths rounded on the back, smooth; ligules (LI, × 8) membranous, 0·3–1 mm. long; blades pointed, 1–6 cm. long, flat or rolled, 1–2·5 mm. wide, smooth beneath, rough on the nerves above and on the margins. Spikes (SP) usually straight and erect, sometimes curved, cylindrical, very slender, stiff, 2–20 cm. long, 1–1·5 mm. in diameter, green or purplish; axis (SP) smooth, jointed; the joints deeply hollowed out on one side, 4–7 (mostly 5) mm. long, breaking horizontally at maturity beneath each spikelet.

Spikelets (SP, × 4) embedded in hollows in the spike-axis, solitary and alternating on opposite sides of the axis, 3–7 (mostly 4–6) mm. long, closely pressed to the axis, falling with the joints of the axis at maturity, 1-flowered (F). Glumes (G$_1$, G$_2$, × 4) equal or nearly so, as long as the spikelet, narrow, pointed, rigid, hardened and thickened, 3–5-nerved, hairless, placed side-by-side in front of and covering the cavity in the axis. Lemma (L, × 4) ovate-oblong to oblong, blunt, as long or nearly as long as the glumes, membranous, finely 3-nerved. Palea (P, × 4) about as long as the lemma. Anthers (ST, × 6) 1·5–4 mm. long. Grain (CE, CH, × 4) tightly enclosed between the glumes and the joint of the spike-axis.

A slender grass, with very narrow brittle spikes; widely distributed along the coasts of the British Isles as far north as E., Mid- and W. Lothian and the Isle of Mull; frequently locally common on the margins of and in salt-marshes, and on waste ground near the sea; flourishing on damp heavy soils, but also found on sandy and gravelly muds, and on sands; on bare ground and scattered among perennial grasses in salt-marsh turf. Also along the shores of W. Europe from Scandinavia to Portugal; rare in the Mediterranean Region. Usually known, incorrectly, as *Lepturus filiformis* or *Pholiurus filiformis*, a Mediterranean Region grass. Flowering: June to August.

When growing amongst other grasses, Sea Hard-grass is often passed by as its very narrow spikes are so similar in appearance to grass culms. It varies considerably in size and habit. Without competition on rich moist soils it forms large tufts with numerous spreading culms; on the other hand plants on dry sands may consist of solitary culms only 3 cm. high.

The species of *Parapholis* have no agricultural value.

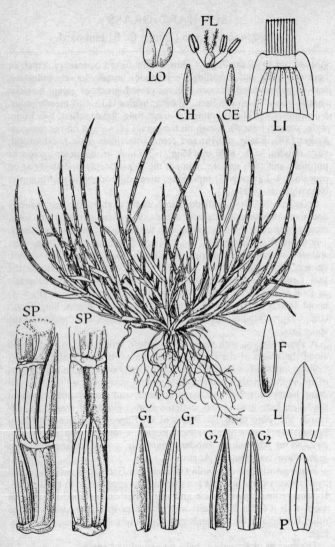

FL

LO

CH CE

LI

SP SP

F

G₁ G₁ G₂ G₂ L

P

Parapholis incurva. Uncommon; salt-marshes.

CURVED SEA HARD-GRASS
Parapholis incurva (L.) C. E. Hubbard

Annual, 2–20 cm. high. Culms loosely to densely tufted, or solitary, prostrate, curved, and ascending, or erect, very slender, rigid, usually much branched in the lower part, smooth, few- to many-noded. Leaves hairless, green; sheaths rounded on the back, smooth; ligules (LI, × 6) 0·5–1 mm. long, membranous; blades finely pointed, 0·4–3 cm. long, 1–2 mm. wide, flat or rolled, smooth beneath, rough on the nerves above and on the margins. Spikes (SP) rigid, curved, or rarely straight, slender, cylindrical, 1–8 cm. long, 1–2 mm. in diameter, green or purplish; axis (SP) smooth, jointed; the joints shorter than the spikelets, deeply hollowed out on one side, 2·5–5 mm. long, breaking horizontally beneath each spikelet at maturity.

Spikelets (SP, × 5) embedded in the hollows in the spike-axis, solitary and alternating on opposite sides of the axis and closely pressed to it, 4–6 mm. long, oblong, 1-flowered (F), falling with the joints of the axis at maturity. Glumes (G_1, G_2, × 5) as long as the spikelet, placed side by side and closing the cavity in the axis, narrowly oblong-subulate, pointed, thick and rigid, hairless, 3–4-nerved. Lemma (L, × 5) slightly shorter than the glumes, lanceolate to narrowly ovate, thinly membranous, finely 3-nerved. Palea (P, × 5) nearly as long as the lemma. Anthers (FL, × 6) 0·5–1 mm. long. Grain (CE, CH, × 5) enclosed between the hardened glumes and the joint of the axis. *Ch. no.* 2n = 38.

Widespread in the Mediterranean Region, extending along the coast of W. Europe to S. and E. England and S. Wales; of uncommon to rare occurrence by the sea from Somerset and Dorset to W. Norfolk, S. Lincolnshire and Yorkshire; in bare places on the more elevated parts of salt-marshes, on gravelly mud banks, and among short grasses on low ledges, in relatively drier places than *Parapholis strigosa*. It occurs occasionally inland as an alien. Introduced into N. and S. America and Australia. Known as Sickle Grass in the United States. Flowering: June and July.

Parapholis incurva is very similar to *P. strigosa*, but is usually smaller and has more rigid shorter curved spikes. It is best recognized by its very small anthers, 0·5–1 mm. long, those of *P. strigosa* being 1·5–4 mm. long. Where the two species grow near each other, it will be found that *P. incurva* flowers a few weeks earlier than *P. strigosa*. The genus *Parapholis* may be recognized by its very slender cylindric spikes, its 1-flowered spikelets being embedded in cavities in the main axis.

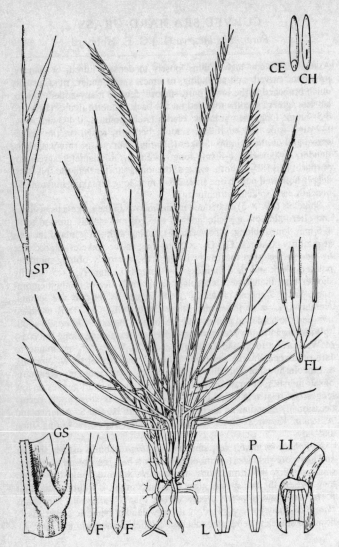

Nardus stricta. Common; acidic grassland.

MAT-GRASS
Nardus stricta L.

A densely tufted perennial, 10–40, rarely up to 60 cm. high, with coarse roots and numerous vegetative shoots closely packed on short rhizomes. Culms erect, slender, wiry, unbranched, 1-noded towards the base, smooth. Leaves greyish-green or green; sheaths smooth, the basal short, crowded, persistent, pale, tough, shining; ligules (LI, × 8) membranous, blunt, up to 2 mm. long; blades bristle-like, sharp-pointed, 4–30 cm. long, tightly inrolled, about 0·5 mm. in diameter, hard, stiff, grooved, minutely hairy in the grooves, or hairless and smooth. Spikes erect, very slender, one-sided, 3–8 cm. long, green or purplish; axis up to 0·8 mm. wide, rough on the margins, produced at the tip into a bristle up to 1 cm. long.

Spikelets (SP, × 3) narrow, finely pointed, 5–9 mm. long, stalkless, loosely to closely overlapping, in two rows along one side of the spike-axis, 1-flowered. Glumes (GS, × 18) persistent; lower very small; upper usually absent. Lemma (F, L, × 3) narrowly lanceolate or lanceolate-oblong, as long as the spikelet, tipped with an awn 1–3 mm. long, 2–3-keeled, rough on the keels, 3-nerved, firm. Palea (P, × 3) slightly shorter than the lemma, 2-nerved. Anthers (FL, × 4) 3·5–4 mm. long. Grain (CE, CH_2, × 4) narrow, 3–4 mm. long, tightly enclosed by and falling with the hardened lemma and palea at maturity. *Ch. no.* 2n = 26.

A tough wiry grass, widespread in the British Isles, being recorded from nearly every county; on heaths and moorland, in hill and mountain grassland; on poor dry to damp sandy and peaty soils; from low elevations to over 910 m.; more common in the west and north. Throughout Europe, in temperate Asia, N.W. Africa, Azores, Greenland, and Newfoundland. Flowering: June to August.

Although this grass is widely distributed, it is less frequent in the south-east, though occasionally quite common on sandy heaths; but in hill and mountain grassland it is often very abundant, dominating extensive areas, and in winter giving a characteristic whitish tone to the slopes. Except in spring when young, it is usually not grazed by cattle or sheep; it quickly becomes fibrous and unpalatable.

The flowers are protogynous, the single minutely hairy stigma protruding from the apex of the floret before the anthers, as in other grasses lacking lodicules. It is stated to be apomictic.

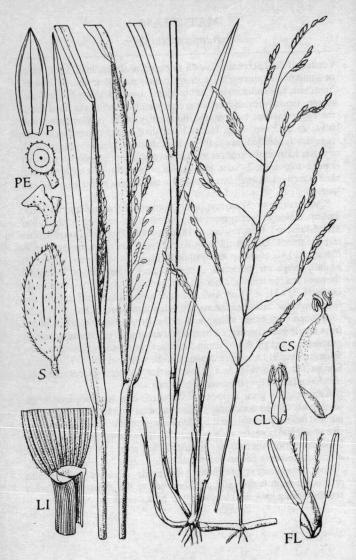

Leersia oryzoides. Rare; wet places.

CUT GRASS
Leersia oryzoides (L.) Swartz

Perennial, 30–120 cm. high, with slender rhizomes, forming loose tufts or patches. Culms erect or ascending, slender to somewhat stout, often branched, few- to many-noded, hairy at the nodes, rough towards the upper nodes, or smooth. Leaves yellowish-green; sheaths rounded on the back, finely ribbed, the upper rough with short stiff reflexed hairs between the ribs; ligules (LI, × 4) up to 1·5 mm. long; blades finely pointed, flat, 8–30 cm. long, 5–10 mm. wide, rough, spiny on the margins. Panicles enclosed in the leaf-sheaths or partially or wholly exserted from them, contracted to very loose, 10–22 cm. long, up to 14 cm. wide; branches spreading, very fine, flexuous, bare in the lower part; pedicels (PE) 0·3–1 mm. long.

Spikelets (S, × 6) overlapping on one side of and towards the tips of the branches, semi-elliptic-oblong, flattened, 4–5 mm. long, pale green, 1-flowered, falling at maturity. Glumes reduced to a narrow rim at the tip of the pedicels (PE). Lemma semi-elliptic-oblong, abruptly pointed, firm, fringed on the keel with stiff spreading hairs and with much shorter ones on the sides, 5-nerved, the outermost nerves marginal. Palea (P, × 6) as long as or slightly longer than the lemma, narrow, 3-nerved, stiffly hairy on the back. Anthers 0·4–0·7 mm. long in closed spikelets (CL, × 10), 1·5–2 mm long in open spikelets (FL, × 10). Grain (CS, × 10) enclosed by the lemma and palea. *Ch. no.* 2n = 48.

A rough-leaved grass of brook and river margins, and ditch bottoms, restricted in the British Isles to the counties of Surrey, Sussex, Hampshire, Somerset, and Dorset. Although relatively rare it may be locally very abundant, as on the rich alluvial soils at Amberley Wild Brooks. Here it fringes the ditches, sometimes scrambling over other waterside plants by means of its hooked sheaths and rough blade-margins. Also in Europe from S. Sweden to Spain, and eastwards to temperate Asia, and N. America. Also known as Rice Grass. Flowering: August to October.

With average spring and summer temperatures, the panicles remain enclosed within or become only partially exserted from the leaf-sheaths. Under such conditions the spikelets are cleistogamous; the anthers being very small, pollination takes place within the closed lemma and palea. When the seasons are exceptionally warm, especially the spring, the panicles become completely exserted. The spikelets are then chasmogamous, the larger anthers hanging from the gaping lemma and palea, so that cross-pollination may take place.

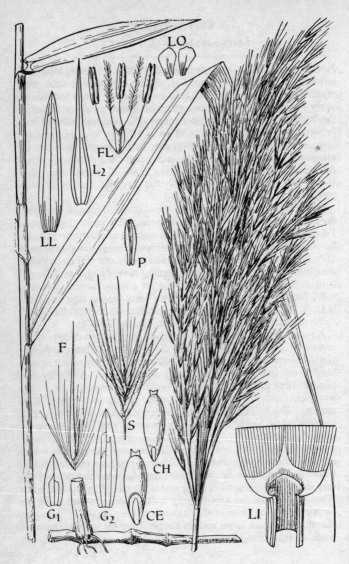

Phragmites communis. Common; wet places.

COMMON REED
Phragmites communis Trin.

A robust perennial, 1·5–3 m. high, spreading by stout creeping rhizomes and stolons. Culms erect, rigid, stout, closely sheathed, many-noded, usually unbranched, smooth. Leaves greyish-green, smooth; sheaths rounded on the back, overlapping; ligule (LI, × 2) a dense fringe of short hairs; blades contracted at the base, long-tapering to a very fine curved or flexuous tip, flat, 20–60 cm. (or more) long, 10–30 mm. wide, tough, closely nerved, ultimately falling from the sheaths. Panicles erect or finally nodding, 15–40 cm. long, loose to dense, soft, purplish or brownish, much-branched, with smooth or nearly smooth branches, hairy at intervals; pedicels short.

Spikelets (S, × 3) lanceolate, at length widely gaping, 10–16 mm. long, 2–6-flowered, with the lowest floret male and the others bisexual, the hairy axis breaking up at maturity beneath each fertile lemma (F). Glumes (G_1, G_2, × 4) persistent, membranous, smooth, 3–5-nerved, the lower half to two-thirds the length of the upper, the upper about half the length of the lowest lemma. Lowest lemma (LL, × 4) narrowly lanceolate, pointed, 9–13 mm. long, membranous, mostly 3-nerved, smooth. Fertile lemmas (F, L_2, × 4) narrower, more finely pointed, thinner, 1–3-nerved, surrounded by white silky hairs (F) up to 9 mm. long from the spikelet-axis. Paleas (P, × 4) 3–4 mm. long. Anthers (FL, × 6) 1·5–2 mm. long. Grain (CE, CH, × 12) enclosed by the thin lemma and palea. *Ch. no.* 2n = 48, 96.

Our tallest native grass, covering large areas of swamp and fen, frequent in the shallow water of rivers and lakes; occurring in most parts of the British Isles, and especially common in the lowlands. Widespread in temperate regions, extending to the tropics. Flowering: end of August to October.

The culms and leaves, being very tough and persistent, are used for thatching, whilst the panicles are dried for decorative purposes. On the margins of rivers and lakes, its network of roots and rhizomes helps in preventing erosion. Var. *variegatus*, with leaves striped yellow and green, is cultivated in parks and gardens.

Two robust exotic grasses, the Giant Reed, *Arundo donax* L., and the Pampas Grass, *Cortaderia selloana* (Schult.) Aschers. & Graebn. (*C. argentea* Stapf) are also cultivated for ornament. The former is similar in habit to *Phragmites*, with 2–6 m. high robust culms, and 30–60 cm. long panicles. The latter forms dense leafy tussocks, with very long, rough-edged crowded leaf-blades, and unisexual panicles up to 120 cm. long. It is sometimes naturalized.

(*Phragmites australis* (Cav.) Trin. ex Steudel)

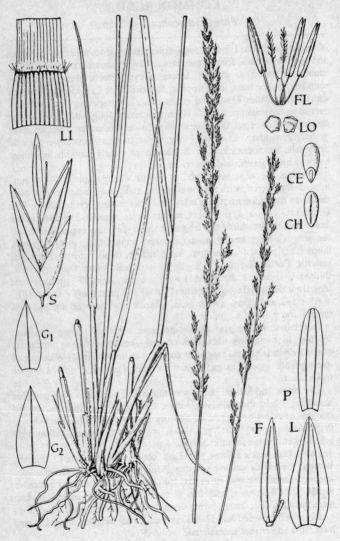

Molinia caerulea. Very common; damp or wet peaty soils.

PURPLE MOOR-GRASS
Molinia caerulea (L.) Moench

A compactly tufted, tough-rooted perennial, 15–120 cm. high, often forming large tussocks. Culms erect, slender to somewhat stout, stiff, smooth, 1-noded towards the base, the basal internode about 5 cm. long, club-shaped. Leaves green; sheaths rounded on the back, smooth, hairy at the top; ligule (LI, × 2) a dense fringe of short hairs; blades long-tapering to a fine point, 10–45 cm. long, flat, 3–10 mm. wide, slightly hairy above or hairless, minutely rough on the margins, falling from the sheaths in winter. Panicles very variable, ranging from very dense and spike-like to open and very loose, dark to light purple, brownish, yellowish, or green, 5–40 cm. long, 1–10 cm. wide; branches slender, smooth or minutely rough; pedicels variable in length.

Spikelets (S, × 6) lanceolate to oblong, 4–9 mm. long, loosely 1–4-flowered, breaking up at maturity beneath each lemma, with a slender rough axis. Glumes (G_1, G_2, × 6) persistent, unequal to nearly equal, lanceolate to ovate or oblong, shorter than the lemmas, membranous; lower 1·5–3 mm. long, 0–1-nerved; upper 2·5–4 mm. long, 1–3-nerved. Lemmas (F, L, × 6) spaced, narrowly lanceolate to narrowly oblong in side view, pointed or blunt, rounded on the back, mostly 4–6 mm. long, 3–5-nerved, firm, smooth. Paleas (P, × 6) with minutely rough keels. Anthers (FL, × 6) 1·5–3 mm. long, purple. Stigmas purple. Grain (CE, CH, × 6) enclosed by the hardened lemma and palea. *Ch. no.* 2n = 18, 36, 90.

A very variable grass, found in most parts of the British Isles, in wet or damp peaty areas on moorland, heaths, commons, and in the fens; usually abundant and frequently dominating large areas, often to the exclusion of other flowering plants; occurring from the lowlands to 1220 m. on Scottish mountains. Widespread in Europe, N.W. Africa, and in S.W. and N. Asia; introduced into N. America. Numerous varieties have been described. Known also as Flying Bent and Purple Melick-grass. Flowering: July to September.

Purple Moor-grass has little agricultural value, its leaves being eaten only when young by cattle and sheep. The leaves arise at two levels on the shoot, some at the base and others about 5 cm. above it. The intervening portion becomes club-shaped in the late summer or autumn, being gradually thickened downwards and filled with food reserves. Var. *variegata*, with the leaves striped green and cream, is cultivated in gardens.

Molinia litoralis Host (*M. altissima* Link) has been recorded from various parts of S. England and Wales; it is said to differ from *M. caerulea* in being taller (1·2–1·6 m.), with larger, mostly looser, panicles (30–50 cm.), longer spikelets (6–9 mm.) and lemmas (6 mm.).

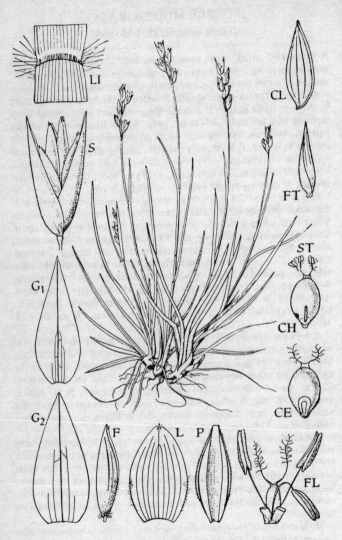

Sieglingia decumbens. Common; moors, heaths.

HEATH GRASS
Sieglingia decumbens (L.) Bernh.

A densely tufted perennial, 10–60 cm. high. Culms erect, spreading, or almost prostrate, slender, stiff, 1–3-noded, smooth. Leaves green; sheaths rounded on the back, usually with fine spreading hairs, bearded at the apex; ligule (LI, × 5) a dense fringe of short hairs; blades with blunt or abruptly pointed tips, 5–25 cm. long, 2–4 mm. wide, flat, or inrolled, stiff, sparsely hairy, or hairless, rough upwards. Panicles narrow, compact, or loose, 2–7 cm. long, bearing 3–12 spikelets; branches erect or spreading, rough, with 1–3 spikelets.

Spikelets (S, × 4) 6–12 mm. (rarely more) long, elliptic or oblong, plump, 4–6-flowered, breaking up at maturity above the glumes, purplish or green. Glumes (G_1, G_2, × 4) persistent, rounded below, keeled above, as long as the spikelet or nearly so, equal, or the lower slightly longer, lanceolate to narrowly ovate, blunt or pointed, 3–5-nerved, with smooth thin translucent sides. Lemmas (F, L, × 4) closely overlapping, 5–7 mm. long, rounded and smooth on the back, broadly elliptic, shortly 3-toothed at the tip, becoming tough and rigid, densely short-bearded at the base, usually short-haired on the margins up to the middle, 7–9-nerved. Paleas (P, × 4) with two short-haired keels. Anthers minute, 0·2–0·4 mm. long (ST), or about 2 mm. long (FL). Grain (CE, CH, × 6) tightly enclosed between the lemma and palea. *Ch. no.* 2n = 18, 24, 36, 124.

Heath Grass occurs on sandy and peaty soils in most parts of the British Isles, being recorded from every county. It is frequent on moorland, heaths, and the poorer types of hill grassland, usually in somewhat moist or wet places; in Ireland it ascends to over 910 m. Also in most parts of Europe, extending into S.W. Asia, N.W. Africa, the Azores, and Madeira. Flowering: June to August.

The flowers are usually cleistogamous, pollination taking place at an early stage within the closed floret (F), the minute anthers (ST) remaining in close contact with the weakly developed stigmas. In such plants the panicles remain contracted. Normal flowering has been observed on several occasions, usually on plants in wet soils; here the much larger anthers (FL) and stigmas become exserted from the open floret, while the panicle-branches spread. Basal spikelets (cleistogenes, CL, FT, × 4) may often be found at the base of the old culms in the axils of the leaf-sheaths; these have minute anthers. The grass is of no agricultural value.

Sieglingia decumbens subsp. *decipiens* Sch. & Bass. from calcareous soils, more slender habit, looser tufts, 7–9 rows of cells in leaf-fold. *Ch. no.* 2n = 24.

(*Danthonia decumbens* (L.) DC.)

351

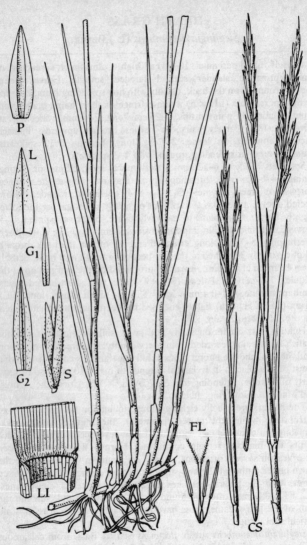

Spartina maritima. Uncommon; salt-marshes.

CORD-GRASS
Spartina maritima (Curt.) Fernald

A stiff perennial, 15–50 cm. high, with tough rhizomes, forming small tufts or loose patches. Culms erect, moderately stout, closely sheathed below, many-noded, smooth. Leaves green or purplish; sheaths persistent, smooth, rounded on the back; ligule (LI, × 4) a dense fringe of short hairs, 0·2–0·6 mm. long; blades erect or spreading slightly, with a fine hard tip, 2–18 cm. long, up to 6 mm. wide, stiff, flat or inrolled, closely ribbed above, smooth, finally disarticulating from the sheaths. Panicles very narrow, exceeding the leaves, erect, 4–10 cm. long, of 1–5 (mostly 2–3) spikes. Spikes spaced, rigid, 3–8 cm. long, one-sided, green or purplish; axis 3-angled, smooth, produced at the tip into a bristle up to 14 mm. long.

Spikelets (S, × 2) closely overlapping, in two rows on one side of and appressed to the spike-axis, falling entire at maturity, flattened, 1-flowered, narrowly oblong, 11–15 mm. long. Glumes (G_1, G_2, × 2) softly short-haired, keeled; lower narrow, up to four-fifths the length of the upper, 1-nerved, firmly membranous; upper linear-lanceolate, as long as the spikelet, firm, except for the membranous margins, 3-nerved. Lemma (L, × 2) a little shorter than the palea, narrowly oblong-lanceolate, minutely hairy upwards, 1-nerved, firm, except for the wide membranous margins. Palea (P, × 2) slightly shorter than the spikelet, 2-nerved, smooth. Anthers (FL, × 2) 4–6 mm. long. Grain (CS, × 2) enclosed by the lemma and palea between the firm glumes. *Ch. no.* $2n = 60$.

A rather uncommon grass of muddy tidal salt-marshes in S. England from S. Lincoln to S. Devon, in S. Wales and S.E. Ireland; unevenly distributed, rare in some districts, in others locally abundant, fringing gullies, and in shallow pans and pools, or amongst *Puccinellia maritima*. Also on the shores of W. Europe from Holland to Spain, at the head of the Adriatic, in N.W. Africa, S. and S.W. Africa. Flowering: July to September.

Distinguished from *S. × townsendii* and *S. anglica* by its shorter growth, tough wiry rhizomes, narrower and shorter leaf-blades (which excepting the uppermost ultimately fall from the sheaths), by its fewer spikes, shorter spikelets, and fertile anthers.

The species of *Spartina* have the following characters in common: ligule a fringe of hairs; spikelets mostly 1-flowered, flattened, falling entire at maturity, in spikes; grain with a long green embryo. The long short-haired stigmas protrude from the spikelet before the anthers, as in other grasses lacking lodicules, thus favouring cross-pollination.

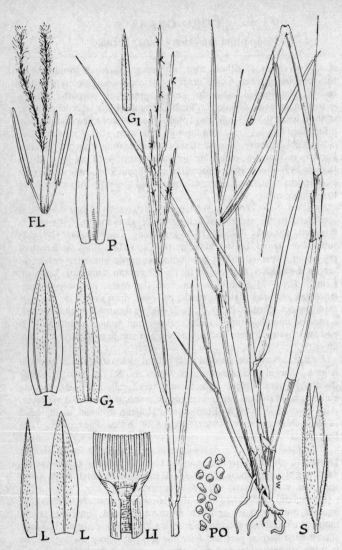

Spartina × *townsendii*. Locally common; coastal mud-flats.

TOWNSEND'S CORD-GRASS

Spartina × *townsendii* H. & J. Groves

A deep-rooting perennial, 30–130 cm. high, with relatively numerous vegetative shoots, forming close tussocks or patches and finally meadows, spreading by extensively creeping scaly rhizomes. Culms erect, slender to stout, many-noded, closely sheathed; sheaths overlapping, rounded on the back, smooth; ligule (LI, × 2½) a dense fringe of silky hairs, 1–2 mm. long; blades tapering to a fine hard point, 6–30 cm. or more long, 4–12 mm. wide, the upper spreading at an angle of 20–45°, flat or rolled, firm, smooth, closely flat-ribbed above. Panicles erect, contracted, linear to narrowly oblong, up to 25 cm. long, of 2–9 spikes, yellow or yellowish-green. Spikes erect, 4–15 cm. long, 2–3 mm. wide, stiff; axis 3-angled, smooth, terminating in a bristle 1–2 cm. or more long.

Spikelets (S, × 2½) closely overlapping, in two rows on one side of and appressed to the axis, narrowly oblong, flattened, 12–18 mm. long, 2–2·5 mm. wide, mostly 1-flowered, minutely and sparsely hairy. Glumes (G_1, G_2, × 2½) keeled, pointed; lower up to two-thirds the length of the upper, 1-nerved; upper as long as the spikelet, oblong-lanceolate, tough except for the membranous margins, 1- or closely 3-nerved. Lemma (L, × 2½) oblong-lanceolate, shorter than the upper glume, keeled, rough on the keel, minutely hairy, 1–3-nerved, with membranous margins. Palea (P, × 2½) slightly longer than the lemma, 2-nerved. Anthers (FL, × 2½) very narrow, 5–8 mm. long, not opening, with sterile pollen (PO). Grain not developed. *Ch. no.* = 62.

Although it has not yet been raised experimentally, there is little doubt that this male-sterile grass is the product of the crossing of *Spartina alterniflora* and *S. maritima*. It was first collected in 1870 at Hythe on the shore of Southampton Water where its putative parents also grew. From there it spread slowly over the tidal mud-flats, new colonies being established from plants and rhizomes uprooted and washed along the Hampshire coast during storms. It is now known from numerous places between Poole Harbour, Dorset, and Chichester Harbour in West Sussex, as well as from localities as far apart as in West Norfolk, Merioneth, and Dublin, where *Spartina* has been introduced. This sterile hybrid is the grass which gave rise, by chromosome doubling, to the fertile *Spartina* with which it has been confused and which is here named *S. anglica*. It is very probable that some of the sterile hybrids are poly-haploids which have originated from *S. anglica* by a halving process, reversing the doubling. Also in France and Denmark. Flowering: July to September.

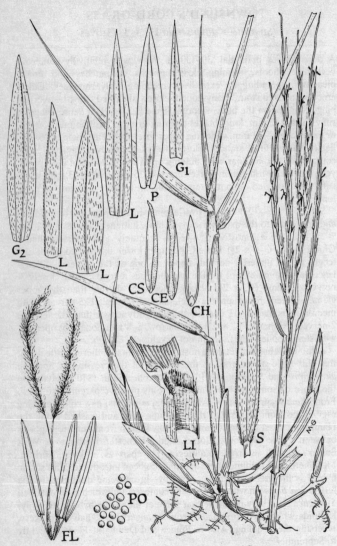

Spartina anglica. Common; coastal mud-flats.

COMMON CORD-GRASS
Spartina anglica C. E. Hubbard

A deep-rooting perennial, 30–130 cm. high, spreading by soft stout fleshy rhizomes, forming large clumps and extensive meadows. Culms erect, stout, many-noded, smooth. Leaves green or greyish-green; sheaths overlapping, rounded on the back, smooth; ligules (LI, × 1½) densely silkily ciliate, with hairs 2–3 mm. long; blades with a fine hard point, 10–45 cm. long, 6–15 mm. wide, flat or inrolled upwards, firm, closely flat-ribbed above, smooth, the upper widely spreading. Panicles erect, finally contracted and dense, 12–40 cm. long, of 2–12 spikes, overtopping the leaves. Spikes erect or slightly spreading, stiff, up to 25 cm. long; axis 3-angled, smooth, terminating in a bristle up to 5 cm. long.

Spikelets (S, × 2½) closely overlapping, in two rows on one side of and appressed to the axis, narrowly oblong, flattened, 14–21 mm. long, mostly 2·5–3 mm. wide, 1- rarely 2-flowered, falling entire at maturity, loosely to closely pubescent. Glumes (G_1, G_2, × 2½) keeled, pointed; lower two-thirds to four-fifths the length of the upper, 1-nerved; upper as long as the spikelet, lanceolate-oblong, tough except for the membranous margins, 3–6-nerved. Lemma (L, × 2½) shorter than the upper glume, lanceolate-oblong, 1–3-nerved, with broad membranous margins, shortly hairy. Palea (P, × 2½) a little longer than the lemma, 2-nerved. Anthers (FL, × 2½) 8–13 mm. long. Grain (CE, CH, CS, × 2½) with a long green embryo, enclosed between the lemma, palea, and glumes. *Ch. no.* 2n = 122–124.

This remarkable grass was first collected at Lymington, Hampshire, in 1892, in the Isle of Wight in 1893, and by 1900 it occurred in scattered patches from Chichester Harbour to Poole Harbour. From then onwards it spread with great rapidity, covering several thousands of acres of tidal mud-flats from Sussex to E. Dorset by 1907, and forming almost 30,000 acres of marshland around the shores of Britain by 1960. Subsequently, it has declined in area due to erosion and species invasion of the marshland limits. It appeared also on the north coast of France. By means of its extensive system of roots and rhizomes it stabilizes soft coastal mud, whilst through the filtering action of its culms and leaves it collects debris and silt, thus raising the level of the mud-flats. It has been much planted in such habitats in the British Isles, Europe and Australasia, in order to protect foreshores from erosion and to reclaim hitherto useless land. Known also as Rice Grass. Flowering: July to November.

Spartina anglica is an amphidiploid derived from the sterile primary hybrid, *S.* × *townsendii*, by doubling of the chromosomes. It may be distinguished from the latter by its mostly broader and more widely spreading upper leaf-blades, longer ligular hairs, and mostly longer, wider, and more hairy spikelets, and its longer, perfect anthers.

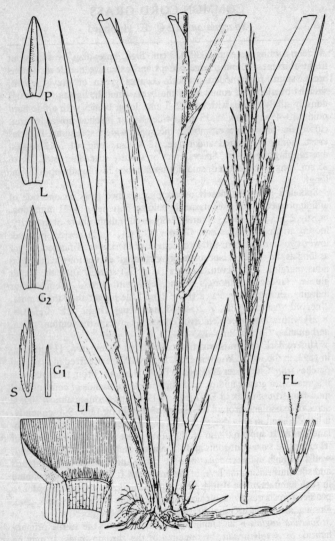

P

L

G₂

G₁

S

LI

FL

Spartina alterniflora. Very rare; coastal mud-flats.

SMOOTH CORD-GRASS

Spartina alterniflora Lois.

A robust perennial, 40–100 cm. high, with fleshy rhizomes, forming clumps or beds. Culms erect, stout, closely sheathed, smooth. Leaves green; sheaths smooth, rounded on the back; ligule (LI, × 4) a dense fringe of hairs 1–1·8 mm. long; blades with a fine hard point, 10–40 cm. long, flat, 5–12 mm. wide, firm, equalling or overtopping the spikes, smooth, closely ribbed above, persistent. Panicles erect, contracted, 10–25 cm. long, up to 3·5 cm. wide, of 3–13 scattered spikes. Spikes erect or slightly spreading, slender; axis 3-angled, smooth, tipped by a bristle 15–27 mm. long.

Spikelets (S, × 2) loosely overlapping, in two rows on one side of and appressed to the axis, lanceolate or narrowly oblong, flattened, 10–18 mm. long, 1-flowered, falling entire at maturity. Glumes keeled, pointed, minutely hairy or rough on the keels, otherwise smooth; lower (G₁, × 2) very narrow, half to four-fifths the length of the spikelet, 1–3-nerved, membranous; upper (G₂, × 2) broader, as long as the spikelet, 5–9-nerved, tough except for the membranous margins. Lemma (L, × 2) slightly shorter than the palea, lanceolate-oblong to narrowly ovate, 1–5-nerved, thin, smooth. Palea (P, × 2) a little shorter than the upper glume, 2-nerved, membranous. Anthers (FL, × 2) 5–7 mm. long. Grain enclosed by the lemma, palea and glumes *Ch. no.* 2n = 62.

A N. American grass, introduced in the early part of the nineteenth century; first noticed by Dr. Bromfield in 1829 in the estuary of the R. Itchen near Southampton. At one time it grew profusely on the tidal mud flats, and spread to other parts of Southampton Water, and along the coast of South Hampshire as far west as Lymington. Since the coming of *Spartina × townsendii* in 1870 and its fertile derivative, *S. anglica*, it has gradually receded, being crowded out by these vigorous and aggressive grasses, until it has now become very rare or perhaps extinct. It was also introduced into the south-east corner of the Bay of Biscay, where it also hybridized with the European species, *S. maritima*, giving rise to *S. × townsendii*. Also known as Many-spiked Cord-grass or American Cord-grass. Flowering: July to November.

Distinguished from *S. maritima*, *S. × townsendii* and *S. anglica* by its almost hairless spikelets, and from the first by its greater size, much longer, persistent leaf-blades, and from the others by its smaller spikelets and anthers, and the 5–9-nerved upper glume. *S. glabra* Muhl. of the coast of E. United States has been planted on a few mud-flats; it differs from *S. alterniflora* by having longer and wider, spreading leaf-blades and more closely imbricate lemmas.

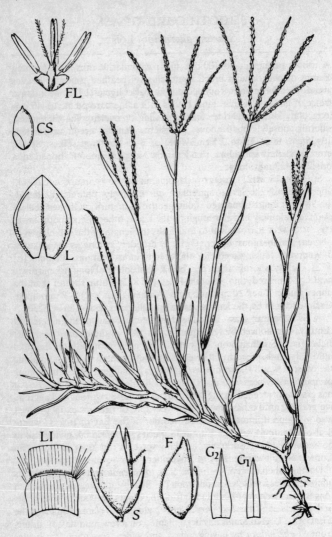

Cynodon dactylon. Rare; coastal sands.

BERMUDA GRASS
Cynodon dactylon (L.) Pers.

A mat-forming perennial, spreading by prostrate runners and scaly rhizomes, the runners branching profusely, rooting at the nodes and developing there short leafy-shoots and flowering culms. Culms erect or bent at the base, 8–30 cm. high, very slender, smooth. Leaves greyish-green or green, loosely short-haired or almost hairless; sheaths rounded, short; ligule (LI, × 4) a dense row of short hairs; blades narrowed to a blunt tip, 2–15 cm. long, 2–4 mm. wide, flat, spreading, minutely rough. Spikes in a cluster of 3–6 at the tip of the culm, very slender, soon spreading, straight or curved, 2–5 cm. long, 1–1·5 mm. wide; main-axes very slender, 3-angled.

Spikelets (S, × 8) without stalks, borne in two rows on one side of and appressed to the axis, overlapping, ovate-oblong, much-compressed, 2–2·8 mm. long, 1-flowered, breaking up at maturity above the glumes, purple or green. Glumes (G_1, G_2, × 8) more or less persistent, equal or slightly unequal, narrow, pointed, keeled, 1-nerved, 1·5–2·3 mm. long, membranous. Lemma (F, L, × 8) as long as the spikelet, boat-shaped, blunt, keeled, 3-nerved, firm, densely and minutely hairy on the keel and often near the margins. Palea about as long as the lemma, 2-keeled. Anthers (FL, × 10) up to 1·5 mm. long. Grain (CS, × 10) tightly enclosed between the hardened lemma and palea. *Ch. no.* 2n = 36.

A low creeping grass, introduced probably long ago into the British Isles, but now so well established in a few sandy maritime localities in S.W. England from Isle of Wight and Dorset to Cornwall and Somerset, in S. Wales and in the Channel Isles, that it has the appearance of a native grass. It was recorded in 1688 by John Ray from between Penzance and Marazion, where it is still locally plentiful. Elsewhere in Britain it occurs occasionally as a chance introduction, in a few places becoming naturalized. A patch on one of the Kew lawns has persisted for many years, the underground rhizomes surviving very severe frosts, whilst the leaves have remained green during periods of extreme drought when our indigenous lawn grasses have become brown, but have been killed in the winter. It is widespread in warm regions, being used extensively as a lawn grass. Like other well-known grasses it has numerous common names, being known as Kweek in S. Africa, Doob in India, Couch in Australia, Bermuda Grass in the United States, and in the British Isles sometimes as Creeping Dog's-tooth-grass or Creeping Finger-grass. Flowering: end of July to September.

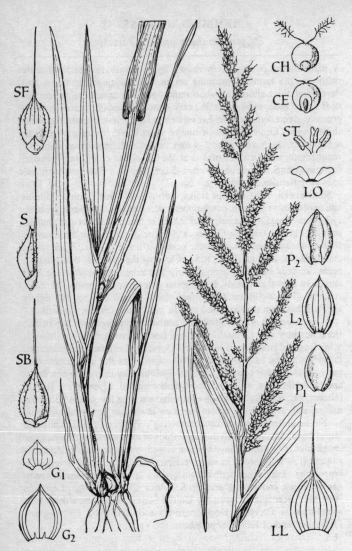

Echinochloa crus-galli. Rare; arable and waste land.

COCKSPUR GRASS
Echinochloa crus-galli (L.) Beauv.

A tufted annual, 30–120 cm. high. Culms erect or spreading, rather stout, usually branched, smooth. Leaves green, hairless; sheaths smooth, keeled; ligules absent; blades finely pointed, 8–35 cm. long, flat, 8–20 mm. wide, soft, rough on the thickened margins, smooth beneath. Panicles lanceolate to ovate, erect or nodding, 6–20 cm. long, up to 8 cm. wide, formed of few to many scattered or clustered spike-like racemes; racemes very dense, green or purplish, up to 6 cm. long, their axes rough, usually also with bristly hairs; pedicels 0·5–2 mm. long.

Spikelets (S, SB, SF, × 4) crowded, in pairs or clusters on one side of the axis, falling entire at maturity, ovate-elliptic in back view, semi-elliptic in side view, 3–4 mm. long, pointed, or awned, with two florets, the lower barren and the upper bisexual. Glumes membranous; lower (G_1, × 4) broad, about one-third the length of the spikelet, 3–5-nerved; upper (G_2, × 4) covering the rounded back of the spikelet, 5-nerved, the nerves bearing short spiny hairs. Lower lemma (LL, × 4) as long as the spikelet, similar to the upper glume but flat or depressed on the back, pointed, or abruptly narrowed into a short cusp or an awn up to 5 cm. long, 5–7-nerved; palea (P_1, × 4) shorter than the lemma. Upper lemma (L_2, × 4) as long as the spikelet, rounded on the back, tough, white or yellowish, smooth; palea (P_2, × 4) as long as the lemma. Anthers (ST, × 4) 1 mm. long. Grain (CE, CH, × 4) tightly enclosed by the hard lemma and palea. *Ch. no.* 2n = 36, 54.

A luscious grass of warm temperate and tropical regions, occasionally appearing on waste and cultivated ground, in warm summers seeding and persisting for a few years. During World War II it was of frequent occurrence as a weed among carrots and other root crops, the seeds of which had come from N. America. Known in the United States as Barnyard Millet. Flowering: August to October.

There are several local races of this grass, and as our plants have come from different areas, they naturally vary considerably in structure. In particular, some have long-awned spikelets, others are awnless, or with awned and awnless spikelets mixed in the same panicle. A few other species of *Echinochloa* are rarely introduced, such as the Asiatic cereal, *Echinochloa frumentacea* Link, on town rubbish-tips, the widespread tropical weed *E. colonum* (L.) Link, on port-dumps, etc., and the N. American *E. pungens* (Poir.) Rydb. in cultivated fields.

Echinochloa utilis Ohwi and Yabuno, derivative of *E. crus-galli of* East Asia, cultivated as Japanese Millet in warm, temperate countries, has broader, longer, purplish or brownish spikelets than *E. frumentacea*.

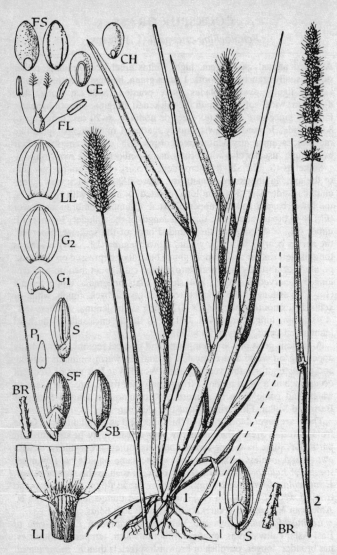

FS

CH

CE

FL

LL

G₂

G₁

P₁

S

BR

SF

SB

LI

S

BR

1

2

Setaria viridis (1) and *S. verticillata* (2). Rare; arable and waste land.

GREEN BRISTLE-GRASS
Setaria viridis (L.) Beauv. (Figure 1)

A loosely tufted annual, 10–60 cm. high. Culms erect, or usually bent at the base, slender, 3–5-noded, branched in the lower part or not, rough towards the panicle. Leaves green; sheaths hairy on the margins, round; ligule (LI, × 4) a dense fringe of silky hairs; blades finely pointed, 3–30 cm. long, flat, 4–10 mm. wide, hairless, minutely rough. Panicles spike-like, very bristly, mostly erect, very dense, cylindrical or tapering upwards, 1–10 cm. long, 4–10 mm. wide (excluding the bristles), greenish or purplish; branches up to 3 mm. long; bristles (BR) straight or wavy, 1–3 beneath each spikelet, up to 10 mm. long, minutely rough.

Spikelets (S, SB, SF, × 6) elliptic-oblong in back view, blunt, semi-elliptic-oblong in side view, 2–3 mm. long, 1-flowered, falling entire at maturity. Glumes (G_1, G_2, × 6) thinly membranous; lower up to one-third the length of the spikelet, ovate, 1–3-nerved; upper covering the whole of the back of the spikelet, 5-nerved. Lower lemma (LL, × 6) resembling the upper glume, 5–7-nerved; palea (P_1, × 6) up to half the length of the lemma, very thin. Upper lemma (FS, back and front views, × 6) as long as the spikelet, elliptic-oblong, blunt, pale, rounded on the back, becoming tough and rigid, very finely wrinkled; palea flat on the back. Anthers (FL, × 8) 0·8 mm. long. Grain (CE, CH, × 6) tightly enclosed by the hardened lemma and palea. *Ch. no.* 2n = 18.

A rather rare weed of cultivated and waste land, occurring occasionally in various parts of the British Isles, but mostly in the south, sometimes persisting from year to year in the same locality. A native of warm-temperate Europe and Asia, introduced into N. and S. America, etc. Flowering: August to October.

Setaria verticillata (L.) Beauv. (Figure 2), Bur or Rough Bristle-grass, of the warm regions of the Old World, is a very rare alien of waste places. It resembles *S. viridis* but has less bristly somewhat interrupted panicles, and reflexed (backward-pointing) teeth on the bristles (BR). *Ch. no.* 2n = 18, 36. *S. italica* (L.) Beauv., Fox-tail or Italian Millet, is cultivated in some warm-temperate countries for its small seeds, which are used as food for cage-birds. It is a derivative of *S. viridis*, from which it may be distinguished by its larger panicles (up to 30 cm. long) and by the upper floret (fruit) becoming detached from the rest of the spikelet at maturity. There are numerous varieties, differing in the shape and size of the panicles, and in the colour of the fruits, these being white, yellow, red, brown, and black. *Ch. no.* 2n = 18.

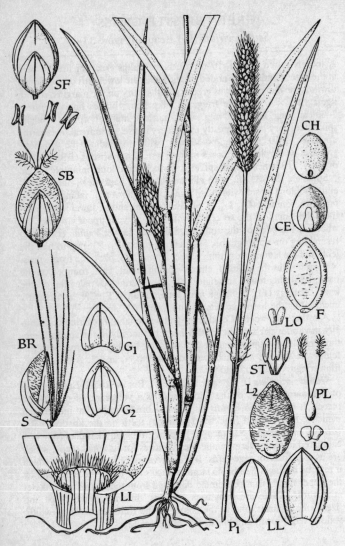

Setaria glauca. Rare; arable and waste land.

YELLOW BRISTLE-GRASS
Setaria glauca (L.) Beauv.

Annual, 6–75 cm. high. Culms loosely tufted or solitary, erect, or bent and ascending, slender, 2–4-noded, rough near the panicle. Leaves green; sheaths smooth, the lower compressed, keeled; ligule (LI, × 4) a dense fringe of fine hairs; blades finely pointed, 6–30 cm. long, flat, 4–10 mm. wide, hairy towards the base, or hairless, minutely rough on the margins. Panicles spike-like, dense, very bristly, erect, cylindrical, 1–14 cm. long, 4–8 mm. wide (excluding the bristles); branches up to 1 mm. long, usually bearing a single spikelet and beneath it 5–10 bristles (BR); bristles fine, minutely rough, straight or wavy, yellowish to reddish-yellow, up to 10 mm. long.

Spikelets (S, SB, SF, × 6) broadly elliptic in back view, blunt, broadly semi-elliptic in side view, about 3 mm. long, falling entire at maturity, 1–2-flowered, with the lower floret male or barren and the upper bisexual. Glumes (G_1, G_2, × 6) broadly ovate, thinly membranous; lower up to half the length of the spikelet, 3-nerved; upper up to two-thirds the length of the spikelet, 5-nerved. Lower lemma (LL, × 6) as long as the spikelet, broad, flat or slightly depressed on the back, 5-nerved; palea (P_1, × 6) flat. Upper lemma (L_2, × 6) as long as the spikelet, broadly boat-shaped, rounded on the back, prominently transversely wrinkled, tough, rigid, becoming yellow or brown; palea as long as the lemma. Anthers (ST, × 6) up to 1·5 mm. long. Grain (CE, CH, × 6) tightly enclosed by the hard lemma and palea. *Ch. no.* 2n = 18, 36.

A rare weed of cultivated and waste land; native of the warm-temperate zone of the Old World, introduced into N. and S. America, Australia, etc. Known also as Glaucous Bristle-grass. Flowering: July to October.

Setaria geniculata (Lam.) Beauv., of the warm parts of America, has been found on port rubbish-tips. It resembles *S. glauca*, but is a perennial, with short hard creeping rhizomes, more slender panicles, and smaller spikelets (2–2·5 mm. long).

Setaria may be distinguished from the species of *Panicum* found on rubbish-tips in the British Isles in the branches of the panicles being produced as one or more bristles beneath the spikelets. That these bristles are modified branches may be deduced from the occasional development of a spikelet at their tips as in *Setaria italica. S. plicata* (Lam.) T. Cooke (*Panicum plicatum* Lam.) is grown in warm greenhouses for its attractive foliage, the leaf-blades being folded lengthways like a fan.

(*Setaria pumila* (Poiret) Schultes.)

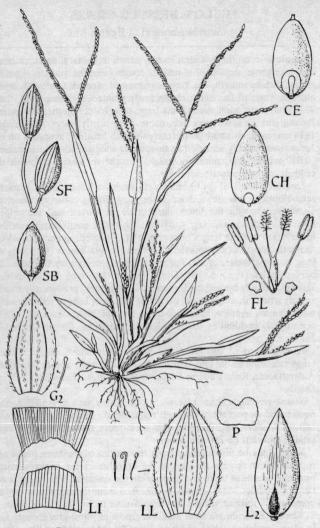

Digitaria ischaemum. Rare; arable and waste land.

SMOOTH FINGER-GRASS

Digitaria ischaemum (Schreb.) Muhl.

A loosely or compactly tufted annual, 10–35 cm. high. Culms ascending, or spreading from a bent base, or prostrate, very slender, 2–4-noded, usually branched, smooth. Leaves green or tinged with purple; sheaths hairless, or with a few hairs at the apex, smooth; ligules (LI, × 5) 1–2 mm. long, membranous; blades narrowly lanceolate, more or less rounded at the base, finely pointed, 2–12 cm. long, 2–7 mm. wide, flat, hairless, minutely rough on the margins. Racemes spike-like, 2–8, borne at or near the apex of the culm, very slender, finally spreading, 1·5–7 cm. long, purplish; raceme-axes narrowly winged, 1 mm. wide, minutely rough on the margins.

Spikelets (SF, SB, × 6) in pairs or threes, on one side of the axis only, contiguous, short- and unequally pedicelled, falling entire at maturity, somewhat flattened on the back, elliptic or oblong-elliptic, rather blunt, 2–2·5 mm. long, 1-flowered. Lower glume outermost, very minute, or suppressed; upper glume (G_2, × 12) elliptic, as long as spikelet or nearly so, 3-nerved, minutely hairy, thin. Lower lemma (LL, × 12) flat on the back, similar in outline and length to the spikelet, 5-nerved, thin, hairy like the upper glume, with a minute palea (P, × 30), but no flower. Upper lemma (L_2, × 12) as long as the spikelet, brown or purplish-brown, rigid except for the flat thin margins folding over the palea, smooth. Anthers (FL, × 12) 0·5–0·7 mm. Grain (CE, CH, × 12) tightly enclosed by the hardened lemma and palea. *Ch. no.* 2n = 36.

A rare grass, established in some sandy fields in S. and S.E. England; occasionally found on waste ground and rubbish dumps near ports. A native of warm-temperate Europe and Asia, introduced into the United States, etc. Also known as Red Millet. Flowering: August and September.

The species of *Digitaria* possess very distinctive inflorescences, their spikelets being borne on very short stalks along one side of the axes of slender spike-like racemes, these being clustered at or near the apex of the culm. In this respect they resemble *Cynodon dactylon*, which is, however, a creeping perennial with hairy ligules, its flattened spikelets compressed from the side and not from the back.

Some species of *Panicum*, such as *P. miliaceum* L. (Common Millet or Broom-corn Millet), the seed of which is fed to cage-birds, and *P. capillare* L., may be found on rubbish tips, etc., in the late summer. They are distinguished from *Digitaria* by their spikelets being arranged in loose panicles.

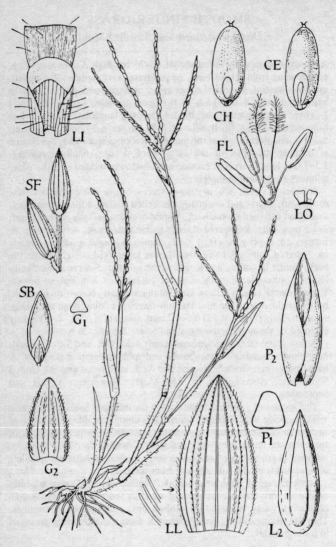

Digitaria sanguinalis. Rare; cultivated and waste land.

HAIRY FINGER-GRASS
Digitaria sanguinalis (L.) Scop.

A loose-growing green or purplish annual, 10–30 (rarely 60) cm. high. Culms mostly ascending from a bent or prostrate base, rooting from the lower nodes, slender, branched or not, 3–8-noded, loosely bearded at the nodes, or hairless and smooth. Leaf-sheaths closely to sparsely hairy from minute tubercles, or hairless, loose; ligules (LI, × 3) 1–2 mm. long, membranous; blades narrowly lanceolate, rounded at the base, finely pointed, 3–10 (rarely 20) cm. long, 3–8 (rarely 14) mm. wide, flat, hairy or hairless, minutely rough on the margins. Racemes spike-like, 4–10 (rarely more or less), clustered at or near the apex of the culm, 4–18 cm. long, very slender, finally spreading; raceme-axes 3-angled, rough on the angles, about 1 mm. wide.

Spikelets (SF, SB, × 6) in pairs, along one side of the racemes, touching, unequally short-pedicelled, falling entire at maturity, somewhat flattened, ovate-elliptic to oblong-elliptic, pointed, 2·5–3·3 mm. long, 1-flowered. Lower glume (G_1, × 12) outermost, minute; upper glume (G_2, × 12) up to half the length of the spikelet, lanceolate to narrowly ovate, pointed, 3-nerved, thin, minutely hairy. Lower lemma (LL, × 12) flat or nearly so on the back, corresponding in length and outline to the spikelet, 7-nerved, minutely rough on the nerves, finely and obscurely hairy, with a minute palea (P_1, × 20), but no flower. Upper lemma (L_2, × 12) as long as the spikelet, pointed, firm, except for the broad thin margins folding over the back of the palea (P_2, × 12), smooth. Anthers (FL, × 20) about 0·6 mm. long. Grain (CE, CH, × 12) tightly enclosed by the hardened lemma and the palea. *Ch. no.* 2n = 36.

An introduced grass of rare occurrence as a weed of cultivated and waste land, railway sidings, docks, and rubbish dumps, mainly in S. England and Wales; also in sandy fields and on roadsides in the Channel Isles. Frequent in the Mediterranean Region and Asia; introduced into N. and S. America, S. Africa, and Australasia. Known as Crab Grass in the United States. Flowering: August to October.

A related species, *D. adscendens* (H.B.K.) Henrard (= *D. ciliaris* (Retz.) Koel.), widespread in the Tropics, and rarely introduced into the British Isles, has a more prominent ligule, and smooth nerves on the lower lemma. *D. ischaemum* (p. 369) differs from both in having smaller blunt spikelets, with the upper glume nearly covering one side of the spikelet and, like the lower lemma, clothed with minute swollen-tipped hairs.

HIGHLAND BENT

Agrostis castellana Boiss. & Reuter

Densely to loosely-tufted perennial; vigorously spreading from stout, short rhizomes. Culms to 100 cm. high, very slender, numerous, curved to erect, 3–4(6)-noded, glabrous, smooth. Panicles linear, loose and spreading, becoming contracted, 4–8 cm. wide, 17–20 cm. long. Leaf sheaths smooth, glabrous. Leaves characteristically blue-green, blades finely acute, linear, flat, to 12 cm. long, 1·5–4·5 mm. wide, minutely rough, closely ribbed. Uppermost ligule to 3 mm. long, remainder shorter, prominent often jagged.

Spikelets of two kinds; terminal and awned or awnless, with 5-nerved lemmas; lateral ones awnless, with 3–5-nerved lemmas; on tips of branches and branchlets. Glumes 2 mm. long, equal or lower one slightly longer (to 3 mm.), green tinged with purple, linear-lanceolate and sharply acute in profile, 1-nerved, keeled; lower rough on keel, upper smooth. Lemmas (1·5–) 2 mm. long, sparsely and minutely pubescent on sides, membranous-hyaline, ovate-oblong, truncate-lobulate; outer lateral nerves sometimes excurrent into awnlets to 0·5 mm. long; thickened base or callus, 2 lateral tufts of white hairs to 0·3 mm. long. Palea two-thirds length of lemma, shallowly 2-lobed, oblong, finely 2-nerved. When present, awns from or near base of lemma, to twice length of lemma. Anthers 1 mm. long. *Ch. no.* 2n = 28 + 2, 42 (for Portuguese material). Grain rounded on the back, with a narrow median groove in front; embryo about quarter of grain, orbicular.

About 400 tonnes of Brown Top seed are imported annually, most of it containing Highland Bent, for sowing on sports turf, in country parks, in reclamation projects and in other semi-natural areas. The cultivar was originally selected in Oregon from naturalized bent grasses although characteristics are strongly suggestive of a Mediterranean origin (bluish-green leaf colour, early heading and drought resistance).

Two varieties identified amongst naturalized and amenity research material examined from this country and New Zealand. Var. *mixta* Hack. has spikelets awned and awnless in the same panicle. Var. *mutica* Hack. has spikelets without awns. Associated with recently sown amenity grassland, as a mixture of forms including true *Agrostis castellana* and possible hybrids between it and *Agrostis tenuis*. Recorded from Hampshire, Middlesex, Norfolk, Gloucestershire and Cornwall. Probably widespread.

Agrostis castellana growing in short turf distinguished from *Agrostis tenuis* by differences in colour and ligule size.

TENTATIVE KEY TO SUBSPECIES OF
FESTUCA RUBRA L.

1 All the leaf-blades setaceous (bristle-like), usually plicate, up to 1·3 mm. wide in side-view or flat, and to 2·7 mm. wide; anthers 2–3 mm. long

2 Plants without rhizomes, densely tufted; outer basal leaf-sheaths glabrous or minutely pubescent; upper glume 3·5–6 mm. long; lower lemmas 5–6·5 mm. long, glabrous or rarely hairy (cultivated or waste ground) ....subsp. **commutata** (135)

2a Plants with short to long rhizomes, loosely to densely tufted, or with scattered shoots and culms

3 Plants compactly tufted or mat-forming, with comparatively short very slender rhizomes; culms 10–48 cm. high; panicles 3–8 cm. long

4 Plants mat-forming; outer basal leaf-sheaths usually glabrous; leaf-blades 0·5–0·7 mm. wide in side view, dark green; lower lemmas 6–7·5 mm. long, rarely less (–5 mm.), always glabrous (salt marshes) ....subsp. **litoralis** (375)

4a Plants forming loose to dense tufts; outer basal leaf-sheaths mostly retrorsely pubescent; leaf-blades 0·6–1·3 mm. wide in side view, becoming whitish-pruinose, or green; lower lemmas 5–5·5 mm. long, rarely more (–6 mm.), glabrous, or pubescent ....subsp.| **pruinosa** (376)

3a Plants loosely to closely tufted, or with scattered vegetative shoots and culms, with relatively long to very long rhizomes:

5 Lemmas (lower) awnless or mucronate, or the upper with awns 0·5–1·5 mm. long; culms mostly scattered, 12–30 cm. high; panicles dense, narrow 3–5 cm. long, densely short villous to hirsute, or ? occasionally glabrous (high altitudes on mountains) .... subsp. **arctica** (379)

5a Lemmas usually awned, the awns 0·5–3 mm. long; glumes glabrous; culms to 85 cm. high

6 Lemmas 4·5–5·5 (rarely to 6) mm. long, glabrous, or shortly pubescent; upper glume 3–4·5 mm. long; basal outer leaf-sheaths densely retrorsely pubescent ....subsp. **rubra** (137)

6a Lemmas 6–8 mm. long, usually densely hairy with spreading hairs, rarely glabrous; upper glume 4·5–7·5 mm. long

7 Plant with long branching rhizomes, on sand dunes; basal outer leaf-sheaths usually glabrous; panicles 7–15 cm. long
subsp. **arenaria** (377)

7a Plant with slender comparatively short rhizomes, at high eleva-

373

tions on mountains; basal outer leaf-sheaths pubescent;
panicles 4·5–6·6 cm. long .... subsp. (ex Cairngorms)
1a All the leaf-blades flat, or only the basal blades plicate and setaceous;
the culm-blades flat; anthers 3–4 mm. long; culms up to 110 cm.
high, relatively stout; basal leaf-sheaths densely pubescent;
lemmas 6–8 mm. long, usually glabrous; panicles 12–22 cm. long,
up to 15 cm. wide:
8 Basal leaf-blades plicate and setaceous, 0·5–1 mm. wide in side view;
culm-blades flat, 1·5–4 mm. wide, 7–11-ribbed above, the ribs
pubescent .... subsp. **megastachys** (378)
8a All leaf-blades flat, 2–5 mm. wide, up to 13-ribbed above, the ribs
pubescent .... subsp. **multiflora** (380)

SLENDER CREEPING RED FESCUE
Festuca rubra subsp. *litoralis* (G. F. W. Meyer) Auquier

Densely tufted or mat-forming perennial, with numerous closely-packed tillers and culms; with short very slender rhizomes, purplish to brown, scaled or sheathed. Outer basal leaf-sheaths usually glabrous, entire. Basal and culm blades slender, dark green, bristle-like, slightly curved, keeled, 0·5–0·7 mm. long (basal blade), 4·5–6·5 mm. long (culm blade). Culms 10–48 cm. high, erect or curved at the base, stiff, 1–2-noded in the lower quarter or third, blackish-purple nodes. Panicle linear, erect, contracted, dense, generally few, sometimes reduced to 2–3 spikelets, green or tinged with purple.

Spikelets relatively large, 7–16 mm. long, 3–9-flowered, without hairs, oblong. Lower lemma 6–7·5 mm. long (rarely 5 mm.), oblong-lanceolate, pointed. Lower glume 3–5 mm. long, upper glume 4–7·5 mm. long. Awnless or with awns 0·5–3 mm. long. Anthers 2–3 mm. long.

Recorded from Norfolk, Suffolk, Sussex, East Lothian, the Channel Isles and Monmouthshire, but probably widespread around the coast. Forms a close green turf on muddy tidal sediment above the zone of or intermixed with *Puccinellia maritima*, *Halimione portulacoides* and *Triglochin maritima*.

Distinguished from subsp. *rubra* by the longer lemmas, glabrous outer leaf-sheaths and long rhizomes.

BLOOMED FESCUE

Festuca rubra subsp. *pruinosa* (Hack.) Piper

Compact to loosely-tufted perennial arising from very short slender wiry upturned rhizomes, to 3·5 mm. long. Outer basal leaf-sheaths covered with downward-pointing hairs, entire. Blades bristle-like, acute to obtuse, whitish-pruinose or green, 3–28 cm. long, 0·6–1·3 mm. wide, 7-nerved, rigid, curved or straight, tightly folded. Culm blades much shorter than the basal blades. Stems 10–48 cm. high, erect, slender, 2–3-noded in the lowest quarter, curved at the lower nodes. Panicles lanceolate to narrowly ovate, to 7·5 mm. long, contracted, erect, purplish.

Spikelets glabrous, 5–7-flowered, oblong, to 11 mm. long, tinged with purple, greyish. Lower lemmas 5–5·5 mm. long, rarely more (to 6 mm.), glabrous or with short hairs, rough at margins. Awns 0·5–2·5 mm. long. Anthers 2–3 mm. long.

Distributed around the coast and recorded from the Shetland Isles, Ireland, the Channel Isles and Somerset. Found on sea-cliffs, stony sea-shores and salt-marshes.

Distinctive on account of its dense habit; very pruinose, very rigid, bristle-like leaf-blades; and tough, short lemmas.

SAND FESCUE

Festuca rubra L. subsp *arenaria* (Osbeck) Syme.

Perennial, forming loosely-tufted patches with solitary culms; long, slender, branching, wiry rhizomes. Culms 20–85 cm. high, erect, slender, curved near the base, 1–3-noded, glabrous, finely striate towards panicle. Basal sheaths glabrous and smooth. Basal leaf-blades bristle-like, folded, up to 45 cm. long, 0·6–1 mm. wide, bluish, striate, 7-ribbed above, ribs green, minutely and densely hairy. Culm leaf-blades are similar to basal blades but prominently 6–9-ribbed above. Panicles erect or nodding, 7–15 cm. long, lanceolate to linear, contracted or loose, with lower branches paired or solitary, unequal, spreading and longer to 4 cm.

Spikelets 7–15 mm. long, shaggy, green, oblong or elliptic-oblong, 4–8-flowered. Lemmas 6–9 mm. long, 3-nerved, sharply pointed, short and soft to densely hairy. Variable in glume length. Anthers 2·6–4·5 mm. long.

Recorded from Norfolk, Essex, Cornwall, Devon, Merioneth, Glamorgan, Kirkcudbrightshire, and the Shetland Isles. Near sea on loose or consolidated sand-dunes, shingle-sand ridges and waste ground.

Festuca rubra L. subsp *megastachys* Gaud.

Loosely tufted or as scattered culms; slender rhizomes. Basal leaf-sheaths densely hairy. Basal leaf-blades bristle-like and folded, 21–65 cm. long, 0·5–1·2 mm. wide. Culm-blades flat 1·5–4 mm. wide, 7–11-ribbed above, ribs pubescent, hard pointed tip. Culms to 110 cm. high, relatively stout, 2–3-noded, erect but curved at the base, striate towards panicle. Panicles erect or nodding, 8–23 cm. long, contracted to 2 cm. wide, dense, green, lanceolate.

Spikelets 9–14 mm. long, 4–9-flowered, green or tinged with purple, without hairs, oblong. Glumes 6 mm. long, keeled. Lemmas 6–8 mm. long, usually hairless.

Scattered localities in Scotland, Wales and E. England. Probably widespread. Associated with sown grassland. Found on grass banks, waste ground, roadside verges and pastures.

Differs from subsp. *rubra* by the much larger spikelets. In var. *pubescens* the outer basal sheaths are densely and minutely pubescent. Spikelets are minutely pubescent.

Festuca rubra L. subsp. *arctica* (Hack.) Govor.

A perennial, forming compact tufts with long ascending rhizomes, numerously ending in shoots. Stems 12–45 cm. high, erect above a curved base, slender, 2–3-noded, smooth, minutely hairy near panicle. Basal outer leaf-sheaths densely covered with backward-pointing or spreading hairs. Inner leaf-sheaths closely covered with minute hairs. Basal leaf-blades bristle-like, curved, blunt, folded, green, 0·5–1·0 mm. wide, 4–18 cm. long. Culm blades 7-ribbed, hairy above, green, blunt, to 6 cm. long. Panicles erect, dense, contracted, oblong to ovate, greyish to purplish-green, 3–5 cm. long.

Spikelets 4–7-flowered, 8 mm. long, pruinose, elliptic-oblong. Glumes glabrous, oblong-lanceolate, sometimes with a few hairs at the tip of the second one. Upper lemmas with awns 0·5–1·3 mm. long. Anthers 2–2·8 mm. long, deep purple. *Ch. no.* 2n = 42.

High altitudes on mountains above 600 m. Scotland, Perthshire and the Shetland Isles.

(*Festuca richardsonii* Hooker)

Festuca rubra L. subsp. *multiflora* (Hoffn.) Wallr.

A compactly tufted perennial with short, spreading, upturned rhizomes. Basal leaf-sheaths densely hairy in upper part, or quite glabrous and smooth, entire. Ligule 0·3 mm. long. Culm leaf-blade 7–13-ribbed above, hairy on ribs, hairless beneath, 15–38 cm. long, minutely rough on margins and towards hard, pointed tip, dark green. Culms slender to relatively stout, not ridged or grooved, slightly curved below mid point then erect, 3-noded in the lower half, hairless, minutely rough near panicle, otherwise smooth, to 90 cm. high. Basal leaf-blades to 60 cm. long, narrowly linear, finely pointed, 5–9-ribbed above. Panicle narrowly ovate to ovate-oblong, erect, inclined or nodding, loose, open, 12–22 cm. long, green; rhachis angular; branches paired and unequal, the lowest 5–11 cm. long, spreading; pedicels 2–4 mm. long.

Spikelets 12–17 mm. long, 3–4 mm. wide, oblong, 7–10-flowered, green. Glumes unequal, acute; lower 2·5–3·5 mm. long, narrowly-lanceolate, keeled, 1-nerved; upper 4·5–7 mm. long, oblong-lanceolate, keeled, 3-nerved. Awns 0·5–3 mm. long. Anthers 3–4 mm. long.

Recorded from E. Perthshire, Surrey and Wicklow. Grassy banks and the margins of recently sown grassland.

Separated from the other rhizomatous taxa of the *Festuca rubra* group by its wide blades, the large inflorescences and spikelets with numerous flowers.

VEGETATIVE CHARACTERS OF GRASSES

The key for the identification of our common grasses, based entirely on differences in their habit and in the structure of their shoots and leaves, is intended for grassland investigators, farmers, greenkeepers, and others requiring the names of grasses when flowers are not available. It is assumed that those using the key are able to recognize the parts of the grass plant, but if this is not so, then they should turn to page 17, where the various organs are described. When there is ample material for examination, a complete plant with rootstock and leafy shoots in good condition should be dug or pulled up and the basal parts washed free of soil.

In the vegetative state it is not always possible to distinguish annuals and biennials from perennials. The former, however, usually have solitary shoots or a few shoots in a loose cluster, their leaves are softer, and the remains of the seed-husks often persist for some time at the base of the shoots. Perennials, on the other hand, usually possess firmer shoots and blades; the former are often coated at the base with old leaf-sheaths or their remains, whilst in many species there are basal buds, rhizomes, or stolons.

In perennials the shoots may be gathered together in loose or dense tufts, or be scattered and even widely separated from each other. If such grasses with spaced shoots are carefully examined, it will usually be found that they are connected by creeping wiry or fleshy stems. When these creeping stems lie on or near the surface of the soil, as in Creeping Bent, they are termed stolons or runners and the plants possessing them are said to be stoloniferous. Alternatively, if the stems are beneath the surface, as in Couch-grass, they are known as rhizomes, and the plants bearing them are rhizomatous. Both stolons and rhizomes develop shoots and roots at the nodes. Stolons are usually green or purplish, and have complete green leaves consisting of sheaths and blades, although the latter may be smaller than usual. Rhizomes, on the other hand, being below ground, are whitish, yellowish, or brown. They bear short whitish or brownish scale-like leaves which are bladeless and only become greenish or purplish where they protrude from the soil. It is sometimes difficult to distinguish stolons from rhizomes, especially where stoloniferous and rhizomatous grasses have formed a close sward or dense turf, or where stolons have become buried and bleached and then resemble rhizomes. In close short turf when stoloniferous grasses are present, some stolons will usually grow over the tops of the other grasses, or their remains may be found at the base of the shoots at ground level. Under such conditions, however, it may be necessary for the grass, of which

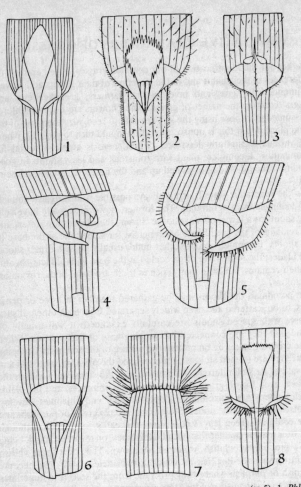

LIGULES AND AURICLES AT JUNCTION OF SHEATH AND BLADE (× 5). 1, *Phleum bertolonii*. 2, *Bromus sterilis*. 3, *Melica uniflora*. 4, *Festuca pratensis*. 5, *Festuca arundinacea*. 6, *Alopecurus pratensis*. 7, *Sieglingia decumbens*. 8, *Anthoxanthum odoratum*.

the name is required, to be transplanted into open ground where it can develop freely without competition.

The vegetative shoots, tillers, or innovations as they are called by botanists, should be examined next, to ascertain whether each of the younger ones has grown straight up from the base within a leaf-sheath, or whether it has grown from a bud which has burst through the base of the leaf-sheath. The first type of growth, called intravaginal, is characteristic of densely tufted grasses such as Sheep's Fescue, whilst the second kind, known as extravaginal, gives rise to loosely tufted or mat-forming plants as in Red Fescue. At this stage the inner basal leaf-sheaths should be studied to find out if they have free margins, that is, with one margin overlapping the other, or joined margins and the sheaths consequently tubular. These characters are most important for distinguishing certain species of *Festuca*, e.g. Sheep's Fescue and Red Fescue, as well as many other grasses. In order to see which type of sheath is present, a basal shoot should be freed of all sheaths except the innermost. Then the young leaf-blade protruding from the sheath should be slowly pulled against the side of the sheath directly opposite to its blade. If the margins of the sheath are free, one margin will be seen moving over the other, whereas in tubular (entire) sheaths, a tear will develop as soon as the pressure of the blade becomes too great. All species of *Bromus*, *Glyceria*, and *Melica* have entire tubular sheaths.

The young leaf-blades are arranged within the sheaths of the shoots in two ways. In the first type the young blade is folded longitudinally about its middle nerve, whereas in the second it is rolled longitudinally with one margin innermost. These differences sometimes distinguish closely related species, as for example, Perennial and Italian Rye-grass. They can be seen best by cutting transversely across the young shoot just below the tip of the sheath with a sharp knife or razor blade, and examining the cut surface with a lens. The folded type of blade will be compressed with its two margins touching, whereas the rolled blade will be more or less rounded with one margin innermost and the other outermost. From such a section it is possible also to ascertain whether the margins of the enveloping leaf-sheaths are free or united. Most grasses with rolled leaf-blades have cylindrical shoots, with their sheaths usually rounded on the back, whilst in those with folded blades the shoots are more or less compressed and flattened, and their sheaths frequently keeled on the back.

In the key, the grasses have been divided into two groups depending on whether their fully developed leaf-blades are normally flat (expanded) as in most pasture and meadow grasses, or stiff and more or less bristle-like as are those of Sheep's Fescue and Mat-grass. In the first group, however, the blades may become rolled or folded when dry conditions prevail. Those of the second group may have a single channel or two to four grooves above, or they may be tightly infolded or inrolled and when opened out rarely more than 2 mm. wide. The margins of the blades are parallel in Blue Sesleria, but in the majority of our grasses the blades taper very gradually towards the apex. The tips of the blades should always be examined, since these show good diagnostic characters. They may be finely pointed (sometimes with the tips needle-like), abruptly pointed, or rather blunt. The blades of *Poa* and *Puccinellia* usually have slightly hooded tips.

A drawing of the ligule, lettered LI, is included in most illustrations. Its shape and size are of considerable value for distinguishing closely related species, such as those of *Poa* and *Agrostis*, as well as many other grasses which superficially resemble each other. It is usually a delicate nerveless whitish membrane, except in certain coarse grasses, for example, Tufted Hair-grass and Marram Grass, in which it is stiff and nerved. In the Common Reed, the Cord-grasses and a few other species, the ligule is represented by a dense row of short fine hairs. Only in Cockspur Grass is it entirely absent. Another kind of out-growth of the leaf, known as an auricle (AU, LI in the illustrations), may be present on each margin of the leaf where the sheath joins the blade. Auricles are usually narrow, pointed, spreading, and somewhat claw-like; they are present in almost all grasses of the Barley and Wheat tribe, *Triticeae* (*Agropyron, Hordeum, Triticum*, etc.), as well as in the Rye-grasses and some species of *Festuca* and *Bromus*.

The presence of hairs on the leaves is often a constant feature of a particular grass. Other grasses may have hairless leaves, or the leaves may bear minute rough points or be quite smooth. For example, those of the Rye-grasses and Bent-grasses are always hairless, those of Soft Brome softly hairy, the sheaths of Rough Meadow-grass frequently minutely rough, whilst those of Meadow-grass are smooth. Hairiness and roughness may extend all over the leaf, or be confined to the sheath or blade, or to one or both surfaces of the latter. Neither hairiness nor the presence of minute rough points is an entirely reliable means of identification, since some species have hairy or hairless, or smooth or rough strains. Cocksfoot, for example, is generally hairless, and Yorkshire Fog normally softly and densely hairy, yet in both these grasses hairy and hairless strains occur.

Among other features of value for recognizing grasses are particular colours, flavours, and smells. Yellowish colorations at the base of the lowest living sheaths are characteristic of Crested Dog's-tail and Tall Oat-grass. The basal living sheaths of Perennial Rye-grass are usually pinkish, those of Meadow Foxtail dark purple or dark brown, whilst the veins of the sheaths of Yorkshire Fog are pinkish. Colour, however, is not always a satisfactory diagnostic character, since even grasses normally green may under dry conditions develop purplish or reddish sheaths, and others become greyish- or bluish-green owing to the formation of a thick skin (cuticle) or the presence of a white wax covering. Some grasses are more readily grazed than others by animals and no doubt have attractive flavours or scents. Water Whorl-grass has slightly sweet shoots, whereas those of Tall Oat-grass are bitter to the taste. A few grasses may be identified by their aromatic leaves, in particular those of Sweet Vernal-grass and Holy-grass, which are scented with coumarin, but the majority of our grasses appear to have no special smell or taste, at least to humans.

The anatomy of the leaves cannot be considered here except to note that many grasses differ very considerably in the arrangement and development of particular tissues and in the structure of the epidermis. Certain anatomical features affect the appearance of the leaves. Thus the presence of strands of fibres (sclerenchyma) is shown externally in the prominent ribbing of the upper surface of the blades of Sea Couch and many other grasses, whilst the presence of large colourless cells on each side of the midrib shows up as two translucent zones in the Sweet-grasses and Meadow-grasses. For further information on the anatomy of the grasses, the reader should see C. R. Metcalfe, *Anatomy of the Monocotyledons*, Vol. 1, 'Gramineae' (1960).

The following key is drawn up like that on page 35, the contrasting characters being arranged in pairs numbered 1 and 1a, and so on, in the manner explained on page 34. One final piece of advice is: gather good and complete specimens and examine them thoroughly before using the key, bearing in mind that plants from moist habitats are usually larger, greener, and less hairy or rough then those of the same species from dry situations.

KEY FOR NAMING THE MORE COMMON
GRASSES BY THEIR VEGETATIVE
CHARACTERS

*The figures in parentheses refer to the pages on which the grasses are
described or mentioned.*

1 Leaf-blades usually flat (opened out), or rolled or folded down the
  middle when dry, mostly not very narrow but if so then not
  bristle-like (to p. 399):
2 Ligule formed by a dense fringe of very short hairs; no auricles
  present at the junction of sheath and blade (to p. 388):
3 Blades 10–30 mm. wide, 20–60 cm. or more long, with long finely
   pointed flexuous tips, tough, closely many-nerved, hairless,
   greyish-green or dull green; sheaths smooth, bearded at the
   junction with the blade when young; plant reed-like; perennial
   with long stout rhizomes and stolons; wet places, in water
                       Phragmites communis (347)
3a Blades up to 15 mm. wide; plants not reed-like:
4 Leaves hairless on the outside at the junction of sheath and blade;
   young leaf-blade rolled in the shoot, the latter more or less
   cylindrical:
5 Leaf-blades prominently and closely ribbed on the upper surface,
    the ribs flat-topped; blades smooth, hairless, green or
    yellowish-green; shoots cylindrical; plants with creeping
    rhizomes:
6 Leaf-blades 6–15 mm. wide, 10–45 cm. long; rhizomes stout,
    soft, fleshy, extensively creeping:
6* Ligules 2–3 mm. long; leaf-blades widely spreading; coastal
    mud-flats .... **Spartina anglica** (357)
6a* Ligules 1–2 mm. long; leaf-blades slightly spreading; coastal
    mud-flats .... **Spartina × townsendii** (355)
6a Leaf-blades up to 6 mm. wide, 2–18 cm. long; rhizomes tough,
    wiry, shortly creeping; ligules 0·2–0·6 mm. long; salt-
    marshes .... **Spartina maritima** (353)
5a Leaf-blades scarcely ribbed above, 3–10 mm. wide, 10–45 cm.
   long, slightly hairy above or hairless, dull green, finely
   pointed; shoot thickened towards the base; tufted perennial,
   with tough cord-like roots; wet peaty places
                       Molinia caerulea (349)
4a Leaves short-bearded with spreading hairs at the junction of
  sheath and blade; blades with abruptly pointed or blunt tips,

2–4 mm. wide, 5–25 cm. long, the youngest folded in the
shoot, afterwards flat or gutter-like, not ribbed above; tufted
perennial; heaths and moors ..... **Sieglingia decumbens** (351)

2a Ligules membranous, variable in length, sometimes short and
obscure, white, cream, green or purplish:

7 Youngest leaf-blade rolled in the shoot, the latter mostly cylindrical;
sheaths usually rounded on the back, or keeled only in the
upper part (to p. 397):

8 Leaves with small narrow white, pale green or purplish claw-like
outgrowths (auricles) at the junction of sheath and blade (to
p. 390):

9 Plants with extensively creeping whitish or brownish rhizomes,
giving rise to scattered shoots or tufts; sheaths open, with
free margins; ligules up to 1 mm. long:

10 Leaf-blades prominently and closely ribbed on the upper
surface, hairless; leaves greyish-green or bluish-grey;
sheaths smooth:

11 Leaf-blades 8–20 mm. wide, up to 60 cm. long, minutely
rough above on the ribs; shoots and rhizomes stout; sand-
dunes ....**Elymus arenarius** (105)

11a Leaf-blades 2–6 mm. wide, often inrolled, 8–35 cm. long,
minutely rough above on the ribs, or smooth; shoots
slender; rhizomes wiry, slender; sand-dunes and salt-
marshes .... **Agropyron pungens** (99)

10a Leaf-blades with the main nerves spaced, not closely ribbed,
3–10 mm. wide, flat, loosely to sparsely hairy or hairless on
the upper surface; ligules less than 1 mm. long; auricles up
to 2 mm. long, finely pointed; shoots slender; leaves dull
green or greyish-green; arable and waste land
Agropyron repens (97)

9a Plants of one to many shoots, in loose to dense tufts; annuals
or perennials, without rhizomes:

12 Leaf-sheaths more or less hairy, especially the lower (to
p. 389):

13 Leaf-sheaths stiffly hairy with long spreading or reflexed hairs,
tubular, but soon splitting; loosely tufted perennials:

14 Ligules up to 6 mm. long, jagged; auricles very small; blades
dull green, 6–16 mm. wide, thinly hairy or hairless,
rough; woods and shaded places ... **Bromus ramosus** (71)

14a Ligules up to 1 mm. long; auricles larger; blades bright
green, 5–14 mm. wide, loosely to sparsely hairy, rough
on the upper surface; woods
Hordelymus europaeus (107)

13a Leaf-sheaths softly or shortly hairy:

13* Tufted perennial, 45–120 cm. high, with slender to some-

what stout culms; ligules 1–3 mm. long; leaf-blades
4–12 mm. wide; sheaths tubular; auricles small; woods
Bromus benekenii (69)

13a* Annuals, or if perennial then with ligules less than 1 mm.
long and leaf-blades 2–6 mm. wide:

15 Shoots very slender; wild grasses; leaf-blades 2–8 mm.
wide:

16 Annual; auricles well developed, up to about 2 mm. long;
leaves light green; blades 2–8 mm. wide, loosely to
sparsely hairy or hairless, rather weak; arable and
waste land .... **Hordeum murinum** (109)

16a Tufted perennial; auricles weakly developed, about
0·5 mm. long; leaves dull green or greyish-green;
blades 2–6 mm. wide, firmer; grassland
Hordeum secalinum (113)

15a Shoots stouter; cultivated cereals; annuals; leaf-blades
mostly wider:

17 Auricles well developed, clasping the shoot, often
minutely hairy on the margins; young blades with short
hairs above; young sheaths densely to loosely short-
haired; Wheat .... **Triticum aestivum** (422)

17a Auricles small, hairless; leaf-sheaths hairy with long and
short hairs; Rye .... **Secale cereale** (424)

12a Leaf-sheaths (lower) hairless:

18 Auricles noticeable (to p. 390):

19 Remains of old leaf-sheaths and culms at the base of plant;
loosely tufted perennials:

20 Auricles and marginal junction of sheath and blade hairless;
leaf-blades bright green, glossy and very smooth
beneath:

21 Leaf-blades 6–16 mm. wide, usually drooping; ligules up
to 2·5 mm. long; woods and shady places
Festuca gigantea (145)

21a Leaf-blades 3–8 mm. wide; ligules up to 1 mm. long;
lowland grassland .... **Festuca pratensis** (141)

20a Auricles and marginal junction of sheath and blade fringed
with minute hairs; leaf-blades dull green, 3–12 mm.
wide, firm, rough above, tough; grasslands
Festuca arundinacea (143)

19a Annuals or biennials; without the remains of old sheaths or
culms at the base:

22 Leaf-blades up to 10 mm. wide, ribbed above, green; shoots
slender (to p. 390):

23 Leaf-blades glossy beneath, hairless; lower sheaths pink to
red; hayfields, waste places **Lolium multiflorum** (151)

23a Leaf-blades dull beneath, shortly and sparsely hairy; lower sheaths whitish or greenish; arable and waste land .... **Hordeum murinum** (109)

22a Leaf-blades wider, not glossy beneath; cultivated cereals:

24 Auricles strongly developed, overlapping and clasping the shoot; leaves green to light green; Barley
Hordeum vulgare and **H. distichon** (424)

24a Auricles weakly developed; leaves bluish-green; Rye
Secale cereale (424)

18a Auricles obscure, very small; leaves bluish-green; blades 1–3·5 mm. wide, minutely hairy or hairless; sheaths smooth; annual; salt-marshes **Hordeum marinum** (111)

8a Leaves without auricles at the junction of sheath and blade, but sometimes hairy there:

25 Leaf-sheaths open, with free margins (at least in the upper half), one margin overlapping the other (to p. 396):

26 Leaf-blades closely and prominently ribbed on the upper surface, with the ribs densely covered with minute white hairs, flat or often inrolled, 2–6 mm. wide; sheaths smooth; perennials with long rhizomes:

27 Ligules 1–3 cm. long, narrow; blades sharp-pointed, up to 60 cm. long, rigid, erect, inrolled or opening out and up to 6 mm. wide, unequally ribbed above, greyish- or bluish-green, or green only beneath; rhizomes stout; stems tough, not brittle; coastal sand-dunes **Ammophila arenaria** (287)

27a Ligules 0·5–1 mm. long; blades fine-pointed, 10–35 cm. long, stiff to rather soft, mostly inrolled and narrower, evenly and closely ribbed above, bluish-grey; sheaths coated with whitish wax when young; rhizomes slender; stems brittle; coastal sand-dunes
Agropyron junceiforme (103)

26a Leaf-blades not as above:

28 Leaves aromatic when bruised (scented with coumarin), loosely to densely bearded with spreading hairs at the junction of sheath and blade, green; ligules 1–5 mm. long, blunt; blades 1·5–9 mm. wide, loosely hairy or hairless; tufted perennial; grassland
Anthoxanthum odoratum (269)

28a Leaves not aromatic; sheaths not bearded at the junction with the blade:

29 Shoots thickened at the base (ground level); the lowest one to three internodes swollen, and more or less bulbous (to p. 391):

30 Roots and bases of lower sheaths orange-yellow at the junction with the shoot; basal internodes bulbous or pear-

shaped; leaves hairless or hairy; nodes usually hairy; rough grassland and arable land

Arrhenatherum elatius var. **bulbosum** (233)

30a Roots and bases of sheaths not yellow; basal internodes of shoot less swollen; blades green or greyish-green, hairless, firm, minutely rough on the nerves; sheaths smooth, the basal becoming dark brown; loosely to compactly tufted perennials:

31 Blades up to 45 cm. long, 3–9 mm. wide; ligules up to 6 mm. long; grassland ....**Phleum pratense** (321)

31a Blades 3–12 cm. long, 2–5 mm. wide; ligules 1–4 mm. long; grassland ....**Phleum bertolonii** (319)

29a Shoots not bulbously thickened at the base:

32 Leaves hairless (to p. 394):

33 Roots and bases of lower sheaths orange-yellow at the junction with the shoot; leaves dull green, bitter to the taste; sheaths smooth; ligules 1–3 mm. long; blades 4–10 mm. wide, 10–40 cm. long, slightly ribbed above, rough; rough grassland **Arrhenatherum elatius** (233)

33a Roots and bases of sheaths not orange-yellow, or if slightly yellowish then with narrower and shorter leaf-blades:

34 Plants with creeping wiry or fleshy white or brownish rhizomes, forming loose to dense tufts or patches; rhizomes bearing scale-leaves without blades; perennials (to p. 392):

35 Leaves green or yellowish-green (to p. 392)·

36 Leaf-sheaths with cross-nerves between the main nerves; rhizomes fleshy; ligules 2·5–16 mm. long; blades finely nerved above, rough towards the tip, 10–35 cm. long, 6–18 mm. wide, broad at the base; wet places ....**Phalaris arundinacea** (273)

36a Leaf-sheaths without cross-nerves; rhizomes wiry:

37 Ligules 4–12 mm. long; leaf-blades closely ribbed on the upper surface, up to 70 cm. long, 4–10 mm. wide, narrowed at the base; damp woods and fens

Calamagrostis epigejos (283)

37a Ligules 0·5–6 mm. long; blades finely ribbed and rough or smooth above:

38 Blades very narrow, rolled or opening out and 1–2 mm. (rarely more wide), firm to stiff, closely few-ribbed above, dull green; ligules longer than wide, narrowed upwards, often pointed; densely tufted perennial; dry grassland

Agrostis canina subsp. **montana** (297)

38a Blades wider, usually flat; ligules very blunt or
   toothed:
39 Blades 1–20 cm. long, medium to dark green;
   ligules hairless; tufts spreading:
40 Ligules shorter than wide, 0·5–2 mm. long; blades
   up to 5 mm. wide; grassland

Agrostis tenuis (299)

40a Ligules as long as or longer than wide, 1·5–6 mm.
   long; blades up to 8 mm. wide; arable and
   waste land, etc. .... **Agrostis gigantea** (301)

39a Blades up to 45 cm. long, rolled or flat, 2–6 mm.
   wide, light green or yellowish-green; ligules
   0·5–2 mm. long, fringed with minute hairs; tufts
   erect; grassland **Brachypodium pinnatum** (91)

35a Leaves greyish-green, very rarely hairless; nodes
   bearded; ligules 1–4 mm. long; blades 4–20 cm.
   long, 3–12 mm. wide; rhizomes well-developed

Holcus mollis (263)

34a Plants without rhizomes, loosely to densely tufted,
   sometimes with stolons creeping over the surface of
   the ground; perennials or annuals:

41 Densely to loosely tufted or stoloniferous, with remains
   of old sheaths at the base; perennials (to p. 393):

42 Leaf-blades very prominently grooved and ribbed
   above, with the ribs very rough, smooth beneath,
   stiff, dark green; ligules very narrow, pointed, firm,
   up to 15 mm. long; densely tufted perennial; wet
   grassland and woods **Deschampsia caespitosa** (251)

42a Leaves not deeply grooved and ribbed; ligules not
   narrow and pointed, usually much shorter:

43 Loosely to densely tufted, without stolons; perennials
   (to p. 393):

44 Leaf-blades 1–4 mm. wide, up to 15 cm. long, green;
   ligules 0·5–2 mm. long:

45 Living basal leaf-sheaths streaked at the base with
   bright yellow, yellowish-brown when old; blades
   glossy beneath, dark green, firm, ribbed above;
   small compact tufts; grassland

Cynosurus cristatus (219)

45a Living basal leaf-sheaths whitish; blades pale
   green, dull beneath, ribbed above; roots often
   yellowish; loosely tufted

Trisetum flavescens (245)

44a Leaf-blades wider, up to 15 mm. wide, 6–40 cm.
   long:

392

46 Ligules up to 2·5 mm. long:

47 Basal leaf-sheaths purplish or deep brown; ligules 1–2·5 mm. long; blades bluntly ribbed above, dull dark green, firm; loosely to compactly tufted; meadows **Alopecurus pratensis** (333)

47a Basal leaf-sheaths greenish or whitish; ligules 0·5–1·5 mm. long; blades finely nerved, pale or bright green, thin; loosely tufted; woods, shaded places .... **Agropyron caninum** (95)

46a Ligules 3–10 mm. long; leaves dull green; blades thin, ribless above, roughish or smooth; loosely tufted; woods .... **Milium effusum** (275)

43a Plants with creeping stolons, rooting at the nodes and producing there loose or compact tufts of leafy shoots; stolons greenish, bearing leaves with blades; leaf-blades ribbed above, rough on the ribs; perennials:

48 Leaf-blades very narrow, mostly 1–2 mm. wide, few-ribbed above, bright green, 2–15 cm. long, soft; ligules longer than wide, 1–4 mm. long, often pointed; stolons with compact tufts of fine leafy shoots at the nodes; damp grassland

      Agrostis canina subsp. **canina** (295)

48a Leaf-blades usually wider, dull green or greyish-green; ligules very blunt:

49 Leaf-sheaths green or purplish; blades slightly keeled beneath; plants with long trailing leafy stolons:

50 Blades 1–10 cm. long, up to 5 mm. wide; ligule 1–6 mm. long; forming a close turf; grassland

      Agrostis stolonifera var. **stolonifera** (303)

50a Blades 6–20 cm. long, 3–7 mm. wide; ligule up to 8 mm. long; not turf-forming; wet places

      Agrostis stolonifera var. **palustris** (303)

49a Leaf-sheaths usually with a whitish wax covering; blades not keeled beneath, 2–12 cm. long, 2–7 mm. wide; ligules 2–5 mm. long; not turf-forming; wet places

      Alopecurus geniculatus (331)

41a Plants without the remains of old sheaths or culms at the base; shoots solitary, or clustered due to branching at the base; annuals or biennials:

51 Leaves pale green or whitish-green; blades smooth on the closely nerved upper surface, 0·5–6 cm. long, up to 4 mm. wide, flat; ligules up to 7 mm. long;

sheaths smooth; sand-dunes

Phleum arenarium (315)

51a Leaves green or greyish-green; blades rough above:

52 Leaf-blades 0·5–3·5 mm. wide, 1–10 cm. long, flat or rolled, closely and finely ribbed or ribless above; sheaths smooth:

53 Ligules 0·3–1 mm. long; blades pointed, dark green; salt-marshes ....**Parapholis strigosa** (339)

53a Ligules 0·5–3 mm. long:

54 Leaf-blades ribbed above, narrowed to a blunt tip, firm; coastal sands

Catapodium marinum (207)

54a Leaf-blades ribless and finely nerved above, finely pointed; dry places **Catapodium rigidum** (205)

52a Leaf-blades wider, up to 15 mm. wide, up to 25 cm. or more long, flat; ligules 2–10 mm. long, often minutely rough on the back; sheaths smooth or rough near the blades:

55 Blades closely and prominently ribbed above, with the ribs rough-pointed, 3–15 mm. wide; ligules 3–10 mm. long, arable and waste land

Apera spica-venti (289)

55a Blades finely ribbed above, with the ribs minutely rough, 2–8 mm. wide; ligules 2–5 mm. long; arable and waste land

Alopecurus myosuroides (325)

32a Leaves more or less hairy:

56 Roots and bases of lower sheaths orange-yellow at the junction with the shoot; leaf-sheaths usually hairless, rarely loosely hairy; blades loosely to sparsely hairy, dull green, finely nerved, bitter to the taste, 4–10 mm. wide; rough grassland …**Arrhenatherum elatius** (233)

56a Roots and sheath-bases not so coloured, or if with yellowish roots then the leaf-sheaths softly hairy and the blades narrower:

57 Leaf-sheaths hairless, smooth; blades very smooth and glossy beneath (to p. 397):

58 Blades up to 40 cm. or more long, 3–6 mm. wide, very finely hair-pointed, coarse, closely nerved, loosely short-haired on the upper surface; ligules 2–5 mm. long; with creeping rhizomes, forming loose tufts or patches; fens and swampy places

Calamagrostis canescens (281)

58a Blades up to 15 cm. long, 1–4 mm. wide, usually hairless, rarely minutely hairy above; ligules 0·5–1·5 mm.

394

long; forming small compact tufts

Cynosurus cristatus (219)

57a Leaf-sheaths loosely to densely hairy:
  59 Basal leaf-sheaths white or suffused with purple, with
     pink or purplish veins; sheaths densely and velvety
     hairy with equally long spreading hairs; ligules
     1–4 mm. long, white, blunt; blades light green or
     greyish-green, 3–10 mm. wide, softly hairy; loosely
     to compactly tufted; grassland

Holcus lanatus (261)

59a Basal leaf-sheaths usually with green veins:
  60 Plants without rhizomes; perennials or annuals:
     61 Leaf-blades 1–4 mm. wide; basal sheaths softly and
        densely hairy; ligules 0·5–2 mm. long:
        62 Compactly tufted; ligules up to 1 mm. long; blades
           often inrolled, very narrow; dry grassland

Koeleria cristata (241)

        62a Loosely tufted; ligules 0·5–2 mm. long; blades
            usually flat; grassland **Trisetum flavescens** (245)
     61a Leaf-blades 4–15 mm. or more wide; basal leaf-
         sheaths loosely to sparsely hairy:
         63 Plants tufted, with remains of old sheaths and culms
            at the base; perennials; leaf-blades loosely hairy
            above:
            64 Lower leaf-sheaths loosely hairy with conspicuous
               spreading or reflexed hairs; blades dull dark
               green, drooping, narrowed towards the sheath;
               ligules 1–6 mm. long; woods

Brachypodium sylvaticum (89)

            64a Lower leaf-sheaths shortly and slightly hairy;
                blades bright or pale green, not gradually
                narrowed at the base; ligules 0·5–1·5 mm. long

Agropyron caninum (95)

         63a Annuals, with solitary shoots, or these branched at
             the base; basal leaf-sheaths loosely to slightly
             hairy; ligules 2–8 mm. long, broad; blades up to
             60 cm. long, 4–15 mm. or more wide, hairy on
             the margins or hairless; arable and waste land
             Avena fatua (237) and other species of **Avena**
             (235, 239, 425)
  60a Plants with creeping wiry rhizomes, forming tufts or
      patches; perennials:
     65 Leaves softly hairy, greyish-green; sheaths with
        spreading or reflexed hairs; ligules 1–4 mm. long;
        blades 4–20 cm. long, 3–12 mm. wide; nodes

densely bearded; shady places; arable land
Holcus mollis (263)

65a Leaves slightly to loosely hairy, yellowish-green or
light green; sheaths with spreading hairs; ligules up
to 1 or 2 mm. long, minutely hairy; blades up to
45 cm. long, 2–6 mm. wide, erect; grassland
Brachypodium pinnatum (91)

25a Leaf-sheaths tubular, without free overlapping margins, but soon
splitting at the top:

66 Leaf-sheaths produced at the apex into a slender bristle 1–4 mm.
long on the side opposite the blade; sheaths usually purplish,
loosely hairy with reflexed hairs, or hairless; blades bright green,
rather thin, 3–7 mm. wide; loose perennial, with slender
rhizomes; woods ....**Melica uniflora** (225)

66a Leaf-sheaths without a bristle at the apex:

67 Leaf-sheaths hairless:

68 Plants densely to loosely tufted, with remains of old sheaths and
culms at the base; perennials; blades usually hairless:

69 Leaf-blades 1–4 mm. wide, very glossy beneath; living basal
sheaths streaked with yellow near junction with shoot; ligules
0·5-1·5 mm. long ....**Cynosurus cristatus** (219)

69a Leaf-blades 3–10 mm. wide, slightly glossy or dull beneath;
living basal sheaths whitish or purplish:

70 Basal sheaths purple, becoming purplish-brown or dark brown;
ligules 1–2·5 mm. long; tip of blade finely pointed;
meadows .... **Alopecurus pratensis** (333)

70a Basal sheaths white, becoming yellowish-brown; ligules
0·5-1·5 mm. long; apex of blade slender but thickened at
the tip; grassland ....**Briza media** (213)

68a Annuals, with solitary shoots or these branched at the base;
ligules 1–2 mm. long; blades 4–10 mm. wide, loosely hairy;
arable and waste land ....**Bromus secalinus** (87)

67a Leaf-sheaths loosely to densely hairy:

71 Plants with creeping wiry rhizomes; perennial; leaves greyish-
green, usually softly hairy, especially the sheaths; nodes
conspicuously bearded; shady places, arable land
Holcus mollis (263)

71a Plants without rhizomes; tufted perennials or annuals:

72 Plants tufted, with remains of old leaf-sheaths at the base;
perennials (to p. 397):

73 Basal leaf-sheaths with pink or purple veins; leaves softly and
densely hairy; blades 3–10 mm. wide, soft; grassland
Holcus lanatus (261)

73a Basal leaf-sheaths with greenish veins; leaves loosely to
sparsely hairy; blades 2–3 mm. wide, tough; calcareous

grassland ....**Bromus erectus** (73)
72a Annuals, with solitary shoots or these branched at the base;
    leaves softly hairy; ligules very thin, whitish; blades not
    ribbed above, soft:
  74 Ligules 1·5–4 mm. long, pointed or toothed; basal sheaths with
      long and short hairs intermixed; young blades slightly
      twisted; arable and waste land ....**Bromus sterilis** (61)
  74a Ligules mostly shorter:
    75 Leaf-sheaths densely and very softly hairy; grassland, waste
        places .... **Bromus mollis** (77)
    75a Leaf-sheaths loosely hairy; grassland, arable land
                      Bromus racemosus (83) & **B. commutatus** (85)
7a Youngest leaf-blade folded lengthwise about the middle nerve in
    the shoot, the latter usually compressed and flattened, rarely
    cylindrical; sheaths frequently keeled:
  76 Lower leaf-sheaths loosely to densely hairy:
    77 Leaf-blades mostly 1–2 mm. wide, folded or inrolled or opening
        out; sheaths hairy with very short hairs; dry grassland
                                         Koeleria cristata (241)
    77a Leaf-blades 2–6 mm. wide; sheaths loosely hairy with
        spreading or deflexed long hairs:
      78 Ligules up to 8 mm. long; blades 2–6 mm. wide, soft, glossy
          beneath; sheaths conspicuously hairy with spreading or
          reflexed hairs; grassland ... **Helictotrichon pubescens** (229)
      78a Ligules up to 3 mm. long; blades 2–3 mm. wide, dull green,
          tough; sheaths sparsely to very thinly hairy; calcareous
          grassland ....**Bromus erectus** (73)
  76a Lower leaf-sheaths hairless, or only very minutely hairy:
    79 Leaves (especially the upper) with small to minute projecting
        pointed whitish outgrowths (auricles) at the junction of
        sheath and blade; blades green, 2–6 mm. wide, glossy and
        very smooth beneath, finely ribbed above; basal sheaths with
        free margins, mostly pink or purple; ligule about 1 mm. long;
        grassland ....**Lolium perenne** (149)
    79a Leaves without projecting auricles:
      80 Living basal leaf-sheaths slightly streaked with yellow in the
          lower part; blades 1–4 mm. wide, glossy beneath; ligules
          0·5–1·5 mm. long; forming small compact tufts; grassland
                                         Cynosurus cristatus (219)
      80a Living basal sheaths whitish, greenish or purplish:
        81 Leaf-sheaths compressed and prominently keeled (to p. 399):
          82 Leaf-sheaths with cross-veins and air-cavities between the
              main nerves; sheaths entire, but soon splitting at the top
              (to p. 398):
            83 Ligules broad and blunt except for a fine median tooth,

3–6 mm. long; blades 7–20 mm. wide, 30–60 cm. long; shoots stout to robust; with long stout rhizomes; wet places .... **Glyceria maxima** (123)

83a Ligules blunt or pointed without a median tooth; blades 1·5–14 mm. wide:

84 Leaf-sheaths rough or minutely hairy near the blade; ligules 2–8 mm. long; blades 3–14 mm. wide; wet places .... **Glyceria plicata** (121)

84a Leaf-sheaths smooth:

85 Leaves green; blades pointed, 3–10 mm. wide; ligules 5–15 mm. long; wet places

Glyceria fluitans (117)

85a Leaves greyish-green or tinged with purple; blades abruptly pointed or blunt, stiff, 1·5–8 mm. wide; ligules 4–9 mm. long; ditches, pond-margins

Glyceria declinata (115)

82a Leaf-sheaths without cross-veins and air-spaces between the nerves, or if not, then the sheaths with free margins (*Catabrosa*):

86 Ligules extremely short, fringed with minute hairs; blades equally wide from the base to the abruptly pointed hooded tip, 2–6 mm. wide, firm, bluish-green above, rough on the margins; calcareous grassland

Sesleria caerulea subsp. **calcarea** (227)

86a Ligule without a hairy fringe:

87 Shoots rather broad, strongly compressed, succulent, with the young whitish basal leaf-sheaths slightly sticky; sheaths with the margins united; ligules 2–12 mm. long; blades finely pointed, 2–14 mm. wide, green or greyish-green; densely tufted; grassland

Dactylis glomerata (215)

87a Shoots narrow, or if rather broad, then with blunt blades and leaf-sheaths with free margins:

88 Leaf-sheaths with free margins, strongly compressed and keeled, with cross-nerves between the main veins; blades equally wide throughout, blunt, 2–10 mm. wide, bright green, smooth, sweet to the taste; ligules 2–8 mm. long; stoloniferous perennial; wet places

Catabrosa aquatica (221)

88a Leaf-sheaths without free margins, but soon splitting at the tip; blades with abruptly pointed or blunt hooded tips:

89 Plants tufted or stoloniferous; perennials or annuals; without rhizomes (to p. 399):

90 Ligules 2–10 mm. long (rarely less), narrowed upwards

398

and sometimes pointed, whitish; blades 1–6 mm.
wide (to p. 399):

91 Perennial, with slender creeping stolons; basal leaf-
sheaths usually purplish or reddish; upper sheaths
usually rough; ligules pointed or blunt, up to
4–10 mm. long; blades very glossy beneath, not
transversely crinkled when young; grassland
Poa trivialis (185)

91a Annual; loosely tufted; basal leaf-sheaths often
whitish; upper sheaths smooth; ligules 1–5 mm.
long; blades transversely crinkled when young,
bright to dark green; arable and waste land
Poa annua (167)

90a Ligules up to 0·5 mm. long, very blunt; blades
1–3 mm. wide, green, usually weak; plants loosely
tufted; woods and shady places
Poa nemoralis (175)

89a Plants with slender creeping rhizomes; perennials:

92 Leaves mostly bright green; ligules usually less than
1 mm. long; blades soft, each generally several
times longer than its accompanying sheath; grassland, etc. .... **Poa pratensis** (189)

92a Leaves mostly greyish-green; ligules about 1 mm. or
more long; blades stiff, up to about twice as long
as the sheath; dry places .... **Poa compressa** (193)

81a Leaf-sheaths rounded on the back, at least in the lower part,
and keeled only towards the blade:

81* Leaf-blades prominently ribbed above, very rough on the
ribs and margins, green; ligules up to 15 mm. long
Deschampsia caespitosa (251)

81a* Leaf-blades not as above; ligules 1–5 mm. long:

93 Leaf-blades bluish-green above, green beneath, stiff to
rigid, 1–5 mm. wide; erect densely tufted perennial; dry
grassland .... **Helictotrichon pratense** (231)

93a Leaf-blades bluish-green or grey-green on both
sides; fleshy, ribbed on the upper surface, 1–4 mm.
wide:

94 Turf-forming, with creeping stolons; salt-marches
Puccinellia maritima (201)

94a Tufted, without stolons; salt-marshes
Puccinellia distans (199)

1a Leaf-blades bristle-like usually inrolled, infolded, grooved or
channelled, narrow:

95 Shoots in small tufts or solitary, with soft fine blades; without old
sheaths or culms at the base; annuals (to p. 400):

96 Ligules up to 5 mm. long; blades hairless, blunt, inrolled, about 0·3–0·5 mm. wide, keeled, folded in the young shoot:

97 Leaf-sheaths minutely rough; blades greyish-green; sandy places
Aira caryophyllea (257)

97a Leaf-sheaths smooth; blades green or reddish; sandy places
Aira praecox (259)

96a Ligules up to 1 mm. long; blades minutely hairy and few-ribbed above, finely pointed, inrolled or flat and 0·5–3 mm. wide, dark to light green; sheaths smooth; arable and waste land
Vulpia bromoides, (155) **V. myuros** (157),
Nardurus maritimus (163)

95a Tufted or mat-forming, or with scattered shoots; with remains of old sheaths and culms at the base; perennials:

98 Ligules obscure or short, blunt, up to 4 mm. long (to p. 401):

99 Roots cord-like, coarse; shoots closely packed on short rhizomes, forming dense tufts; sheaths smooth, the basal tough and shining; ligules up to 2 mm. long; blades sharp-pointed, rigid, hard, grooved, about 0·5 mm. wide, the outer horizontally spreading; moors, heaths .... **Nardus stricta** (343)

99a Roots fine, slender; basal sheaths not hard and shining:

100 Ligules very short and obscure, mostly 0·5 mm. or less (to p. 401):

101 Densely tufted, without rhizomes or stolons:

102 Leaf-sheaths with free margins, one overlapping the other; blades tightly infolded or channelled, stiff to rigid:

103 Leaf-blades hair-like or bristle-like, 0·2–0·6 mm. wide, bright to dark green:

104 Leaf-blades 0·2–0·4 mm. wide; acid grassland
Festuca tenuifolia (127)

104a Leaf-blades 0·3–0·6 mm. wide; heaths, hill and mountain grassland .... **Festuca ovina** (129)

103a Leaf-blades 0·5–1 mm. wide, bluntly keeled, greyish-green or slightly bluish-green; dry grassland
Festuca longifolia (131)

102a Leaf-sheaths tubular, but soon splitting; blades green, 0·6–1 mm. wide, bluntly keeled
Festuca rubra subsp. **commutata** (135)

101a Rhizomatous; with slender creeping whitish or brownish scaly rhizomes:

105 Shoots rounded; basal sheaths often purplish, densely short-hairy or hairless, entire, but soon splitting; blades channelled above, 0·5–1 mm. wide, infolded, up to 2 mm. wide when opened out, dark green or grey-green, glossy beneath, minutely hairy and few-ribbed above; grassland
Festuca rubra subsp. (137)

105a Shoots compressed; basal sheaths keeled, smooth, open with free margins; blades folded about the midrib, bluntly keeled, 1–2 mm. wide when opened out, green, hairless or minutely hairy above; dry grassland

Poa angustifolia (187)

100a Ligules 0·5–4 mm. long:

106 Basal leaf-sheaths usually softly and shortly hairy; dry grassland .... **Koeleria cristata** (241)

106a Basal leaf-sheaths hairless:

107 Leaf-blades 0·3–1 mm. wide, inrolled or channelled, or opening out and up to 3 mm. wide:

108 Densely tufted, without rhizomes or stolons; leaf-blades pliant but rather stiff, 0·3–0·8 mm. wide, infolded or channelled, bright green; ligules 0·5–3 mm. long; moors, heaths ....**Deschampsia flexuosa** (249)

108a Densely tufted or mat-forming, with rhizomes or stolons; leaf-blades flat or inrolled, soft to firm; ligules up to 4 mm. long:

109 Grass with wiry rhizomes; leaves firm; dry grassland

Agrostis canina subsp. **montana** (297)

109a Grass with slender creeping stolons, producing tufts of fine soft leafy shoots at the nodes; damp grassland

Agrostis canina subsp. **canina** (295)

107a Leaf-blades 0·2–0·3 mm. wide, channelled above, minutely rough beneath, green or greyish-green, hairless; ligules narrow, 2–4 mm. long; densely tufted; heaths and moors

Agrostis setacea (293)

98a Ligules 1–3 cm. long, narrow; blades greyish or whitish-green, up to 60 cm. long, sharp-pointed, tightly inrolled, closely ribbed above, the ribs minutely hairy, smooth beneath; plants with extensively creeping rhizomes; sand-dunes

Ammophila arenaria (287)

THE 'SEEDS' OF GRASSES

The term seed is commonly applied in the grasses to a wide range of fruiting bodies far from uniform in size and structure. It includes the naked (huskless) grains of Bread-wheat, Rye, and numerous tropical grasses, as well as those seeds in which the grains are enclosed in various types of husk such as one finds in cultivated and wild oats and in our pasture grasses. If the oat seed be closely examined, it will be seen that the grain is tightly embraced by two hard husks technically known as lemma and palea. Seeds of most British grasses are of this type. In many kinds, the lemma and particularly the palea frequently adhere so closely to the grain that it is difficult to remove them without damaging the latter. It should be noted that this form of seed is a later stage of development of the floret which is illustrated in the drawings under the letters F and FS, so that these may be used for comparison. Whenever possible, drawings of the grains, lettered C, CE, CH, and CS, are also included in the illustrations. The letter C stands for caryopsis, the term used by botanists for the grain of grasses; CE and CH are its back and front views showing respectively the embryo and the hilum, whilst CS is the side view.

Before describing the different kinds of seeds, it will help us in classifying them if we consider how they become detached from the parent plant. In wild British grasses this is brought about by the development of narrow zones of special tissue in various parts of the seed-head along which clean-cut fractures occur as soon as the seed is ripe. These fracture lines may be at right-angles to the axis in which they develop, but more often they are oblique, forming an acute angle with it, and leading to the formation of a hard-pointed and frequently bearded spur at the base of the seed. In most of our grasses the fracture takes place in the spikelet-axis beneath each fertile lemma; but there are some kinds in which it occurs only beneath the lowest of several lemmas (*Melica* etc.), below a single spikelet or cluster of spikelets (*Hordeum*), or rarely in the main-axis of the seed-head (*Parapholis*). Grasses with naked seeds do not grow naturally in the British Isles, although they are frequent in two large tropical genera, *Sporobolus* and *Eragrostis*, some species of which are occasionally introduced. In these the grain is exposed and ultimately shed when a fracture develops at the base of the supporting lemma allowing it to fall from the spikelet. The naked seeds of the cereals, Bread-wheat and Rye, are cleaned of the enveloping lemma and palea by threshing, there being no fracture lines to free the grain from the seed-head. Thus it will be seen that the position of the fracture lines determines to a certain extent the form of the seed and whether one or more grains are present in the same seed unit. Among wild and cultivated British grasses the following types of seed may be recognized.

1. Seed consisting of the grain only (Bread-wheat, Rye).
2. Seed consisting of the grain loosely to tightly enclosed by the lemma and palea;
   A. Seed with a small joint of the spikelet-axis attached to the base adjacent to the palea (numerous grasses, including species of *Bromus, Cynosurus, Dactylis, Festuca, Glyceria, Lolium, Poa*, etc.)
   B. Seed without a joint of the spikelet-axis at the base (*Agrostis, Milium, Nardus, Phleum*, etc.)
3. Seed consisting of two or more lemmas, with one or more grains (*Anthoxanthum, Arrhenatherum, Hierochloë, Melica, Phalaris*, etc.).
4. Seed consisting of a single complete spikelet, with usually one grain (*Alopecurus, Digitaria, Echinochloa, Holcus, Polypogon, Setaria, Spartina*, etc.).
5. Seed consisting of a cluster of three or more spikelets (*Hordeum* spp., *Phalaris paradoxa*).
6. Seed cylindrical, consisting of a single spikelet embedded in a joint of the spike-axis (*Parapholis*).

In many seeds the lemma and palea completely envelop the grain, protecting it from damage during growth and at maturity. Some lemmas and paleas are like membranous skins whilst others are of a papery or leathery nature. In many of our grasses the lemma and palea adhere so closely to the grain that they can only be loosened by soaking in water. They may be flattened, hollowed out or winged, and consequently more easily dispersed by the wind. Many bear hairs, teeth, barbs, bristles, or awns, by means of which they adhere to animals and other moving objects, the seeds thereby becoming more widely spread than would otherwise be possible. Hairs may be evenly distributed over the surface of the lemmas, or alternatively they may be restricted to parts of these scales, for example to the upper part, to the nerves, or to the extreme base. They vary considerably in length, density, softness, or rigidity. The keels of the paleas provide useful diagnostic characters, some being fringed with very short hairs, others rough with minute teeth or points or even quite smooth. The position and form of these outgrowths should be carefully observed in order that the seeds may be compared with the drawings and descriptions. Similarly the position of the awns or bristles should be accurately noted. They may arise at the base of the lemma, or at any point on its back, or from or near its tip. The awns are mostly illustrated in the dried state as this is the usual condition of the seed, but on soaking in water it will be observed that bent and twisted awns straighten out. The lemma and palea also vary considerably in size,

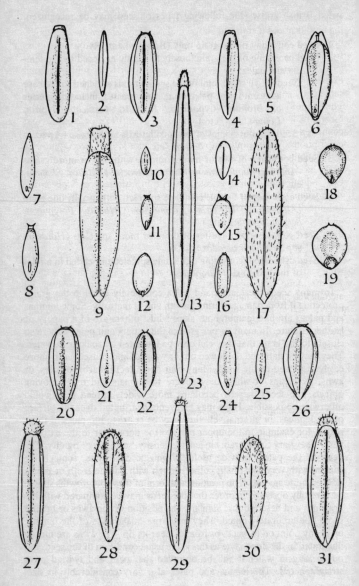

shape, colour, and nervation. These structural differences, together with the modifications mentioned above, and similar variations in the glumes, provide excellent characteristics for distinguishing the seeds of one grass from those of another.

If it is not possible to identify the seeds after a thorough external examination, they should be soaked in cold water until the husks are sufficiently softened for removal without damage to them or the grain. The shape, apex, and nervation of the lemma and palea may then be ascertained more accurately with the aid of × 10 or × 20 lens, and compared with the drawings labelled L, LL, L₂, P, as well as with the descriptions. When confirmatory characteristics are required, one may often obtain them from an examination of the minute scales (lodicules) at the base of the grain on the side facing the lemma. There are normally two lodicules in British grasses, except in the genera *Alopecurus*, *Anthoxanthum*, *Nardus*, and *Spartina*, from which they are absent. They are joined laterally in *Glyceria* and *Melica*, but free from each other in all other British grasses. Differences in their size, shape, toothing, and hairiness may be seen in the drawings lettered LO.

The grains provide valuable diagnostic characters, certain of which are included in the key as supplementary aids to identification. There is a wide range in size from the very small ones of *Phleum* and *Agrostis*, 1–2 mm. long, to those of *Avena*, up to 20 mm. in length. They may be angular, circular, or flattened. Some are longitudinally grooved, channelled, or flat along one side and rounded or keeled on the other. Occasionally they are very hard and flinty as in *Glyceria*, whilst others are relatively soft. Particular attention should be paid to the shape and size of the embryo (CE) and hilum (CH), both of which are usually shown in the illustrations. In *Spartina* it will be seen that the embryo is green and unusually long, occupying the whole of one side of the grain. In the majority of our grasses, however, it rarely reaches half the length of the grain and is usually much shorter. Very important distinctions are provided by the hilum, which is found on the opposite side of the grain to the embryo and is usually of a deeper colour than the rest of the grain. In *Bromus*, *Festuca*, *Avena*, *Agropyron*, and other genera it takes the

GRAINS OF GRASSES (CH, × 6). 1, *Lolium perenne*. 2, *Trisetum flavescens*. 3, *Festuca rubra*. 4, *Vulpia bromoides*. 5, *Nardus stricta*. 6, *Cynosurus echinatus*. 7, *Dactylis glomerata*. 8, *Deschampsia flexuosa*. 9, *Hordeum murinum*. 10, *Agrostis gigantea*. 11, *Phragmites communis*. 12, *Anthoxanthum odoratum*. 13, *Bromus sterilis*. 14, *Molinia caerulea*. 15, *Briza media*. 16, *Cynosurus cristatus*. 17, *Avena fatua*. 18, *Phleum pratense*. 19, *Echinochloa crus-galli*. 20, *Festuca arundinacea*. 21, *Poa pratensis*. 22, *Glyceria fluitans*. 23, *Alopecurus pratensis*. 24, *Puccinellia maritima*. 25, *Holcus lanatus*. 26, *Melica uniflora*. 27, *Agropyron caninum*. 28, *Helictotrichon pratense*. 29, *Brachypodium sylvaticum*. 30, *Arrhenatherum elatius*. 31, *Bromus mollis*.

form of a fine line as long as the grain, whereas in *Poa, Puccinellia, Agrostis*, and other grasses, it is like a dot at the base of the grain. Among other things to be looked for on the grain are hairs or appendages. For example, species of *Bromus, Brachypodium, Hordeum*, and related genera are characterized by a minutely hairy knob-like outgrowth at the tip of the grain, whilst the grains of *Avena* and *Arrhenatherum* are clothed with fine silky hairs.

For those who have the use of a compound microscope and are able to make microscopic preparations, the anatomy of the lemma and its epidermis (skin) may be investigated, the latter in particular showing minute differences between allied species. This is also true of the outer covering of the grain, but such studies are beyond the scope of this work. It may be possible, however, to examine the starch granules which are tightly packed and occupy the whitish central portion of the grain. In *Bromus, Brachypodium, Agropyron*, and other genera of the tribe *Triticeae* (*Hordeeae*) the granules are entire (simple) and rounded or angular; on the other hand, in *Avena, Festuca, Lolium*, and most of our grasses the granules are composed of a number of angular fragments and are described as compound.

The following key or guide for the identification of the seeds of our common grasses should be used only after several seeds typical of a large number have been studied thoroughly and their structure ascertained. The contrasting characters are arranged in pairs numbered 1 and 1a, and so on, in the manner explained on page 34. A warning is necessary for those who may examine seeds from lawn- or fodder-grass mixtures, since in the process of cleaning, hairs, bristles, and awns may sometimes be partially or wholly removed. In addition, where the seed is formed of more than one lemma and palea (enclosing the grain), some of the extra scales may become detached, or damaged.

KEY FOR NAMING THE MORE COMMON
GRASSES BY THEIR 'SEEDS'

The figures in parentheses refer to the pages on which the grasses are described or mentioned.

1 Seed consisting of the naked grain only, this minutely hairy at the tip; hilum a fine line as long as the grain, in a narrow groove:

 2 Grains plump, elliptic to oblong, 5–8·5 mm. long, 3–4 mm. wide, whitish, yellow, reddish or brown; Wheat
Triticum aestivum (425)

 2a Grains relatively narrower, oblong, 7–10 mm. long, brownish-olive, greyish-brown; Rye ....**Secale cereale** (425)

1a Seed formed by the grain wholly or partially covered by the lemma and palea and, in some grasses, also by the glumes:

 3 Seed formed of a cluster of three spikelets attached to part of the spike-axis; hilum a long fine line; grain tightly embraced by the lemma and palea, minutely hairy at the tip; glumes and lemmas awned:

  4 Glumes of the central spikelet of each three spikelets fringed with hairs in the lower part; fertile lemma 7–12 mm. long, tipped with a straight awn 18–50 mm. long **Hordeum murinum** (109)

  4a Glumes all hairless, rough; fertile lemma 6–9 mm. long, tipped with an awn 6–24 mm. long:

   5 Glumes of the lateral spikelets of each three spikelets dissimilar, one bristle-like, the other widened at the base; awn of fertile lemma up to 24 mm. long .... **Hordeum marinum** (111)

   5a Glumes of the lateral spikelets similar, both bristle-like; awn of fertile lemma 6–12 mm. long ......**Hordeum secalinum** (113)

 3a Seed formed by a single spikelet or more often by a single floret, the grain in the latter case enclosed by the lemma and palea:

  6 Seed formed by a single spikelet, with two glumes at the base and one or more florets above them (to p. 408):

   7 Spikelet with 3 to 10 lemmas, these 7–13 mm. long, exceeding the glumes, with or without an awn up to 10 mm. long from their tips; grain hairy at the tip, its hilum a long fine line:

    8 Lemmas tough and rigid, with prominently thickened nerves in the upper part .... **Agropyron pungens** (99)

    8a Lemmas firm, with finer nerves .... **Agropyron repens** (97)

   7a Spikelet with only 1 or 2 lemmas; grain hairless, with a small hilum at the base:

    9 Spikelets 14–21 mm. long, narrow, flattened, hairy, formed of 2 glumes, as well as the lemma and palea, enclosing the grain;

grain 10 mm. or more long, with a long green embryo
Spartina anglica (357)

9a Spikelets 2–7 mm. long; grain with a small obscure embryo at
the base:

10 Spikelets without awns; seed cylindrical, formed of the spikelet
embedded in the thickened joint of the spike-axis, hairless,
3–7 mm. long ....**Parapholis strigosa** (339)

10a Spikelets awned, flattened:

11 Glumes each with a fine awn 4–7 mm. long from the tip,
minutely rough, 2–3 mm. long; lemma delicate, about half
the length of the glumes, smooth and shining

Polypogon monspeliensis (309)

11a Glumes without awns; lemma usually awned:

12 Seed formed of two whitish, greyish or dull purplish glumes
enclosing two florets (two lemmas and two paleas), the
lower floret with grain; lower glume 1-nerved:

13 Upper lemma with a curved or hook-like awn (up to 2 mm.
long) hidden by the glumes ....**Holcus lanatus** (261)

13a Upper lemma with a slightly bent awn (3·5–5 mm. long)
protruding from the glumes .... **Holcus mollis** (263)

12a Seed formed of two glumes and a single lemma enclosing
the grain; palea absent; both glumes 3-nerved; grains
compressed; lemma awned:

14 Margins of glumes united only near the base; keels of
glumes fringed with fine hairs, the glumes hairy also on
the sides:

15 Spikelets 4–6 mm. long; awn exceeding the glumes by
3–5 mm. .... **Alopecurus pratensis** (333)

15a Spikelets 2·5–3·5 mm. long; awn exceeding the glumes by
2–3 mm. ....**Alopecurus geniculatus** (331)

14a Margins of glumes united for up to half their length; keels
of glumes minutely hairy, very narrowly winged; spikelets 4·5–7 mm. long; awn exceeding the glumes by
4–8 mm. ....**Alopecurus myosuroides** (325)

6a Seed formed of a single floret (lemma, palea, and grain) or of two
or more florets, but in both cases without glumes at the base:

16 Seed formed of more than one floret, usually two or three (to
p. 409):

17 Seeds awned, the awns arising on the back of or from near the
base of the lemmas (to p. 409):

18 Lemmas 8–22 mm. long; grain hairy all over with appressed
fine hairs; hilum a long fine line (to p. 409):

19 Awns 3–5·5 cm. long; lemmas 2 to 3, bearded at the base,
mostly stiffly hairy above, 15–22 mm. long

Avena ludoviciana (239)

19a Awns up to 1·7 cm. long; lemmas 2 to 3, short-bearded at the base, hairless or loosely and softly hairy above, 8–10 mm. long ....**Arrhenatherum elatius** (233)

18a Lemmas up to 4 mm. long, the lower two hairy, brown except for the white tips, without paleas, awned, with the awns up to 9 mm. long, enclosing the fertile awnless shining brown lemma and palea which envelop the grain

Anthoxanthum odoratum (269)

17a Seeds awnless, 3–7 mm. long or with a short awn up to 5 mm. long from or near the tip:

17* Lemmas closely fringed on the keel with very short stiff hairs or with short rough points, awnless or with a very short straight awn from the tip .... **Dactylis glomerata** (215)

17a* Lemmas not as above:

17** Upper of two lemmas awned from just below the tip:

17† Awn curved or hook-like, up to 2 mm. long

Holcus lanatus (261)

17a† Awn slightly bent, 3·5–5 mm. long .. **Holcus mollis** (263)

17a** All lemmas awnless:

20 Seed formed of one fertile smooth lemma and palea enclosing the grain and two to three sterile lemmas in a club-shaped mass at the apex, 4–7 mm. long; grain rounded on the back, with a long fine line-like hilum

Melica uniflora (225)

20a Seed formed of one fertile lemma and palea enclosing the grain and with two small sterile lemmas at the base only; grain with a small basal or short hilum:

21 Seeds 3–4 mm. long; sterile lemmas 1–1·5 mm. long, hairy; fertile lemma hairy in the upper part

Phalaris arundinacea (273)

21a Seeds 5–6 mm. long; sterile lemmas 3–4·5 mm. long, hairless; fertile lemma becoming hairless and glossy

Phalaris canariensis (271)

16a Seed formed of a single floret, that is with a lemma and palea wholly or partly enclosing the grain, and without any sterile lemmas at its base:

22 Lemmas surrounded by long silky white hairs arising from the base or from a piece of the spikelet-axis at the base of the lemma, the hairs from one-third the length of to much longer than the lemma (to p. 410):

23 Lemmas delicate, thinly membranous (to p. 410):

24 Lemmas 9–13 mm. long, slender, finely pointed, narrowly lanceolate, 1–3-nerved; enveloping hairs about three-fourths the length of the lemma, arising on the spikelet-axis at the base of the lemma; palea one-fourth to one-

third the length of the lemma; embryo one-third of the grain ....**Phragmites communis** (347)

24a Lemmas 2·5–3 mm. long, lanceolate-oblong, 3–5-nerved; enveloping hairs arising at the base of the lemma; palea about two-thirds the length of the lemma; embryo one-fourth of the grain:

25 Enveloping hairs shortly exceeding the tip of the lemma
Calamagrostis canescens (281)

25a Enveloping hairs up to twice as long as the lemma
Calamagrostis epigejos (283)

23a Lemmas hardened, tough, 8–12 mm. long, minutely rough, laterally compressed, narrow; basal hairs up to about one-third the length of the lemma; hilum a fine line
Ammophila arenaria (287)

22a Lemmas with a tuft of short hairs at the base, or hairless there, but if with hairs up to 5 mm. long, then the lemma bearing a bent and twisted awn on the back:

26 Lemmas with three small firm teeth at the tip, awnless, tough and rigid, rounded on the back, short-haired on the margins and at the base, 5–7 mm. long, 7–9-nerved; minute anthers usually enclosed in the floret at the tip of the grain; hilum narrow, about half the length of the grain

Sieglingia decumbens (351)

26a Lemmas not three-toothed at the tip, but if appearing so then the apex very thin and whitish:

27 Lemmas pointed or blunt at the tip, without an awn (bristle) at the tip or on the back (to p. 415):

28 Lemmas very thin, delicate, pale, glistening, smooth or nearly so, hairless or with a few minute hairs at the base and on the nerves, 1·5–3 mm. long; no joint of spikelet-axis present at base of seed; hilum very small, at the base of the grain (to p. 411):

29 Seeds lanceolate to ovate, oblong, or elliptic, pointed; lemma ovate to oblong, hairless on the nerves; grain narrowly grooved on one side:

30 Palea half to three-fourths the length of the lemma:

31 Lemmas always 5-nerved; seeds silvery-grey to straw-coloured, narrowly ovate to elliptic or oblong
Agrostis stolonifera (303)

31a Lemmas mostly 3-nerved:

32 Seeds oblong or elliptic, plump, yellowish or straw-coloured, glossy; grain about 1·3 mm. long
Agrostis gigantea (301)

32a Seeds lanceolate to narrowly ovate or oblong, light to

dull grey or straw-coloured; grain about 1 mm. long
Agrostis tenuis (299)
30a Palea minute; lemma 4–5-nerved
Agrostis canina (295–7)
29a Seeds broader, broadly elliptic-oblong to broadly elliptic
or rotund; lemma very broad, very blunt, minutely hairy
on the nerves, 5–7-nerved; palea nearly as long as the
lemma; grain plump, not grooved, yellowish:
33 Lemma 1·3–2 mm. long .... **Phleum bertolonii** (319)
33a Lemma 2–2·5 mm. long ....**Phleum pratense** (321)
28a Lemma firm to hard and thickened, but sometimes thin and
translucent at the margins and tip, greenish, yellowish,
or purplish, hairy or hairless:
34 Seeds compressed from the side, keeled, triangular in transverse section; joint of spikelet-axis present on one side
at base of seed (to p. 412):
35 Keel of lemma usually closely fringed with very short stiff
hairs, or only rough-pointed; lemma 4–7 mm. long,
lanceolate to oblong and pointed in side view, 5-
nerved, without a web of hairs at the base
Dactylis glomerata (215)
35a Keel of lemma very softly hairy or hairless and smooth:
36 Spikelet-axis short-haired; lemma 3-nerved, with thin
whitish margins, 3·5–5·5 mm. long, hairless or downy-
hairy all over, without a web of hairs at the base; palea
projecting from the side of the lemma, 2-toothed at
the tip; hilum narrow, short . **Koeleria cristata** (241)
36a Spikelet-axis smooth, rarely minutely rough; lemmas 5-
nerved, 2–4 mm. long, often softly hairy on the lower
part of the nerves and keel, frequently with a web of
curly hairs at the base, with membranous tips and
margins; palea blunt; hilum dot-like:
37 Keels of palea mostly closely fringed with short hairs;
lemma without a web of hairs at the base, hairy on
all the nerves and keel, or hairless, finely 5-nerved,
2·5–4 mm. long ....**Poa annua** (167)
37a Keels of palea minutely rough; lemma mostly hairy on
the keel and on the outer (marginal) nerves, or hairless on the latter:
38 Lemma hairy on the keel only or rarely hairless there,
the marginal nerves hairless, distinctly 5-nerved,
with a web of hairs at the base, narrowly oblong and
pointed in side view, 2·5–3·5 mm. long
Poa trivialis (185)

411

38a Lemma hairy on the keel and on the marginal nerves, finely 5-nerved, blunt or rather blunt in side view:

39 Inner pair of lateral nerves very faint and indistinct and the lemma appearing 3-nerved:

40 Spikelet-axis minutely rough; lemma with or without a web of hairs at the base, 2·6–3·6 mm. long
Poa nemoralis (175)

40a Spikelet-axis smooth; lemmas 2·5–3 mm. long:

41 Tip of lemma golden or brownish; lemma with a web of hairs at the base ....**Poa palustris** (181)

41a Tip of lemma whitish, greenish, or purplish; lemma with or without a web of hairs at the base
Poa compressa (193)

39a Inner pair of lateral nerves fine yet visible; web of hairs present at base of lemma; spikelet-axis smooth:

42 Lemmas 2–3 mm. long ....**Poa angustifolia** (187)

42a Lemmas 3–4 mm. long .... **Poa pratensis** (189)

34a Seeds narrowly to broadly rounded on the back, the lemma with or without the middle-nerve projecting, more or less boat- or barge-shaped, or only laterally compressed and keeled in the upper part, rarely 2–3-keeled (*Nardus*):

43 Lemmas very broad, cordate at the base, rounded or hooded at the apex, deeply concave, with broad firmly membranous margins, hairless, 7–9-nerved; grains compressed, flat in front, rounded on the back:

44 Lemmas 2–3·5 mm. long and wide; grains about 1 mm. long ....**Briza minor** (209)

44a Lemmas 3·5–4 mm. long and wide; grains about 2 mm. long ....**Briza media** (213)

43a Lemmas narrower, lanceolate to oblong or elliptic, never cordate at the base; grain not compressed as above:

45 Lemmas very smooth, glossy, brown, finely 5-nerved, tightly embracing the glossy palea by the margins, 2·5–3·5 mm. long, ovate to elliptic; seeds plump, hard; without a joint of the spikelet-axis at the base of the seed ....**Milium effusum** (275)

45a Lemmas and paleas not glossy and very smooth all over, usually rather dull to very dull, except sometimes for the shining membranous margins:

46 Lemmas prominently 3-nerved (to p. 413):

47 Seeds narrowly lanceolate or lanceolate-oblong, finely pointed, 5–9 mm. long, without a joint of the spikelet-axis at the base; lemmas 2–3-keeled,

412

minutely rough on the keels; hilum a short fine line
Nardus stricta (343)

47a Seeds wider, not finely pointed, with a joint of the spikelet-axis at the base:

48 Lemmas pointed or slightly blunt, narrowed upwards, lanceolate to ovate, 4–6 mm. long, hairless; hilum a long fine line .... **Molinia caerulea** (349)

48a Lemmas very blunt (truncate), elliptic-oblong to oblong, 2·5–3·5 mm. long, smooth, or sometimes minutely hairy on the nerves; hilum basal, prominent .... **Catabrosa aquatica** (221)

46a Lemmas 5–9-nerved; joint of the spikelet-axis on one side at the base of each seed:

49 Grains hairy at the tip, or all over; hilum a long fine line:

50 Lemmas densely hairy with short soft hairs, lanceolate, pointed, 1–2·5 cm. long; grain hairy at the tip
Elymus arenarius (105)

50a Lemmas hairless, sometimes rough:

51 Grains hairy only at the tip; lemma oblong or lanceolate-oblong, 5-nerved:

52 Lemmas 7–13 mm. long, slightly pointed or blunt:

53 Lemmas with prominent thickened nerves in the upper part, very tough and rigid
Agropyron pungens (99)

53a Lemmas with finer nerves, thinner and less tough
Agropyron repens (97)

52a Lemmas 11–20 mm. long, blunt or slightly hollowed out at the tip
Agropyron junceiforme (103)

51a Grains hairy all over with appressed hairs; seeds plump and smooth below, narrowed above and rough there on the nerves; lemma 7–9-nerved; Oat .... **Avena sativa** (17, 425)

49a Grains hairless:

54 Lemmas more or less pointed, or at least narrowed upwards, mostly with firm tips (to p. 414):

55 Seeds bright yellow or brown, lanceolate, pointed; lemmas 3–4 mm. long, finely 5-nerved, minutely rough .... **Cynosurus cristatus** (219)

55a Seeds not so coloured, but if brown then larger or not rough, usually straw-coloured, greenish or tinged with purple, or dull brown:

56 Lemmas 2–3·5 mm. long (to p. 414):

57 Lemmas oblong or narrowly elliptic in side view,

413

slightly pointed or somewhat blunt; paleas
minutely granular on the back between the
keels; hilum dot-like, near the base of the
grain:

58 Lemmas 2–2·5 mm. long
Catapodium rigidum (205)

58a Lemmas 2·5–3·8 mm. long
Catapodium marinum (207)

57a Lemmas lanceolate to lanceolate-oblong in side
view, finely pointed, 2·5–3·5 mm. long,
minutely rough near the tips; paleas smooth
between the keels; hilum a long fine line
Festuca tenuifolia (127)

56a Lemmas 5–9 mm. long; hilum a long fine line:

59 Lemmas with a firm pointed tip, rough in the
upper part, 6–9 mm. long; seeds lanceolate to
lanceolate-oblong **Festuca arundinacea** (143)

59a Lemmas slightly pointed or blunt, smooth,
5–8 mm. long:

60 Seeds oblong or lanceolate-oblong, barge-shaped:

61 Spikelet-axis cylindrical; grains broadly oblong
Festuca pratensis (141)

61a Spikelet-axis compressed; grains narrowly
oblong .... **Lolium perenne** (149)

60a Seeds elliptic to ovate, plump, hard
Lolium temulentum (153)

54a Lemmas with rather broad or broad blunt lobed or
toothed thin tips:

62 Lemmas smooth except for fine hairs near the base,
very blunt, 5-nerved; hilum dot-like, near the
base of the grain; lodicules 2-toothed, free from
each other:

63 Lemmas 3–5 mm. long **Puccinellia maritima** (201)

63a Lemmas 2–2·5 mm. long **Puccinellia distans** (199)

62a Lemmas minutely rough, hairless, 7-nerved; hilum
a long fine line; lodicules truncate, laterally fused;
grains dark brown or blackish, very hard:

64 Lemmas 3–5 mm. long (to p. 415).

65 Lemmas very blunt, not toothed at the tip; palea
with a blunt tip:

66 Paleas with wingless rough keels
Glyceria maxima (123)

66a Paleas with the keels narrowly winged near the
tip .... **Glyceria plicata** (121)

65a Lemmas mostly 3-toothed or 3-lobed at the tip;

palea with a sharply 2-toothed tip

Glyceria declinata (115)

64a Lemmas 6–7·5 mm. long; palea sharply 2-toothed

Glyceria fluitans (117)

27a Lemmas with an awn (bristle) arising from or near the tip or on the back:

67 Lemmas bearing an awn on the back at or near or below the middle, the lower part of the awn frequently twisted and brown, the upper part greenish (to p. 416):

68 Lemmas 9–20 mm. long, bearing an awn 1·2–4 cm. long from about the middle of the back; grains hairy at the top or all over, with a long line-like hilum:

69 Seeds bearded at the base with hairs 1–5 mm. long, with a thickened smooth scar at the base of the lemma:

70 Awns 1·2–2·2 cm. long; lemmas 5-nerved, minutely rough upwards; grains hairy only at the tip:

71 Basal tuft of hairs 1–2 mm. long; lemmas 10–17 mm. long; awn from just above the middle of the lemma

Helictotrichon pratense (231)

71a Basal tuft of hairs 2–5 mm. long; lemmas 9–14 mm. long; awn from about or just below the middle of the lemma .... **Helictotrichon pubescens** (229)

70a Awns 2·5–4 cm. long; lemmas 7–9-nerved, mostly stiffly hairy, 1·4–2 cm. long; grains hairy all over

Avena fatua (237)

69a Seeds hairless at the irregularly fractured base, the lemma without a scar at the base:

72 Lemmas each tipped with two fine bristles 3–7 mm. long, hairy in the upper part or hairless; awns bent, twisted in the lower part .... **Avena strigosa** (235)

72a Lemmas slightly toothed or blunt at the tip, without bristles at the tip, hairless; awns straight or curved

Avena sativa (17, 425)

68a Lemmas 1·5–4·5 mm. long, bearing an awn 2–9 mm. long; grains hairless; hilum small, at or near the base of the grain:

73 Awn from about or just above the middle of the lemma, 5–9 mm. long, bent and twisted in the lower part; lemma 4–5·5 mm. long, minutely hairy at the base, narrowed at the tip into two very short fine bristle points; grain enclosed by the firm back of the lemma

Trisetum flavescens (245)

73a Awn from near the base or one third above the base of the lemma:

74 Lemmas blunt to very blunt and minutely toothed when

opened out, membranous; awn from near the base of
the lemma:

75 Seeds with conspicuous tufts of hairs at the base up to
1·5 mm. long; hairy joint of spikelet-axis present at
base of seed; lemmas 2·5–5·5 mm. long; paleas as
long or nearly as long as the lemmas:

76 Awns straight, up to 4 mm. long; lemmas 2·5–4 mm.
long ....**Deschampsia caespitosa** (251)

76a Awns bent at about the middle, twisted in the lower
part, 4–7 mm. long; lemmas 3·5–5·5 mm. long
Deschampsia flexuosa (249)

75a Seeds with an obscure tuft of minute hairs at the base;
no joint of spikelet-axis at base of seed; lemmas
1·5–2·5 mm. long; awn bent at and twisted below the
middle or straight, up to 4·5 mm. long; palea minute:

77 Basal hairs of seed very obscure; lemma 1·5–2 mm.
long .... **Agrostis canina** (295–7)

77a Basal hairs of seed about 0·5 mm. long; lemma
2–2·5 mm. long ....**Agrostis setacea** (293)

74a Lemmas narrowed into a finely and minutely 2-toothed
tip, rough in the upper part, 2–2·5 mm. long,
minutely bearded at the base, dark brown; awn arising
about one-third above the base of the lemma, up to
5·5 mm. long, bent and twisted below the middle
Aira praecox (259) and **A. caryophyllea** (257)

67a Lemma bearing an awn from or very near the tip, or from
between two apical teeth, the awn straight, wavy, or
curved, but never bent and closely twisted below the
middle:

78 Awns mostly 10–20 cm. long, straight and very stiff
Hordeum vulgare (425) and **H. distichon** (425)

78a Awns up to 3 cm. long, but usually much shorter:

79 Keels of palea usually minutely rough or nearly smooth,
very rarely closely fringed with minute hairs; awn from
or very near the tip of the lemma (to p. 419):

80 Lemmas laterally compressed, keeled, the keel closely
fringed with short stiff hairs, or only rough; lemmas
lanceolate to oblong in side view, 4–7 mm. long, each
tipped with an awn-point up to 1·5 mm. long, 5-
nerved .... **Dactylis glomerata** (215)

80a Lemmas rounded on the back, or if at all compressed
and keeled then the awn more than 1·5 mm. long:

81 Seeds bright yellow or brown, 3–4 mm. long; lemmas
minutely rough, each tipped with an awn-point up to

1 mm. long, finely 5-nerved

Cynosurus cristatus (219)

81a Seeds not so coloured, but if brownish then the seeds larger or not rough:

82 Lemma 3-nerved, with the nerves rough, narrowly lanceolate or lanceolate-oblong, finely pointed, 5–9 mm. long, each tipped with an awn 1–3 mm. long; seed without a joint of the spikelet-axis at the base ....**Nardus stricta** (343)

82a Lemmas 5–9-nerved; seed with a joint of the spikelet-axis at the base:

83 Grains hairless, very rarely with a few obscure hairs at the tip and then the seeds narrowly lanceolate and 5–8 mm. long (*Festuca heterophylla*) (to p. 418):

84 Awns 0·5–6 mm. long; lemmas lanceolate or oblong-lanceolate, 3·5–9 mm. long, 5-nerved:

85 Grains minutely and obscurely hairy at the tips; lemmas 5–8 mm. long, each with a fine awn 1·5–6 mm. long at the tip

Festuca heterophylla (133)

85a Grains hairless at the tip:

86 Lemmas 2·5–6 mm. long, rough in the upper part, rarely short-haired all over:

87 Lemmas mostly 2·5–4:5 mm. long, each tipped with a fine awn up to 1·5 mm. long:

87* Lemmas 2·5–3·5 mm. long

Festuca tenuifolia (127)

87a* Lemmas mostly 3·5–4·5 mm. long

Festuca ovina (129)

87a Lemmas mostly 4–6 mm. long, each tipped with a fine awn 0·5–4 mm. long **Festuca rubra** (135–7), [see also **F. longifolia** (131)]

86a Lemmas 6–9 mm. long, each tipped with an awn 1–4 mm. long ......**Festuca arundinacea** (143)

84a Awns 5–18 mm. long:

88 Lemmas 2·5–3 mm. long, minutely rough above the middle, 5-nerved, awned from near the tip, with the fine straight awn 5–10 mm. long; hilum very small, at the base of the grain

Apera spica-venti (289)

88a Lemmas 5–9 mm. long:

89 Lemmas very narrow, finely pointed, linear-lanceolate in side view, minutely rough

upwards, each tipped with a fine awn up to 15 mm. long; seed cylindrical; hilum a long fine line

Vulpia bromoides (155) and **V. myuros** (157)

89a Lemmas wider, lanceolate to narrowly oblong or ovate in side view:

90 Lemmas lanceolate, minutely rough upwards, gradually narrowed to a fine point, each terminated by a fine straight 6–16-mm.-long awn; grain with a prominent white apical appendage; hilum minute, near the base of the grain ....**Cynosurus echinatus** (217)

90a Lemmas oblong or lanceolate-oblong in side view, broadly rounded on the back, smooth or minutely rough; hilum a long fine line:

91 Awns usually flexuous, 10–18 mm. long, from the pointed tips of the lemmas; spikelet-axis minutely hairy   **Festuca gigantea** (145)

91a Awns straight or nearly so, from just below the blunt or minutely 2-toothed tips of the lemmas; spikelet-axis smooth:

92 Lemmas oblong or lanceolate-oblong; seeds narrow; awns fine, up to 10 mm. long

Lolium multiflorum (151)

92a Lemmas elliptic to ovate; seeds plump; awns stouter, up to 20 mm. long

Lolium temulentum (153)

83a Grain with a small pale hairy appendage at the tip of the brown part; hilum a long fine line; lemmas 6–15 mm. long:

93 Lemmas 5-nerved, 7–13 mm. long, mostly hairless; keels of paleas rough (to p. 419):

94 Awns up to 10 mm. long, usually much shorter, straight; lemmas somewhat keeled, hairless at the base; spikelet-axis minutely rough or smooth:

94* Lemmas tough and rigid, with prominently thickened nerves in the upper part

Agropyron pungens (99)

94a* Lemmas firm, but thinner and with finer nerves

Agropyron repens (97)

94a Awns 7–20 mm. long, straight or flexuous; lemmas without keels, minutely bearded at the base; spikelet-axis minutely hairy

Agropyron caninum (95)

93a Lemmas 7-nerved:
  95 Paleas minutely and closely hairy on the keels;
    lemmas 6–11 mm. long, rounded on the back;
    lodicules fringed with minute hairs:
    96 Awns 1–5 mm. long, straight; lemmas mostly hair-
      less ....**Brachypodium pinnatum** (91)
    96a Awns up to 12 mm. long, often flexuous; lemmas
      usually shortly and stiffly hairy

              Brachypodium sylvaticum (89)
  95a Paleas minutely rough on the keels; lemmas
    10–15 mm. long, more or less keeled especially
    in the upper part; awns 2–8 mm. long; lodicules
    hairless:
    97 Lemmas shortly hairy near the margins and on the
      back; awn from near the tip of the lemma
               Bromus ramosus (71)
    97a Lemmas hairless, rarely softly hairy all over; awn
      from the tip of the lemma

               Bromus erectus (73)
79a Keels of paleas loosely fringed with short stiff spreading
  hairs; awns from just below the entire or two-toothed
  tip of the lemmas; grain with a pale hairy appendage
  at the tip; hilum a long fine line:
  98 Lemmas narrowly lanceolate in side view, 13–36 mm.
    long, with a straight awn 15–60 mm. long:
    98* Lemma 22–36 mm. long (apical teeth 4–7 mm.); awns
      3·5–6 cm. long ....**Bromus diandrus** (67)
    98a* Lemma 13–23 mm. long (apical teeth 1–2 mm.); awns
      1·5–1·8 cm. long ....**Bromus sterilis** (61)
  98a Lemmas wider, obovate or elliptic, widest at or above
    the middle, 5·5–11 mm. long; awns 3–10 mm. long:
    99 Hairy top of grain visible at the tip of the lemma;
      lemmas 5·5–6·5 mm. long, usually hairless

               Bromus lepidus (79)
    99a Hairy top of grain enclosed by lemma and palea;
      lemmas 6·5–11 mm. long:
    100 Paleas slightly shorter than the lemmas; grains not
      inrolled; margins of lemma slightly curved inwards
      or flat (to p. 420)
    101 Lemmas usually hairless (to p. 420):
    102 Lemmas 6–8·5 mm long (to p. 420):
    103 Lemmas relatively thin, with the nerves prominent
               Bromus thominii (77)
    103a Lemmas tough, smooth, with the nerves not
      raised ....**Bromus racemosus** (83)

102a Lemmas 8–11 mm. long, rather tough, the nerves not raised .... **Bromus commutatus** (85)

101a Lemmas usually softly hairy, 8–11 mm. long, relatively thin, with the nerves prominent
Bromus mollis (77)

100a Paleas as long as the lemmas; grain inrolled and narrow; lemmas 7–9 mm. long, hairy or hairless, with tightly inrolled margins **Bromus secalinus** (87)

THE USES OF GRASSES

The true grasses form one of the larger groups and undoubtedly the most important family of flowering plants, exceeding all others in the amount, variety, and value of their products, and in the number of their individuals. Directly or indirectly, they provide man and his domestic animals with the principal necessities of life; they add diversity to the landscape and stability to the ground surface, and they have ornamental and amenity applications.

From the cereals – wheat, barley, oats and rye in cool regions, and rice, maize and millets in warmer lands – enormous crops of grain are harvested, rich in starch and containing fats, proteins, minerals and vitamins. These grains are the source of flours and meals used in bread-making and in the preparation of various foodstuffs, as well as in the manufacture of a large range of products including adhesives, cosmetics, plastics and oils. The sweet sap of sugar-cane and varieties of sorghum yields much of our sugar, besides syrup and molasses. Alcoholic beverages, spiritous liquors and industrial alcohol are all made from the grains of cereals and from sugar molasses. Citronella-, lemon-, and vetiver-grasses of the tropics are famous for the aromatic oils distilled from their leaves or roots.

The fibres of the leaves and stems of esparto and halfa (two grasses of the Mediterranean Region) and of some bamboos and certain tropical grasses are employed in the manufacture of writing and packing papers of the highest quality, and of cards and boards. The stems and leaves of grasses with a high fibre content are also made into straw hats, sandals, screens, mats, ropes and brushes, and are used for thatching houses and stacks. Bamboos are the largest grasses, with exceptionally strong woody culms or stems up to 30 m. high. These are of great value for building houses, making furniture, and for many other purposes.

Natural grasslands (savannah, steppe and prairie) and man-made ones (ley, pasture and meadow) supply stock of all kinds, as well as other grazing animals, with their chief supply of fodder. Comparatively few species of our grasses are of outstanding value for forage purposes, but of these there are numerous variants both naturally derived and artificially produced. Some, from our old grasslands, have the most desirable qualities; others are of little use to the farmer. They vary considerably in size, form, rapidity of growth and leafiness, in the proportion of vegetative shoots to flowering culms, hardiness (winter greenness), disease and drought resistance, persistence, palatability, and in their capacity to withstand cutting, heavy grazing and trampling. In the past it was customary for the farmer to sow a seed-mixture of many species and strains, hoping that some would survive and prove suitable for the

421

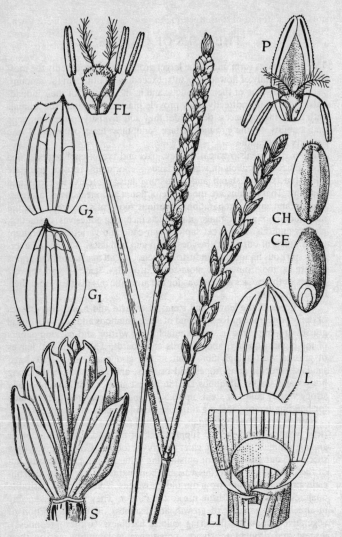

Wheat, *Triticum aestivum*, spikes, × ⅔; rest, × 3.

situation, soil, and purpose (grazing or hay) for which they were sown. Nowadays it is the practice to sow seeds of specified strains derived from a few species where the requirement is a suitability for grazing, hay, silage or ley pasture.

It is in connection with unsound agricultural practices that man becomes aware of one of the greatest assets of grasses, for when he allows them to be destroyed by excessive grazing or unwise cultivation, the soil, losing its protective covering of leaves and stems and the binding network of roots and rhizomes, soon suffers erosion by the action of wind and rain. The disastrous effects of such bad farming are fortunately rarely encountered in the British Isles, but in many overseas countries where grasses have been killed, over large areas much or all of the top soil has been washed or blown away and the farms have become derelict.

Grasses play an important role in the stabilization of ground associated with industrial, transport or residential development, where the covering must be of aesthetic value and manageable. Near the sea, a covering of grass may bind the surface against the ravages of the tides or even assist the process of sedimentation. In many instances, aesthetic value must be combined with practical application. If the grass is to be used for a recreational area, it must provide an even surface capable of sustaining heavy wear often at a time of limited growth.

Recognition of the vitally important role of grasses has been signalled by a wealth of international research. In this country, research is concentrated in long-established centres dealing with the breeding, selection and field trials of grasses for different uses. At the Welsh Plant Breeding Station, Aberystwyth, in particular, the late Sir R. George Stapledon and the late Professor T. J. Jenkin, their colleagues and successors, selected and bred the famed 'S' numbers. Similar work took place at the Scottish Plant Breeding Station, Corstorphine (later at Pentlandfield), at the Plant Breeding Institute, Cambridge, and also at several public and private breeding grounds. Extensive research on grasses and grasslands, their structure, improvement and use, is carried out at the Grassland Research Institute, Hurley, near Maidenhead. The Institute was originally conceived under the far-sighted direction of the late Dr William Davies, and recently a new research station sited on Devonshire farmland has been added to its existing centre. In most parts of the British Isles there are advisory officers of the Agricultural Development Advisory Service (formerly the National Agricultural Advisory Service) – specialist seedsmen and expert farmers – who can give information on forage grassland problems. The subject of amenity grassland is the province of the long-established Sports Turf Research Institute at Bingley in West Yorkshire, where research and advisory staff deal with the suitability of grasses for a wide range of playing surfaces.

An account of the specialized use of grasses should not neglect the

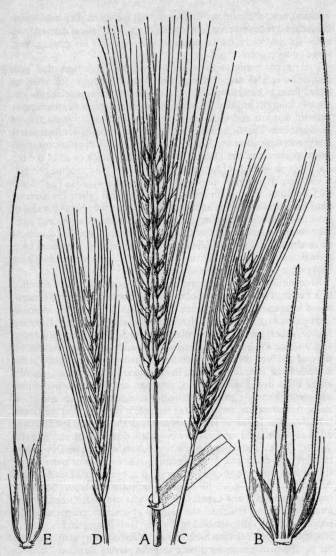

Barleys, *Hordeum vulgare* (A, B), *and H. distichon* (C); Rye,
Secale cereale (D, E); spikes, × ⅔. B, E, spikelets, × 2.

natural order of plants; the diversity of our countryside affords a great deal of pleasure to millions of people.

Cereals in Britain

Numerous agricultural varieties of wheat, barley, and oats are cultivated here, but only a few kinds of rye. Information concerning them may be found in the books listed in the bibliography (p. 447) and in the publications of the Ministry of Agriculture, Fisheries, and Food, and the National Institute of Agricultural Botany, Cambridge. They are classified under eight botanical species, which may be separated from each other by the characters given in the following key.

The figures given in brackets are the pages on which illustrations are to be found

1 Leaves without auricles at the junction of sheath and blade; spikelets borne on stalks, arranged in loose or contracted panicles:
  2 Lemmas each with two fine bristles 3–9 mm. long from the apex, also with an awn 20–35 mm. long from the back; Bristle or Small Oat
      Avena strigosa (234)
  2a Lemmas without bristles at the apex, only slightly toothed there, awned or awnless on the back:
    3 Lemmas hairless at the base, fracturing horizontally at the base from the spikelet-axis; Common Oat   **Avena sativa** (18, 20)
    3a Lemmas usually with few to several hairs at the base, fracturing obliquely at the base from the spikelet-axis; Red or Algerian Oat ....**Avena byzantina**
1a Leaves with claw-like auricles at the junction of sheath and blade; spikelets stalkless, borne in dense spikes:
  4 Spikelets solitary at each node (joint) of the spike-axis:
    5 Glumes broad, bulging on the back, 5–7-nerved; spikelets 2–5-flowered: lemmas broad, rough on the keels, awned or awnless:
      6 Glumes keeled in the upper half only; stems generally hollow; Bread Wheat ....**Triticum aestivum** (422)
      6a Glumes keeled from base to apex; stems solid and filled with pith in the upper part, or thick-walled; Rivet or Cone Wheat
          Triticum turgidum
    5a Glumes very narrow, 1-nerved; spikelets usually 2-flowered; lemmas narrow, stiffly hairy on the keels, long-awned; Rye
          Secale cereale (424)
  4a Spikelets in threes at each node (joint) of the spike-axis:
    7 Spikes with six longitudinal rows of fertile spikelets; all the spikelets of each cluster of three producing seed; Four-rowed and Six-rowed Barley ....**Hordeum vulgare** (424)
    7a Spikes with two longitudinal rows of fertile spikelets; the middle

spikelet of each three producing seed, the other two spikelets sterile or male; Two-rowed Barley   **Hordeum distichon** (424)

Forage Grasses

Forage grasses play a major part in the rural economy of the British Isles. The majority of farmers derive a substantial portion of their income from grazing animals, and many of the holdings are entirely pastoral. More than three-quarters of the food required by cattle, sheep and horses is obtained from herbage, either as pasture or as conserved fodder. About a third of the enclosed land comprises permanent pastures and meadows, and a similar area is occupied by sown swards of various ages. The bulk of the herbage in these fields consists of grasses. Animals grazing the moorlands, heaths and marshes also derive most of their nourishment from grasses, for which they forage among heather, gorse, bracken, rush, sedge and other coarse vegetation.

The older swards (permanent grassland) contain many species of grass, very few of which are cultivated for sowing in leys on arable land, or used to reseed grassland. The indigenous species that are cultivated, in descending order of importance, are Perennial Rye-grass (*Lolium perenne*), Large-leaved Timothy-grass (*Phleum pratense*), Cocksfoot (*Dactylis glomerata*), Meadow Fescue (*Festuca pratensis*), and Tall Fescue (*Festuca arundinacea*), and interest in the last three is diminishing. However, several other species deserve a mention, since they are the principal components of most permanent pastures and meadows, and because they usually reappear, sooner or later, in sown swards. Common Bent (*Agrostis tenuis*), Creeping Bent (*Agrostis stolonifera*), Yorkshire Fog (*Holcus lanatus*), Red Fescue (*Festuca rubra*), Rough Meadow-grass (*Poa trivialis*), and Meadow Fox-tail (*Alopecurus pratensis*) all make significant contributions to the total supply of forage from enclosed grassland. Many other grasses are equally widespread, but usually more thinly distributed: they include Smooth Meadow-grass (*Poa pratensis*), Sweet Vernal-grass (*Anthoxanthum odoratum*), Crested Dog's-tail (*Cynosurus cristatus*), Small-leaved Timothy-grass (*Phleum bertolonii*) and Golden Oat-grass (*Trisetum flavescens*). Yet others are locally dominant, e.g. Soft Brome (*Bromus mollis*) in upland meadows, Floating Fox-tail (*Alopecurus geniculatus*) and Tufted Hair-grass (*Deschampsia caespitosa*) on wet lands.

The predominant grasses in an established sward usually give a good indication of its productivity. The principal grasses of the moorlands are Purple Moor-grass (*Molinia caerulea*) and Mat-grass (*Nardus stricta*). The poorest of the enclosed grassland is characterized by an abundance of Red Fescue (*Festuca rubra*), Creeping Soft-grass (*Holcus mollis*) or Upright Brome (*Bromus erectus*), slightly better swards by Common Bent (*Agrostis tenuis*), Creeping Bent (*Agrostis stolonifera*) or Yorkshire

Fog (*Holcus lanatus*). Further up the scale, these grasses become less dominant, while species of *Poa*, *Alopecurus*, and *Phleum*, *Dactylis glomerata* and *Lolium perenne* become more frequent. In the best old pastures, Perennial Rye-grass (*Lolium perenne*) may occupy more than a third of the ground, and other species in that group form a larger proportion than *Agrostis*, *Holcus* and *Festuca*. In old meadows on fertile land, Meadow Fox-tail (*Alopecurus pratensis*) is often the dominant grass. However, the greater part of our semi-natural grassland is dominated by the *Agrostis/Holcus/Festuca* complex; and many of the sown swards are invaded as they age – first by Annual Meadow-grass (*Poa annua*) and Rough Meadow-grass (*Poa trivialis*), then by *Agrostis* and *Holcus*, and eventually by many other indigenous grasses.

Thus most of the forage obtained from permanent swards, and much of that from sown swards, is produced by species of *Agrostis*, *Holcus*, *Poa*, *Festuca rubra* and other non-cultivated species. While these grasses are rated inferior to Perennial Rye-grass (*Lolium perenne*) in potential yield, length of productive season, palatability and nutritive value, few of them fall so far short of that standard as to qualify for the disparagement frequently heaped on 'permanent grass'. As plants, they are patently adapted to the environment in which they exist – an environment that would need considerable amelioration before the cultivated species could perform well. And they are edible: the stems of many grasses, and the leaves of some, become very tough when mature and are then rejected by the grazing animals, but the immature tissue of most of our native grasses is accepted. The hairy foliage of species of *Holcus*, *Bromus*, *Hordeum* and *Agropyron* is often avoided by grazing animals; but whether food uptake is depressed or not when they have less choice is a moot point.

We are fortunate in Britain that the dominant species of grasses of our grazing lands produce usable forage. However, some are capable of higher yields than others. The obvious candidates for sowing are species which respond best to manuring, have a long productive season and are outstanding in nutritive value.

PERENNIAL RYE-GRASS (*Lolium perenne*)

Lolium perenne is an obvious choice for sowing because of its response to manuring, its long productive season and its outstanding nutritive value. It has the added advantage that the seedlings develop rapidly and compete strongly with any weeds that threaten the establishment of a sward. It also stands up well to the heavy trampling and defoliation that go with intensive stocking. At a given stage of growth, the forage has a higher content of digestible organic matter than that of either Large-leaved Timothy-grass (*Phleum pratense*) or Cocksfoot (*Dactylis glomerata*). Within this one species there are forms whose flowering dates differ by about three weeks, so that a farmer, from *Lolium perenne* alone, can have a sequence of crops at an appropriate stage for mowing or grazing throughout the long growing season. Modern breeding methods, pioneered in the 1920s at the Welsh Plant Breeding Station, have given us leafy, persistent varieties – some diploid, some tetraploid – of both early and late types. The British-bred varieties are winter-green, yet sufficiently hardy for all but the most elevated land and the extreme north-east. Tetraploid varieties and those from continental sources are preferred in the coldest regions. The tetraploid varieties are also favoured by farmers in some other eastern districts, where they appear to recover more rapidly after cutting or grazing in hot, dry weather. When a heavy crop is cut for hay, *Lolium perenne* is slightly more difficult to handle than other cultivated perennial grasses. However, on the more intensive farms grass is mown at an early stage and ensiled, and *Lolium perenne* is as suitable for this process as it is for grazing.

These are some of the reasons why *Lolium perenne* is now by far the most important component of seed mixtures for leys of three years or longer duration, and for permanent pasture.

LARGE-LEAVED TIMOTHY-GRASS (*Phleum pratense*)

Phleum pratense is a late-flowering grass and starts its growth later than Perennial Rye-grass (*Lolium perenne*) in most districts, but in the north-east, where *Lolium perenne* may be set back by a hard winter, it is a reliable source of relatively early grazing. Its suitability for haymaking makes it a popular grass in the north, where a large proportion of the grass crop has to be saved for winter feeding. Many seed mixtures sown in other regions also have a complement of *Phleum pratense*. In short-term leys intended for mowing, the erect, earlier maturing varieties are normally used, but the later-flowering, densely tillered varieties are prescribed for long-term pastures.

COCKSFOOT (*Dactylis glomerata*)

Dactylis glomerata was included in the majority of seed mixtures for three- to four-year leys earlier in this century, but, as evidence of the superior nutritive value of *Lolium perenne* emerged, even the leafy varieties of *Dactylis glomerata* declined in popularity. This grass still has some adherents in eastern England because of its ability to recover during hot, dry weather. In the north-east, some use is made of hardy varieties from Denmark to ensure some 'early' grazing – as in the case of *Phleum*.

MEADOW FESCUE (*Festuca pratensis*)

Festuca pratensis shares many qualities with Perennial Rye-grass (*Lolium perenne*), but is comparatively slow in establishment and much less competitive. Non-Rye-grass mixtures, based on *Festuca pratensis* and Large-Leaved Timothy-grass (*Phleum pratense*), enjoyed a brief spell of popularity among farmers interested in exploiting clovers, but these leys proved very prone to invasion by weed grasses; and little use is now made of *Festuca pratensis*.

TALL FESCUE (*Festuca arundinacea*)

Festuca arundinacea grows earlier in spring than the other cultivated perennials. In this respect, a sward of *Festuca arundinacea* can match Italian Rye-grass (*Lolium multiflorum*). The seedlings are slow to develop, and special care is required in order to establish a sward; but, once, established, this is a very persistent grass, even on cold, wet land, and is capable of a high yield. It flowers very early, and must be defoliated frequently if forage of good quality is to be obtained. It is seldom sown, except by green-crop driers, who value its capacity to grow early and provide a steady supply of material for processing throughout the summer.

ITALIAN RYE-GRASS (*Lolium multiforum*) AND HYBRIDS

The only exotic forage grass in general use is *Lolium multiflorum*. It develops even more rapidly than Perennial Rye-grass (*Lolium perenne*) and, when established, grows earlier in the spring. However, it is a short-lived perennial and its principal use is in one- and two-year leys, though a small amount of it is often included in seeds mixtures for longer leys to boost yield in the first season. Introduced into Britain in 1840, Italian Rye-grass was soon widely adopted as a companion for Broad Red Clover in one-year leys. Today it is more often sown alone because, on arable land and intensive grass farms, the one-year ley usually receives generous dressings of nitrogenous fertilizer to produce early pasture and bulky crops of material for conservation. Modern varieties will yield for two years, but leys sown for two years usually consist of a mixture of *Lolium multiflorum* and *Lolium perenne*. The two species hybridize, and bred varieties of the hybrid are replacing *Lolium multiflorum* in leys used intensively for two to four years.

Although *Lolium multiflorum* and its hybrid derivatives grow more rapidly than *Lolium perenne* in spring, they flower at the same time as intermediate varieties of *L. perenne*, and the two species are comparable in nutritive value at that stage. Unlike the bred varieties of *L. perenne*, all varieties of *L. multiflorum* and hybrid Rye-grass produce flowering stems throughout the summer, and need to be mown or grazed frequently in order to maintain quality in the herbage.

Plant breeders have provided us with many varieties of all these cultivated grasses and are continually seeking to improve upon existing stock. Their products are screened and tested in field trials at sites throughout the British Isles. Lists of recommended varieties, with information on the main characteristics of each, are regularly issued by the National Institute of Agricultural Botany (for England and Wales), by the Scottish Agricultural Colleges, and by the Departments of Agriculture in Northern Ireland and Eire.

Weed Grasses in Agriculture

Nowadays, the tendency in cereal and pasture farming is towards the use of monocultures, where the emphasis can be placed on the size, timing and quality of the yield. Under such conditions any intruding plant species may be regarded as a weed, although its presence may be tolerated at a later stage of the ley or in permanent grassland. Generally, a weed species may be undesirable due to its unpalatability and contamination of the crop, its poor comparative yield and its competition for space and nutrient supply with the sown species.

Whereas the presence of broad-leaved weeds has been controlled by the use of selective weedkillers, there are still certain grass weeds which prove troublesome within a grass-type crop. These include Black Grass (*Alopecurus myosuroides*), Bristle Oat (*Avena strigosa*), Common Wild Oat (*Avena fatua*), Black Bent or Red Top (*Agrostis gigantea*), Couch (*Agropyron repens*), Annual Meadow-grass (*Poa annua*), and Rough Meadow-grass (*Poa trivialis*). Creeping Soft-grass (*Holcus mollis*) is a pest in some areas and the Sterile Brome (*Bromus sterilis*) is increasing in others.

Selective weedkillers are available to deal with Black Grass and Wild Oats, and the seedling stage of Annual Meadow-grass. Less selective chemicals can be used during a fallow period against the rhizomatous Couch and Black Bent.

Sand- and Mud-Binding Grasses

By providing a cover for the surface and a fine network of roots in the soil, most grasses prevent erosion by wind and water, especially on hill and mountain slopes, river-sides, and on muddy and sandy sea-shores. Certain species, however, are more suitable than others for this purpose, particularly those with deep root-systems, extensively creeping rhizomes, or stolons, as well as other special modifications which enable them to grow in relatively unfavourable situations.

On flats subject to flooding by river water, and on river-banks, the tall rhizomatous grasses, Reed Canary-grass (*Phalaris arundinacea*), and Reed Sweet-grass (*Glyceria maxima*) protect the ground from erosion and form a close growth of succulent stems and leafage which may be grazed by cattle when the area is not too wet. The Common Reed (*Phragmites communis*) also covers large areas in such habitats, and its leaves and stems are valuable for thatching houses and stacks. Two short grasses, spreading by creeping rooting stolons, Marsh Bent (*Agrostis stolonifera* var. *palustris*), and Rough Meadow-grass (*Poa trivialis*) will form a close growth on river- and stream-banks, or round lakes and ponds.

There are several grasses which may be used for the control of drifting sand of coastal dunes. The most important of these is the well-known Marram Grass (*Ammophila arenaria*), the rhizomes of which spread rapidly through loose sand, branching and rooting profusely, and giving rise to erect leafy shoots capable of growing up through gradually increasing layers of sand. It has been extensively planted on large dunes at various points on our coasts and has been most successful in consolidating such areas. Hybrid Marram (× *Ammocalamagrostis baltica*) has also been planted for the same purpose with good results. On small dunes and the lower parts of large ones nearest to the sea, Sand Couch (*Agropyron junceiforme*) is a very valuable pioneer, stabilizing the sand by means of its creeping rhizomes and leafy shoots. Once the sand has been partially fixed, the Sand Fescue (*Festuca rubra* subsp. *arenaria*), by means of its fine roots, rhizomes, and shoots, assists in binding it still firmer. Lyme Grass (*Elymus arenarius*) is another valuable consolidator of drifting sand; it is frequently associated with Marram Grass and has often been planted in coastal dunes. Where there is shingle mixed with sand, or the terrain is a gravelly mud, the Sea Couch (*Agropyron pungens*) is important as a stabilizer.

On tidal mud-flats, flooded at high water, the Common Salt-marsh-grass (*Puccinellia maritima*) spreads over the bare mud by means of its creeping rooting stolons gradually forming the short dense turf of a salt-marsh. Its stiffly erect stems and leaves trap silt and fine debris and the surface of the marsh is very gradually raised until the maritime strains of Red Fescue (*Festuca rubra* subsp. *litoralis*) can gain a foothold and spread to form a continuous turf. On the bare soft mud on the seaward side of such salt-marshes, in pans and along creeks and channels in the salt-marshes, and in similar situations at the foot of sea-banks where no other grasses can exist, Common Cord-grass (*Spartina anglica*) has been very extensively planted to protect foreshores and reclaim mud-flats. Small tufts are put out in rows where, if the local conditions are suitable, the plants spread rapidly by their stout rhizomes and in good seasons by seed, soon linking up to form a continuous meadow. As the tides advance and recede, the rigid erect stems and leaves of this grass collect silt and debris so that besides consolidating the mud by its roots and rhizomes, the surface of the mud-flat is raised. Before planting *Spartina anglica* one must consider whether its growth is likely to cause serious inconvenience or obstruction by silting up estuaries and harbours and damage to beds of shell-fish. The sterile primary hybrid, Townsend's Cord-grass (*Spartina* × *townsendii*) forms a closer growth on mud-flats than does Common Cord-grass, but spreads more slowly, being limited to vegetative propagation by its rhizomes and vegetative shoots.

Amenity Grassland

Amenity grassland may be considered to be all grass with recreational, functional or aesthetic value, which is not primarily intended for agricultural production. A survey commissioned by the Natural Environment Research Council estimated that in 1973 amenity grassland covered about 850,000 ha. in the United Kingdom, or nearly 4 per cent of the land surface. This can be categorized according to the intensity of use and management.

Slightly over half (470,000 ha. in 1973) is more or less 'natural' grassland. Part of it, designated 'untrampled open spaces' (about 65,000 ha.) and including airfields and railway and motorway embankments, may have been artificially created, but is not subject to any serious pressure of human use (sport, walking, car parking, etc.). The other and larger part (about 405,000 ha.), designated 'semi-natural trampled open spaces', is by definition more subject to human use than the previous category but includes many long-established and often very diverse types of grassland: golf course 'roughs', rural road verges, country parks, open nature reserves, etc. Both these major categories of grassland are likely to be subject to systematic management of some sort, though it is often deliberately kept to a minimum. Much of this grassland, with a wide diversity of grasses and plants growing and flowering freely, is amenity grassland only in the widest sense.

The narrower and perhaps more conventional idea of amenity grassland is represented by the two remaining categories, totalling 380,000 ha. in 1973. About 110,000 ha can be described as 'intensively managed', and consists of sports turf and grass playing-fields of all kinds. Another 270,000 ha., designated 'man-made trampled open spaces', includes domestic lawns, urban parks and road verges. These areas are subject to use, or 'wear', of varying intensity and destructiveness, from people engaged in sport or recreation and also sometimes from horses. There is also relatively obvious management of such areas, ranging from 'low maintenance' regimes consisting of one or two cuts per year to a very high input of labour, fertilizer and other resources on top-quality sports facilities. The heavier the wear and the more intensive the management, the fewer the grass species able to tolerate such treatment. These comparatively few species are conveniently termed 'turf grasses' to denote their special suitability for surfaces intended for sport or recreation. They are, broadly, the 'lawn grasses' of earlier editions of this book, though emphasis nowadays is on wear which must be supported and repaired, and ease and infrequency of mowing, rather than on the fine texture and elegance which were once the principal criteria.

The relative merits of the main turf grasses under United Kingdom conditions

Turf grass	Persistence under close mowing (5 = best)	Low growth (5 = lowest growing)	Tolerance of heavy wear (5 = most tolerant)
Velvet Bent (*Agrostis canina* subsp. *canina*)	5	4	2
Brown Top (*Agrostis tenuis*) and Highland Bent (*A. castellana*)	5	3–4	2
Creeping Bent (*Agrostis stolonifera*)	5	4	2
Fine-leaved Sheep's Fescue (*Festuca tenuifolia*)	3	3	1
Hard Fescue (*Festuca longifolia*)	4	3	1
Subspecies of Red Fescue (*Festuca rubra*): Chewings Fescue (subsp. *commutata*)	4	3	2
Slender creeping Red Fescue (subsp. *litoralis*)	4	2–3	2
Strong creeping Red Fescue (subsp. *rubra*)	3	1–2	1
Crested Dog's-tail (*Cynosurus cristatus*)	2	3	2
Rough Meadow-grass (*Poa trivialis*)	2	3	½
Smooth Meadow-grass (*Poa pratensis*)	3	2–4	4–4½
Small-leaved Timothy-grass (*Phleum bertolonii*)	3	3	3½
Large-leaved Timothy-grass (*Phleum pratense*)	2	2–3	3½–4
Perennial Rye-grass (*Lolium perenne*)	1–2	1–2	4½–5

(Adapted from *Turfgrass 1982*, published by the Sports Turf Research Institute)

The main sown turf grasses for the United Kingdom are shown in the table (p. 433), placed in an order which broadly – though not precisely – indicates their suitability for turf in three respects, namely, persistence under close mowing, low growth, and tolerance of heavy wear.

All these turf grasses are available as certified seed of named cultivars (cultivated varieties). They are mostly selected or bred for use in intensively managed turf, though they can also be produced for less intensive maintenance or special conditions such as high salinity or contamination by heavy metals. There is some overlap with agricultural use, particularly in Timothy and Perennial Rye-grass. For example, the well-known cultivar of Perennial Rye-grass (*Lolium perenne*), 'Aberystwyth S. 23', has long been a valuable component of turf grass mixtures: nowadays, however, there is increasing reliance on turf-type cultivars when Perennial Rye-grass is used. The main species, in order of importance as denoted by seed weight sold each year, are Perennial Rye-grass (*Lolium perenne*), Red Fescue as Chewings Fescue (*Festuca rubra* subsp. *commutata*), Slender creeping Red Fescue (*Festuca rubra* subsp. *litoralis*), and Strong creeping Red Fescue (*Festuca rubra* subsp. *rubra*), the Bent-grasses as mainly Brown Top (*Agrostis tenuis*) with Highland Bent (*A. castellana*), and Smooth Meadow-grass (*Poa pratensis*).

In addition to these sown species, Annual Meadow-grass (*Poa annua*) is an important unsown constituent of many turf areas in the United Kingdom, particularly those mown close and subject to heavy wear. Some types of Annual Meadow-grass, which are in fact more or less long-lived perennials, are very persistent under close mowing and are tolerant of wear, as well as being low-growing. They are thus rated highly although they do have certain faults. Some professional turf managers accept Annual Meadow-grass as a useful, or even essential, turf grass; others regard it as a weed to be eliminated from the turf as completely as possible by appropriate management.

Most new turf sports areas are established from seed. Only a small proportion are established from sod, i.e. by laying pieces of mature turf. This is partly because until recently there was very little sod that would meet the requirements of professional users. The erstwhile small supply (principally of that specialized commodity, sea-marsh turf) is now being substantially augmented by cultivated sod, consisting of good turf grasses grown specifically for sod production on natural soils or special growing mediums. Sod lifted from old agricultural pastures has always been more acceptable for domestic and landscaping use than for sport, but even for these markets good cultivated sod is preferable and is now gaining in popularity.

(a) *Fine turf*. For very fine sports turf (e.g. for golf and bowling greens) and high quality ornamental areas such as lawns, likely to be mown regularly to about 5 mm., the two main sown species are Brown Top or Common Bent (*Agrostis tenuis*) and Chewings Fescue (*Festuca rubra* subsp. *commutata*) as a seeds mixture of about 20 per cent and 80 per cent respectively, by weight. The bent is more tolerant of really close mowing than the fescue, and will be the dominant partner on most soils if supplied with adequate water and nitrogenous fertilizer. The fescue, however, will be more important in drier and less fertile conditions, for example on a sandy soil receiving little or no fertilizer. Both grasses will adapt to fairly acid conditions, the bent rather more successfully; and in such conditions there will be relatively little competition from other species. If acidity is reduced and if moisture and fertility are ample, Annual Meadow-grass is likely to invade the turf.

The Chewings Fescue can be partly replaced by some fine-leaved types of Creeping Red Fescue, especially in dry or saline situations, for instance on the sea-coast. The bent normally used nowadays is the cultivar Highland Bent (Agrostis castellana). It is well adapted to United Kingdom conditions but it may be partly replaced by bent cultivars of *Agrostis tenuis*, or by Creeping Bent (*Agrostis stolonifera*) or Velvet Bent (*Agrostis canina* subsp. *canina*).

Occasionally, fine turf is established from bent alone, either Creeping Bent or a mixture of species, but this runs the risk of damage from disease and loses the flexibility of response to environment and management which a mixture of two or more species is intended to give.

(b) *Heavy-duty sports turf*. At the opposite extreme of intensive management from the golf or bowling green is the rugger or soccer pitch, mown at 20 mm. or taller. The most important sown grass is Perennial Rye-grass (*Lolium perenne*), though even here Annual Meadow-grass often invades to become an almost equal partner. Turf-type cultivars of Perennial Rye-grass are now giving better wear tolerance than cultivars bred for agriculture, and are increasingly overshadowing the other components of the typical playing-field mixture – Smooth Meadow-grass (*Poa pratensis*), Red Fescue (*Festuca rubra* subsps.) and Brown Top (*Agrostis tenuis*). The Smooth Meadow-grass can contribute a useful amount of wear tolerance, and recovery after wear from its rhizomes: it is particularly important on sandy soils. The value of the fescue and bent is questionable, although they can increase ground cover before a pitch is used. They can perhaps contribute to the structure of the grass playing-surface in some ways, but their value under heavy wear is negligible. Only on a close-mown area such as a hockey pitch, or where a football pitch has to serve as a cricket outfield in summer, is there an obvious merit in these grasses.

(c) *Other types of sports turf.* There are now various types of grass playing-surfaces, in mowing height somewhere between fine turf and football pitches, which have helped to fill a gap which has existed for many years between fescue and bent (tolerant of close-mowing but not of wear) and Perennial Rye-grass (tolerant of wear but not of close-mowing). Smooth Meadow-grass (*Poa pratensis*) and Small-leaved Timothy-grass (*Phleum bertolonii*) partly filled this gap. The turf-type cultivars of Perennial Rye-grass seem likely to fill it more successfully.

Racecourses have special requirements, for which the most wear-tolerant of currently used turf grasses are often adequate. It is uncertain whether other, more robust, grasses can be found for such a purpose, or whether completely different solutions to problems of heavy wear will have to adopted.

TURF GRASS MIXTURE FOR NON-INTENSIVE MANAGEMENT

Compared with the intensively managed types of amenity grassland, mainly used for sport, the non-intensive or 'low maintenance' types of amenity grassland are more diverse: Firstly, the range of possible treatment can vary from quite frequent mowing to as few as one or two cuts per year. In the latter case, many species can flourish as they never could in regularly mown turf, and there can even be deliberate encouragement of many non-grass species. Secondly, wear on such areas is – or should be – relatively light, and this also encourages marginal species. Thirdly, specialized environments (very wet or dry, or those shaded or contaminated in various ways) are often recognized as unsuitable for intensive use, and species are selected in an attempt to match the particular environmental conditions.

For all these reasons, seeds mixtures for such areas are often complex, containing scarce and expensive seed of unusual species which may often be unnecessary. Much can be done with basic turf grasses. The various fine-leaved fescues and bents can form low-growing swards requiring relatively little mowing, particularly in acid or infertile conditions. Smooth Meadow-grass (*Poa pratensis*) and some low-growing cultivars of Creeping Red Fescue (*Festuca rubra* subsps.) can be used on dry or rather alkaline soils. On very wet soils, Rough Meadow-grass (*Poa trivialis*) or Timothy-grass (*Phleum* sp.) may be useful. For rapid cover of newly sown areas, some cultivars of Perennial Rye-grass or Creeping Red Fescue may be sown because of their quick initial growth; they may also be used as 'nurse-crops' for other grass or plant species which establish more slowly – a combination of non-persistent cultivars and judicious cutting being intended to ensure the disappearance of the nurse crop after initial soil stabilization and moisture conservation.

Key for the Identification of Grasses in Turf

This key is provided for the benefit of greenkeepers and others who do not wish to use the longer one on page 387. The figures in parentheses refer to the pages on which the grasses are described and illustrated.

1 Leaf-blades normally flat, or rolled or folded lengthwise during dry weather, soft to firm but never bristle-like (if not, then to 1a on page 439):

2 Ligule formed by a dense fringe of very short hairs; leaves bearded with spreading hairs at the junction of sheath and blade; blades 2–4 mm. wide, blunt or abruptly pointed, folded in the shoot, afterwards flat or gutter-like; tufted perennial; Heath Grass

Sieglingia decumbens (351)

2a Ligules membranous, variable in length, sometimes short and obscure:

3 Young leaf-blade rolled in shoot, the latter mostly cylindrical, circular in transverse section; sheaths mostly rounded on the back (if not, then to 3a on p. 438):

4 Leaves loosely to densely bearded with spreading hairs at the junction of sheath and blade, aromatic when bruised, green; ligules 1–5 mm. long, blades 1·5–5 mm. wide, finely pointed; tufted perennial; Sweet Vernal-grass

Anthoxanthum odoratum (269)

4a Leaves not so bearded or aromatic when bruised:

5 Shoots usually swollen or bulbous at the base; leaves dull, tapering, green or greyish-green, ribbing not conspicuous, finely pointed, hairless:

6 Leaf-blades 2–5 mm. wide. Ligules 1–4 mm. long. Sometimes with leafy stolons; Small-leaved Timothy-grass

Phleum bertolonii (319)

6a Leaf-blades longer and wider to 9 mm., perhaps twisting. Ligules up to 6 mm. long; Large-leaved Timothy-grass

Phleum pratense (321)

5a Shoots not thickened at the base:

7 Leaves loosely to densely hairy especially on the sheaths, green or greyish green (if not, then to 7a on p. 440):

8 Basal leaf-sheaths white or suffused with purple, with pink or purplish veins (if not, then to 8a on p. 440):

9 Nodes downy or almost hairless; no rhizomes; leaf blades 3–10 mm. wide; ligules 1–4 mm. long; Yorkshire Fog

Holcus lanatus (261)

9a Nodes bearded; rhizomes; leaf-blades 3–8 mm. wide,

pointed; ligules 1–5 mm. long; Creeping soft-grass
Holcus mollis (262)

8a Basal leaf-sheaths usually with green veins; blades 1–2·5 mm.
wide; ligules up to 1 mm. long; Crested Hair-grass
Koeleria cristata (241)

7a Leaves and nodes hairless:
10 Leaves strongly ribbed, glossy below; living basal sheaths
yellow or yellow-brown; ligules 0·5–1·5 mm. long; plants
compactly tufted; Crested Dog's-tail
Cynosurus cristatus (219)

10a Leaves dull green; blades finely pointed:
11 Plants with whitish or brownish wiry rhizomes creeping
through the soil and bearing brownish scale leaves;
perennials, forming loose to dense tufts or patches:
12 Ligules mostly shorter than broad, 0·5–1 mm. wide;
Common Bent or Brown Top ... **Agrostis tenuis** (299)

12a Ligules as long as or longer than broad, 1–5 mm. long:
13 Leaf-blades 2–6 mm. wide; ligules equally wide throughout,
very blunt or toothed; plants loosely tufted; Red Top
or Black Bent .... **Agrostis gigantea** (301)

13a Leaf-blades 1–3 mm. wide; ligules narrowed upwards or
pointed, plants densely tufted; Brown Bent
Agrostis canina subsp. **montana** (297)

11a Plants always without underground rhizomes, but sometimes with surface runners (stolons) bearing green leaves,
otherwise loosely to densely tufted:
15 Leaf-blades 1–3 mm. wide, soft, usually bright green;
ligules often pointed or narrowed upwards; Velvet
Bent ....**Agrostis canina** subsp. **canina** (295)

15a Leaf-blades up to 5 mm. wide, firm, dull green to greyish-
green; ligules equally wide throughout, very blunt;
Creeping Bent, White Bent or Fiorin
Agrostis stolonifera (303)

3a Young leaf-blade folded lengthwise about the middle nerve in the
shoot, the latter sometimes more or less compressed, and the
sheaths frequently keeled, especially in the upper part, rarely
rounded on the back:
16 Leaves with small pointed outgrowths (auricles) on the margins
at the junction of sheath and blade; blades pointed or blunt,
2–6 mm. wide, green, very glossy beneath, strongly ribbed
above; living basal sheaths usually red or red-purple; ligules
about 1 mm. long; plants tufted; Perennial Rye-grass
Lolium perenne (149)

16a Leaves without auricles; basal leaf-sheaths whitish or greenish,

438

or streaked with bright yellow, rarely purplish or reddish:

17 Leaf-blades finely pointed; plants tufted, perennials:

18 Shoots very slender; sheaths rounded on the back; blades 1–3 mm. wide, glossy beneath; base of sheath yellow or yellow-brown; ligules 0·5–1·5 mm. Crested Dog's-tail
Cynosurus cristatus (219)

18a Shoots relatively stout, sheaths compressed and keeled; blades 2–8 mm. wide, dull green; ligules 2–6 mm. long; Cocksfoot
Dactylis glomerata (215)

17a Leaf-blades with abruptly pointed or blunt hooded tips; sheaths compressed and keeled; the blade bearing a characteristic 'tramline' being transparent lines either side of the midrib:

19 Ligules 1–5 mm. or more long, narrowed upwards; blades 1–5 mm. wide:

20 Plants tufted, possibly with short stolons or prostrate stems rooting at nodes; blades transversely crinkled when young, yellowish-green or green; basal sheaths often whitish; usually flowering in short turf; Annual Meadow-grass
Poa annua (167)

20a Plants with leafy creeping stolons, perennial; blades not transversely crinkled, often bright green, very glossy beneath; basal sheaths often purplish or reddish; Rough Meadow-grass .... **Poa trivialis** (185)

19a Ligules 0·3 to less than 1 mm. long, very blunt:

21 Plants loosely tufted, without rhizomes, blades usually weak, 1–3 mm. wide; Wood Meadow-grass **Poa nemoralis** (175)

21a Plants with slender creeping scaly rhizomes; blades firm, 2–4 mm. wide; Smooth Meadow-grass
Poa pratensis (189)

1a Leaf-blades bristle-like, usually tightly infolded or inrolled, narrowly grooved or channelled on the upper side, very narrow, usually hairless:

22 Roots cord-like; shoots closely packed on short rhizomes forming dense tufts; basal sheaths tough and shining; ligules about 1 mm. long; blades sharply pointed, rigid; Mat-grass
Nardus stricta (343)

22a Roots very slender; basal sheaths not hard and shining:

23 Ligules extremely short and obscure, less than 0·5 mm. long (to p. 440):

24 Plants densely tufted, without rhizomes (to p. 440):

25 Leaf-sheaths open, with free margins, one overlapping the other; leaf-blades 0·2–0·6 mm. wide (to p. 440):

26 Leaf-blades mostly 0·2–0·3 mm. wide, 3–5-nerved; Fine-leaved Sheep's Fescue .... **Festuca tenuifolia** (127)

26a Leaf-blades mostly 0·4–0·6 mm. wide, 7-nerved; Hard Fescue
Festuca longifolia (131)

25a Leaf-sheaths tubular but soon splitting; blades 0·6–1 mm. wide; Chewings Fescue
Festuca rubra subsp. **commutata** (135)

24a Plants with slender, creeping, whitish or brownish, scaly rhizomes forming loosely to densely tufted or with scattered shoots:

27 Plants compactly tufted or mat-forming, with comparatively short, very slender rhizomes:

28 Plants mat-forming; outer basal leaf-sheaths usually glabrous; leaf-blades 0·5–0·7 mm. wide in side view; dark green (on salt marshes); Slender creeping Red Fescue
Festuca rubra subsp. **litoralis** (375)

28a Plants forming loose to dense tufts; outer basal leaf-sheaths mostly with backward-pointing hairs. Leaf-blades 0·6–1·3 mm. wide in side view, becoming whitish-pruinose or green; Bloomed Fescue
Festuca rubra subsp. **pruinosa** (376)

27a Plants loosely to closely tufted, with scattered vegetative shoots:

30 Relatively long to very long rhizomes. Basal outer leaf-sheaths densely covered with backward pointing hairs; Strong creeping Red Fescue ....**Festuca rubra** subsp. **rubra** (137)

30a Long, branching rhizomes. Basal outer leaf sheaths usually smooth (on sand dunes); Sand Fescue.
Festuca rubra subsp. **arenaria** (377)

23a Ligules 0·5–3 mm. long; leaf-blades 0·3–0·8 mm. wide, bright green; leaf-sheaths open; plants densely tufted, usually without rhizomes; Wavy Hair-grass ....**Deschampsia flexuosa** (249)

Ornamental Grasses

There is now such an abundance of beautiful flowering and foliage plants, it may seem presumptuous for a grass-specialist to advocate the wider use of grasses for the adornment of parks, gardens, and woodlands. It is true their flowers cannot compete in colour, scent, and splendour with the lily or the rose, nevertheless they possess distinctive types of foliage and flower-head which provide a very pleasing setting for more showy plants. For practical purposes ornamental grasses may be divided into two groups, depending on whether they are grown for their attractive flower-heads or for their graceful and unusual foliage.

For a more extensive account of ornamental grasses of use in the gardens of Western Europe and those with similar climatic conditions, the reader should consult the second Supplement (1968) to the Royal Horticultural Society's *Dictionary of Gardening*.

I. GRASSES WITH DECORATIVE FLOWER-HEADS

These include all those grasses which, because of their delicately branched, plume-like, feathery, bristly, spiky, or coloured flower-heads, or because of the regular form of their individual spikelets, are suitable as decorative material. Their flower-heads can be used in the fresh or dried state; in the latter condition especially during the winter months, when fresh flowers are not so plentiful. They may be displayed in vases, baskets, and bouquets, or on confectionery, either mixed together, or associated with other dried flowers such as the colourful 'Everlastings' (*Helichrysum bracteatum*). Most grasses of this kind are easy to grow. Many are annuals or biennials which can be cultivated with a high degree of success even on relatively poor soils, provided they receive sufficient moisture. Seeds should be sown very thinly in March, April, and May, in irregular patches when sown with other plants for the adornment of borders, or in wide rows for cutting. The perennials can also be raised from seed, but they are generally best increased by division of the root-stocks in autumn or spring. The flower-heads must be cut in dry weather and at the stage when the anthers are beginning to be exserted. The lower leaves should be removed and the stems tied in small bunches and hung in a cool dark airy room where the flower-heads can dry quickly, retaining a good fresh colour. After drying, they may be dyed, if so desired, with various bright colours.

There are very numerous grasses which can be grown for their flower-heads; only a few are listed below. In addition to these, many of our native grasses have very elegant inflorescences suitable for drying.

A. ANNUALS OR BIENNIALS. 1, With attractive spikelets: *Avena sterilis, Briza maxima, B. minor, Bromus arvensis, B. briziformis, B. macrostachys, B. madritensis, Desmazeria sicula,* 2, With delicate and profusely branched flower-heads: *Agrostis nebulosa, Aira elegans, Apera spica-venti, Panicum capillare.* 3, With spike-like flower-heads: *Lolium temulentum, Phalaris canariensis, P. minor.* 4, With bristly or feathery flower-heads: *Cynosurus echinatus, Echinochloa crus-galli, Elymus caput-medusae, Lagurus ovatus, Lamarckia aurea, Polypogon monspeliensis, Setaria glauca, S. viridis.* 5, With unusual flower-heads: *Aegilops ovata, A. ventricosa, Coix lacryma-jobi, Eleusine indica.*

B. PERENNIALS. 1, With loose or contracted and plume-like flower-heads: *Briza media, Chionochloa conspicua* ('*Danthonia cunninghamii*') *Cortaderia richardii* ('*conspicua*'), *C, selloana, Miscanthus sinensis, Panicum virgatum, Stipa arundinacea, S. calamagrostis, S. pennata, Uniola latifolia.* 2, With spike-like flower-heads: *Elymus arenarius,*

Hordeum jubatum, *Hystrix patula*, *Melica altissima*, and its var. *purpurea*.

II. GRASSES WITH ATTRACTIVE FOLIAGE

Such grasses are useful for a variety of situations, including borders, formal gardens, rockeries, isolated beds on lawns, shrubberies, and screens, wild gardens, woodland glades, stream- and lake-sides. With few exceptions they are readily propagated by division of the rootstock, preferably in autumn but also in early spring. The leaves may be variegated with green and white, cream, or yellow, or be yellowish, bluish- or silvery-grey, purple, or green.

A. VARIEGATED LEAVES. Because of longitudinal stripes of silvery- or creamy-white, yellow or gold, alternating with the natural green of the leaf, grasses with variegated leaves brighten borders (etc.) over a long period, especially before and after their showy companions have flowered. The following species all have variegated varieties, mostly known as var. *variegatus* or *variegata*: *Alopecurus pratensis*, *Arrhenatherum elatius*, *Arundo donax*, *Cortaderia selloana*, *Dactylis glomerata*, *Glyceria maxima*, *Holcus mollis*, *Molinia caerulea*, *Phalaris arundinacea* var. *picta*, and *Spartina pectinata*. *Miscanthus sinensis* var. *zebrinus* has the leaves transversely and irregularly barred with yellowish-green.

B. COLOURED (NOT GREEN) LEAVES. With bluish- or silvery-grey leaves: *Elymus arenarius*, *Festuca glauca*, *Poa glauca*. With golden or yellow leaves, usually known as var. *aureus* or *aurea*: *Alopecurus pratensis*, *Dactylis glomerata*, *Milium effusum*, and *Phragmites communis*. With purple leaves: *Zea mays* var. *purpurea*.

C. GREEN OR GREENISH LEAVES. The Pampas Grass, *Cortaderia selloana* (*C. argentea*,*Gynerium argenteum*), is perhaps the most widely cultivated ornamental grass. Its large dense tussocks of graceful curved narrow leaves, surmounted by the tall erect or spreading plumes produced in autumn, are especially suitable for isolated beds on lawns where, when in flower, they are often the most conspicuous feature of the landscape. Besides male and female plants, there are several horticultural varieties, some with silvery, others with purplish or reddish plumes. Var. *pumila*, a shorter variety about 4 ft. high, is suitable for small gardens. *C. richardii* ('*conspicua*') is similar to *C. selloana* in its garden uses, but flowers earlier, in July and August. *Arundo donax*, *Erianthus ravennae*, *Miscanthus sacchariflorus* and *M. sinensis*, besides numerous bamboos, are other useful tall grasses, suitable for large beds, shrubberies, and woodlands.

GRASSES FOR WET PLACES. The variegated varieties of *Glyceria maxima*, *Molinia caerulea*, *Phalaris arundinacea*, and *Phragmites communis*, are suitable for planting on the banks of streams and lakes. Indian Rice,

Zizania aquatica, a tall grass, with green leaves and attractive panicles, may also be grown in lakes.

GRASSES FOR SHADY PLACES. The following grasses flourish in glades and open spaces in woodlands, positions difficult to fill with other plants: *Brachypodium sylvaticum*, *Bromus ramosus*, *Festuca heterophylla*, *F. tenuifolia*, *Hordelymus europaeus*, *Melica uniflora*, *Milium effusum*, *Poa chaixii*, and *P. nemoralis*. All have elegant flower-heads, dark green leaves and, with the exception of the rhizomatous *Melica*, form compact tufts.

BAMBOOS. These belong to a separate group of grasses having woody branched stems which even in our climate reach considerable heights, especially in the south and west, where some kinds may be 20–30 ft tall. Besides being important ornamental plants, they are also valuable for hedges and screens, whilst their mature canes are used as stakes. The young shoots of some species of *Phyllostachys* are edible, being cooked in the same manner as asparagus. In the British Isles most species require protection from north and east winter winds, and ample moisture in the summer. They are best grown on slopes facing south or west, in dells, by the side of streams and lakes, and in the shelter of trees. Some species have a definite life-cycle, flowering and seeding at intervals of about 15, 30, 60, and 120 years, after which the whole plant dies. For example, *Phyllostachys aurea* flowers about every 15 years, whilst *Arundinaria nitida*, introduced in 1889, has not yet flowered in cultivation. The following is a short list of those grown successfully in the London area: *Arundinaria anceps*, *A. auricoma*, *A. fastuosa*, *A. fortunei*, *A. graminea*, *A. japonica*, *A. murielae*, *A. nitida*, *A. simoni*, *A. vagans*, *Sasa palmata*, *S. tessellata*, *S. veitchii*, *Phyllostachys aurea*, *P. castillonis*, *P. flexuosa*, *P. henonis*, *P. nigra*, *P. viridi-glaucescens*, and *Shibataea kumasasa*.

CLASSIFICATION OF GRASSES

The true grasses belong to the family of flowering plants known as the *Gramineae*. They may be classified either by grouping species and genera in a purely arbitrary or artificial manner without considering possible relationships or their evolution; or, alternatively, by arranging them in a hypothetically natural system. In the first form of classification all genera possessing one distinctive feature in common as, for example, solitary spikes, might be grouped together, as in fact they were about 200 years ago. In the second arrangement, however, only those grasses closely resembling one another in a large number of characteristics would be associated in the same division of the family. In this more natural scheme, botanists frequently introduce their evolutionary theories, commencing their system with the grasses they regard as most ancient and concluding with those they consider the most recently evolved, but as so few remains of grasses have been preserved as fossils, we know very little about the ancient grasses, and in fact nothing which will help us in preparing our classifications. Instead the grass-specialist has had to rely more on morphological and other important characteristics which appear to be reliable indicators of close relationship, and to group together those grasses sharing the greatest number of such features, and to regard as the most primitive those which possess structural details similar to those of other groups of flowering plants considered to have an earlier origin.

In the past the classification of grasses into genera and into the larger groups – subtribes and tribes – has been largely based on the structure and arrangement of their spikelets, as these show a greater range of visible distinguishing features than do other parts of the grass plant. For many years, however, it has been obvious that such systems founded mainly on spikelet- and inflorescence-structure are unreliable guides to relationship and, moreover, that generally they are not in agreement with modern generic groupings based on anatomical, cytological, chemical, ecological, physiological and other specialist branches of botanical research. Although very considerable progress in this wider field has been made during the past forty years, and the results used in preparing several more satisfactory groupings than hitherto, very numerous detailed investigations, particularly in the cyto-genetical and physiological fields, are required before our present schemes of classification can be still further improved.

Intensive studies of the grass spikelet have shown that differences in flower and grain structure are correlated with important anatomical, cytological and physiological distinctions. Thus the shape, size, and number of the lodicules, the presence and kind of appendages at the apex of the ovary, the type of stigmatic hair, the structure of the grain, especially the composition of the layers of cells enclosing the starchy central part, the form of the starch granules, the shape, relative size, and structure of the embryo, and the form of the hilum of the grain, have all proved of much value in providing clues to relationships. The form of the first green leaf of the grass-seedling, whether erect and narrow or broad and spreading (often horizontally), has been found to be correlated with differences in anatomy and cytology. Anatomical studies have revealed important characteristics in the arrangement and form of the chlorophyll-containing tissues, in the number and structure of the sheaths around the vascular bundles, in the form of the epidermal cells, especially the shape of those containing silica, and the presence or absence and shape of the two-celled micro-hairs. These differences in anatomical structure are generally associated with distinctions in the sizes, shapes, and basic numbers of the chromosomes. For further information on this subject the reader is referred to the section on *Gramineae* by the author in J. Hutchinson's *British Flowering Plants*, 1948, and especially to W. Edwin Booth's *Agrostology*, 1964.

The genera and intergeneric hybrids (prefixed by ×) of grasses described in this book are classified in the following 19 tribes.

The figures in parentheses give the pages of the descriptions and illustrations for each

1. Tribe **Bromeae**. *Bromus* (60–87).
2. Tribe **Brachypodieae**. *Brachypodium* (88–91).
3. Tribe **Hordeeae** (or **Triticeae**.) *Agropyron* (92–103), *Triticum* (422), *Secale* (424), *Elymus* (104–5), *Hordelymus* (106–7), *Hordeum* (108–13, 424).
4. Tribe **Glycerieae**. *Glyceria* (114–23).
5. Tribe **Festuceae**. *Festuca* (124–45), × *Festulolium* (146–7), *Lolium* (148–53), *Vulpia* (154–61), *Nardurus* (162–3), *Poa* (164–93), *Puccinellia* (194–203), *Catapodium* (204–7), *Briza* (208–13), *Dactylis* (214–15), *Cynosurus* (216–19), *Catabrosa* (220–21).
6. Tribe **Meliceae.**, *Melica* (22).
7. Tribe **Seslerieae**. *Sesleria* (226–7).
8. Tribe **Aveneae**. *Helictotrichon* (228–31), *Arrhenatherum* (232–3), *Avena* (234–9), *Koeleria* (240–43), *Trisetum* (244–5), *Deschampsia* (246–53), *Corynephorus* (254–5), *Aira* (256–9), *Holcus* (260–63), *Hierochloë* (264–5), *Anthoxanthum* (266–9).
9. Tribe **Phalarideae**. *Phalaris* (270–73).
10. Tribe **Milieae**. *Milium* (274–5).
11. Tribe **Agrostideae (Agrosteae)**. *Calamagrostis* (276–83), × *Ammocalamagrostis* (284–5), *Ammophila* (286–7), *Apera* (288–91), *Agrostis* (292–305, 372), × *Agropogon*, (306–7), *Polypogon* (308–9),

Differences between Grasses, Rushes, and Sedges

Grasses have such a very distinctive form of growth and flower-head that usually there is little chance of confusing them with other groups of flowering plants, except perhaps the rushes and sedges which have grass-like leaves. The rushes belong to the family *Juncaceae*, represented in the British Isles by the genera *Juncus* and *Luzula*. These differ from grasses in possessing flowers with 6 perianth segments and have a 1–3-celled capsular fruit containing 3 to many seeds. On the other hand, the grasses usually have 2 very small perianth segments (lodicules) hidden by the lemma and palea, and a single-seeded fruit. The sedges belong to the family *Cyperaceae*, of which the genera *Blysmus*, *Carex*, *Cladium*, *Cyperus*, *Eleocharis*, *Eriophorum*, *Kobresia*, *Rhynchospora*, *Schoenus* and *Scirpus*, occur in the British Isles. They resemble grasses in having greenish, purplish, or brownish flower-heads, but there is only one scale beneath each flower instead of two as in grasses. In addition their stems are usually 3-angled and solid whereas those of grasses are cylindrical or flattened and mostly hollow between the nodes.

BIBLIOGRAPHY

(A) STRUCTURE, CLASSIFICATION, DISTRIBUTION AND ECOLOGY
OF GRASSES

ARBER, A. *The Gramineae: a Study of Cereal, Bamboo and Grass*, 1934;
reprinted 1965, with 32 pp. introduction by W. D. Clayton

ARMSTRONG, S. F. *British Grasses and their Employment in Agriculture*,
3rd edn., 1948.

BARNARD, C. (ed.) *Grasses and Grasslands*, 1964.

BEWS, J. W. *The World's Grasses*, 1929.

BOOTH, W. E. *Agrostology*, 1964.

BURR, S., and TURNER, D. M. *British Economic Grasses: their identification by the Leaf-Anatomy*, 1933.

DARLINGTON, C. D., and WYLIE, A. P. *Chromosome Atlas of Flowering
Plants*, 1955.

HUTCHINSON, J. *Families of Flowering Plants*, vol. 2, *Monocotyledons*,
1934; 2nd edn., 1959.

HUTCHINSON, J. *British Flowering Plants*, 1948.

MCCLURE, F. A. *The Bamboos: A Fresh Perspective*, 1966.

METCALFE, C. R. *Anatomy of the Monocotyledons*, vol. 1, *Gramineae*,
1960.

PERRING, F. H., and WALTERS, S. M. (eds.) *Atlas of the British Flora*,
1976.

PERRING, F. H. *Critical Supplement to the Atlas of the British Flora*, 1968.

TANSLEY, A. G. *The British Isles and their Vegetation*, 1939.

TROUGHTON, A. *The Underground Organs of Herbage Grasses*, 1957.

WARD, H. H. *Grasses*, 1901.

Botanical Society of the British Isles: Abstracts and notes.
Journal of Ecology.
Proceedings of the Botanical Society of the British Isles.
Reports of the Botanical Society and Exchange Club of the British Isles,
1879–1948.
Watsonia: Journal of the Botanical Society of the British Isles.
Year Book of the Botanical Society of the British Isles, 1949–53.

(B) BRITISH AND FOREIGN FLORAS AND PLANT-LISTS

ASCHERSON, P., and GRAEBNER, P. *Synopsis der Mitteleuropäischen
Flora*, vol. 2, part 1 (1898–1902).

BABINGTON, C. C. *Manual of British Botany*, 10th edn., 1922.

BENTHAM, G., and HOOKER, J. D. *Handbook of the British Flora*, 7th
edn., 1924 and 1930.

BUTCHER, R. W. *A New Illustrated British Flora*, 2 vols., 1961.

CLAPHAM, A.R., TUTIN, T. G., and WARBURG, E. G. *Flora of the British Isles*, 1952; 2nd edn., 1962.

DRUCE, G. C. *British Plant List*, 2nd edn., 1928.

FOURNIER, P. *Les Quatre Flores de la France*, 2nd edn., 1961.

HEGI, G. *Illustrierte Flora von Mittel-Europa*, 2nd edn., vol. 1, 1936.

HERMANN, F. *Flora von Nord- und Mitteleuropa*, 1956.

HITCHCOCK, A. S. *Manual of the Grasses of the United States*, 2nd edn. 1951.

HOOKER, J. D. *Student's Flora of the British Islands*, 3rd edn., 1884.

HUSNOT, T. *Graminées*, 1896–99.

HYDE, H. A., and WADE, A. E. *Welsh Flowering Plants*, 2nd edn., 1957.

HYLANDER, N. *Nordisk Kärlväxtflora*, vol. 1, 1953.

JANSEN, P. *Flora Neerlandica*, vol. 2, *Gramineae*, 1951.

KLAPP, E. *Taschenbuch der Gräser*, 10th edn., 1974.

KOMAROV, V. L. (ed.) *Flora of the U.S.S.R.*, vol. 2, English translation, 1963.

LID, J. *Norsk og Svensk Flora*, 1963.

PARNELL, R. *The Grasses of Britain*, 1842–45.

ROUY, G. *Flore de France*, vol. 14, 1913.

SYME, J. T. BOSWELL *English Botany*, vol. 11, 1872.

TUTIN, T. G., HEYWOOD, D. M., VALENTINE, D. H., WALTERS, S. M., and WEBB, D. A. *Flora Europaea*, vol. 5, 1980.

WEBB, D. A. *An Irish Flora*, 5th edn., 1967.

WEIMARCK, H. *Skånes Flora*, 1963.

(C) GRASSES AND GRASSLANDS (AGRICULTURAL)

CHARLES, A. H., and HAGGAR, R. J. *Changes in Sward Composition and Productivity*, 1979.

DAVIES, W. 'The Grassland Map of the British Isles' (*Journal of the Ministry of Agriculture*, vol. 48, 112, 1941).

DAVIES, W. *The Grass Crop: its Development, Use and Maintenance* 1952 and 1960.

ELLIOT, R. H. *The Clifton Park System of Farming, and Laying Down Land to Grass*, 5th edn., 1943.

FORBES, T. J., DIBB, C., GREEN, J. O., HOPKINS, A., and PEEL, S. *Factors Affecting the Productivity of Permanent Grassland*, 1980.

FRANKLIN, T. B. *British Grasslands from the Earliest Times to the Present Day*, 1953.

GREEN, J. O. *A Sample Survey of Grasslands in England and Wales*, 1982.

HALL, M. (ed.) 'Five Hundred Varieties of Herbage and Fodder Plants', *Commonw. Bur. Pastures and Field Crops, Bulletin*, 39, 1948.

HOLMES, W. *Grass: Its Production and Utilization*, 1980.

MOORE, I. *Grass and Grasslands*, 1966.

ROBINSON, D. H. *Good Grassland*, 1947.

SEMPLE, A. T. *Improving the World's Grasslands*, 1952.

SPEDDING, C. R. W., and DIEKMAHNS, E. C. *Grasses and Legumes in British Agriculture*, 1972.

STAPLEDON, R. G. *The Plough-up Policy and Ley Farming*, 1939.

STAPLEDON, R. G., and HANLEY, J. A. *Grassland, its Management and Improvement*, 1927.

STAPLEDON, R. G., and DAVIES, W. *Ley Farming*, 1948.

WATSON, J. S. *Grassland and Grassland Products*, 1951.

WATSON, J. S., and NASH, M. J. *The Conservation of Grass and Forage Crops*, 1960.

WRIGHT, C. E. *Physiology and Herbage Production*, 1981.

The Grassland Research Institute: Reports.

Grass Drying, *Ministr. of. Agric. Bulletin*, no. 157, 1953.

Grass and Forage Science.

Grass and Grassland, *Ministr. of Agric. Bulletin*, no. 154, 1966.

Herbage Abstracts; Herbage Reviews, 1933–40.

Hill Farming Research Organisation: Reports.

Journal of Applied Ecology.

National Institute of Agricultural Botany, Farmers Leaflets (Varieties of herbage grasses, and cereals).

United States Dept. Agriculture Year Book, Grass, 1948.

Welsh Plant Breeding Station, Reports.

(D) CEREALS

BEAVEN, E. S. *Barley*, 1947.

BURTT-DAVY, J. *Maize*, 1914.

COPELAND, E. B. *Rice*, 1924.

GRIST, D. H. *Rice*, new edn., 1963.

HECTOR, J. M. *Introduction to the Botany of Field Crops*, vol. 1, *Cereals*, 1936.

HUNTER, H. *Oats: their Varieties and Characteristics*, 1924.

HUNTER, H. *The Barley Crop*, 1952.

PEACHEY, R. A. *Cereal Varieties in Great Britain*, 1951.

PERCIVAL, J. *The Wheat Plant*, 1921.

PERCIVAL, J. *Wheat in Great Britain*, 2nd edn., 1948.

SCHIEMANN, E. *Weizen, Roggen, Gerste, systematik geschichte und verwendung*, 1948.

SNOWDEN, J. D. *The Cultivated Races of Sorghum*, 1936.

WALLACE, H. A., and BRESSMAN, E. N. *Corn and Corn Growing* [Maize], 5th edn., 1952.

WEATHERWAX, P. *The Story of the Maize Plant*, 1923.

Field Crop Abstracts.
Plant-Breeding Abstracts.

(E) LAWNS AND SPORTSGROUNDS

BEARD, J. B. *Turfgrass: Science and Culture*, 1973.

BRADSHAW, A. D., and CHADWICK, M. J. *The Restoration of Land*, 1980.

DAWSON, R. B. *Practical Lawn Craft*, 6th edn., 1968.

DUFFEY, E., *et al. Grassland Ecology and Wildlife Management*, 1974.

ESCRITT, J. R. *A B C of Turf Culture*, 1978.

ESCRITT, J. R. *Lawns*, 1979.

GOOCH, R. B., and ESCRITT, J. R. *Sports Ground Construction – Specifications*, National Playing Fields Association, 1975.

HESSAYON, D. G. *Be Your Own Lawn Expert*, 2nd edn., 1967.

RORISON, I. H., and HUNT, R. (eds.) *Amenity Grassland: an ecological perspective*, 1980.

Journal of the Sports Turf Research Institute.
S.T.R.I. specialist bulletins, e.g. Turfgrass 1982, Turfgrass diseases, and Fertilizers in Turf Culture.
Proceedings of International Turfgrass Research Conferences. (Harrogate 1969; Blacksburg, Virginia 1973; Munich 1977; Guelph, Ontario 1981.)

(F) MISCELLANEOUS REFERENCE WORKS

CHITTENDEN, F. J. (ed.) *Dictionary of Gardening*, 4 vols. plus centre Suppls. 1951–1968. (Includes grasses of use in horticulture.)

FORSYTH, A. A. 'British Poisonous Plants', *Ministry of Agriculture Bulletin*, no. 161, 1954.

FRYER, J. D., and EVANS, S. A. *Weed Control Handbook*, 1968.

SALISBURY, E. *Weeds and Aliens*, 1961.

SAMPSON, K., and WESTERN, J. H. *Diseases of British Grasses and Herbage Legumes*, 2nd edn., 1953.

SIMPSON, N. D. *A Biographical Index of the British Flora*, 1960.

GLOSSARY

acuminate: gradually tapering to a point.

acute: sharply pointed.

adhere: touching, but not grown together.

alternate: not opposite; applied to spikelets placed at different levels in spikes or racemes.

annual: plants completing their life-cycle within one year.

anther: portion of stamen bearing the pollen grains, borne on a stalk (filament) in grasses.

apiculate: with a small point at the apex.

apomictic: producing viable seeds without fertilization (sexual fusion).

appendage: attachment or secondary part, such as the hairy projection on the top of the ovary and grain in *Bromus*.

appressed: one organ pressed against another but not united with it.

aquatic: living in water.

aristate: bearing an awn.

articulate: jointed; provided with nodes and internodes such as the spike of *Parapholis* and the axes of many spikelets; usually fracturing at the nodes.

ascending: sloping or curving upwards; applied to stems which curve from the base upwards.

auricle: applied to small claw- or ear-like outgrowths at the junction of the sheath and blade of some grasses.

awn: slender bristle-like projection from the back or tip of the glumes and lemmas in some grasses; straight or bent.

awned: provided with an awn, in contrast to awnless.

axil: angle made by one part of a plant with another part, such as that between a branch and the main-axis of the flower-head.

axis: main stem of the plant, or of the flower-head (*rhachis*), or spikelet (*rhachilla*).

barbed: provided with backward pointing teeth, like the bristles of *Setaria verticillata*.

bearded: furnished with stiff hairs, as at the base of the floret and seed in some grasses.

biennial: plants completing their life-cycle within two years.

bisexual: having both sexes (stamens and ovary) present in the same floret or spikelet.

blade: part of the leaf above the sheath, also known as the lamina, often flat, but sometimes bristle-like.

bract: much-reduced leaf of the flower-head, such as the glumes and lemmas.

branch: a lateral growth from the main stem; in a panicle the main divisions are branches.

branchlet: division of a branch.

bristle: stiff hair, or a very fine straight awn, also applied to the upper part of the awn.

bristly: bearing stiff hairs.

bulbous: swollen base of the stem resembling a bulb.

caespitose: tufted.

calcareous: chalky or limy.

callus: hard basal projection at the base of the floret or spikelet where these form the seed-units of some grasses.

capillary: hair-like.

caryopsis: naked grass-fruit or grain in which the seed coat is united with the ovary wall.

chartaceous: papery texture.

chasmogamous: florets opening normally.

chlorophyll: green colouring matter of the plant.

chromosomes: microscopic bodies found in the nuclei at the time of division. In the vegetative cells two sets of these are normally present, their number (*diploid*, written 2n) usually being constant in a species. The numbers, where known, are given at the end of the descriptions.

ciliate: fringed with hairs (cilia).

cleistogamous: applied in grasses to florets which do not open, fertilization taking place within the closed lemma and palea as in some spikelets of *Leersia* and *Sieglingia*.

collar: whitish, yellowish, or purplish zone at the junction of the leaf-sheath and blade.

compressed: flattened, usually laterally as in the spikelets of *Alopecurus*, or the basal leaf-sheaths of species of *Poa*.

concave: curving inwards; hollowed out.

contiguous: touching each other at the margins.

continuous: not articulate or breaking up; applied to the axis of the spike of *Agropyron repens* or that of the spikelet of *Arrhenatherum*.

contracted: said of panicles in which the branches are erect and close to the main-axis.

convolute: one margin rolled over the other.

cordate: heart-shaped; with a rounded lobe on each side at the base, such as the lemma of *Briza*.

coriaceous: leathery texture.

culm: stem of grasses.

cuneate: wedge-shaped.

cusp: small sharply pointed projection.

deciduous: falling off at maturity or end of life, such as the ripe spikelets or their parts, or the blades of some grasses.

decumbent: with stem lying on the ground.

deflexed: bent backwards or downwards, such as hairs on some leaf-sheaths.

dense: applied to flower-head when crowded with spikelets.

digitate: fingered, as the inflorescence of *Digitaria* and *Cynodon*.

diploid: plant having two sets of chromosomes in its nuclei.

disarticulating: fracturing at the nodes, as the axis of the spikelet of many grasses.

distichous: arranged in two rows, as the leaves of grasses.

distinct: separate, not joined.

ear: flower-head of grasses, usually applied to that of wheat, rye, and barley.

effuse: spreading widely.

elliptic: widest about the middle, gradually narrowed to both ends; about twice as wide as long; if longer or wider, would be described as narrowly or broadly elliptic.

emarginate: shallowly notched at the tip.

embryo: rudiment of the plant in the seed.

empty glumes: two empty bracts at the base of the spikelet; here known as the lower and upper glumes.

endemic: native to one country or area.

endosperm: nutritive tissue in the seed.

entire: not divided or cut at the margins or tip.

epidermis: outermost layer of cells on the stems and leaves etc.

exserted: projecting, such as the lemma from the glumes in some grasses.

extravaginal: applied to the young vegetative shoot when it grows up outside the leaf-sheath owing to its bud bursting through the base of the sheath; contrasting with intravaginal.

fertile: capable of bearing viable seeds, or of good pollen in the case of stamens.

filament: stalk of anther.

filiform: thread-like.

flexuous: wavy, as the branches of some panicles.

floret: lemma and palea with the enclosed flower; florets may be bisexual and perfect, or unisexual and male or female, or barren (neuter), or reduced to the lemma.

flowering glume: here called lemma, the lower of two bracts enclosing the flower.

folded: applied to leaf-blades folded lengthwise about the midrib, with upper surface within.

free: not joined; the margins of the leaf-sheath may be free or joined.

fruit: ripened ovary; in grasses applied to the naked grain, or to the grain plus the bracts enclosing it.

geniculate: bent abruptly like a knee = kneed, said of the culms and awns so bent.

gibbous: bulging or swollen on one side.

glabrescent: becoming hairless.

glabrous: without hairs.

glaucous: bluish-green, often owing to a white wax or to a thick white skin covering the green stems, leaves, and spikelets.

globose: shaped like a globe.

glume: two (usually) empty bracts at the base of the spikelet, called the lower and upper glumes; *Hüllspelze* (German).

grain: caryopsis or naked seed of grasses.

gynoecium: female part of flower.

habit: appearance, or form of growth of a plant.

habitat: natural place of abode or area of occupation of a plant.

herbaceous: not woody; green and of a soft texture.

hermaphrodite: with both male and female organs.

hexaploid: having 6 sets of chromosomes in its nuclei.

hilum: in the grain of grasses marking the point of attachment of the ovule to the ovary wall.

hirsute: clothed with rather long hairs.

hispid: stiffly hairy.

husk: applied to the scales (glumes and lemmas) covering the grain of grasses.

hyaline: translucent and delicate tissue.

hybrid: progeny of a cross between two different species or plants of lower grade than a species.

imbricate: overlapping, such as the spikelets in *Alopecurus*.

included: not projecting; the lemma is sometimes hidden by the glumes.

incurved: curved gradually inwards.

indehiscent: not opening.

indurated: hardened and toughened.

inflexed: turned sharply inwards, as the margins of paleas and lemmas.

inflorescence: flower-head terminating the stem (and its branches); in grasses, a panicle, raceme, or spike, or reduced to a single spikelet.

innovation: basal vegetative shoot of a grass.

internode: portion between two successive nodes (e.g. of the culm, flower-head or spikelet).

interrupted: not continuous; said of panicles not dense throughout.

intravaginal: applied to the young vegetative shoot when it grows up within the enveloping sheath; contrasting with extravaginal.

involute: with the margins rolled inwards (e.g. of a leaf-blade).

joint: used for the node of the culm; also applied to the internodes of the spike-axis and the spikelet-axis; such axes are said to be jointed.

keel: sharp fold or ridge at the back of a compressed sheath, blade, glume, lemma, or palea; such parts are said to be keeled.

lamina: blade of the grass leaf.

lanceolate: lance-shaped, widest in the lowest third and gradually narrowed upwards; length to breadth in ratio of about 3 to 1; if narrower or wider would be described as narrowly or broadly lanceolate.

lateral: on the side; such as lateral nerves on each side of the middle nerve.

lax: loose; said of panicles which are not dense.

lemma: lower of two bracts enclosing the flower, sometimes called flowering glume or valve; *glumelle inférieure* (French); *Deckspelze* (German).

ligule: outgrowth at the inner junction of the leaf-sheath and blade, often membranous, sometimes represented by a fringe of hairs.

linear: long and narrow, with parallel sides, ratio of length to breadth = 12 or more to 1; as in leaf-blades of many grasses.

lobe: a division, such as the apical teeth or segments of a lemma, then said to be lobed.

lodicules: minute scales (usually two) outside the stamens and ovary; probably the vestiges of the perianth (petals and sepals); *glumellules* (French).

lower palea: = lemma.

meadow: a grassy field cut for hay, afterwards often grazed.

membranous: translucent, thin and dry, not green.

mucro: short fine point, a minute awn; organs with a mucro are said to be mucronate.

muticous: without awn or mucro.

naked: without scales or hairs.

nerve: applied to slender veins or ribs of leaves, glumes, lemmas and paleas; e.g. the paleas are usually 2-nerved.

nodding: inclined from the vertical, said of such panicles and spikelets.

node: point on stem or axis at which a leaf or bract arises.

oblanceolate: lanceolate outline inverted.

oblique: slanting.

oblong: with parallel sides, longer than wide in the ratio of about 2 to 1; if longer or wider would be described as narrowly or broadly oblong.

obovate: ovate outline inverted.

obtuse: blunt; applied to the tip of a leaf or bract.

open: loose; such as in panicles with separate spaced spikelets.

opposite: borne at same level on opposing sides of axis.

orbicular: circular.

ovary: female part of flower enclosing the ovule.

oval: elliptic.

ovate: egg-shaped in outline, widest in the lowest third, gradually narrowed to base and apex; length to breadth in ratio of about 3 to 2; if longer or wider would be described as narrowly or broadly ovate.

ovoid: egg-shaped solid.

ovule: borne in the ovary, developing into the seed after fertilization.

palea: upper of two bracts enclosing the flower, sometimes called the upper palea or valvule; *glumelle supérieure* (French); *Vorspelze* (German).

panicle: branched flower-head, with main-axis, divided branches and stalked spikelets, ranging from very dense and spike-like to very diffuse.

pasture: enclosed grassland grazed by animals.

pedicel: applied to the stalk of the spikelet.

pendulous: hanging down or drooping.

perennial: of more than two years' duration.

perfect: applied to florets having male and female organs, and to anthers with good pollen.

pericarp: skin of grass fruit; ripened wall of ovary.

persistent: remaining attached to axis after maturity, such as leaf-blades, or glumes of spikelet.

petiole: stalk of leaf.

pilose: softly hairy with rather long hairs.

pollen: grains in anther containing male element.

polymorphic: variable; applied to species comprising a wide range of forms.

polyploid: species having more than two sets of chromosomes in the nuclei of the vegetative cells.

procumbent: lying on or trailing over the ground.

proliferous: bearing vegetative buds or miniature plants at the tips of the spikelets.

prostrate: flat on the ground.

protandrous: stamens maturing before the female part of the flower.

protogynous: female part of flower maturing before the stamens.

pruinose: covered with a whitish deposit.

pubescent: shortly and softly hairy.

pungent: sharply and stiffly pointed.

raceme: unbranched flower-head, with the spikelets stalked directly on the axis.

recurved: curved backwards.

reflexed: bent or turned backwards or downwards.

rhachilla (or *rachilla*)*:* term for main-axis of spikelet.

rhachis (or *rachis*)*:* term for main-axis of flower-head.

rhizome: underground stem, bearing scale-like leaves.

rib: main or prominent nerves on leaves; leaves with such nerves are said to be ribbed.

rootstock: basal part of plant in soil.

runner: trailing or prostrate stem, rooting at the nodes and there giving rise to vegetative shoots and culms.

salting: salt-marsh.

salt-marsh: coastal or estuarine inter-tidal mud flats, with grasses and other plants.

scabrid: rough.

scale: miniature leaf without blade, found at the base of stems and on rhizomes.

secund: directed to one side; a one-sided spike or raceme.

sessile: without a stalk.

setaceous: bristle-like.

sheath: lower part of the leaf surrounding stem; also called vagina.

simple: not divided.

smooth: used to indicate lack of minute rough points and hairs.

solitary: borne singly.

spike: unbranched flower-head, bearing stalkless spikelets.

spikelet: unit of the grass flower-head, generally composed of 2 glumes and one or more flowers each borne between a lemma and palea; *épillet* (French); *Äehrchen* (German).

spike-like: resembling a spike, applied to dense racemes and panicles.

spreading: directed outwards, e.g. the culms, or the branches of panicles.

stamen: male (pollen-bearing) part of flower.

stem: main-axis of plant, bearing leaves and flower-head = culm.

sterile: not producing viable seeds or pollen.

stigma: receptive part of female organ which receives the pollen.

stolon: prostrate or creeping stem, rooting at the nodes and there giving rise to vegetative shoots and culms.

striate: longitudinally grooved.

style: connection between stigma and ovary.

subulate: very narrow and pointed.

tapering: gradually narrowed.

terete: circular in section, not angled or grooved.

terminal: at the tip.

tetraploid: plant with 4 sets of chromosomes in its nuclei.

triangular: shaped as a triangle.

triploid: plant with 3 sets of chromosomes in its nuclei.

truncate: ending abruptly as though cut off, very blunt.

tuft: loose, compact or dense cluster of vegetative shoots and/or stems.

tumid: swollen, plump.

turgid: swollen.

unisexual: of one sex only.

upper palea: = palea.

valve: = lemma.

valvule: = palea.

viviparous: see proliferous.

INDEX TO COMMON NAMES

In addition to those indexed below, other common names for our grasses will be found in A Dictionary of English Plant Names *by J. Britten and R. Holland (1886).* The Concise British Flora in Colour *by W. Keeble Martin (1965),* English Names of Wild Flowers *by J. G. Dony, F. H. Perring and C. M. Rob (1980) and in the numerous county floras*

INDEX TO BOTANICAL NAMES

The figures refer only to the pages on which the grasses are described or mentioned. In addition to the names used in this book, numerous names at one time given to British grasses, but now regarded as synonyms, are included. The names adopted are as far as possible in accordance with the international code of botanical nomenclature (1966)

Agrostis canina var. montana Hartm. = subsp. montana
  canina × A. stolonifera, 297, 303
  canina × A. tenuis, 297
  capillaris auct. brit. = A. tenuis
  capillaris L. *see* Agrostis tenuis
  capillaris var. nigra (With.) Druce = A. gigantea
  castellana Boiss. and Reuter, 372
  curtsii Kerguélen *see* Agrostis setacea Curt.
  densissima (Hack.) Druce = A. stolonifera
  gigantea Roth, 301
  gigantea × A. stolonifera, 301, 303
  gigantea × A. tenuis, 301
  hyperborea Laest. = A. canina subsp. montana
  interrupta L. = Apera interrupta
  maritima Lam. = A. stolonifera
  nigra With. = A. gigantea
  palustris Huds. = A. stolonifera var. palustris
  pumila L. = A. tenuis
  pusille Dum. = Agrostis canina subsp. montana
  semiverticillata (Forsk.) C. Christ., 305
  semiverticillata × stolonifera, 305
  setacea Curt., 293
  spica-venti L. = Apera spica-venti
  spica-venti subsp. interrupta (L.) Hook. f. = Apera interrupta
  spica-venti var. interrupta (L.) Hook. f. = Apera interrupta
  stolonifera L., 303
  stolonifera subsp. gigantea (Roth) Maire & Weill. = Agrostis gigantea
  stolonifera var. gigantea (Roth) Koch = A. gigantea
  stolonifera var. palustris (Huds.) Farw., 303
  stolonifera var. stolonifera, 303
  stolonifera × A. canina, 297, 303
  stolonifera × A gigantea, 301, 303
  stolonifera × A. semiverticillata, 305
  stolonifera × A. tenuis, 299, 303
  stolonifera × Polypogon monspeliensis = × Agropogon littoralis
  tenuis Sibth., 299
  tenuis var. nigra (With.) Druce = A. gigantea
  tenuis × A. canina, 297, 299
  tenuis × A. gigantea, 299, 303
  tenuis × A. stolonifera, 299, 303
  ventricosa Gouan = Gastridium ventricosum
  verticillata Vill. = A. semiverticillata
  vinealis Schreber. = Agrostis canina subsp. montana
  vulgaris With. = A. tenuis
  vulgaris var. nigra (With.) Druce = A. gigantea
Aira alpina L. = Deschampsia alpina
  aquatica L. = Catabrosa aquatica
  caerulea L. = Molinia caerulea
  caespitosa L. = Deschampsia caespitosa
  caespitosa subsp. alpina (L.) Hook. f. = Deschampsia alpina
  caespitosa var. vivipara Anders. = Deschampsia caespitosa var. vivipara
  canescens L. = Corynephorus canescens
  capillaris Host = A. elegans
  caryophyllea L., 257
  caryophyllea var. multiculmis Dum. = A. multiculmis (Dum.) Dum.
  cespitosa = caespitosa
  cristata L. = Koeleria cristata
  cupaniana Guss., 257
  discolor Thuill. = Deschampsia setacea
  elegans Willd., 257

elegantissima Schr. *see* Aira elegans Willd.
flexuosa L. = Deschampsia flexuosa
flexuosa subsp. uliginosa (Weihe) Hartm. = Deschampsia setacea
flexuosa var. montana L. = Deschampsia flexuosa var. montana
laevigata Sm. = Deschampsia alpina
major Syme subsp. alpina (L.) Syme = Deschampsia alpina
major subsp. caespitosa (L.) Syme = Deschampsia caespitosa
multiculmis (Dum.) Dum., 257
Aira praecox L., 259
setacea Huds. = Deschampsia setacea
uliginosa Weihe = Deschampsia setacea
Alopecurus aequalis Sobol., 327
aequalis × geniculatus = A. × haussknechtianus
agrestis L. = A. myosuroides
alpinus Sm., 335
alpinus var. watsonii Syme, 335
× brachystylus *see* Alopecurus × hybridus Wimm.
bulbosus Gouan, 329
fulvus Sm. = A. aequalis
geniculatus L., 331
geniculatus subsp. bulbosus (Gouan) Hook. f. = A. bulbosus
geniculatus subsp. fulvus (Sm.) Hartm. = A. aequalis
geniculatus var. aequalis (Sobol.) Fiori = A. aequalis
geniculatus var. bulbosus (Gouan) Sond. = A. bulbosus
geniculatus var. fulvus (Sm.) Hampe = A. aequalis
geniculatus var. pronus Mitt. = A. × hybridus
geniculatus × A. aequalis = A. × haussknechtianus
geniculatus × A. pratensis = A. × hybridus
× haussknechtianus Aschers. & Graebn., 331
× hybridus Wimm., 331
monspeliensis L. = Polypogon monspeliensis
myosuroides Huds., 325
ovatus Knapp = A. alpinus
palustris Syme subsp. bulbosus (Gouan) Syme = A. bulbosus
palustris subsp. fulvus (Sm.) Syme = A. aequalis
palustris subsp. geniculatus (L.) Syme = A. geniculatus
pratensis L., 333
pratensis × A. geniculatus = A × hybridus
pronus Mitt. = A. × hybridus
× Ammocalamagrostis baltica (Fluegge ex Schrad.) P. Fourn., 285
Ammophila arenaria (L.) Link, 287
arenaria × Calamagrostis epigejos = × Ammocalamagrostis baltica
arundinacea Host = A. arenaria
baltica (Fluegge ex Schrad.) Dum. = × Ammocalamagrostis baltica
breviligulata Fernald., 287
Anisantha diandra (Roth) Tutin = Bromus diandrus
gussonii (Parl.) Nevski = Bromus diandrus
madritensis (L.) Nevski = Bromus madritensis
rigida (Roth) Hyl. = Bromus rigidus
sterilis (L.) Nevski = Bromus sterilis
tectorum (L.) Nevski = Bromus tectorum
Anthoxanthum aristatum Boiss., 267
odoratum L., 269
odoratum var. puelii (Lec. & Lam.) Coss. & Dur. = A. puelii
puelii Lecoq & Lamotte, 267
Apera intermedia Hack., 291
interrupta (L.) Beauv., 291
spica-venti (L.) Beauv., 289
Arrhenatherum avenaceum Beauv. = A. elatius
bulbosum (Willd.) C. Presl = A. elatius var. bulbosum

elatius (L.) Beauv. ex J. & C. Presl, 26, 233
elatius subsp. bulbosum (Willd.) Hyl. = var. bulbosum
elatius var. bulbosum (Willd.) Spenn., 233
pratense (L.) Samp. = Helictotrichon pratense
pubescens (Huds.) Samp. = Helictotrichon pubescens
tuberosum (Gilib.) F. W. Schultz = A. elatius var. bulbosum
Arundo arenaria L. = Ammophila arenaria
baltica Fl. ex Schrad. = × Ammocalamagrostis baltica
calamagrostis L. = Calamagrostis canescens
canescens Weber = Calamagrostis canescens
Arundo donax L., 347
epigejos L. = Calamagrostis epigejos
neglecta Ehrh. = Calamagrostis stricta
phragmites L. = Phragmites communis
stricta Timm = Calamagrostis stricta
vulgaris Lam. = Phragmites communis
Atropis borreri (Bab.) K. Richt. = Puccinellia fasciculata
distans (L.) Griseb. = Puccinellia distans
maritima (Huds.) Griseb. = Puccinellia maritima
× pannonica Hack. = Puccinellia × pannonica
Avena alpina Sm. = Helictotrichon alpinum
barbata Broth., 235
bulbosa Willd. = Arrhenatherum elatius var. bulbosum
byzantina C. Koch, 425
elatior L. = Arrhenatherum elatius
fatua L., 237
fatua subsp. sativa (L.) Thell. = A. sativa
fatua var. fatua, 237
fatua var. glabrata Peterm., 237
fatua var. pilosa Syme, 237
fatua var. pilosissima S. F. Gray = var. fatua
fatua × A. sativa, 237
flavescens L. = Trisetum flavescens
ludoviciana Durieu, 239
nodosa Walker = Arrhenatherum elatius var. bulbosum
persica Steud., 239
pratensis L. = Helictotrichon pratense
pubescens Huds. = Helictotrichon pubescens
sativa L., 17, 235, 425
sativa × A. fatua, 237
sterilis L., 239
sterilis subsp. ludoviciana (Dur.) Gill. & Magne = A. ludoviciana
sterilis var. ludoviciana (Dur.) Husn. = A. ludoviciana
strigosa Schreb., 235, 425
Avenastrum pratense (L.) Jess. = Helictotrichon pratense
pubescens (Huds.) Jess. = Helictotrichon pubescens
Avenula praeusta (Reichenb.) J. Holub. *see* Helictotrichon alpinum (Sm.) Henrard
pratensis (L.) Dumort. *see* Helictotrichon pratense (L.) Pilger
Avenula pubescens (Huds.) Dumort. *see* Helictotrichon pubescens (Huds.) Pilger

Baldingera arundinacea (L.) Dum. = Phalaris arundinacea
Brachypodium distachyon (L.) Beauv., 89
pinnatum (L.) Beauv., 91
pinnatum var. pubescens S. F. Gray, 91
sylvaticum (Huds.) Beauv., 89
Briza maxima L., 211
media L., 213
minor L., 209
Bromus arvensis L., 75
asper Murr. = B. ramosus

tectorum var. longipilus Borb. = var. hirsutus
thominii Hard., 77
unioloides H. B. K., 71
willdenowii Kunth *see* Bromus unioloides H. B. K.

Calamagrostis arenaria (L.) Roth = Ammophila arenaria
    calamagrostis (L.) Karst. = C. canescens
    canescens (Weber) Roth, 283
    canescens × stricta, 279, 281
    epigejos (L.) Roth, 283
    epigejos var. densiflora Ledeb., 283
    epigejos × Ammophila arenaria = × Ammocalamagrostis baltica
    × gracilescens (Blytt) Blytt, 281
    hookeri (Syme) Druce = C. stricta
    lanceolata Roth = C. canescens
    neglecta G., M. & S. = C. stricta
    neglecta subsp. stricta = Calamagrostis stricta
    neglecta var. hookeri (Syme) Druce = C. stricta
    scotica (Druce) Druce, 277
    stricta (Timm) Koel., 279
    stricta var. hookeri Syme = C. stricta
    stricta × C. canescens, 279, 281
    strigosa auct. brit. = C. scotica
    strigosa (Wahl.) Hartm., 277
× Calammophila baltica = × Ammocalamagrostis baltica
Capriola dactylon (L.) Kuntze = Cynodon dactylon
Catabrosa aquatica (L.) Beauv., 221
    aquatica subsp. minor (Bab.) Perring & Sell = var. uniflora
    aquatica subsp. monantha Haas = var. uniflora
    aquatica var. grandiflora Hack., 221
    aquatica var. littoralis Parn. = var. uniflora
    aquatica var. minor Bab. = var. uniflora
    aquatica var. subtilis Fries = var. uniflora
    aquatica var. uniflora S. F. Gray, 221
Catapodium loliaceum (Huds.) Link = Catapodium marinum
    marinum (L.) C. E. Hubbard, 207
    marinum × C. rigidum, 207
    rigidum (L.) C. E. Hubbard, 205
    rigidum subsp. majus (C. B. Presl) Perring & Sell = var. majus
    rigidum var. majus (C. B. Presl) Lousley, 205
Ceratochloa carinata (Hook. & Arn.) Tutin = Bromus carinatus
    unioloides (Willd.) Beauv. = Bromus unioloides
Chamagrostis minima (L.) Borkh. ex Wibel = Mibora minima
Cortaderia argentea (Nees) Stapf = C. selloana
    selloana (J. A. & J. H. Schult.) Aschers. & Graebn., 347
Corynephorus canescens (L.) Beauv., 255
Cuviera europaea (L.) Koel. = Hordelymus europaeus
Cynodon dactylon (L.) Pers., 361
Cynosurus cristatus L., 219
    echinatus L., 217

Dactylis aschersoniana Graebn. = D. polygama
    glomerata L., 215
    glomerata subsp. aschersoniana (Graebn.) Thell. *see* Dactylis aschersoniana
    Graebn.
    glomerata var. collina Schlechtd., 215
    polygama Horvat., 215
Danthonia decumbens (L.) DC. = Sieglingia decumbens
Demazeria = Desmazeria
Deschampsia alpina (L.) Roem. & Schult., 253
    caespitosa (L.) Beauv., 251

caespitosa subsp. parviflora (Thuill.) Javorka & Soo = var. parviflora
caespitosa var. parviflora (Thuill.) Coss. & Germ., 251
caespitosa var. vivipara S. F. Gray, 253
cespitosa = caespitosa
cespitosa subsp. alpina (L.) Tzvelev *see* Deschampsia alpina Roem. & Schult.
cespitosa subsp. cespitosa *see* Deschampsia caespitosa subsp. parviflora (Thuill.) Javorka & Soo
discolor (Thuill.) Roem. & Schult. = D. setacea
flexuosa (L.) Trin., 249
flexuosa var. montana (L.) Huds., 249
setacea (Huds.) Hack., 247
Desmazeria loliacea (Huds.) Nym. = Catapodium marinum
marina (L.) Druce = Catapodium marinum
rigida (L.) Tutin = Catapodium rigidum
Deyeuxia hookeri (Syme) Druce = Calamagrostis stricta
neglecta Kunth = Calamagrostis stricta
neglecta var. scotica Druce = Calamagrostis scotica
scotica Druce = Calamagrostis scotica
strigosa auct. brit. = Calamagrostis scotica
Digitaria adscendens (H. B. K.) Henrard, 371
ciliaris (Retz) Koel = Digitaria adscendens
humifusa Pers. = Digitaria ischaemum
ischaemum (Schreb.) Muhl., 369
sanguinalis (L.) Scop., 371
Digraphis arundinacea (L.) Trin. = Phalaris arundinacea

Echinochloa colonum (L.) Link, 363
crus-galli (L.) Beauv., 363
frumentacea Link, 363
pungens (Poir.) Rydb., 363
utilis Ohwi and Yabuno, 363
Elymus arenarius L., 105
caninus (L.) L. *see* Agropyron donianum F. B. White
caninus (L.) L. *see* Agropyron caninum (L.) Beauv.
Elymus europaeus L. = Hordelymus europaeus
farctus subsp. boreali-atlanticus (Simonet & Guinochet) Melderis. *see* Agropyron junceiforme (A. & D. Löve) A. & D. Löve
geniculatus Curt., ? = E. arenarius
pungens (Pers.) Melderis. *see* Agropyron pungens (Pers.) Roem. & Schult.
pycnanthus × Elymus farctus subsp. boreali-atlanticus *see* Agropyron × obtusiusculum Lange
repens (L.) Gould *see* Agropyron repens (L.) Beauv.
repens subsp. arenosus (Petif.) Melderis. *see* Agropyron maritimum (Koch & Ziz) B. de Lesdain
Elytrigia juncea auct. = Agropyron junceiforme
junceiformis A. & D. Löve = Agropyron junceiforme
× obtusiuscula (Lange) Hyl. = Agropyron junceiforme × A. pungens
pungens (Pers.) Tutin = Agropyron pungens
repens (L.) Nevski = Agropyron repens

Festuca adscendens Retz. = × Festulolium loliaceum
aetnensis (Tin.) Richt. = Vulpia ambigua
altissima All., 125
ambigua Le Gall = Vulpia ambigua
arenaria Osb. = F. rubra var. arenaria
arenaria var. glabrata Lebel = F. juncifolia var. glabrata
arundinacea Schreb., 143
arundinacea × F. gigantea = F. × gigas
arundinacea × Lolium multiflorum, 147
arundinacea × Lolium perenne, 147

467

arvernensis Auquier, K. & M.D. *see* Festuca glauca Lam.
× aschersoniana Dorfl., 141
borreri Bab. = Puccinellia fasciculata
× braunii K. Richt. = × Festulolium braunii
× brinkmanni A. Br. = × Festulolium brinkmannii
bromoides L. = Vulpia bromoides
caesia Sm. = F. glauca var. caesia
calamaria Sm. = F. altissima
capillata Lam. = F. tenuifolia
capillaris Liljebl. = Puccinellia capillaris
ciliata Danth. = Vulpia ciliata
ciliata Danth. var. ambigua (Le Gall) Towns. = Vulpia ambigua
ciliata var. glabra Towns. = Vulpia ambigua
danthonii Aschers. & Graebn. = Vulpia ciliata
danthonii var. ambigua (Le Gall) Druce = Vulpia ambigua
decidua Sm. = F. altissima
decumbens L. = Sieglingia decumbens
dertonensis (All.) Aschers. & Graebn. = Vulpia bromoides
dumetorum L., 139
dumetorum f. glabrata (Lebel) Litard. = F. juncifolia var. glabrata
duriuscula L. = F. rubra
duriuscula auct. = F. longifolia
duriuscula var. dumetorum (L.) Gaud. = F. dumetorum
elatior L., 141, 143
elatior subsp. arundinacea (Schreb.) Hack. = F. arundinacea
elatior subsp. pratensis (Huds.) Hack. = F. pratensis
elatior var. arundinacea (Schreb.) Celak. = F. arundinacea
elatior var. pratensis (Huds.) Hack. = F. pratensis
fallax Thuill. = F. rubra subsp. commutata
fluitans L. = Glyceria fluitans
gigantea (L.) Vill., 145
gigantea × F. arundinacea, 145
gigantea × F. pratensis, 145
gigantea × Lolium perenne, 147
× gigas Holmb., 145
glauca Lam., 131
glauca var. caesia (Sm.) K. Richt., 131
heterophylla Lam., 133
× holmbergii Dörfl. = × Festulolium holmbergii
juncifolia St.-Amans, 139
juncifolia var. glabrata (Lebel), 139
loliacea Huds. = × Festulolium loliaceum
longifolia Thuill., 131
longifolia var. villosa (Schrad.) Howarth, 131
marina L. = Catapodium marinum
maritima L. = Nardurus maritimus
Festuca megalura Nutt. = Vulpia megalura
membranacea (L.) Druce = Vulpia membranacea
myuros L. = Vulpia myuros
myuros subsp. ambigua (Le Gall) Syme = Vulpia ambigua
myuros subsp. pseudomyuros (Soy.-Will.) Hayw. = Vulpia myuros
myuros subsp. sciuroides (Roth) Hayw. = Vulpia bromoides
nigrescens Lam. *see* Festuca rubra subsp. commutata Gaud.
oraria Dum. = F. rubra var. arenaria
ovina L., 129
ovina subsp. capillata (Lam.) Schinz & Kell. = F. tenuifolia
ovina subsp. rubra (L.) Hook. f. = F. rubra
ovina subsp. tenuifolia (Sibth.) Peterm. = F. tenuifolia
ovina subsp. vulgaris (Koch) Schinz & Kell. = F. ovina
ovina var. capillata (Lam.) Alef. = F. tenuifolia

ovina var. hispidula (Hack.) Hack., 129
ovina var. tenuifolia (Sibth.) Dum. = F. tenuifolia
ovina var. vivipara L., 129
ovina var. vulgaris Koch = F. ovina
ovina × F. tenuifolia, 127
pratensis Huds., 141
pratensis var. loliacea (Huds.) With. = × Festulolium loliaceum
pratensis × F. arundinacea = F. × aschersoniana
pratensis × F. gigantea = F. × schlickumii
pratensis × Lolium multiflorum, 147
pratensis × Lolium perenne, 147
richardsonii (Hooker) see Festuca rubra subsp. arctica (Hack.) Govar.
rigida (L.) Rasp. = Catapodium rigidum
rigida var. patens (C. B. Presl) Lousley = Catapodium rigidum var. majus
rottboellia Aschers. & Graebn. = Catapodium marinum
rottboellioides Kunth = Catapodium marinum
rubra L., 135, 137, 373–80
rubra subsp. arctica (Hack.) Govar., 379
rubra subsp. arenaria (Osbeck) Syme, 377
rubra subsp. commutata Gaud., 135
rubra subsp. dumetorum (L.) Guad. see F. dumetorum
rubra subsp. duriuscula (L.) Gaud. = F. rubra subsp. rubra
rubra subsp. fallax (Thuill.) Hack. = F. rubra subsp. commutata
rubra subsp. juncifolia (St.-Amans) Litard. = F. juncifolia
rubra subsp. litoralis (G. F. W. Meyer) Auquier, 375
rubra subsp. megastachys (Gaud.), 378
rubra subsp. multiflora (Hoffn.) Wallr., 380
rubra subsp. pruinosa (Hack.) Piper, 376
rubra subsp. rubra, 137
rubra var. arenaria Fries = F. rubra subsp. arenaria
rubra var. dumetorum (L.) Hartm. see F. dumetorum
rubra var. fallax (Thuill.) Hack. = F. rubra subsp. commutata
rubra var. heterophylla (Lam.) Mut. = F. heterophylla
rubra var. pruinosa (Hack.) Howarth = F. rubra subsp. pruinosa
rubra × Vulpia bromoides, 155
rubra × Vulpia membranacea, 161
rubra × Vulpia myuros, 157
sabulicola Duf. = F. juncifolia
× schlickumii Grantz., 141, 145
sciuroides Roth = Vulpia bromoides
supina auct. brit. = F. ovina var. vivipara
sylvatica Huds. = Brachypodium sylvaticum
sylvatica Vill. = F. altissima
tenuifolia Sibth., 127
tenuifolia var. hirtula (Hack. ex Travis) Howarth, 127
tenuifolia × F. ovina, 127
trachyphylla (Hack.) Kraj. = F. longifolia
uniglumis Sol. = Vulpia membranacea
vivipara (L.) Sm., 129
× Festulolium braunii (K. Richt.) A. Camus (Festuca pratensis × Lolium multif-
    lorum), 147
    brinkmannii (A. Br.) A. & G. (Festuca gigantea × Lolium perenne), 147
    holmbergii (Dörfl.) P. Fourn. (Festuca arundinacea × Lolium perenne), 147
    loliaceum (Huds.) P. Fourn. (Festuca pratensis × Lolium perenne), 147

Gastridium australe Beauv. = G. ventricosum
    lendigerum (L.) Desv. = G. ventricosum
    phleoides (Nees & Meyen) C. E. Hubbard, 311
    ventricosum (Gouan) Schinz & Thell., 311
Gaudinia fragilis (L.) Beauv., 245

Glyceria aquatica (L.) Wahlb. = G. maxima
   aquatica (L.) J. & C. Presl = Catabrosa aquatica
   borreri (Bab.) Bab. = Puccinellia fasciculata
   capillaris (Liljebl.) Wahlb. = Puccinellia capillaris
   declinata Bréb., 115
   distans (L.) Wahlenb. = Puccinellia distans
   distans var. prostrata Beeby = Puccinellia capillaris
   festuciformis auct. brit. = Puccinellia maritima
   fluitans (L.) R. Br., 117
   fluitans subsp. plicata (Fries) Hayw. = G. plicata
   fluitans × G. declinata, 115, 117
   fluitans × G. plicata = G. × pedicellata
   loliacea (Huds.) Wats. = Catapodium marinum
   maritima (Huds.) Wahlb. = Puccinellia maritima
   maxima (Hartm.) Holmb., 123
   × pedicellata Towns., 119
   plicata Fries, 121
   plicata var. declinata (Bréb.) Druce = G. declinata
   procumbens (Curt.) Dum. = Puccinellia rupestris
   rigida (L.) Sm. = Catapodium rigidum
   rupestris (With.) E. S. Marshall = Puccinellia rupestris
   salina Druce = Puccinellia distans × maritima
Gynerium argenteum Nees = Cortaderia selloana

Helictotrichon alpinum (Sm.) Henrard, 231
   pratense (L.) Pilger, 231
   pubescens (Huds.) Pilger, 229
Hierochloë borealis Roem. & Schult. = H. odorata
   odorata (L.) Beauv., 265
Holcus lanatus L., 261
   mollis L., 263
   mollis var. parviflorus Parin., 263
   mollis × H. lanatus, 263
   odoratus L. = Hierochloë odorata
Homalocenchrus oryzoides (L.) Poll. = Leersia oryzoides
Hordelymus europaeus (L.) Harz, 107
Hordeum distichon L., 113, 425, 426
   europaeum (L.) All. = Hordelymus europaeus
   glaucum Steud., 109
   gussonianum Parl. = H. hystrix
   hystrix Roth, 111
   jubatum L., 113
   leporinum Link, 109
   marinum Huds., 111
   maritimum Stokes ex With. = H. marinum
   murinum L., 109
   murinum subsp. glaucum (Steud.) Tzvelev see Hordeum glaucum Steud.
   murinum subsp. leporinum (Link) Arcangeli see Hordeum leporinum Link
   nodosum L., 113
   polystichon Hall. = H. vulgare
   pratense Huds. = H. secalinum
Hordeum sativum Pers. = H. vulgare
   secalinum Schreb., 113
   secalinum × Agropyron repens, 113
   stebbinsii Covas = H. glaucum
   sylvaticum Huds. = Hordelymus europaeus
   tetrastichum Koern. = H. vulgare
   vulgare L., 113, 424, 425

Knappia agrostidea Sm. = Mibora minima

Koeleria albescens DC., 241
  britannica (Domin) Druce, 241
  cristata (L.) Pers., 241
  cristata × K. vallesiana, 243
  gracilis Pers. = K. cristata
  gracilis subsp. britannica Domin = K. cristata
  gracilis var. britannica Domin = K. cristata
  macrantha (Ledeb.) Schultes *see* Koeleria cristata (L.) Pers.
  phleoides Pers., 243
  pseudocristata Domin = K. cristata
  splendens (Pourr.) Druce = K. vallesiana
  valesiaca Gaud. = K. vallesiana
  vallesiana (Honck.) Bertol., 243
  vallesiana × K. cristata and K. britannica (Domin) Druce, 243

Lagurus ovatus L., 313
Leersia oryzoides (L.) Swartz, 345
Lepiurus strigosus Dum. = Parapholis strigosa
Leptothrix europaea (L.) Dum. = Hordelymus europaeus
Lepturus filiformis (Roth) Trin., 339
  incurvatus (L.) Trin. = Parapholis incurva
  incurvus (L.) Druce = Parapholis incurva
Leymus arenarius (L.) Hochst. = Elymus arenarius
Lolium arvense With. = L. temulentum L. arvense
  × hybridum Hausskn. = L. multiflorum × L. perenne
  italicum A. Br. = L. multiflorum
  linicola A. Br. = L. remotum
  multiflorum Lam., 151
  multiflorum var. italicum (A. Br.) Beck = L. multiflorum
  multiflorum × Festuca arundinacea = × Festulolium
  multiflorum × L. perenne, 151
  perenne L., 149
  perenne subsp. italicum (A. Br.) Syme = L. multiflorum
  perenne subsp. multiflorum (Lam.) Husnot = L. multiflorum
  perenne var. aristatum Schum. = Lolium multiflorum
  perenne var. italicum Parn. = L. multiflorum
  perenne var. multiflorum Parn. = L. multiflorum
  persicum Boiss. & Hoh., 153
  remotum Schrank, 153
  rigidum Gaud., 153
  temulentum L., 153
  temulentum var. arvense Liljebl., 153
  westerwoldicum auct. =L. multiflorum
Lophochloa cristata (L.) Hyl. *see* Koeleria phleoides Pers.

Melica altissima L., 223
  caerulea (L.) L. = Molinia caerulea
  ciliata L., 223
  montana Huds. = M. nutans
  nutans L., 223
  uniflora Retz., 225
Mibora minima (L.) Desv., 337
  verna Beauv. = M. minima
Milium effusum L., 275
  lendigerum L. = Gastridium ventricosum
  scabrum Rich., 275
  vernale L. subsp. scabrum (Rich.) Paunero = M. scabrum
Molinia altissima Link = Molinia litoralis
  caerulea (L.) Moench, 349
  caerulea subsp. arundinacea (Schrank) H. Paul *see* Molinia litoralis Host

471

depauperata Lindl. = M. caerulea
litoralis Host, 349
maxima Hartm. = Glyceria maxima

Nardurus maritimus (L.) Murb., 163
Nardus stricta L., 343

Oryza oryzoides (L.) Brand. = Leersia oryzoides

Panicum capillare L., 369
  colonum L. = Echinochloa colonum
  crus-galli L. = Echinochloa crus-galli
  frumentaceum Roxb. = Echinochloa frumentacea
  glabrum Gaud. = Digitaria ischaemum
  glaucum L. = Setaria glauca
  humifusum (Pers.) Kunth = Digitaria ischaemum
  ischaemum Schreb. = Digitaria ischaemum
  italicum L. = Setaria italica
  lutescens Weig. = Setaria glauca
  miliaceum L., 369
  plicatum Lam. = Setaria plicata
  pumilum Poiret = Setaria glauca
  sanguinale L. = Digitaria sanguinalis
  verticillatum L. = Setaria verticillata
  viride L. = Setaria viridis
Parapholis incurva (L.) C. E. Hubbard, 341
  strigosa (Dum.) C. E. Hubbard, 339
Phalaris angusta Nees, 271
  arundinacea L., 273
  arundinacea var. picta L., 273
  canariensis L., 271
  minor Retz., 271
  paradoxa L., 271
  paradoxa var., appendiculata (Roem. & Schult.) Chiov. = P. paradoxa var.
    praemorsa
  paradoxa var. praemorsa Coss. & Dur., 271
Phalaroides arundinacea (L.) Rausch = Phalaris arundinacea
Phleum alpinum L., 323
  alpinum var. commutatum (Gaud.) Koch = P. alpinum
  arenarium L., 315
  asperum Jacq. = P. paniculatum
  bertolonii DC., 319
  boehmeri Wibel = P. phleoides
  commutatum Gaud. = P. alpinum
  exaratum Griseb., 315
  graecum Boiss. & Heldr. = P. exaratum
  nodosum L. = P. pratense
  paniculatum Huds., 315
  phalaroides Koel. = P. phleoides
  phleoides (L.) Karst., 317
  pratense L., 321
  pratense subsp. nodosum (L.) Peterm. = P. pratense
  pratense subsp. bertolonii (DC.) Bornm. *see* Phleum bertolonii DC.
  pratense subsp. vulgare (Celak.) Aschers. & Graebn. = P. pratense
  pratense var. bertolonii (DC.) Link = P. bertolonii
  pratense var. nodosum (L.) Huds. = P. pratense
  subulatum (Savi) Aschers. & Graebn., 315
  tenue Schrad. = P. subulatum
Pholiurus filiformis (Roth) Trin., 339
  incurvus (L.) Schinz & Thell. = Parapholis incurva

472

rupestris With. = Puccinellia rupestris
serotina Ehrh. = P. palustris
subcaerulea Sm., 191
subcompressa Parn. = P. compressa
sudetica Haenke = P. chaixii
Poa sylvatica Poll. = Festuca altissima
sylvatica Vill. = P. chaixii
trivalis L., 185
Polypogon × littoralis Sm. = × Agropogon littoralis
lutosus (Poir.) Hitchc., 307
maritimus Willd., 309
monspeliensis (L.) Desf., 309
monspeliensis × Agrostis stolonifera = × Agropogon littoralis
semiverticillatus (Forsk.) Hyl. = Agrostis semiverticillata
viridis (Gouan) Breistr. *see* Agrostis semiverticillata
Psamma arenaria (L.) Roem. & Schult. = Ammophila arenaria
baltica (Fl. ex Schrad.) Beauv. ex Roem. & Schult. = × Ammocalamagrostis
baltica
Puccinellia borreri (Bab.) Hitchc. = Puccinellia fasciculata
capillaris (Liljebl.) Jansen, 197
capillaris × P. maritima, 197
distans (L.) Parl., 199
distans subsp. borealis (Holmberg) W. E. Hughes *see* Puccinellia capillaris (Liljebl.) Jansen
distans var. prostrata (Beeby) Druce = P. capillaris
distans × P. maritima, 199
distans × P. rupestris, 199, 203
fasciculata (Torr.) Bickn., 195
× hybrida Holmb., 199
× krusemanniana Jansen & Wacht., 203
maritima (Huds.) Parl., 201
maritima × P. capillaris, 197
maritima × P. distans, 199
maritima × P. rupestris, 203
× mixta Holmb., 197
× pannonica (Hack.) Holmb., 199, 203
pseudodistans (Crép.) Jansen & Wacht., 199
retroflexa (Curt.) Holmb. = P. distans
rupestris (With.) Fern. & Weath., 203
rupestris × P. distans, 199, 203
rupestris × P. maritima, 203

Roegneria canina (L.) Nevski = Agropyron caninum
doniana (F. B. White) Meld. = Agropyron donianum

Savastana odorata (L.) Scribn. = Hierochloë odorata
Schedonorus benekenii Lange = Bromus benekenii
Sclerochloa borreri (Bab.) Bab. = Puccinellia fasciculata
distans (L.) Bab. = Puccinellia fasciculata
loliacea (Huds.) Woods ex Bab. = Catapodium marinum
maritima (Huds.) Lindl. ex Bab. = Puccinellia maritima
multiculmis subsp. borreri (Bab.) Syme = Puccinellia fasciculata
multiculmis subsp. distans (L.) Syme = Puccinellia distans
patens C. B. Presl = Catapodium rigidum var. majus
procumbens (Curt.) Beauv. = Puccinellia rupestris
rigida (L.) Link = Catapodium rigidum
rigida var. major C. B. Presl = Catapodium rigidum var. majus
rupestris (With.) Britt. & Rendle = Puccinellia rupestris
Scleropoa loliacea (Huds.) Gren. & Godr. = Catapodium marinum
rigida (L.) Griseb. = Catapodium rigidum

rigida var. major (C. B. Presl) Lousley = Catapodium rigidum var. majus
rigida var. patens Willk. = Catapodium rigidum var. majus
Secale cereale L., 424, 425
Serrafalcus arvensis (L.) Godr. = Bromus arvensis
   commutatus (Schrad.) Bab. = Bromus commutatus
   interruptus (Hack.) Druce = Bromus interruptus
   japonicus (Thunb.) Wilmott = Bromus japonicus
   mollis (L.) Parl. = Bromus mollis
   pratensis (Ehrh. ex Hoffm.) Wilmott = Bromus commutatus
   racemosus (L.) Parl. = Bromus racemosus
Serrafalcus secalinus (L.) Bab. = Bromus secalinus
Sesleria albicans Kit. in Schult. = S. caerulea subsp. calcarea
   caerulea (L.) Ard., 227
   caerulea subsp. calcarea (Celak.) Hegi, 227
   caerulea var. calcarea Celak., 227
   caerulea var. luteo-alba Opiz, 227
   calcarea Opiz = S. caerulea subsp. calcarea
   deyliana A. & D. Löve = S. caerulea subsp. calcarea
   varia (Jacq.) Wettst. = S. caerulea subsp. calcarea
Setaria geniculata (Lam.) Beauv., 367
   glauca (L.) Beauv., 367
   italica (L.) Beauv., 365
   lutescens (Weig.) F. T. Hubbard = S. glauca
   plicata (Lam.) T. Cooke, 367
   pumila (Poir.) Roem. & Schult. = S. glauca
   verticillata (L.) Beauv., 365
   viridis (L.) Beauv., 365
Sieglingia decumbens (L.) Bernh., 351
   decumbens subsp. decipiens Sch. & Bass
Spartina alterniflora Lois, 359
   alterniflora × S. maritima = S. × townsendii
   anglica C. E. Hubbard, 357
   glabra Muhl., 359
   maritima (Curt.) Fernald, 353
   maritima × S. alterniflora = S. × townsendii
   neyrautii Fouc. = S. × townsendii
   stricta (Ait.) Roth = S. maritima
   × townsendii H. & J. Groves, 355
Sturmia minima (L.) Hoppe = Mibora minima

Trichoon phragmites (L.) Rendle = Phragmites communis
Triodia decumbens (L.) Beauv. = Seiglingia decumbens
Trisetum flavescens (L.) Beauv., 245
   pratense Pers. = T. flavescens
Triticum acutum DC. = Agropyron acutum
   aestivum L., 422, 425
   alpinum G. Don = Agropyron donianum
   biflorum auct. = Agropyron donianum
   caninum L. = Agropyron caninum
   caninum var. biflorum Mitt. = Agropyron donianum
   caninum var. glaucescens (Lange) A. & G. = Agropyron caninum var. glaucum
   donianum (F. B. White) Wilmott = Agropyron donianum
   junceum L. = Agropyron junceum (L.) Beauv.
   junceum auct. brit. = Agropyron junceiforme
   junceum subsp. pungens Pers. = Agropyron pungens
   laxum Fries = Agropyron × laxum
   littorale Host = Agropyron
   loliaceum (Huds.) Sm. = Catapodium marinum
   maritimum L. = Nardurus maritimus
   pungens Pers. = Agropyron pungens

repens L. = Agropyron repens
repens subsp. pungens (Pers.) Sowerby = Agropyron pungens
repens var. pungens (Pers.) Duby = Agropyron pungens
sativum Lam. = T. aestivum
turgidum L., 425
vulgare Vill. = T. aestivum

Vulpia ambigua (Le Gall) A. G. More, 159
aetnensis Tin. = Vulpia ambigua
bromoides (L.) S. F. Gray, 155
bromoides × Festuca rubra, 155
ciliata Dum., 159
ciliata subsp. ambigua (Le Gall) Stace & Auquier *see* Vulpia ambigua (Le Gall)
A. G. More
danthonia (Aschers. & Graebn.) Volk = Vulpia ciliata
Vulpia dertonensis (All.) Gola = V. bromoides
megalura (Nutt.) Rydb., 157
membranacea (L.) Dum., 161
membranacea × Festuca rubra, 161
myuros (L.) C. C. Gmel., 157
myuros × Festuca rubra, 157
sciuroides (Roth) C. C. Gmel. = V. bromoides
uniglumis (Sol.) Dum. = V. membranacea
unilateralis (L.) Stace *see* Nardurus maritimus (L.) Murbeck

Weingaertneria canescens (L.) Bernh. = Corynephorus canescens

Zerna benekenii (Lange) Lindm. = Bromus benekenii
erecta (Huds.) S. F. Gray = Bromus erectus
inermis (Leyss.) Lindm. = Bromus inermis
ramosa (Huds.) Lindm. = Bromus ramosus

READ MORE IN PENGUIN

READ MORE IN PENGUIN

SCIENCE AND MATHEMATICS

Six Easy Pieces Richard P. Feynman

Drawn from his celebrated and landmark text *Lectures on Physics*, this collection of essays introduces the essentials of physics to the general reader. 'If one book was all that could be passed on to the next generation of scientists it would undoubtedly have to be *Six Easy Pieces*' John Gribbin, *New Scientist*

A Mathematician Reads the Newspapers John Allen Paulos

In this book, John Allen Paulos continues his liberating campaign against mathematical illiteracy. 'Mathematics is all around you. And it's a great defence against the sharks, cowboys and liars who want your vote, your money or your life' Ian Stewart

Dinosaur in a Haystack Stephen Jay Gould

'Today we have many outstanding science writers ... but, whether he is writing about pandas or Jurassic Park, none grabs you so powerfully and personally as Stephen Jay Gould ... he is not merely a pleasure but an education and a chronicler of the times' *Observer*

Does God Play Dice? Ian Stewart

As Ian Stewart shows in this stimulating and accessible account, the key to this unpredictable world can be found in the concept of chaos, one of the most exciting breakthroughs in recent decades. 'A fine introduction to a complex subject' *Daily Telegraph*

About Time Paul Davies

'With his usual clarity and flair, Davies argues that time in the twentieth century is Einstein's time and sets out on a fascinating discussion of why Einstein's can't be the last word on the subject' *Independent on Sunday*